TENDER
OFFERS

TENDER OFFERS

DEVELOPMENTS AND COMMENTARIES

Edited by MARC I. STEINBERG

Quorum Books

Westport, Connecticut • London, England

Library of Congress Cataloging in Publication Data

Main entry under title:

Tender offers.

  Bibliography: p.
  Includes index.
  1. Tender offers (Securities)—Law and legislation—
United States.   I. Steinberg, Marc I.
KF1477.T45   1985   346.73'0666   84-24947
ISBN 0-89930-088-X (lib. bdg.)   347.306666

Library of Congress Catalog Card Number: 84-24947
ISBN 0-89930-088-X

First published in 1985 by Quorum Books

Greenwood Press
A division of Congressional Information Service, Inc.
88 Post Road West, Westport, Connecticut 06881

Printed in the United States of America

10 9 8 7 6 5 4 3 2 1

Contents

Acknowledgments

I owe many thanks to a number of individuals for helping to bring about the successful completion of this project. Foremost, I express my appreciation to the contributors whose efforts made the project a reality. The professionalism, scholarship, and insights contained in their commentaries should provide useful guidance to the resolution of the multifaceted issues associated with the tender offer phenomenon.

I also thank my research assistants at the University of Maryland School of Law, Ms. Joan Karwasinski, Mr. H. Haywood Miller, Mr. Gregory Neville, and Ms. Patricia Prestigiacomo, for their editorial contributions, as well as Ms. Ann Garrett for her secretarial assistance. Last, but certainly not least, I wish to dedicate this book to my sister, Nancy Gossman, and her family, her husband, Robert, and daughters, Julie, Wendy, and Jennifer.

TENDER
OFFERS

Introduction

This book represents an effort to collect in one source a treatment of many of the timely and provocative issues associated with the tender offer phenomenon along with a diversity of viewpoints on how a number of these issues should be resolved. Although the nature of this project precludes thorough examination of the multitude of subjects relating to tender offers, the book succeeds in comprehensively addressing many of the key topics. For example, the contributors analyze such issues as:

—Tender offer litigation

—The constitutional dimensions of state antitakeover statutes

—Target managements' conduct in fending off hostile bidders

—The SEC's Advisory Commission Report of Recommendations on Tender Offers

—SEC tender offer rules

—Definition of the term "tender offer"

—Insider trading in the tender offer context

—Proposals for tender offer reform

The book's contributors offer diverse viewpoints and represent many of the leading authorities in the securities law field. They include a former SEC commissioner, former and current top-level SEC staff members,* the inside general counsel to a major corporation, respected private practitioners, and leading academicians.

---

*As will be disclosed in their commentaries, members of the SEC staff are expressing their own views and not necessarily those of the Commission. The same should be said for other contributors who are expressing solely their own views.

The publication of this book comes at a time when tender offer regulation, on both a federal and state level, is undergoing intense scrutiny. Congressional, SEC, and academic proposals abound. The proper application of the business judgment rule is being debated as is the role of state antitakeover statutes in the regulatory framework. The enactment of significant federal legislation remains a distinct possibility. It is hoped that the commentaries contained herein will add meaningfully to the dialogue now taking place and will serve as a useful source for the resolution of these difficult issues.

As a final note, a number of the commentaries contained in this book were written in 1984, hence they do not reflect the multitude of developments which have taken place in this rapidly changing area since then.

I

THE SEC ADVISORY COMMITTEE REPORT ON TENDER OFFERS

The Securities and Exchange Commission (SEC) Advisory Commission on Tender Offers was established in February 1983 by Chairman John S. R. Shad, with the concurrence of the other commissioners.[1] The formulation of the Advisory Commission was hardly surprising in view of the intensity of concerns that had been generated from the recent explosion of tender offer activity.[2] Responding to this development, the Senate Commission on Banking, Housing, and Urban Affairs expressed its interest, urging in a bipartisan letter to Chairman Shad that "the public interest and the Congress would be best served by a broad study of the many issues surrounding tender offers and particlarly hostile offers, and, therefore, [it] encourage[d] the Commission panel to be comprehensive in both its approach and charter."[3]

The Advisory Commission was not without its critics. Although initially composed of sixteen acknowledgeably competent members, some observers felt that the SEC had "stacked the deck" by appointing persons who had a vested interest in the perpetuation of the current system.[4] After being requested by the Senate Banking Commission to add individuals who hopefully would have different perspectives, the Commission responded by selecting former Supreme Court Justice Arthur J. Goldberg and Jeffrey B. Bartell, Esq., a former Wisconsin securities commissioner.[5] Significantly,

---

1. Securities Exchange Act Release No. 19528, 48 Federal Register 9111 (1983).

2. *See* Sommer, *The SEC's Advisory Commission on Tender Offers: Whatever Happened to State Law?*, 16 Rev. Sec. Reg. 833 (1983).

3. *See* SEC Advisory Commission on Tender Offers, Report of Recommendations 134-136 (July 8, 1983).

4. *See* New York Times, July 9, 1983, § 2, at 32, 37; Fortune, June 27, 1983, at 32, 36.

5. *See* discussion in Sommer, *supra* note 2, at 833.

both Justice Goldberg and Mr. Bartell strongly disagreed with the Commission's Report of Recommendations.[6]

After meeting in full session on six occasions, the Advisory Commission issued its Report of Recommendations in July 1983. The Report, consisting of fifty recommendations in six general areas,[7] covers the broad spectrum of tender offer regulation. The impact and scope of these recommendations fall into several categories: "some are aspirational and state very broad conclusions and objectives of regulation, others simply confirm and endorse present rules and practices, others recommend modest modifications of the present regulatory scheme, some are simply pious platitudes, and others would work radical changes in the regulation of changes in control of corporations."[8]

As mentioned above, there were those on the Commission who disagreed with the Report's focus and proposals. Justice Goldberg asserted that the Report largely ignored the protection of the public interest as well as the plight of the small shareholder.[9] Mr. Bartell dissented due to the Commission's failure to recommend more stringent regulation of partial and two-tier offers and its desire to abolish state corporation laws that restrict the ability of out-of-state corporations to engage in takeover transactions.[10] Messrs. Easterbook and Jarrell, on the other hand, disagreed with the Report's "plea for more regulation," a result that would make "[s]hareholders in bidders, targets, and bystanders alike ... the losers" and would cause "[t]he economy as a whole [to] suffer."[11]

---

6. *See* SEC Advisory Commission Report, *supra* note 3, at 122-146.

7. The six general areas were: (1) economics of takeovers and their regulation, (2) objectives of federal regulation of takeovers, (3) regulation of acquirers of corporate counsel, (4) regulation of opposition to acquisitions of control, (5) regulation of market participants, and (6) interrelationships of various regulatory schemes.

8. Sommer, *supra* note 2, at 834.

9. *See* SEC Advisory Commission Report, *supra* note 3, at 122-141 (Separate Statement of Arthur J. Goldberg). Justice Goldberg called for significant changes in the tender offer framework, including the appointment by the SEC of an independent review person to evaluate the fairness and economic impact of applicable offers; the imposition of a freeze period, such as 120 days, to permit competing bids and antitrust determinations to be made; and the prohibition, or more stringent regulation, of a number of offensive and defensive maneuvers.

10. *Id.* at 142-146 (letter from Jeffrey B. Bartell, Esq., to Mr. Dean LeBaron, Chairman of the SEC Advisory Commission on tender offers). Concluding, Mr. Bartell asserted, "as a general statement of the direction in which tender offer regulation should be headed, I believe Justice Goldberg's report is valuable and on target." *Id.* at 146.

11. *Id.* at 70 (Separate Statement of Professor Frank H. Easterbrook and Mr. Gregg A. Jarrell). At another point, Messrs. Easterbrook and Jarrell assert: "Given the Ad-

In the ensuing commentary, Linda C. Quinn, Esq., and David B. H. Martin, Esq., provide a detailed overview and analysis of the Advisory Commission's Report.[12] They also discuss subsequent developments and issues that are now being explored with a greater sense of urgency, largely due to the Commission's Report of Recommendations. For example, based on the Commission's Report and the debate generated thereby, the SEC has adopted amendments to Rule 10b-4 prohibiting "hedged" tendering,[13] has issued a release requesting public comments on two-tier pricing in tender offers as well as non-tender offer purchase programs,[14] and has delivered a proposed legislative package to Congress.[15] In addition, several bills have been introduced in Congress that address perceived abuses and deficiencies in the tender offer framework.[16]

Thus, the Advisory Commission's most notable accomplishment has been to induce long-overdue SEC and Congressional attention to the controversial issues present in the tender offer context. Irrespective of whether one agrees with the recommendations proffered and the rationales set forth, attention finally has been focused on many of the key issues. Although we must wait for the hopefully enlightened resolution of these issues, at the very least, a significant step forward has been taken.

---

visory Committee's determination to regulate bids at almost every turn, we would ban defensive tactics outright. That is the rule in the United Kingdom, and it is the recommendation of every economically sophisticated commentator." *Id.* at 100 (and sources cited therein). *See also* DeMott, *Current Lessons in Tender Offer Regulation: Lessons from the British*, 58 N.Y.U. L. Rev. 945 (1983).

12. Professor Ted J. Fiflis also provides an extensive analysis of the Advisory Commission Report in the "Panel Discussion" contained herein. Also, portions of the Report are discussed by several commentators, including Peter Brennan, Esq., A. A. Sommer, Esq., and Professors Sargent and Steinberg.

13. *See* Securities Exchange Act Release No. 20799, 49 Federal Register 13867 (1984). Rule 10b-4 is discussed in the "SEC Tender Offer Rules" section contained herein.

14. *See* Securities Exchange Act Release No. 21079, 16 Sec. Reg. & L. Rep. (BNA) 1119 (1984). Two-tier offers are discussed in a number of the commentaries, including those by Linda C. Quinn, Esq., and David B. H. Martin, Esq., by Messrs. Goelzer and Cohen, and by Professor Steinberg.

15. *See* S. 2782, H.R. 5693 *reprinted in* 16 Sec. Reg. & L. Rep. (BNA) 793, 913, 1102 (1984) (proposing, *inter alia*, to close the "ten-day window" currently available under Section 13(d) of the Exchange Act between the time the threshold triggering disclosure is reached and the time actual disclosure must be made, to prohibit the payment of "greenmail" by target management with certain exceptions, and to prohibit the granting of "golden parachutes" once a tender offer has commenced).

16. *See, e.g.*, the several bills discussed in 16 Sec. Reg. & L. Rep. (BNA) 913, 1102 (1984) (e.g., S. 2754, 2777, 2782, 2783, 2785; H.R. 3165, 4357, 5693, 5694).

The SEC Advisory Committee on Tender Offers and Its Aftermath— A New Chapter in Change-of-Control Regulation

LINDA C. QUINN and DAVID B. H. MARTIN, JR.*

I. INTRODUCTION

The first half of the 1980's has witnessed significant and complex realignments in the U.S. capital markets. Nowhere has the quest for capital during this period been more popularized than in the widely followed tender offer and proxy contests for control of U.S. companies. These dramas have captured the fancy of the press, polarized the theories of commentators, and taxed the stamina of the players. Sensing the upheaval of which these contests are a part, government has sought to discern with greater precision their workings and to test the premises and the effectiveness of the laws that apply to those transactions. In doing so, fundamental issues of corporate governance and federal-state relationships have been raised.

In the area of federal securities laws, the process of analysis and appraisal was initiated by the Securities and Exchange Commission in February of 1983, when it established a special panel, the Advisory Committee on Tender Offers, to review the techniques for the acquisition of control of public companies and the laws applicable to such transactions.[1] The Advisory Committee presented its recommendations on July 8, 1983. On March 1984,

*Ms. Quinn is the executive assistant to Chairman John S. R. Shad of the Securities and Exchange Commission. She served as the staff director of the Commission's Advisory Committee on Tender Offers and as the associate director of the Division of Corporation Finance responsible for the Office of Tender Offers. Mr. Martin is special counsel to Chairman Shad and served as secretary to the Advisory Committee. As a matter of policy, the Commission disclaims responsibility for any private publication by any of its employees. The views expressed in this article are those of the authors and do not necessarily represent views of the Commission or the authors' colleagues on the staff.

1. The Commission established the Advisory Committee on February 25, 1983 (Release No. 34-19528 (February 25, 1983)), in accordance with the provisions of

the Commission testified on its views concerning the Commission's recommendations and commenced implementation of a program of legislative and regulatory initiatives to revise the regulatory framework governing control acquisitions in a number of areas.[2] This commentary describes the working of the Advisory Committee, the recommendations that resulted, and the Commission's response to those recommendations.

II. THE ADVISORY COMMITTEE

A. Reasons for Its Creation

Since the Williams Act was adopted in 1968,[3] takeover practices in the United States have undergone fundamental changes. In the first five years of the Williams Act, there was an average of only 54 tender offers per year. With the contest between Inco Canada and United Aircraft Corp. for ESB Incorporated in 1974, acknowledged by most to mark a watershed in takeover activities, hostile tender offers became an acceptable method of acquisition. Since then, tender offers have averaged 131 per year.[4]

---

the Federal Advisory Committee Act, as amended, 5 U.S.C. App. 1 (1976 & Supp. V 1981).

2. Appendix A (following this chapter) sets forth each of the Advisory Committee's recommendations along with a summary notation as to the Commission's position on each proposal. These positions were voted on by the Commission in public session on March 13, 1984, and later issued by way of written testimony by Commission Chairman John S. R. Shad before the Subcommittee on Telecommunications, Consumer Protection, and Finance of the House Committee on Energy and Commerce on March 28, 1984. Appendix B (following Appendix A) lists members of the SEC Advisory Committee on Tender Offers.

3. 15 U.S.C. §§ 78 m(d), 78m(e), 78n(d)-(f). Until 1968 tender offers were essentially unregulated. The Williams Act amended the Securities Exchange Act of 1934 [hereinafter cited as Exchange Act] (15 U.S.C. §§ 78a-78kk (1976 & Supp. VI 1982), *as amended by* Act of June 6, 1983, Pub. L. No. 98-38) to provide for federal regulation of tender offers.

4.

Fiscal Year	Number of Tender Offers[a]	Fiscal Year	Number of Tender Offers[a]
1965	105[b]	1975	113
1966	77[b]	1976	100
1967	113[c]	1977	162[d]
1968	115[c]	1978	179
1969	70	1979	147
1970	34	1980	104
1971	43	1981	205[e]
1972	50	1982	117
1973	75	1983	92
1974	105	1984	121

Most dramatic of the more recent changes has been the introduction of the "billion-dollar takeover bid" in the three-bidder contest for Conoco, Inc., in the summer of 1981. In that contest, more than $20 billion of credit was lined up by the participants. When the bidding was over, Conoco shareholders accepted Du Pont's tender offer of $7.8 billion—$3.087 billion in cash, the rest in Du Pont common stock. Since the takeover of Conoco, there have been successful cash bids for Gulf Corporation ($13.3 billion), Shell Oil Company ($5.5 billion), Marathon Oil ($3.750 billion), CitiServices ($1.920 billion), and Texas Gas Resources ($1.637 billion). Today, size clearly no longer provides immunity from the takeover bid.

Along with increased size and competitiveness in bidding, complex and creative bidding strategies have evolved. These strategies have included toehold acquisitions, "creeping" tender offers, front-end–loaded bids, and innovative uses of multiple prorationing pools.

Changes in bidding strategies and the apparent vulnerability to takeover of any issuer, irrespective of size, have evoked a wave of new defensive strategies. There has been the "Pac-Man" defense, where the target company makes a responding counter offer for the stock of the bidder; the defensive issuer reacquisition of shares, where the target makes a competing bid for its own stock or announces a buying program for shares in the market; and, most recently, the "poison pill," where the target issues a preferred stock dividend that provides for conversion into the stock of the bidder at a prescribed rate if the bidder succeeds in seizing control of the target. Anti-takeover provisions, only a few years ago pronounced useless, are once again in vogue. An increasing number of issuers have resorted to super-majority vote requirements, nonvoting common stock, limitations on the total voting power to be held by a single person, and "fair-price" provisions. Also reflective of management's perception of vulnerability to takeover is the accelerating implementation of share repurchases at a premium to market, so called greenmail and golden parachute arrangements—compensation

---

[a]Data for fiscal year 1969 and following have been obtained from the Commission and represent tender offers commenced.

[b]These figures were obtained from a study entitled "Tactics of Cash Takeovers Bids," prepared by Professors Samuel L. Hayes, III, and Russell A. Taussig, 45 Harv. Bus. Rev. 135 (1967), which was submitted in 1967 to the Senate and House committees holding hearings on the bill that became the Williams Act. The figures are based on a calendar rather than fiscal year. *See* Hearings on H.R. 14475, S.510 before the Subcomm. on Commerce and Finance of the House Comm. on Interstate and Foreign Commerce, 90th Cong., 2d Sess. 21 (1968).

[c]These figures were obtained from W. T. Grimm & Co. They are based on a calendar year and represent tender offers commenced. Grimm has indicated that it obtained this information from news stories in the financial press and that the figures include tender offers for companies not subject to Section 12 under the Exchange Act but do not include tender offers for securities other than common stock.

[d]In 1977, the federal government changed its fiscal year. Accordingly, this figure is based on an extended fiscal year from July 1, 1976 to September 30, 1977.

[e]Includes approximately seventy offers by one bidder as part of a single program.

provisions that trigger upon the change of control or other events related to change of control. Buybacks, such as Texaco's $1.28 billion repurchase of its shares from the Bass Brothers and Disney's $325.3 million repurchase of its shares from Reliance Holdings, have provoked a storm of criticism. As to golden parachutes, at least 40 percent of the Fortune 1000 corporations now protect their top officers with employment contracts. Of those, more than one-third have specific change-of-control triggers.[5]

With these changes in takeover practices have come changes in the regulatory structure governing such practices. States, whose initial attempts to regulate the tender offer process through antitakeover legislation were struck down by the courts,[6] have renewed their efforts to regulate takeovers. Seeking to withstand constitutional challenge, some have incorporated new takeover provisions in their corporate or other statutes. Maryland, for example, has amended its corporate statute to require that any transaction with the holders of more than 10 percent of a company's voting power, subject to a shareholder vote, must be approved by 80 percent of the shares and two-thirds of the disinterested shareholders *unless* certain value and other standards are met.[7] Ohio has adopted takeover legislation that would require shareholder approval prior to the consummation of specified "control acquisitions," unless the charter or bylaws of an issuer otherwise provide.[8] Hawaii regulates additional purchases of securities or corporate assets by holders of 10 percent or more of the voting securities of a Hawaii corporation under an environmental protection mandate.[9] Pennsylvania, reflecting a variation of the British system, has adopted legislation that requires a person who owns at least 30 percent of a company's voting power to purchase for cash at fair value any stock tendered to it by the remaining shareholders.[10]

All of these developments have made tender offers front-page news and raised substantial public and Congressional concern. In view of these developments and the fundamental issues they have raised, the Securities and Exchange Commission undertook a reexamination of the takeover process and a reevaluation of the laws that govern the process. As a first step, the Commission established the Advisory Committee to review the techniques for the acquisition of control of public companies and the laws applicable to such transactions.

---

5. Survey of Employment Contracts and "Golden Parachutes" among the Fortune 1,000, Ward Howell International, Inc., September 27, 1982.

6. Judicial invalidation of state takeover laws culminated in the Supreme Court's decision in Edgar v. MITE Corp., 457 U.S. 624 (1982), which held the Illinois Business Takeover Act unconstitutional.

7. Md. H.B. 1 (June 21, 1983).

8. Ohio Rev. Code Ann. §§ 1701.01(2)(1), 1701.48, 1701.831, 1707.42.

9. Hawaii Environmental Disclosure Act, Hawaii Rev. Stat. § 343D (1982).

10. Pa. Bus. Corp. § 910.

B. Establishment of the Advisory Committee

The Commission first discussed the idea of a comprehensive reevaluation of tender offer regulation at an open meeting on December 15, 1982. On that occasion, the Commission, by a 3 to 2 vote, amended Rule 14d-8 under the Exchange Act to extend proration rights from 10 days to the entire period the offer remains open.[11] In debating the proposed amendments to the rule, the Commission agreed that there should be a study of the entire tender offer process and regulatory framework.[12] Two months later, the Commission established the Advisory Committee.

Initially, the Commission appointed to the Advisory Committee sixteen members who had been prominently and actively involved in the tender offer area as institutional investors, bidders, targets, arbitrageurs, investment and commercial bankers, attorneys, accountants, and recognized authorities. Shortly thereafter, two additional members, a former Supreme Court justice and a former state securities commissioner, were added.[13] Concern was expressed in some quarters as to the makeup of the panel, particularly because many members had business that relied heavily on tender offers and worked on Wall Street. Those concerns seemed ultimately to dissipate in the face of the wide-ranging and spirited debate that characterized the Advisory Committee's meetings. Indeed, many of the Committee's final recommendations were openly styled as compromise positions between conflicting views on the panel.

The degree to which the Advisory Committee embodied a broad spectrum of positions was best reflected in two of the three Separate Statements submitted with the Report. Professors Easterbrook and Jarrell, a law professor and an economist respectively, prepared a Separate Statement recommending repeal of the Williams Act. Former Supreme Court Justice Arthur Goldberg issued a statement in which he called for greater regulation of tender offers, including what would amount to a public interest review prior to consummation of a transaction. Bevis Longstreth, then an SEC commissioner, referred to these statements as "outriggers" that stabilized the Report.

C. The Advisory Committee's Meetings

The Commission requested the Advisory Committee to report out by July 1983. The Commission had been requested by 12 members of the Senate

---

11. 17 C.F.R. § 240.14d-8. Rule 14d-8 requires a bidder in an oversubscribed partial offer to accept securities on a pro rata basis according to the number of securities deposited by each security holder during the period the offer remains open.

12. *See* Release No. 34-19336 (December 15, 1982).

13. A list of the Advisory Committee members is included at Appendix B.

Committee on Banking, Housing, and Urban Affairs ("Senate Banking Committee") to complete and forward the Advisory Committee's Report to Congress by July 31, 1983.[14] Given its deadline for completion, the Advisory Committee developed a schedule of work that included at least one meeting a month for the full committee and numerous interim meetings of various working groups.

The Advisory Committee's first meeting was held on March 18, 1983, at the Commission's main offices in Washington, D.C. During this session, the Committee formulated an agenda of main topic areas to be addressed. These included the economics of tender offers, the basic objectives of the appropriate regulation of change-of-control transactions, the specific regulations governing conduct of bidders, targets, and market participants, and the interrelationship of federal takeover regulation and other regulatory systems such as tax and antitrust. At this meeting, the Committee also appointed as its chairman Dean LeBaron, President of Batterymarch Financial Management, and divided itself into six working groups or subcommittees. Finally, the Advisory Committee used the occasion of its first meeting and a subsequent Federal Register publication[15] and news release to solicit public comment on the issues it was to consider. As would be the case with subsequent meetings, roughly 20 members of the press and 80–100 members of the public attended this session.

The Advisory Committee's second and third meetings were held in New York City on April 15 and May 13, 1983. At these meetings, the Committee's working groups reported, both orally and in writing, on the status of their efforts. In preparation for the meetings, the subcommittees not only exchanged papers and research but also met with representatives of various government agencies, including the Treasury Department, the Federal Trade Commission, and the Federal Reserve.

At its meeting on May 13, the Advisory Committee focused on the tender offer experience and regulatory response in Great Britain. John M. Hignett and Peter Lee, Director-General and Deputy Director-General of the London Panel on Takeovers and Mergers, who previously had provided the Committee a paper on the British system, were in attendance and participated in the Committee's discussions. The British regulatory system was a model against which the U.S. system and the Advisory Committee's proposals were measured throughout the Committee's work. Elements of that system, particularly the requirement to make a tender for all of a company where an acquisition would bring someone's holdings over 30 percent, were of great interest to certain Committee members who took issue with hostile, partial, or two-tier offers.

On June 2, the Committee held a meeting in New York City for the

---

14. *See* letter dated February 1, 1983, to Chairman Shad from the Senate Banking Committee, which is included in the Advisory Committee's Report at 158.

15. *See* Release No. 34-19634 (March 30, 1983).

purpose of receiving presentations from certain commentators and other interested parties. As a result of the earlier solicitation for public comment, the Committee received forty-four comment letters, including fourteen current articles and papers. The hearings on June 2 gave the Committee an opportunity to confer with commentators regarding their views. Thirty-two people participated in this session.[16]

The Committee's fifth and next-to-last meeting was at the Commission's main offices in Washington, D.C., on June 10. On this occasion, the Advisory Committee considered and reached final agreement on the recommendations that would form the basis for its final Report. The final Report itself was presented to the Commission during the Committee's last meeting on July 8 at the Commission's main offices.[17]

III. THE ADVISORY COMMITTEE'S RECOMMENDATIONS

The Advisory Committee's Report contained fifty recommendations ranging from those defining the underlying premises of the proposed regulatory framework to specific suggestions for amendments to existing rules. Advisory Committee Chairman Dean LeBaron highlighted several themes that trace through the proposals in his transmittal letter to the Commission.

One principal theme was the Committee's finding as to the economic consequences of tender offers. The Committee concluded that tender offers are not per se beneficial or detrimental to the economy or the securities markets in general or to issuers or shareholders specifically.[18] Takeovers and related activities represent a valid method of capital allocation,[19] the regulation of which should be limited to the purpose of protecting shareholders and the integrity of the capital markets. As Chairman LeBaron stated in his transmittal letter:

> The Committee respects the free market forces in the operation of the U.S. securities markets. Academic evidence is widespread that the

---

16. Statements presented at these hearings, as well as all comment letters and minutes of Committee meetings are available at the Commission's Public Reference Room in File No. 265-15.

17. *See* Advisory Committee on Tender Offers, Report of Recommendations (July 8, 1983) [hereinafter cited as Report].

18. Some members argued that there is empirical evidence that tender offers create real value for bidders' and target companies' shareholders and that they thus should be encouraged. At the other end of the spectrum, other members identified detriments to tender offers. The majority of the Committee, however, found neither argument wholly persuasive.

19. In this regard, it is significant that hostile takeover contests, which have resulted in so much attention to the change-of-control area, in recent years have represented only around one-third of tender offers commenced.

takeover process is at least not demonstrably harmful to shareholders and some evidence points to its systematic benefits. We would be reluctant to restrict a process which seems to work reasonably well with the possibility that we might incur some unintended harm.

Having concluded that the regulatory structure should not be styled so as to promote or deter takeovers, the Committee reached a second tenet—that takeover regulation should not be designed to favor either the bidder or the target. This theme of regulatory neutrality was sounded by Congress in its adoption of the Williams Act, and the Committee reaffirmed that premise.

The third, and in many respects paramount, theme in the Committee's proposals was that the purpose of any regulation of the process should be the protection of shareholders and the integrity and effectiveness of the markets. This also was a reendorsement of a stated purpose of the Williams Act.

The final theme in the Committee's proposals was that of the balance between state and federal law. This theme was perhaps the least developed and the most ambiguous in the Committee's Report. The lack of clarity no doubt reflected the difficulty the Committee had in resolving the inherent tension in the present system, which as a general rule allocates regulation of bidders to federal law and regulation of targets to state law. Thus, although the Advisory Committee recognized that takeovers take place in the national securities market, and in so doing impliedly endorsed a uniform structure of regulation, it also posited that federal takeover regulation should not preempt substantive state corporation law, "except to the extent necessary to eliminate abuses or interference with the intended functioning of federal takeover regulation." In general, the Committee believed that the business judgment rule should continue to govern target company activities. This conceptual pole ultimately attracted criticism for two reasons. First, to some the proposition seemed disingenuous, given the Advisory Committee's proposals to prohibit certain charter and bylaw provisions and to require advisory votes on various issues. These recommendations seemed to some a most basic interference with the corporate governance process.[20] Second, it did not acknowledge the difficulties that some have identified with the application of the business judgment rule in the context of a hostile takeover bid, particularly where shareholders have not voted on the transaction in question.[21]

---

20. *See, e.g.*, Sommer, *The SEC's Advisory Committee on Tender Offers: Whatever Happened to State Law?* 16 Rev. Sec. Reg. 833 (1983).

21. *See* Gutman, *Tender Offer Defensive Tactics and the Business Judgment Rule*, 58 N.Y.U. L. Rev. 621 (1983); Prentice, *Target Board Abuse of Defensive Tactics:*

A. Regulation of Bidders

Proceeding from these basic propositions, the Committee recommended four major revisions in the regulation of bidders. The first of these recommendations was the removal of regulatory disincentives to exchange offers. Upon this proposal there was little disagreement. Because of the need under the Securities Act of 1933 ("Securities Act")[22] to register securities to be offered in exchange and the delay inherent in that process, particularly because of the expansive disclosure required to be included in the registration statement, bidders, to whom time is of the essence, have been deterred from using securities as consideration in tender offers. Bidders also have been discouraged from use of the exchange offer, because under current Commission rules an exchange offer may not commence until the Commission has declared the registration effective. The Committee specifically recommended that the integration of disclosure under the Securities Act and the Exchange Act, currently permitted by the Commission in securities offerings for cash, should be extended to exchange offers.[23] Along with streamlining the disclosure process, the Committee also recommended that bidders be permitted to commence their bids upon filing of a registration statement and to receive tenders prior to the effective date of the registration statement, subject to the shares being withdrawable prior to effectiveness.[24]

A second major concern of the Committee with the then current process was the ability of those seeking to acquire control of a public company to accumulate large holdings, perhaps even effective control, without adequate notice to the shareholders or the market and without providing shareholders an opportunity to share in the control premium. To address this concern, the Committee made two principal proposals.

The first related to reports of significant shareholdings. Under Section 13(d) of the Exchange Act, a person acquiring more than 5 percent of a class of specified equity securities of a public company is required to file with the Commission and the issuer a Schedule 13D that discloses his holdings and his intention with respect to such investment. That disclosure is not required until the tenth day from the triggering acquisition, until which date the acquirer may continue to buy additional securities. The

---

Can Federal Law be Mobilized to Overcome the Business Judgment Rule? 8 J. Corp. L. 337 (1983); Note, *Misapplication of the Business Judgment Rule in Contests for Corporate Control,* 76 Nw. U.L. Rev. 980 (1982). *See also* Harrington, *If It Ain't Broke, Don't Fix It: The Legal Propriety of Defenses against Hostile Takeover Bids,* 34 Syracuse L. Rev. 977 (1983).

22. 15 U.S.C. §§ 77a-77aa (1976 & Supp. VI 1982).

23. *See* Report, *supra* note 17, at Recommendation 11.

24. *Id.* at Recommendation 12.

Committee found that the ten-day window presented substantial opportunity for abuse and undermined the purpose of Section 13(d) to provide timely notice of potential changes in control of the issuer. It thus recommended that the filing window be closed and that the Schedule 13D be filed forty-eight hours prior to any acquisition of shares that would result in beneficial ownership of more than 5 percent of the class.[25]

As a further response to open market accumulation programs, the Committee also recommended that any any acquisition resulting in a holding of more than 20 percent of a class of voting securities be required to be made by a tender offer.[26] Underlying this proposal was the view that control is essentially a corporate asset and that shareholders should have an equal opportunity to shares in any premium paid for such asset. In the Committee's opinion, such opportunity would best be assured by imposing the substantive protections of the tender offer process.

The third principal recommendation with respect to bidders addressed the issues raised by partial bids. Public concern with partial bids has been particularly strong in recent years with the advent of "two-tier" or "front-end-loaded" bidding strategy. Such a strategy involves a tender offer for a minimum control amount at a high premium, followed by an acquisition of the remaining outstanding shares at a significantly lower price—usually by way of a second-step merger. Critics argue that with such an acquisition, shareholders have no choice but to participate in the first-step tender offer. The alternative of selling shares in the lower priced second step is not attractive. Thus, even if there may be a bid with a higher price than the combined or "blended" price of the two-tier offer, shareholders may feel compelled to accept the first-step tender offer.

Partial bids and other acquisitions of less than all the outstanding stock historically have been quite common in the United States. Partial bids, including two-tier offers, have accounted for approximately one-half of the offers commenced in fiscal years 1982 and 1983.

The use of the two-tier bid, however, is a recent phenomenon. It results in part from the fortuitous convergence of several factors: the demise of the state takeover statutes that generally had required a long proration period, the adoption by the Commission of a twenty-business-day minimum offering period in 1980,[27] and the minimum ten-calendar-day prorationing period prior to 1983. The contest for Conoco dramatically illustrated the strategic advantages of offering shareholders a higher price for shares tendered early. The experience dispelled the conventional wisdom that an offer for all the shares would necessarily be the winning bid and that a second-

---

25. *Id.* at Recommendation 13.
26. *Id.* at Recommendation 14.
27. *See* Rule 14e-1 under the Exchange Act (17 C.F.R. § 240.14e-1).

step acquisition had to be done at, or even above, the tender offer price to be successful. Since the Conoco contest, the basic tenet of bidding strategy is to offer a substantially lower price to those shareholders who delay and whose shares are taken in the second-step transaction.

The Committee expressed concern about the coercive elements of both partial and two-tier bids[28] and the potential such bids provide for abusive tactics and practices. At the same time, the Committee acknowledged the significant role of partial acquisitions in the economy. Thus, rather than recommending the prohibition or substantial restriction of partial offers and two-tier bids, the Committee proposed the imposition of a regulatory disincentive for any partial two-tier offer—a two-week extension of the minimum offering period beyond that applicable to full bids.[29]

In considering the issues involved in open market accumulation programs and partial offers, the Committee gave considerable thought to adoption of requirements similar to those provided in the British City Code on Takeovers and Mergers.[30] While that system had considerable attractions, the Committee opted for a more evolutionary approach, particularly in view of its concerns for the economic consequences of limiting partial acquisitions. The Committee did note in its Report, however, that in the event its recommendations concerning open market purchases and partial bids did not adequately serve the purposes of such recommendations, the Commission should reconsider incorporation of some features of the British system.

The Committee's last major proposal in the regulation of bidders' activities was the elimination of the requirement that the shareholders be permitted to withdraw shares tendered to one bidder upon the commencement of a competing bid.[31] The Committee took issue with a system that permitted a second bidder in effect to control the timing of the first bidder's offer. The Committee determined that this tipped the regulatory balance directly in favor of the second bidder and, because the second bidder is frequently a white knight, indirectly in favor of the target company. The Committee

---

28. As some Commission members pointed out, the pure partial offer is perhaps the ultimate two-tier bid: the first step being the partial tender offer, the second being the open market. Assuming the bidder is successful, the market price for remaining outstanding shares may be significantly lower than the price offered in the tender offer.

29. See Report, supra note 17, at Recommendation 16.

30. The element of the British system that received the greatet attention was the general requirement that where an acquisition would result in a holding of more than 30%, the acquirer must proceed by way of a tender offer for all the shares. Such a system had some appeal, because it would tend to address concerns regarding not only two-tier pricing but also open market purchase programs.

31. See Report, supra note 17, at 28-29. This proposal was framed not in a specific recommendation but rather in the text of the Report as a Committee conclusion.

defined as a fundamental precept that a bidder should control its own bid. It also recommended, however, that shareholders be permitted to withdraw their shares thoughout the minimum offering period, rather than for the first three quarters as currently exists.[32]

B. Regulation of Targets

Under current law, the activities of the bidder are largely regulated by federal law, while the response of the target company generally is governed by state corporate law. In determining whether the current allocation makes sense, the Committee had to balance two of its basic principles: minimal preemption of the traditional state corporate law, on the one hand, and maintenance of the integrity of the national securities market in which tender offers take place, on the other. The Committee struck the following balance.

First, it recommended the continued preeminence of state corporate law governing management's response to a specific offer in which management is making a business judgment.[33] Second, it recommended that federal law prohibit action by an issuer or a state that would generally restrict the transfer of control across the board without reference to a specific offer. The second point rested on the grounds that such restriction reflected no business judgment on the merits of a particular proposed business combination but rather sought to impede any takeover. The Committee concluded this was an undue interference with the functioning of the national capital markets. In this regard, the Committee recommended a prohibition of antitakeover provisions in companies' charters and bylaws, as well as state statutes.[34]

Generally, under the Committee's proposals, defensive actions by an issuer in response to a specific offer would be governed by the business judgment rule and other principles of fiduciary duty imposed under state corporate law. Such actions would include self-tenders, countertenders and sales of "crown jewels."[35] Two exceptions to this general principle of state regulation of defensive responses were recommeded. The Committee proposed that during a tender offer there should be a rule similar to that of the New York Stock Exchange, which requires shareholder approval of the issuance of a significant percentage of a class of a company's voting securities.[36] It also recommended a requirement of shareholder approval of an issuer's repurchase of its shares at a premium to market from a person who

---

32. *Id.* at Recommendation 17.

33. *Id.* at Recommendation 33.

34. *Id.* at Recommendation 35. *See also* Recommendation 34.

35. *Id.* at Recommendation 39-42.

36. *See* NYSE Company's Manual A-284; Report, *supra* note 17, at Recommendation 41. The NYSE rule sets the limit at 18.5%, while the Committee used 15% in its recommendation.

had acquired such shares within two years of the purchase.[37] The latter recommendation was designed to discourage "greenmail."

Acutely aware of the political issues in prohibiting adoption of antitakeover provisions in issuers' charters or bylaws, the Committee recommended two alternative interim measures until such prohibitions could be effected. One such recommendation was to require that supermajority vote provisions be adopted initially by the same supermajority level of vote and ratified every three years.[38] Underlying this recommendation was the apparent assumption that while issuers might possibly be willing to undertake the costs and efforts of obtaining the supermajority vote once, the renewal vote requirement was certain to deter most from seeking to adopt these types of provisions. The second alternative interim measure recommended by the Committee was the annual disclosure of, and shareholder advisory vote on, the issuer's various change-of-control provisions and policies—for example, supermajority provisions, provisions restricting the principle of one share–one vote (other than cumulative voting), and standstill agreements.[39] The shareholder vote would not be binding but rather would advise the board of directors of shareholders' views on these matters.

A final Committee recommendation of some note was its proposal regarding change-of-control compensation. The Committee did not find that "golden parachutes" have a deterrent effect on takeovers. It was well aware, however, of the general belief that such arrangements represent gross overreaching by management and a failure to place the interests of the shareholders foremost. The mistrust of the process arising from this widespread public perception compelled the Committee to recommend that such arrangements be prohibited once a takeover of the issuer had commenced.[40] Under the Committee's proposal, compensation arrangements adopted prior to a threatened takeover would be disclosed in the proxy statement and subject to an advisory vote of the shareholders; adoption of such arrangements during a tender offer would be prohibited. The recommendation struck a balance between the interest of free bargaining of management and the concerns of those troubled by the propriety of management "feathering its own nest."

IV. COMMISSION RESPONSE

A. The Commission's Findings

Upon receiving the Advisory Committee's Report, the Commission forwarded it to Congress. In so doing, however, the Commission did not

---

37. *See* Report, *supra* note 17, at Recommendation 43.
38. *Id*. at Recommendation 36.
39. *Id*. at Recommendation 37.
40. *Id*. at Recommendation 38.

express any views on the recommendations. Rather, the Commission requested in-depth study of all the proposals by its staff. That process[41] culminated in an open meeting on March 13, 1984, at which the Commission arrived at a position with respect to each of the Committee's fifty recommendations.[42] With the exception of two releases in rulemaking projects that had been underway prior to completion of the Advisory Committee's Report,[43] this was the first occasion upon which the Commission addressed the proposals. Two weeks later, on March 28, Chairman Shad restated the Commission's formal positions in testimony before the Subcommitttee on Telecommunications, Consumer Protection, and Finance of the House Committee on Energy and Commerce.

In considering the recommendations of the Advisory Committee, the Commission was guided by four basic premises: (1) that tender offers are a valid method of capital allocation, and, therefore, regulation should be imposed only where necessary to protect shareholders and the integrity and efficiency of the national securities trading market; (2) that tender offers are transactions in the national trading markets, and, therefore, their regulation should be at the federal level; (3) that target company shareholders, not incumbent management, should ultimately determine the success or failure of a tender offer bid; and (4) that state corporate law should govern the actions of a target company management except where such action frustrates the takeover process and the efficiency of the national trading market to the detriment of shareholders.

Applying these premises, the Commission concurred in thirty-four of the

---

41. Along with its own research and analysis, the staff had the benefit of a number of articles that addressed the Advisory Committee's recommendations. *See*, e.g., Greene, *Tender Offer Committee's Suggestions No Surprise*, Legal Times (Wash.), Aug. 8, 1983, at 13; Lowenstein, *Regulation of Tender Offers, A Critical Comment*, 16 Rev. Sec. Reg. 829 (1983); Sommer, *The SEC's Advisory Committee on Tender Offers: Whatever Happened to State Law?* 16 Rev. Sec. Reg. 833 (1983).

42. *See* Appendix A (following this chapter).

43. Release No. 34-20581 (January 19, 1984). In this release the Commission adopted Rule 17Ad-14 (17 C.F.R. § 240.17Ad-14), which requires bidders' tender agents to establish during tender offers an account with qualified registered securities depositories to permit financial institutions participating in such depository system to use the services of the depository to tender shares if desired. The Advisory Committee had recommended adoption of this rule. *See* Report, *supra* note 17, at Recommendation 48. *See also* Release No. 33-6486 (September 23, 1983). In this release, the Commission adopted certain revisions to its disclosure rules which established new requirements as to compensation of highly paid executives. One element of these revisions related to disclosure of change-of-control compensation. *See* Item 402(e) of Regulation S-K (17 C.F.R. § 229.402(e)). In adopting this provision, the Commission noted the Advisory Committee's Recommendations 37 and 38.

Advisory Committee's proposals. As well as agreeing with most of the Commission's basic policy recommendations, the Commission supported the proposals to put cash and exchange offers on a more equal regulatory footing (Recommendations 11 and 12), to require target companies to make shareholder lists available to bidders and those engaged in a proxy solicitation (Recommendation 22), and to prohibit hedged and multiple tendering (Recommendations 44 and 46). The Commission also endorsed the Committee's proposal to prohibit a management buyback of recently accumulated blocks of stock at a premium, unless approved by shareholders or accompanied by an equivalent offer to all shareholders (Recommendation 43). The Commission agreed with the Committee that such management activities erode confidence in the national securities markets and the takeover process and that such repurchases provide management the ability to block bids and inhibit potential takeovers by using corporate assets to buy out prospective bidders. The Commission rejected the argument that the risks of failure for a first bidder are so substantial that the buyback possibility is necessary to encourage first bids. The Commission concluded that shareholders' interests are better served by reducing the risk to first bidders by eliminating management's ability to use the assets and authorized equity of a target company to frustrate a bid, while at the same time removing the disincentives to exchange offers and eliminating the ability of competing offers to reopen withdrawal rights of other offers.

The Commission modified thirteen of the Advisory Committee's recommendations, a number to a large extent, and wholly disagreed with six of the Committee's recommendations. The Commission agreed that the ten-day filing window of Section 13(d) of the Exchange Act should be closed (Recommendation 13), but it rejected the Committee's proposal that this be done by preacquisition notice. The Commission had significant concerns with the economic consequences of a preacquistion filing of Schedule 13D and proposed instead, consistent with the existing requirement of the Williams Act, to require a filing *after* crossing the threshold and before additional acquisitions are made.

As to the timing provisions of tender offers, the Commission modified the Advisory Committee findings that the proration and withdrawal rights should be provided for the defined minimum offering period to provide simply that proration and withdrawal rights exist for the entire duration of an offer, however long. The Commission did endorse the Committee's recommendation that a competing bid should not automatically trigger extension of withdrawal rights in other bids. It did not support certain other elements of the timing proposals that would extend the minimum offering period for full bids to thirty calendar days and for partial bids to forty-five days (Recommendations 17 and 18).

While agreeing with the Advisory Committee that shareholders would be better served if there were no charter or bylaw provisions that discouraged takeovers, the Commission was unwilling to preempt state corporate law on such a fundamental issue. Therefore, the Commission did not endorse the Committee's recommendation of federal prohibition or regulation of such provisions (Recommendation 35).

The Commission, however, was prepared to recommend federal regulation of three specific target management tactics that can prevent or inhibit tender offers and thus deny shareholders the opportunity to accept or reject a bid. First, the Commission concluded, as did the Advisory Committee (Recommendation 41), that the issuance of shares and concomitant placement of votes in hands friendly to incumbent management should be proscribed when undertaken during a tender offer. The Commission proposed, therefore, that issuances in excess of 5 percent of a class of securities or voting power during a tender offer be prohibited unless approved by shareholders.

Second, the Commission concluded that defensive issuer reacquisitions by tender offer and defensive publicly announced market-buying programs likewise blocked tender offers and rejected the Committee's recommendation that they continue to be tested by the business judgment rule (Recommendation 39). The Commission would prohibit such defensive actions unless approved by shareholders. Some have sought to justify issuer tender offers as providing a second step to shareholders where there is only a partial bid. These tender offers are generally subject to the condition that, if the initial bid is withdrawn, the issuer tender offer can likewise be terminated. The Commission found the purpose of the issuer tender offer to be two-fold. First, it is to attract shares into management's hands and thus prevent the first bidder from obtaining the minimum number of shares being sought. If the first bid does not get its minimum, it is usually terminated. Once the third-party bid is eliminated, the issuer tender offer can be withdrawn, and shareholders will receive nothing. Second, the target company bid is designed to make the issuer less attractive. Essentially, the target company is threatening the bidder that if it proceeds with its bid, the bidder will end up with a company substantially less valuable because of a major equity redemption. The Commission also disagreed with the Committee's recommendations concerning advisory voting (Recommendations 37 and 38) and counter tender offers (Recommendation 40).

One of the most notable and fundamental disagreements with the Advisory Committee's recommendations was the Commission's refusal to endorse the application of the business judgment rule to change-of-control transactions to permit virtually unfettered management defensive actions. The Commission, rejecting the Advisory Committee's position, stated that shareholders' interest required greater judicial sensitivity to the potential conflict of interest between shareholders and management of the target company in these situations. However, as with charter and bylaw antitakeover provisions, the Commission was not prepared to support federal preemption of state corporate law on so fundamental and broad an issue as defining directors' fiduciary responsibilities. Finally, the Commission found it needed more study of the problems cited by the Committee in, and the consequences of inhibiting, creeping tender offers and partial and two-tier bids. (Recommendations 14 and 16).

B. Rulemaking and Legislative Initiatives

Implementation of the Commission's program to revise the regulatory framework governing acquistion of control will proceed on three fronts.

1. Rulemaking

Following Chairman Shad's testimony before the House Subcommittee on March 28, the Commission initiated a series of rulemaking projects to effect certain recommendations.

a. Rule 10b-4

The Commission amended Rule 10b-4 under the Exchange Act to prohibit hedged and multiple tendering. *See* Release No. 34-20799 (March 29, 1984). Adoption of these amendments, which had been proposed prior to the establishment of the Advisory Committee (*see* Release No. 34-18050 (August 21, 1981)), implemented Advisory Committee Recommendations 44 and 46. Later, in Release No. 34-21049 (June 14, 1984), the Commission proposed further amendments to Rule 10b-4 to require the person who tenders shares by guarantee of delivery to deliver all of the shares subject to the guarantee to the offeror. This proposal also would extend prohibition of hedged tendering to cover the writing of certain exchange-traded call options. Adoption of these proposed amendments would implement Advisory Committee Recommendation 47.

b. Equalization of Cash and Exchange Offers

The Commission agreed with the Advisory Committee's proposal to extend the concept of integrated disclosure to exchange offers. In Release No. 33-6534 (May 9, 1984), the Commission proposed a new form of registration, Form S-4, for exchange offers and other business combinations. An essential concept in this proposed new form was that the integration of disclosure under the Securities Act and the Exchange Act, previously effected in other registration forms, could be applied in the context of a business combination. Adoption of Form S-4 was to be an implementation of Advisory Committee Recommendation 11.

The Advisory Committee also recommended that bidders be permitted to commence exchange offers upon filing of a Securities Act registration statement and to receive tenders prior to the effective date of that registration statement. *See* Recommendation 12. The Commission agreed with this recommendation and initiated a rulemaking project to consider possible amendments to rules under both the Securities Act and the Exchange Act to effect the Advisory Committee's proposal. The primary issues in effecting Recommendation 12 are the definition of sale under the Securities Act which includes acceptance of payment for registered securities even if rescindable and the consequences of facilitating publicly leveraged takeovers.

c. Other Rule Revisions

Other areas to be the subject of rulemaking projects include: (1) extension of withdrawal rights throughout the offer and the elimination of automatic extension of withdrawal rights upon commencement of a competing bid (Recommendation 17), (2) extension of withdrawal and proration rights and the minimum offer period for a specified time following the announcement of any increase in the price or the number of shares sought (Recommendation 18), (3) the inclusion of key conditions to an offer in a summary advertisement used to commence a tender offer (Recommendation 20), (4) a requirement to deliver shareholder lists (Recommendation 22), and (5) the equalization of proration periods for competing issuer and third-party tender offers (Recommendation 39b).

As noted by the Advisory Committee, the takeover process includes proxy contests as well as equity acquisition transactions, and, to be effective and rational, the regulatory framework governing the different methods of control acquisition must take into account the consequences to the whole process (Recommendation 10). The Commission has commenced a reexamination of its rules governing proxy contests.

2. Legislative Proposals

Certain of the Commission's proposals fell outside the scope of its rulemaking authority. These primarily involved proposals regarding defensive measures by target companies. The Commission forwarded to Congress on May 21, 1984, a proposed legislative package to accommodate these recommendations.[44] The Commission's legislative proposal contained five substantive elements: (1) an amendment to Section 13(d) of the 1934 Act to grant rulemaking authority to the Commission to specify the filing deadline "after" an acquisition bringing a beneficial holding above 5 percent and to prohibit additional purchases until the required disclosure has been provided to the market,[45] (2) a proscription of target company share repur-

---

44. This legislation, entitled the Tender Offer Reform Act of 1984, was introduced in the House by Congressman Timothy Wirth (D-Colo.) on May 22, 1984, as H.R. 5693, and in the Senate by Senator Alfonse D'Amato (R-N.Y.) on June 20, 1984, as S. 2782.

45. This evolved from the Advisory Committee's Recommendation 13—the proposal to close the 10-day filing window in Section 13(d).

chases during certain tender offers,[46] (3) a proscription of specified share issuances during certain tender offers and proxy contests,[47] (4) a proscription of increases to executive compensation during certain tender offers,[48] and (5) a restriction on certain stock repurchases of recently acquired blocks of securities at a premium to market.[49] As a result of a number of large mergers and corporate control transactions, particularly in the oil industry, in the spring of 1984 there developed significant interest on Capitol Hill in the Advisory Committee's Report, specifically, and in the whole area of change-of-control regulation, generally. The by-product of this Congressional attention was the introduction not only of the Commission's proposed legislation but also of numerous other pieces of legislation that presented alternative approaches to a number of common issues. It is unclear, at this writing, what the outcome of this flurry of legislative activity will be. The review of principal topics that follows may well reflect areas of Congressional interest in subsequent sessions.

a. Improving Communications between Issuers and Beneficial Owners

Shortly after the Advisory Committee's Report, the Commission adopted outstanding proposed amendments to Rules 14a-3, 14b-1, and 17a-3 under the Exchange Act. *See* Release No. 34-20021 (July 28, 1983). These amendments require broker-dealers to give names of consenting beneficial holders to issuers of securities that such broker-dealers hold in street name. The purpose of these amendments was to facilitate direct communication between issuers and shareholders. The amendments had evolved from another Commission-sponsored panel, its Advisory Committee on Shareholder Com-

---

46. *See* Report, *supra* note 17, at Recommendation 39a. The Commission's legislative proposal would only restrict golden parachutes and issuer reacquisitions and issuances *during* tender offers that were both unconditional with respect to at least 10% of the target's securities and at least a 25% premium. As the Commission explained in the memorandum accompanying its legislative proposal, it was concerned that without any thresholds for application, the legislation would place undue power in the hands of bidders to block or inhibit legitimate corporate actions, thus disrupting the careful balance between bidders and targets, and that the threat to commence a tender offer could become a new type of coercive tactic. If the prohibitions contained in the legislation could be triggered by any tender offer for the issuer's securities, the Commission was concerned that a bidder could make an offer below market or at a minimal premium, or an offer subject to conditions unlikely to be satisfied, solely to restrict the target's ability to engage in legitimate corporate activities.

47. *Id.* at Recommendation 41.
48. *Id.* at Recommendation 38a.
49. *Id.* at Recommendation 43.

munications, and the Tender Offer Advisory Committee had supported generally the effort to effect better communications between issuers and
beneficial holders. Because the Commission did not have jurisdiction over
proxy processing by banks, the new rules were limited to broker-dealers.
To remedy that imbalance, the Commission proposed a legislative amendment to Section 14(b) of the Exchange Act that would bring banks within
the Commission's proxy oversight. That legislation was introduced by Congressman Timothy E. Wirth (D-Colo.) on May 22, 1984, as H.R. 5696. A
similar bill was introduced by Senator Alfonse M. D'Amato (R-N.Y.) on June
20, 1984, as S. 2785.

b. Greenmail

The spring of 1984 witnessed a series of highly publicized share repurchases at prices above the prevailing market, so-called greenmail.[50] These
transactions stirred significant interest in Congress. As a result, greenmail
was the subject of action not only in the Commission's legislative initiative
but also in separate pieces of legislation, most of which included the same
provision as in the Commission's legislative package, that is, a requirement
that any repurchase of shares at a price above market, from any person who
holds more than 3 percent of the class to be purchased and who has held
such securities for less than two years, be approved by a majority of the
shareholders or be made on equal terms to all shareholders. See S. 2700,
2754, 2777, and 2779.

c. Golden Parachutes

As with "greenmail," the subject of executive compensation during tender
offers, so-called golden parachutes, held a particular Congressional fasci-
nation apart from other change-of-control—related issues. Thus, the Commission's proposal, which would amend Section 14 of the Exchange Act to
prohibit any increase in current or future compensation of an officer or
director during certain classes of tender offers, was introduced not only as
part of the larger tender offer package but also as an amendment to Senator
Jake Garn's (R-Utah) omnibus banking bill (S. 2700). Alternatively, Congress
also adressed golden parachutes as a tax issue. The Tax Reform Act of 1984
(H.R. 4170) contained a provision that subjects "parachute payments" to
an excise tax in the hands of the employee and also makes them nonde-
ductible to the employer. A "parachute payment" was defined in this legislation as an amount exceeding three times average earnings over the

---

50. These transactions included repurchases by Walt Disney Productions from
Saul P. Steinberg, by Texaco from Bass Brothers Enterprises, by Warner Commu-
nications from Rupert Murdoch, by St. Regis from Sir James Goldsmith, by Superior
Oil from T. Boone Pickens, by American Can from Carl Icahn, and by Gulf and
Western from Carl Lindner.

previous five years. Golden parachutes also were treated in amendments to other tax bills. *See* S. 2323, H.R. 2163, and H.R. 4357.

d. Business Judgment

Although the Commission made no specific proposals regarding its concern about the application of the business judgment rule in change-of-control transactions, legislators picked up on the Commission's comment and introduced legislation that would redefine the business judgment rule in the corporate control contest. Specifically, Congressman Wirth proposed legislation (*see* H.R. 5695 and 5972) that would shift the burden of proof to management in a change-of-control situation to prove "by a preponderance of the evidence that the transaction complained of is both prudent for the issuer and fair to the issuer's shareholders." The bill also would give both shareholders and the Commission the right to sue to enjoin the transaction. That provision was also introduced in the Senate. *See* S. 2777 and 2779. With virtually no comment and apparently little notice, the bill was drafted to apply to any change-of-control transaction, whether management is in favor or opposed. This would seem to bring even negotiated mergers under federal regulation on such basic issues as the substantive fairness of the transaction.

e. Other Provisions

Other legislation involving takeovers found its way into the record during the spring of 1984. One item involved a proposed restriction on bidders (*see* S. 2783 and H.R. 5694) based on a proposal submitted by Martin Lipton, a member of the Advisory Committee. It required that an acquistion resulting in ownerhip of more than 10 percent of the voting power of an issuer be by tender offer for all the outstanding shares at a price equal to the highest price paid by the bidder for that stock during the preceding twelve months. Other proposals included a requirement that directors of certain corporations hold at least 1,000 shares of those corporation (S. 2797) and, in an attempt to curtail hostile bids, that a takeover must be approved by a majority of the independent directors of the target company (H.R. 5137). Finally, at least one bill attempted a comprehensive overhaul of takeover regulation. *See* H.R. 5914.

3. Further Study

The Commission expressed reservations with two Advisory Committee recommendations (14 and 16) that were addressed to perceived problems in the area of creeping tender offers and two-tier bidding practices. In expressing its reservation, the Commission indicated that it believed further study of the issues underlying these recommendations was required. On June 21, 1984, the Commission issued a release requesting public comment on the Advisory Committee's recommendations, as well as on other proposals, in the area of two-tier pricing in tender offers and non-tender offer purchase programs. *See* Release No. 34-21079. This release also published a report by the Commission's chief economist on tender offers for calendar years 1981–1983.

V. CONCLUSION

The long-term significance of the Advisory Committee Report likely lies not so much in the Committee's specific recommendations but in its initiation of a substantive debate on fundamental issues involving control of public companies and the relation of federal and state regulation of corporate control transactions: whether the public interest is best served by a system that permits hostile takeovers; whether tender offers for control and mergers are sufficiently alike to require comparable substantive regulation, or sufficiently different to justify primary federal regulation of tender offers and primary state regulation of mergers; and, finally, whether the interests of shareholders should be the primary concern in resolving these issues.

APPENDIX A: COMMITTEE RECOMMENDATIONS AND COMMISSION POSITIONS (AS ADOPTED AT ITS MEETING ON MARCH 13, 1984)

Recommendations	Commission Position
I. *Economics of Takeovers and Their Regulation*	
1. The purpose of the regulatory scheme should be neither to promote nor to deter takeovers; such transactions and related activities are a valid method of capital allocation, so long as they are conducted in accordance with the laws deemed necessary to protect the interests of shareholders and the integrity and efficiency of the capital markets	The Commission agrees with this general proposition.
2. There is no material distortion in the credit markets resulting from control acquisition transactions, and no regulatory initiative should be undertaken to limit the availability of credit in such transactions or to allocate credit among such transactions.	The Commission has limited expertise in this area but agrees with this general proposition.

II. *Objectives of Federal Regulation of Takeovers*

3. Takeover regulation should not favor either the acquirer or the target company but should aim to achieve a reasonable balance, while at the same time protecting the interests of shareholders and the integrity and efficiency of the markets.

The Commission agrees with this general proposition. It requires no specific action.

4. Regulation of takeovers should recognize that such transactions take place in a national securities market.

The Commission agrees with this general proposition. That agreement, however, should not be construed to justify a wholesale preemption of state corporate law.

5. Cash and securities tender offers should be placed on an equal regulatory footing so that bidders, the market and shareholders, and not regulation, decide between the two.

The Commission supports the general proposition that regulatory disincentives to exchange offers should be minimized to the extent consistent with investor protection. Implementation of this recommendation and Recommendations 11 and 12 will be the final major steps in the integration of disclosure requirements under the Securities Act and the Exchange Act.

6. Regulation of takeovers should not unduly restrict innovations in takeover techniques. These techniques should be able to evolve in relationship to changes in the market and the economy.

The Commission agrees with this general proposition.

7. Even though regulation may restrict innovations in takeover techniques, it is desirable to have sufficient regulation to insure the integrity of the markets and to protect shareholders and market participants against fraud, nondisclosure of material information, and the creation of situations in which a significant number of reasonably diligent small shareholders may be at a disadvantage to market professionals.

The Commission agrees with this general proposition.

8. The evolution of the market and innovation in takeover techniques may from time to time produce abuses. The regulatory framework should be flexible enough to allow the Commission to deal with such abuses as soon as they appear.

The Commission agrees with this general proposition.

9. a. *State Takeover Law.* State regulation of takeovers should be confined to local companies.

The Commission agrees with this general proposition.

b. *State Corporation Law.* Except to the extent necessary to eliminate abuses or interference with the intended functioning of federal takeover regulation, federal takeover regulation should not preempt or override state corporation law. Essentially the business judgment rule should continue to govern most such activity.

The Commission agrees with the Advisory Committee's recognition of the general preeminence of state corporate law with respect to the internal affairs of a corporation. However, in the application of the business judgment rule in a change-of-control context, the Commission believes that shareholders would be better served if the courts gave greater recognition to potential conflicts of interest between management and shareholders.

c. *State Regulation of Public Interest Businesses.* Federal takeover regulation should not preempt substantive state regulation of banks, utilities, insurance companies, and similar businesses, where the change-of-control provisions of such state regulation are justified in relation to the overall objectives of the industry being regulated, do not conflict with procedural provisions of federal takeover regulation, and relate to a significant portion of the issuer's business.

The Commission agrees with this general proposition.

d. *Federal Regulation.* Federal takeover regulation should not override the regulation of particular industries, such as banks, broadcast licensees, railroads, ship operators, nuclear licensees, etc.

The Commission agrees with this general proposition.

e. *Relationships with Other Federal Laws.* Federal takeover regulation should not be used to achieve antitrust, labor, tax, use of credit, and similar objectives. Those objectives should be achieved by separate legislation or regulation.

The Commission agrees with this general proposition.

III. *Regulation of Acquirers of Corporate Control*

10. Any regulation of one or more change-of-control transactions by either the Congress or the Commission should address the effects of such regulation in the context of all control acquisition techniques.

The Commission agrees with this general proposition.

11. The concept of integration of disclosure under the Securities Act of 1933 and the Securities Exchange Act of 1934, previously effected by the Commission in securities offerings for cash, should be extended to exchange offers.

The Commission agrees with this general proposition.

12. Bidders should be permitted to commence their bids upon filing of a registration statement and receive tenders prior to the effective date of the registration statement. Prior to effectiveness, all tendered shares would be withdrawable. Effectiveness of the registration statement would be a condition to the exchange offer. If the final prospectus were materially different from the preliminary prospectus, the bidder would be required to maintain, by extension, a 10-day period between mailing of the amended prospectus and expiration, withdrawal, and proration dates. This period would assure adequate dissemination of information to shareholders and the opportunity to react prior to incurring any irrevocable duties.

The Commission agrees with this recommendation generally, reserving judgment on specific means of effecting the proposal.

13. No person may acquire directly or indirectly beneficial ownership of

The Commission endorses closing the 10-day window period in

more than 5% of an outstanding class of equity securities unless such person has filed a Schedule 13D and that schedule has been on file with the Commission for at least 48 hours. Such person may rely on the latest Exchange Act report filed by the target company that reports the number of shares outstanding. The acquirer would have to report subsequent purchases promptly as provided by current law.

Section 13(d). The Commission opposes a preacquisition filing requirement and proposes instead a requirement of immediate public announcement, next-day filing of the Schedule 13D and/or a standstill until filing.

14. No person may acquire voting securities of an issuer, if, immediately following such acquisition, such person would own more than 20% of the voting power of the outstanding voting securities of that issuer unless such purchase were made (i) from the issuer or (ii) pursuant to a tender offer. The Commission should retain broad exemptive power with respect to this provision.

The Commission has serious reservations about this recommendation. Further study of the economic implications for the entire change-of-control area is required.

15. The Committee encourages the Commission to study means to strengthen the concept and definition of "group" or concerted activity.

The Commission has reviewed its rules and interpretations in light of this recommendation and concluded that additional action is not necessary at this time. The Commission will continue to monitor this area.

16. The minimum offering period for a tender offer for less than all the outstanding shares of a class of voting securities should be approximately two weeks longer than that prescribed for other tender offers.

The Commission is sensitive to the Committee's concerns regarding two-tier and partial offers but is not certain that the Committee's recommendation is the best way to address these concerns. This issue requires further study.

17. The minimum offering period for an initial bid should be 30 calendar days; for subsequent bids the minimum offering period should be 20 calendar days, provided that the subsequent bid shall not terminate before the 30th calendar day of the initial bid. In each case, the mini-

The Commission believes the tender offer process should not be permitted to become so complex that it is understood only by investment professionals. *See* Recommendation 32. The Committee's recommendations with respect to the timing of tender

mum offering period will be subject to increase, if the bid is a partial offer. The period during which tendering shareholders will have proration and withdrawal rights should be the same length as the minimum offering period.

offers are too complex and may disadvantage nonprofessional shareholders. Shareholders would be better served by a system that simply provides for prorationing and withdrawal throughout the offering period and a required minimum 20-business-day offering period. The Commission endorses the Committee's proposal to eliminate the automatic extension of withdrawal rights upon commencement of a competing bid.

18. The minimum offering period and prorationing period should not terminate for five calendar days from the announcement of an increase in price or number of shares sought.

The Commission agrees that the offering period should be extended if there is an increase in price or the number of shares sought. Since prorationing and withdrawal rights are proposed to be required throughout an offer, any extension of the offer will automatically extend such rights. The Commission reserves judgment on the length of the extension, pending public comment on a proposed rule change.

19. Where the bidder discloses projections or asset valuations to target company shareholders, it must include disclosure of the principal supporting assumptions provided to the bidder by the target.

The Commission does not endorse this recommendation at this time.

20. The Commission should review its disclosure rules and the current disclosure practices of tender offer participants to eliminate unnecessary or duplicative requirements, as well as inordinately complex or confusing disclosures. The Commission's rules should require a clear and concise statement of the price, terms, and key conditions of the offer. In addition, the Commission should amend its rules to permit inclusion of the key conditions in a summary advertisement used to commence an offer.

The Commission agrees with this general recommendation.

21. The Commission should continue its efforts to facilitate direct communications with shareholders whose shares are held in street name.

The Commission agrees with this general recommendation.

22. The Commission should require under its proxy and tender offer rules that a target company make available to an acquirer, at the acquirer's expense, shareholder lists and clearinghouse security position listings within five calendar days of a bona fide request by an acquirer who has announced a proxy contest or tender offer. The Commission should consider prescribing standard forms (written or electronic) for the delivery of such information.

The Commission agrees with this general recommendation.

23. Tender offer reply forms should be standardized to the extent possible to facilitate handling by brokerage firms, banks, and depositaries.

The Commission agrees with this general recommendation.

24. Except to the extent there already exists such a requirement in a particular context, the price paid by an acquirer unaffiliated with the target company should not be required to be "fair" nor should federal law provide for state law–type appraisal rights.

The Commission agrees with this endorsement of current law.

25. All shareholders whose shares are purchased in a tender offer should be entitled to the highest per share price paid in the offer.

The Commission agrees with this endorsement of current federal securities regulation.

26. Current prohibitions of the purchase by a bidder of target company shares other than under the offer should be continued.

The Commission agrees with this endorsement of current federal securities regulation.

27. All time periods should be defined in terms of calendar days.

The Commission believes that all time periods should continue to be defined in terms of business days.

28. "Commencement" of a tender offer should continue to be determined by present rules, and time periods should continue to run from that date.

The Commission agrees with this endorsement of current federal securities regulation.

29. Offering documents that are required to be mailed should be mailed within seven calendar days of commencement by announcement.

The Commission agrees with this recommendation.

30. Voluntary extensions may be made by the offeror with any type of offer at any time before the commencement of the first trading day after the expiration date of the offer.

The Commission agrees with this endorsement of current federal securities regulation.

31. Approval by shareholders of a bidder with respect to an acquisition should continue to be an internal matter between shareholders and management, subject only to applicable state law.

The Commission agrees with this endorsement of current law.

32. The takeover process should not be permitted to become so complex that it is understood only by investment professionals.

The Commission agrees with this general proposition.

IV. *Regulation of Opposition to Acquisitions of Control*

33. The Committee supports a system of state corporate laws and the business judgment rule. No reform should undermine that system. Broadly speaking, the Committee believes that the business judgment rule should be the principal governor of decisions made by corporate management, including decisions that may alter the likelihood of a takeover.

Qualified by its concerns regarding the application of the business judgment rule in change-of-control situations (*see* Recommendation 9(b)), the Commission agrees with this general proposition.

34. State laws and regulations, regardless of their form, that restrict the ability of a company to make a tender offer should not be permitted, because they constitute an undue burden on interstate commerce. Included in this category should be statutes that prohibit completion of a tender offer without target company shareholder approval and broad policy legislation written so as to impair the ability to transfer corporate control in a manner and

The Commission agrees with this general proposition.

time frame consistent with the federal tender offer process. An exception to this basic prohibition may be appropriate where a significant portion of the target company is in a regulated industry and where special change-of-control provisions are vital to the achievement of ends for which the industry is regulated. Where such change-of-control provisions cannot be justified in relation to the overall objectives of the industry regulations or where only a small portion of the target company is in the regulated industry, there should not be an automatic impediment to the completion of a tender offer. Rather, the tender offer should be completed with the regulated business placed in trust during any postacquisition approval period. Further, no such regulation should interfere with the procedural provisions under the Williams Act.

35. Congress and the Commission should adopt appropriate legislation and/or regulations to prohibit the use of charter and bylaw provisions that erect high barriers to change of control and thus operate against the interests of shareholders and the national marketplace.

The Commission shares the serious concerns of the Advisory Committee with respect to the effects of these devices but is not prepared at this time to concur in such a broad intrusion into state corporate law.

36. To the extent not prohibited or otherwise restricted, companies should be permitted to adopt provisions requiring supermajority approval for change-of-control transactions only where the ability to achieve such a level of support is demonstrable.

   a. Any company seeking approval of a charter or bylaw provision that requires, or could under certain circumstances require, the affirmative vote of more than the minimum specified by state law should be required to obtain that same level of approval in passing the provision initially. Ratification

The Commission agrees with the Advisory Committee that implementation of supermajority voting requirements should require comparable votes for adoption. As noted with respect to Recommendation 35, however, the Commission is not prepared at this time to concur in such a broad intrusion into state corporate law. The Commission does not agree that such provisions should be subject to reratification after adoption.

should be required every three years.

b. Where a charter or bylaw provision provides a formula for the required level of approval, which level cannot be determined until the circumstances of the merger are known, the formula shall be limited by law so as to require a vote no higher than the percentage of votes actually ratifying the charter or bylaw provision. Ratification should be required every three years.

c. For a nationally traded company that has adopted a supermajority provision prior to the date of enactment of this recommendation, and for a local company with a supermajority provision which becomes nationally traded at a later date, shareholders must ratify the supermajority provision within three years after such date and continue to ratify such provision every three years thereafter.

37. The Commission should designate certain change-of-control–related policies of corporations as "advisory vote matters" for review at each annual shareholders' meeting for the election of directors and for disclosure in the proxy statement.

   a. *Matters Covered.* Advisory vote matters should include:

      i. *Supermajority provisions.* To the extent not prohibited or otherwise restricted, charter provisions requiring more than the statutorily imposed minimum vote requirement to accomplish a merger, including provisions requiring supermajority approval under special conditions (*e.g.,* "fair value" and "majority of the disinterested shareholders" provisions);

The Commission supports 37(b) and will propose for comment the concept of annual disclosure of certain change-of-control–related policies. The Commission believes that the concept of advisory voting is problematic, however, and does not at this time support that element of the recommendation.

ii. *Disenfranchisement.* Charter provisions (other than cumulative voting and class voting) that abandon the one share–one vote rule based on the concentration of ownership within a class (*e.g.*, formulas diluting voting strength of 10% shareholders and "majority of the disinterested shareholders" approval requirements);

iii. *Standstill agreements.* Current agreements with remaining lives longer than one year that restrict or prohibit purchases or sales of the company's stock by a party to the agreement; and

iv. *Change-of-control compensation.* Arrangements that provide change-of-control–related compensation to company managers or employees.

b. *Proxy Statement Disclosure.* Companies should be required to disclose all advisory vote matters in a "Change of Control" section of the proxy statement.

c. *Vote.* Shareholders should be requested to vote on an advisory basis as to whether they are or continue to be in favor of the company's policy with respect to the advisory vote matters disclosed in the proxy statement. The board would not be bound by the results of the advisory vote but could, in its own judgment, decide whether company policy should be changed on the advisory vote matters. The outcome of an advisory vote would have no legal effect on an existing agreement.

38. a. *Change-of-Control Compensation during a Tender Offer.*

The Commission shares the Committee's concerns with the

The board of directors shall not adopt contracts or other arrangements with change-of-control compensation once a tender offer for the company has commenced.

b. *Change-of-Control Compensation prior to a Tender Offer.*

    i. *Disclosure.* The issuer should disclose the terms and parties to contracts or other arrangements that provide for change-of-control compensation in the Change of Control section of the annual proxy statement.

    ii. *Advisory Vote.* At each annual meeting, shareholders should be requested to vote, on an advisory basis, as to whether the company should continue to provide change-of-control compensation to its management and employees. The board would not be obligated by the results of the vote to take any specific steps, and the outcome of the vote would have no legal effect on any existing employment agreement.

adoption of change-of-control compensation in the face of a takeover and concurs in the Committee's judgment that such activities may so undermine the public's confidence in the integrity of the takeover process as to require a federal response. The Commission would suggest distinguishing between arrangements entered into after a takeover is threatened and those adopted in the ordinary course of business. This avoids the substantial problems of separating "golden parachutes" from ordinary employment contracts. As noted with Recommendation 37, the Commission does not favor advisory votes at this time. The Commission does agree that, as is currently required, issuers should disclose change-of-control–related compensation, regardless of the timing of its adoption.

39. a. In general, target company self-tenders should not be prohibited during the course of a tender offer by another bidder for the target company.

    b. Once a third-party tender offer has commenced, the target company should not be permitted to initiate a self-tender with a proration date earlier than that of any tender offer commenced prior to the self-tender.

The Commission believes defensive issuer tender offers should be prohibited. In the interim, prior to such prohibition, the Commission agrees with this recommendation.

40. There should be no general prohibition of the counter tender offer as a defense. The employment of the counter tender offer should be prohibited, however, where a bidder

The Commission has serious concerns about the use of counter tender offers as defensive tactics. Management should bear the burden of proving that a

has made a cash tender offer for 100% of a target company.

counter tender offer is not motivated by management's self-interest and reflects a reasonable business judgment.

41. Contracts for the sale of stock or assets to preferred acquirers should continue to be tested against the business judgment rule. During a tender offer, however, the issuance of stock representing more than 15% of the fully diluted shares that would be outstanding after issuance should be subject to shareholder approval.

The Commission supports the concept of requiring shareholder approval for the issuance of any securities representing more than 5% (not 15% as proposed by the Committee) of the class to be outstanding after issuance during a tender offer or proxy contest. Included within this concept would be options, warrants, convertible and other securities. The Commission supports the general proposition that state corporate law, subject to revised application of the business judgment rule in takeovers, should govern disposition of assets during a tender offer.

42. The sale of significant assets, even when undertaken during the course of a tender offer, should continue to be tested against the business judgment rule.

The Commission supports this general proposition, subject to revised application of the business judgment rule.

43. Repurchase of a company's shares at a premium to market from a particular holder or group that has held such shares for less than two years should require shareholder approval. This rule would not apply to offers made to all holders of a class of securities.

The Commission agrees with this recommendation.

V. *Regulation of Market Participants*

44. The Commission should continue the current prohibition on short tendering set forth in Rule 10b-4. To ensure the effectiveness of that provision, the Commission also specifically should prohibit hedged tendering.

The Commission agrees with this recommendation.

45. In furtherance of the policy goals of Rule 10b-4, the Commission generally should require in a partial offer

The Commission agrees with this recommendation.

that all shares tendered pursuant to a guarantee be physically delivered, rather than permitting delivery only of the certificates for those shares to be actually purchased by the bidder.

46. Rule 10b-4 should be amended to include a specific prohibition of multiple tendering.

The Commission agrees with this recommendation.

47. The Commission should revise its interpretation of Rule 10b-4 so that for the purposes of determining whether a person has a "net long position" in a security subject to the tender offer, call options on such security which a person has sold and which a person should know are highly likely to be exercised prior to expiration of the offer shall be deemed to constitute sales of the security underlying such options and therefore netted against such person's position in that security.

The Commission believes that the proposed interpretation is too subjective, thus making it difficult to administer and enforce. Therefore, the Commission does not endorse this recommendation but intends to study the problem further.

48. Without commenting on the technical aspects of the proposal, the Committee recommends adoption of the Commission's proposed Rule 17Ad-14 under the Exchange Act.

The Commission has adopted Rule 17Ad-14.

VI. *Interrelationship of Various Regulatory Schemes*

49. Federal securities regulation of acquisition of corporate control should not impede or otherwise handicap the necessary and appropriate workings of federal antitrust regulations designed to review transactions for antitrust implications prior to their consummation.

The Commission agrees with this general proposition.

50. Premerger notification waiting periods under the Hart-Scott-Rodino Antitrust Improvements Act should be modified so as to take account of the required minimum offering period prescribed under the Williams Act and to avoid, to the extent practicable, delay in completion of a tender offer due to antitrust review.

The Commission agrees with this general recommendation.

APPENDIX B: MEMBERS OF THE SECURITIES AND EXCHANGE COMMISSION ADVISORY COMMITTEE ON TENDER OFFERS

Dean LeBaron, Chairman
President
Batterymarch Financial Management

Jeffrey B. Bartell, Esq.
Quarles & Brady

Michael D. Dingman
President
The Signal Companies, Inc.

Frank H. Easterbrook
Professor of Law
The University of Chicago
The Law School

Joseph H. Flom, Esq.
Skadden, Arps, Slate, Meagher & Flom

Honorable Arthur J. Goldberg
Former Associate Justice of the
Supreme Court of the United States

Robert F. Greenhill
Managing Director
Morgan Stanley & Co., Inc.

Ray J. Groves
Chairman and Chief Executive
Ernst & Whinney

Alan R. Gruber
Chairman and Chief Executive Officer
Orion Capital Corporation

Edward L. Hennessy, Jr.
Chairman of the Board
Allied Corporation

Gregg A. Jarrell, Ph.D.
Senior Economist
Lexecon Inc.

Robert P. Jensen
Chairman and Chief Executive Officer
E. F. Hutton LBO, Inc.

Martin Lipton, Esq.
Wachtell, Lipton, Rosen & Katz

Robert E. Rubin
Partner
Goldman, Sachs & Co.

Irwin Schneiderman, Esq.
Cahill Gordon & Reindel

John W. Spurdle, Jr.
Senior Vice President
Morgan Guaranty Trust Company of
New York

Jeff C. Tarr
Managing Partner
Junction Partners

Bruce Wasserstein
Managing Director
The First Boston Corporation

II

CONSTITUTIONAL DIMENSIONS OF STATE TAKEOVER STATUTES

In *Edgar v. MITE Corp.*,[1] The United States Supreme Court, in an opinion written by Justice White, held that the Illinois Business Takeover Act[2] was unconstitutional on interstate commerce grounds.[3] The Court reasoned that the burdens imposed on interstate commerce were excessive in relation to the local interests served.[4] Another portion of Justice White's opinion, not joined in by a majority of the Court, asserted that the Illinois Act was unconstitutional under the Supremacy Clause.[5] As to this aspect of the opinion, Justices Powell and Stevens, in separate concurrences, indicated that an argument can be made that a state may provide special protection to incumbent management and allow such management to consider pertinent noninvestor interests in responding to a hostile tender offer.[6]

---

1. 102 S. Ct. 2629 (1982).

2. Ill. Rev. Stat., Ch. 121-1/2, ¶ 137.51 *et seq.* (1979). The Illinois Act, which applied to target corporations having as few as 10% of their shareholders resident in that state, imposed a twenty-day precommencement notification requirement upon the offeror and authorized the Illinois secretary of state to hold hearings to determine whether the tender offer was substantively fair. If the secretary held such a hearing, the Act directed him to deny registration to the tender offer if he found that the offer "fail[ed] to provide full and fair disclosure to the offerees of all material information concerning the take-over offer, or that the take-over offer [was] in equitable or work[ed] or tend[ed] to work a fraud or deceit upon the offerees."

3. 102 S. Ct. at 2643.

4. *Id.*

5. *Id.* at 2636-2637. Justice White, reasoning that the Illinois Act conflicted with the Williams Act's policy of neutrality, asserted: "Congress sought to protect the investor not only by furnishing him with the necessary information but also by withholding from management or the bidder any undue advantage that could frustrate the exercise of an informed choice."

6. *Id.* at 2648 (Stevens, J., concurring in part and concurring in the judgment)

In the aftermath of *MITE*, several state statutes, having similar provisions to the Illinois Act, were declared unconstitutional by the lower federal courts.[7] Cognizant of the constitutional infirmities of their takeover statutes, a number of states, with Maryland, Ohio, and Pennsylvania being the initiators, have responded by enacting "second-generation" statutes which seek to pass constitutional scrutiny.[8]

The first commentary in this section by Messrs. Goelzer and Cohen provides a comprehensive overview of *MITE* and its progeny, assesses the constitutionality under the Supremacy and Commerce Clauses of the second-generation state takeover statutes, and discusses the pertinent recommendations in this area by the SEC Advisory Committee on Tender Offers. The authors assert that state statutes, which have the effect of blocking or inhibiting tender offers for widely held public companies, should be declared unconstitutional. Moreover, by impairing the free trading of securities in the national securities markets, these state statutes conflict with the investor protection objectives underlying the federal securities laws. As an additional reflection, Messrs. Goelzer and Cohen astutely observe that "[p]erhaps paradoxically, continued state efforts to regulate tender offers for corporations with a national shareholder constituency have . . . had the perverse effect of strengthening the hand of advocates of direct federal inroads into state corporate law."

("I am not persuaded . . . that Congress' decision to follow a policy of neutrality in its own legislation is tantamount to a federal prohibition against state legislation designed to provide special protection for incumbent management."); *id.* at 2643 (Powell, J., concurring in part) ("I agree with Justice Stevens that the Wiliams Act's neutrality policy does not necessarily imply a congressional intent to prohibit state legislation designed to assure—at least in some circumstances—greater protection to interests that include but often are broader than those of incumbent management."). *See generally* Humphrey, *State Tender Offer Statutes*, 61 N.C.L. Rev. 554 (1983); Langevoort, *State Tender Offer Legislation: Interests, Effects, and Political Competency*, 62 Cornell L. Rev. 213 (1977); Sargent, *On the Validity of State Takeover Regulation: State Responses to* MITE *and* Kidwell, 42 Ohio St. L.J. 689 (1981).

7. *See, e.g.*, Telvest, Inc. v. Bradshaw, 697 F.2d 576 (4th Cir. 1982); Martin Marietta Corp. v. Bendix Corp., 690 F.2d 558 (6th Cir. 1982); National City Lines, Inc. v. LLC Corp., 687 F.2d 1122 (8th Cir. 1982). *See also* Agency Rent-A-Car, Inc., v. Connolly, 686 F.2d 1029 (1st Cir. 1982).

8. *See, e.g.*, Md. Bus. & Assoc. Code §§ 3-202, 3-601-03, 8-801(12)-(14); Ohio Rev. Code §§ 1701.01, 1701.831; Pa. Stat. Ann. tit. 15, §§ 408, 409.1, 910. For commentary on these statutes, see Kreider, *Fortress without Foundation? Ohio Takeover Act II*, 52 U. Cin. L. Rev. 108 (1983); Scriggins & Clarke, *Takeovers and the 1983 Maryland Fair Price Legislation*, 43 Md. L. Rev. 266 (1984); Steinberg, *The Pennsylvania Anti-Takeover Legislation*, 12 Sec. Reg. L.J. 184 (1984). These statutes are discussed herein by Messrs. Goelzer and Cohen, Professor Sargent, and L. P. Scriggins, Esq.

The second commentary by Professor Mark Sargent addresses the second-generation state takeover statutes and their vulnerability to challenge under the Commerce Clause. Professor Sargent recognizes that these second-generation statutes do not regulate the tender offer process *per se*. Rather, they are forms of corporate internal affairs regulation, a function which has traditionally been within the purview of the states.[9] Accordingly, the outcome of a constitutional challenge to these statutes is difficult to predict. This uncertainty is due to the novel questions raised regarding the nature and weight of a state's interest in its own corporate laws and the extent to which state internal affairs regulation can burden interstate commerce. Professor Sargent concludes that these questions can be resolved only through a convergence of constitutional and economic analyses.

---

9. *See generally* Burks v. Lasker, 441 U.S. 471 (1979); Santa Fe Industries, Inc. v. Green, 430 U.S. 462 (1977); Ferrara & Steinberg, *A Reappraisal of* Santa Fe: *Rule 10b-5 and the New Federalism*, 129 U. Pa. L. Rev. 263 (1980).

The Empires Strike Back—
Post–*MITE* Developments in
State Antitakeover Regulation

DANIEL L. GOELZER and ALAN B. COHEN*

I. INTRODUCTION

In *Edgar v. MITE Corp.*, the Supreme Court decisively rejected the notion that a particular state may regulate a nationwide tender offer commenced and conducted in accord with the Williams Act.[1] In *MITE*, the Court invalidated the precommencement disclosure, hearing, and merit review provisions of the Illinois Business Takeover Act[2] on the ground that the statute violated the Commerce Clause of the United States Constitution. *MITE* resolved most, but not all, of the questions regarding the constitutionality of the "first generation" of state takeover statutes.[3] However, several states read *MITE* narrowly and have amended their takeover statutes in an effort

---

*Daniel L. Goelzer is general counsel and Alan B. Cohen is special counsel for the Securities and Exchange Commission. As a matter of policy, the Securities and Exchange Commission disclaims responsibility for any private publication or statement of any of its employees. The views expressed herein are those of the authors and do not necessarily represent the views of the Commission or its staff. *See* 17 C.F.R. 200.735-4(e). This chapter is copyright © 1985 by Daniel L. Goelzer and Alan B. Cohen.

1. Edgar v. MITE Corp., 457 U.S. 624 (1982). The Williams Act, 82 Stat. 454, codified at 15 U.S.C. §§ 78m(d)-(e) and 78n(d)-(f), added new §§13(d), 13(e), and 14(d)-(f) to the Securities Exchange Act of 1934. Of direct relevance to *MITE*, Section 14(d)(1) of the Exchange Act requires an offeror seeking to acquire more than 5% of any class of equity security by means of a tender offer to first file a Schedule 14D-1 with the Securities and Exchange Commission.

2. Ill. Rev. Stat., Ch. 121 1/2, § 137.51 *et seq.* (Supp. 1980).

3. A typical pre-*MITE* statute defines a takeover bid as

the acquisition of or offer to acquire, pursuant to a tender offer or request or invitation for tenders, any equity security of a corporation organized under

to preserve state ability to regulate at least some aspects of tender offers, with the consequence of frustrating or preventing the operation of nation-wide tender offers or open market purchase programs aimed at companies incorporated in that state or otherwise having substantial contact with the state. While these responses are imaginative, their constitutionality is open to question.

This commentary analyzes post-*MITE* state takeover statutes that are premised on state authority to regulate the structure of domestic corpo-rations and the rights of shareholders. Ohio and Maryland are the primary examples of jurisdictions that have taken this avenue to achieve a pattern of state regulation that is constitutional within the strictures of *MITE*.[4] Other areas which some states apparently believe are unaffected by *MITE* include takeover regulation under the rubric of environmental protection and state antifraud and "penalty box" disclosure provisions.

Aggressive state responses to *MITE* may well produce a federal counter-reaction. The recent report of the Securities and Exchange Commission's Tender Offer Advisory Committee[5] and the Congressional response to that

---

the laws of this state or having its principal place of business or substantial assets within this state, if after acquisition thereof the offeror would, directly or indirectly, be a record or beneficial owner of more than __% of any class of the issued and outstanding equity securities of such corporation.

N.Y. Bus. Corp. Law § 1001(a) (McKinney); Ky. Rev. Stat. § 292.560(1).

Typical pre-*MITE* state takeover statutes require the bidder to file with the state and deliver to the subject company a disclosure document and then wait a fixed period of time, usually twenty days, *before* commencing its takeover bid. Perhaps the greatest delay mechanism in first-generation state takeover laws is the hearing requirement. Most jurisdictions provide that a state administrative hearing may be required before any takeover bid can commence, with the subject company often enjoying at least the right to request a hearing and sometimes to demand one. The statutes typically provide that, until the hearing requirements are satisfied, the take-over bid may not be made anywhere in the nation.

The language of a typical state statute, despite the lack of a specific reference to open market purchases, has been construed as covering open market purchases above the percentage threshold specified in the statute. *See, e.g.*, Esmark, Inc. v. Strode, 639 S.W.2d 768 (Ky. Sup. Ct. 1982). Other jurisdictions include open market purchases more explicitly in their definition of "takeover bid." *See, e.g.*, Hawaii Rev. Stat. § 417E-1(7), N.H. RSA § 421-A:2(VI). Five percent and 10 percent are typical percentage thresholds employed in state statutes. *See, e.g.*, 70 Pa. Cons. Stat. Ann. § 73 (Purdon) (5% standard); Va. Code § 13.1-529 (i) (10% standard).

4. Pennsylvania and Wisconsin have also enacted statutes modeled on the Ohio and Maryland legislation.

5. Advisory Committee on Tender Offers—Report of Recommendations (July 8, 1983). The Report was published by Commerce Clearing House as Fed. Sec. L. Rep. No. 1028, a Special Report dated July 15, 1983.

report both suggest the serious possibility of federal legislation preempting components of state corporation law that shield management defensive tactics. Perhaps paradoxically, continued state efforts to regulate tender offers for corporations with a national shareholder constituency have thus had the perverse effect of strengthening the hand of advocates of direct federal inroads into state corporate law.

II. *MITE* AND ITS PROGENY

An important premise underlying enactment of the Williams Act was the Congressional desire to maintain regulatory neutrality between bidder and target company. The Williams Act reflects a Congressional determination that tender offers should not be deterred. Instead, the Williams Act seeks to regulate tender offers and open market purchase programs only to the extent necessary to protect shareholders and investors. The Williams Act was "designed to require full and fair disclosure for the benefit of investors while at the same time providing the offeror and management equal opportunity to fairly present their case."[6]

A tender offer—or an open market purchase program—seeking the shares of a company with a nationwide shareholder constituency does not lend itself to state-by-state regulation. Transactions that are national in scope and that implicate the functioning of the national securities markets are most effectively policed federally, not by the varying philosophies and goals of fifty different states. In *Edgar v. MITE*, the Supreme Court applied these principles to state regulation of a nationwide tender offer.

A. The *MITE* Holding

The Illinois Business Takeover Act,[7] the statute at issue in *MITE*, required a tender offeror to notify the secretary of the state of Illinois twenty business days before commencement of a tender offer.[8] The secretary of state was empowered to convene a hearing, and the tender offer could not proceed until that hearing was completed.[9] One function of the hearing was to permit the secretary of state to review the substantive fairness of the tender offer; were an offer found "unfair," it could be permanently blocked.[10]

MITE Corp. initiated a tender offer for Chicago Rivet & Machine Co., by filing a Schedule 14D with the Securities and Exchange Commission pur-

---

6. S. Rep. No. 550, 90th Cong., 1st Sess. 3 (1967).
7. *See* note 2 *supra.*
8. *Id.* at §§ 137.54.A, 137.54.E.
9. *Id.* at § 137.57.A.
10. *Id.* at § 137.57.E.

suant to the Williams Act.[11] MITE Corp. made no effort to comply with the Illinois Business Takeover Act; rather, it commenced an action in federal court challenging the constitutionality of the statute and obtained a permanent injunction against its enforcement.[12] The Court of Appeals for the Seventh Circuit affirmed,[13] and the Supreme Court accepted, the case for review.[14]

Justice White's opinion, in which only the chief justice joined entirely, held (1) that the Illinois statute unduly favored incumbent management and thus contravened the Supremacy Clause of the U.S. Constitution, because it upset the neutrality policy which is the object of federal tender offer regulation, as embodied in the Williams Act, and (2) that the statute directly restrained interstate commerce in violation of the Commerce Clause.[15] Five justices joined in part, but not all, of the Commerce Clause holding; thus, a majority of the Court[16] held that the Illinois statute was void, because it imposed burdens on interstate commerce that were excessive in light of Illinois' interests.[17]

Justice White's Commerce Clause opinion had two branches. In the first (in which only three other justices joined), he noted that the statute regulated interstate transactions taking place wholly outside of Illinois (in this case purchases by a Delaware corporation of shares owned by non-Illinois residents). Thus, the statute constituted a "direct" restraint on interstate commerce and was, therefore, void, even without an inquiry into the state interests involved.[18] The second branch of Justice White's Commerce Clause opinion, in which five justices concurred and which stands as the opinion of the Court, was based on *Pike v. Bruce Church, Inc.*[19] In that 1970 case, the Court held that a statute which has only an incidental effect on interstate commerce is valid "unless the burden imposed on such commerce is clearly excessive in relation to the putative local benefits."[20] As the Court stated in *MITE*:

---

11. 457 U.S. at 627.

12. *Id.* at 628-29.

13. MITE Corp. v. Dixon, 633 F.2d 486 (7th Cir. 1980).

14. 457 U.S. at 630.

15. 457 U.S. at 626. Justice White's opinion was fully in accord with the Commission's position *amicus curiae*.

16. The chief justice and Justices White, Powell, Stevens, and O'Connor.

17. 457 U.S. at 643-44. Justice Blackmun joined the Supremacy Clause discussion but not that pertaining to the Commerce Clause. Justices Marshall, Brennan, and Rehnquist dissented on the ground that the case was moot; they declined to discuss the case on the merits.

18. 457 U.S. at 643.

19. 397 U.S. 137 (1970).

20. *Id.* at 142.

> While protecting local investors is plainly a a legitimate state objective, the state has no legitimate interest in protecting non-resident shareholders. Insofar as the Illinois law burdens out-of-state transactions, there is nothing to be weighed in the balance to sustain the law.[21]

Five of the six justices reaching the merits in *MITE* expressly held that the Act was invalid on Commerce Clause grounds, because it placed a substantial burden on interstate commerce which outweighed any local benefits.[22] Thus, it seems clear that the standard against which state statutes that frustrate or regulate nationwide tender offers must be measured is whether the burden placed on interstate commerce outweighs the state interest involved. State interests of the sort asserted in *MITE* have already been held insufficient to justify burdening commerce, where their effect is to block out-of-state securities transactions.

B. *MITE* in the Lower Courts

Several courts, both state and federal, have applied the Supreme Court's Commerce Clause holding in *MITE* to particular state takeover statutes. These decisions, dealing with both tender offers and open market purchase programs, have been uniformly adverse to state regulation. As *MITE* has been applied to various state antitakeover statutes, it has become increasingly clear that minor variations on the Illinois theme do not change the ultimate result. As detailed below, these cases make clear that state officials cannot, consistent with the Commerce Clause, interpose their judgment to halt, or even to delay, a nationwide tender offer or open market purchase program.

The leading post-*MITE* appellate opinion arises out of the widely publicized mega-corporate battles for control of Cities Service and Martin Marietta. Mesa Petroleum Co. and Occidental Petroleum Co. each commenced hostile tender offers for Cities Service Co.; Bendix Corp. tendered for Martin Marietta Corp. Mesa, Occidental, and Bendix all sought to enjoin enforcement of the Oklahoma Takeover Bid Act.[23] These actions were consolidated, and in *Mesa Petroleum v. Cities Service Co.*,[24] the Tenth Circuit invalidated the Oklahoma Act. The Oklahoma statute, like the Illinois Act in *MITE*, empowered a state official to convene a hearing and to halt indefinitely the consummation of the tender offer[25] unlike the Illinois Business Takeover Act, the Oklahoma law did not, however, require a filing with the state

---

21. 457 U.S. at 644.
22. *Id.* at 646.
23. 71 O.S. § 431 *et seq.* (1981).
24. 715 F.2d 1425 (10th Cir. 1983).
25. 71 O.S. § 431 *et seq.* (1981).

before commencement of an offer. The court rejected the contention that the absence of precommencement filing requirement was sufficient to distinguish *MITE*. The court dismissed this argument as

> fall[ing] within Judge Learned Hand's category of "distinctions without a difference." The essential point is bellwether clear: under the Oklahoma Act the Administrator may halt, indefinitely, a nationwide tender offer if he finds the disclosure to be inadequate.[26]

The Tenth Circuit emphasized that the central problem with both the Illinois Act in *MITE* and the Oklahoma act in *Mesa* was the "provision which allowed the state ... effectively to block a nationwide tender offer."[27] The decision in *Mesa* clearly indicates that states which have merely removed their precommencement filing requirement have not thereby preserved the validity of their statutes.[28]

The force of the *MITE* holding is not limited to acquisitions by tender offer; the Supreme Court's reasoning has also been applied to state laws which seek to regulate open market purchases of securities. In *Sharon Steel Corp v. Whaland*,[29] Nashua Corp., a Delaware corporation with its principal place of business in New Hampshire, sought to bar further open market purchases of its stock by Summit Systems, Inc., a wholly owned subsidiary of Sharon Steel Corp.[30] The New Hampshire commissioner of insurance,

---

26. 715 F.2d at 1429.

27. *Id*.

28. New Hampshire and Indiana, among other jurisdictions, have amended their takeover statutes since the *MITE* decision by removing the precommencement filing provision invalidated in *MITE*. New York and Massachusetts are among those states which lacked a precommencement filing requirement, even pre-*MITE*. Indiana requires the offeror to file its registration statement "immediately before" making a takeover offer, Ind. Code § 23-2-3.1-3 (Supp. 1983); New Hampshire requires the registration statement to be filed on the date the takeover bid is commenced. N.H. RSA § 421-A:3 (Supp. 1983). However, both jurisdictions have retained the most onerous features of the pre-*MITE*-type statutes in that they continue to impose hearing requirments and continue the authority of the state administrator to halt a nationwide offer.

29. 121 N.H. 607, 433 A.2d 1250 (1980), *vacated and remanded*, 458 U.S. 1101 (1982), *opinion on remand*, [1983-84 Transfer Binder] Fed. Sec. L. Rep. (CCH) ¶ 99,528 (N.H. Sept. 30, 1983). The Commission participated, *amicus curiae*, in this litigation to urge, both before and after the *MITE* decision, the court to invalidate the New Hampshire takeover statute.

30. These purchases consisted of nine separate open market transactions consummated by registered broker-dealers on the New York Stock Exchange or on the over-the-counter market for listed securities.

acting under a state statute[31] that purported to subject "takeover bids" for New Hampshire "target companies" to a variety of prepurchase disclosure and hearing requirements, entered an order barring further purchases by Summit. "Takeover bid" was broadly defined to include open market purchase programs and private purchases that result in the purchaser's owning more than 5 percent of a class of the target's equity securities.[32] In effect, these provisions created a potential delay of up to four months, plus the duration of the hearings, from the time a prospective purchaser must disclose its intentions to the time that the purchases may be consummated.

The New Hampshire Supreme Court, reversing its pre-*MITE* position,[33] invalidated the New Hampshire statute.[34] The court found the statute unconstitutional under the *MITE* majority's analysis of permissible state indirect burdens on interstate commerce: "[T]he statutory definition of a target company is broader than necessary to insure that the state is regulating only corporations that have both substantial assets and shareholders in New Hampshire."[35]

Other federal and state decisions reach the same result. In *Telvest, Inc. v. Bradshaw*,[36] the Fourth Circuit held the Virginia takeover statute[37] unconstitutional when applied to open market purchase programs. The portion of the Virginia law at issue severely restricted an acquirer's ability to make open market purchases without becoming subject to an extensive state administrative review. In *Esmark, Inc. v. Strode*,[38] the Kentucky Supreme Court struck down the Kentucky takeover statute[39] when applied to open market purchase programs, on Supremacy and Commerce Clause grounds. The court found the provisions of the Kentucky statute to be substantially similar to the Illinois law invalidated in *MITE*.[40] In *Martin Marietta Corp. v. Bendix Corp.*,[41] the Sixth Circuit held that the antifraud provisions of the

---

31. N.H. RSA § 421-A *et seq.* (1981).

32. *Id*. at 421-A:2 (VI).

33. 121 N.H. 607, 433 A.2d 1250 (1981).

34. During the course of the litigation, the New Hampshire takeover statute, RSA chapter 421-A, was amended by Laws 1983, chapter 144, effective August 6, 1983. However, the New Hampshire Supreme Court did not rule on the amended statute.

35. [1983-84 Transfer Binder] Fed. Sec. L. Rep. (CCH) ¶ 99,528, at 97,036.

36. 697 F.2d 576 (4th Cir. 1983).

37. Va. Code § 13.1-529 *et seq*.

38. 639 S.W. 2d 768 (Ky. 1982).

39. Ky. Rev. Stat. § 292.560 *et seq*.

40. 639 S.W. 2d 768 (Ky. 1982).

41. 690 F.2d 558 (6th Cir. 1982).

Michigan statute,[42] even if applied only to Michigan shareholders, violated the Commerce Clause, because these provisions prevented Michigan citizens from participating in a nationwide tender offer and reduced the chances for a national tender offer to succeed.[43]

Overall, these cases illustrate that *MITE* does not permit a state official to intervene in a nationwide tender offer or open market purchase program. The common thread in these opinions is that, both in tender offer and open market purchase program contexts, a state official cannot be empowered to determine whether a nationwide transaction may go forward.

III. THE STATE CORPORATION LAW LOOPHOLE— AMENDMENTS IN REACTION TO *MITE*

Several states have reacted to *MITE* by casting their takeover statutes in the form of traditional state corporation law. These states have utilized one or both of two approaches: (1) affording minority shareholders authority to disapprove transactions in the shares of a domestic corporation which effectuate a change in control or (2) regulating the price to be paid when minority shareholders are "frozen out" in the second step of a merger transaction. Both approaches rely on the states' well-established power to regulate the internal affairs of a domestic corporation. The Ohio statute is the prototype for the first approach; Maryland law is the prototype for the second.

A. Revised Ohio Statute[44]

1. Description

Under the revised Ohio statute, prior shareholder authorization by majority vote of the disinterested shareholders[45] is required before consummation of "control share acquisitions" of an Ohio corporation with 50 or more shareholders that has its principal place of business, principal executive offices, or substantial assets within Ohio.[46] A control share acquisition is defined as an acquisition of shares

> that, when added to all other shares in respect of which . . . [the purchaser] may exercise or direct the exercise of voting power . . . would

---

42. Michigan Takeover Offers Act, §§ 451.901-917.

43. 690 F.2d at 567.

44. Ohio Rev. Code Ann. § 1701.01 *et seq.* (Page).

45. *Id.* at § 1701.01(Y) (Page).

46. *Id.* at § 1701.831 (Page).

entitle such person... directly or indirectly... to exercise... voting power... in the election of directors within any of the following range of such voting power:

(a) one-fifth or more but less than one third...;

(b) one-third or more but less than a majority...;

(c) a majority or more of such voting power.[47]

In short, shareholder authorization—prior to consummation—must be secured for any share purchases that result in the buyer's ownership crossing the 20 percent, 33⅓ percent, and 50 percent thresholds. Prior approval is not required for purchases within these zones (*i.e.*, a purchase raising the ownership percentage from 24 percent to 32 percent). Moreover, the acquirer is excluded from participation in the approval process; the shares owned by a prospective purchaser seeking shareholder authorization to acquire more shares are defined under the Ohio statute as "interested shares"[48] and may not be voted in favor of the proposed control share acquisition.[49]

The statute requires that the prospective purchaser furnish the subject corporation an "acquiring person statement" which must set forth "in reasonable detail" the terms of the proposed acquisition.[50] The special meeting of shareholders which must vote on the proposed acquisition need not take place until fifty days after the "acquiring person statement" is received by the corporation.[51] By majority vote, the shareholders may further condition the consummation of a control share acquisition by requiring "consent to such acquisition by directors based on a determination by the directors of the best interests of the... corporation and its shareholders."[52] The Ohio statute applies to tender offers, open market purchases, and privately negotiated transactions.[53] Shareholders (by amending the articles or bylaws

---

47. *Id.* at § 1701.01(Z) (1) (Page).

48. *Id.* at § 1701.01 (CC) (Page). In addition to the prospective purchaser, (1) all elected or appointed officers of the subject company and (2) directors who are also employees are owners of "interested shares." A majority of shares voted at the meeting of shareholders called to vote on the acquisition and a majority of shares voted by disinterested shareholders are required for approval of a control share acquisition. Conceivably, even if a majority of shares voted by disinterested shareholders approve the acquisition, directors or officers holding a large percentage of the share could block the acquisition, because a majority of shares voted at the meeting would then not be in favor of the acquisition.

49. *Id.* at § 1701.831 (E) (Page).

50. *Id.* at § 1701.831 (B) (Page).

51. *Id.* at § 1701.831 (C) (Page).

52. *Id.* at § 1701.11(B) (8) (Page).

53. *Id.* at § 1701.01(Z) (1), (2) (Page). The statute provides no exception from its definition of "control share acquisitions" for open market purchases or privately

of the corporation) can, however, exempt their corporation from the new statute.[54]

2. Validity

Whether one agrees or disagrees, as a policy matter, with the notion that shareholders should be permitted to disapprove share acquisitions to which the company itself is not a party, it is clear that the effect of the Ohio statute would be similar to that of the Illinois Business Takeover Act invalidated in *MITE*. An analysis of the constitutionality of the new statute should also produce a similar result.

a. Commerce Clause

The new Ohio statute is patently detrimental to national trading in the securities of Ohio corporations. The statute reduces, if not eliminates, the likelihood of hostile bids for shares of Ohio corporations and, presumably, depresses share prices at the expense of investors, with the effect of protecting incumbent management. These results are accomplished in a manner which burdens commerce wholly external to Ohio. The statute imposes a trading freeze on open market and privately negotiated purchases—even those occurring outside Ohio among non-Ohio residents—pending shareholder approval. Any purchaser wishing to cross an ownership threshold must initiate a shareholder review process. For example, a 2 percent shareholder residing in Maine cannot sell his shares to a 19 percent shareholder living in California without the requisite shareholder approval.

Because out-of-state securities transactions are burdened (indeed, they are halted until the Ohio statute is complied with—a condition which may prove impossible to fulfill), the statute's extraterritorial impact likely renders it invalid under *MITE*'s application of the *Pike v. Bruce Church* Commerce Clause analysis. As the Supreme Court stated in *MITE*, "[i]nsofar as the ... law burdens out-of-state transactions, there is nothing to be weighed in the balance to sustain the law."[55] Based on their views in *MITE*, at least four justices would presumably also strike down the Ohio statute as unconstitutional *per se* under *Shafer v. Farmers Grain* because it constitutes direct regulation of out-of-state transactions.

Proponents of the new Ohio statute rely on the theory that Ohio has plenary power to regulate the internal affairs of a corporation incorporated under its laws; at minimum, they assert that the state interest in such regulation outweighs any burden that the statute imposes on interstate commerce. Indeed, in adopting the statute, the Ohio General Assembly specifically

---

negotiated purchases. An exception is provided for mergers which already require shareholder approval, if the Ohio corporation is a party to the agreement of merger.

54. *Id.* at § 1701.831 (E) (Page).

55. 457 U.S at 644.

found that tender offers give rise to "basic issues concerning internal cor-porate affairs."[56] However, the Supreme Court in *MITE* decisively rejected this notion. The Court stated that the internal affairs doctrine:

> is of little use to the state in this context. Tender offers contemplate transfers of stock by stockholders to a third party and do not them-selves implicate the internal affairs of the target company.[57]

It is logical to argue that other third-party transfers of stock, such as open market purchases and privately negotiated purchases, likewise do not im-plicate the internal affairs of corporations since, like tender offers, they "contemplate transfers of stock by stockholders to a third party."[58] There-fore, the internal affairs doctrine is an insufficient foundation on which to rest the Ohio statute's heavy burden on interstate commerce.

b. Supremacy Clause

In *MITE*, while the majority of the Court did not reach the Supremacy Clause argument (since a number of justices chose not to participate on the merits because of their view that the case had become moot), no justice disagreed with it. The Ohio statute offends the Supremacy Clause because it is contrary to both the goals and the letter of the federal law. The hearings prior to the 1968 enactment of the federal scheme of tender offer regula-tion—the Williams Act—emphasized the need to get information to the investor by allowing both the offeror and the incumbent managers of a target company to present fully their arguments and then to let the investor decide for himself[59] whether to sell or retain his shares. Congress's intention was that shareholders, in their capacity as potential sellers, informed through full disclosure by both sides in the contest, resolve disputes over corporate control: "This bill is designed to make the relevant facts known so that shareholders have a fair opportunity to make their decision."[60] Similarly, the Williams Act requires postpurchase disclosure of acquisitions, which result in ownership over 5 percent.[61]

A requirement that acquisitions be contingent upon shareholder approval

---

56. Ohio Rev. Ann. § 1707.99 (§3) (A) (3) (Page).

57. 457 U.S. at 645.

58. *Id.*

59. *See generally*, Full Disclosure of Corporate Equity Ownership and in Cor-porate Takeover Bids: Hearings on S. 510 before the Subcomm. on Securities of the Senate Comm. on Banking and Currency, 90th Cong., 1st Sess. at 71-76, 84-85, 87, 98, 105, 108-11, 139-40, 150 and 165 (1967).

60. S. Rep. No. 550, 90th Cong., 1st Sess. 3 (1967); H.R. Rep. No. 1711, 90th Cong., 2d Sess. 4 (1968).

61. Section 13(d) of the Securities Exchange Act of 1934, 15 U.S.C. 78m(d).

is not consistent with this federal regulatory scheme. The Ohio Act may have market effects, including the potential for market disruption and shareholder confusion, which are directly contrary to the objectives of federal securities regulation. For example, price gyrations unrelated to fundamental share values would undoubtedly occur as investors speculate during the lengthy period prior to shareholder approval, should any investor be so bold as to attempt a "control share acquisition" of an Ohio corporation.

Similarly, the Ohio statute takes away from individual investors the ability to decide whether or not to sell their shares, in a tender offer or to any other large-block acquirer, without the approval of their fellow shareholders. The Ohio statute block purchases and sales by investors living throughout the country, pending shareholder approval, regardless of whether the purchase offer is extended to all shareholders (as in a tender offer) or merely to a few shareholders (as in an open market or privately negotiated purchase program). This shareholder approval condition hinders the free transfer of securities. Ironically, the Ohio Act raises the anomaly that control of an Ohio corporation may be easier to achieve through a proxy contest, rather than a tender offer, because, in a proxy contest, the insurgent may vote his shares in favor of his proposals or director nominees. The new Ohio law deprives him of even this ordinary incident of share ownership.

Finally, the shareholder approval provisions of the Ohio statute may disrupt the operation of Commission rules regulating the commencement of tender offers.[62] If Ohio law is interpreted to permit the bidder to commence, but not consummate, its tender offer before shareholder approval is obtained,[63] it is theoretically possible for a bidder to comply with both federal and Ohio law by holding tendered shares in a depositary pending the outcome of the shareholder vote. However, the Ohio shareholder approval provisions will force the bidder to postpone the purchase of tendered securities and to abandon its offer, if shareholder approval is not obtained. This is inconsistent with federal regulation, which contemplates that a bidder for shares should be able to buy tendered shares after the expiration of the minimum tender offer period.[64]

The Ohio statute will eventually be challenged by a prospective purchaser of shares in an Ohio corporation. *MITE* emphasized the preeminence of investor choice and the unconstitutionality of any state efforts which burden out-of-state securities transactions. Accordingly, the Ohio statute will, in all probability, be struck down, most likely on the ground that it imposes an unconstitutional burden on interstate commerce, but also possibly, as we

---

62. *See* SEC Rule 14d-2.

63. This is the most plausible interpretation of § 1701.831. The Ohio statute does not expressly restrict the commencement of a tender offer, but it does make commencement prior to shareholder approval impractical.

64. *See, e.g.*, SEC Rules 14d-1, 14e-1.

have seen, because it conflicts with the pattern of federal regulation and is preempted by such regulation under the Supremacy Clause.

B. Revised Maryland Statute[65]

1. Description

On June 21, 1983, the Maryland legislature enacted antitakeover legislation that typifies a second approach to post-*MITE* state tender offer regulation. The new Maryland law seeks to regulate the price paid when minority shareholders are "frozen out" in the second step of a transaction. The avowed intent of this legislation is to ensure that shareholders receive a "fair price" for their shares in a two-tier tender offer.[66]

The statute's provisions apply to "business combinations" involving "interested stockholders" of Maryland corporations.[67] A "business combination" includes any merger, consolidation, or share exchange by a corporation with any "interested shareholder" (or any other corporation which is or after the transaction would be an affiliate of an interested stockholder), unless the transaction does not alter the contract rights of the stock or convert any outstanding shares of stock.[68] Under this definition, unless an acquisition involves a share exchange, the commencement or consummation of the first step will not be affected. It is apparently the "freezeout" of the remaining shareholders via the second-step merger or consolidation that the statute seeks to regulate.

An "interested stockholder" is defined as a person who owns (beneficially, directly, or indirectly) 10 percent or more of the outstanding vote stock of a Maryland corporation.[69] A business combination with an "interested stockholder" must be recommended by the board of directors and must be approved by a vote of (1) 80 percent or more of the company's outstanding shares and (2) 66⅔ percent or more of the shareholders other than the interested stockholder,[70] unless certain exemptions or fair-price exceptions are applicable.

The statute contains numerous exemptions,[71] including exemptions for (1) close corporations, (2) corporations with fewer than 100 stockholders,

---

65. Md. Corps. & Assn's Code Ann. §§ 3-601 *et seq.*

66. *See* Washington Post, June 22, 1983, at C6.

67. Md. Corps. & Assn's Code Ann. § 3-601(E). Other aspects of the legislation's definition of "business combination" deal with the sale or lease of assets, the issuance of securities of the coporation to interested stockholders, liquidation, and recapitalization plans. These aspects of the statute are not dealt with herein.

68. *Id.* at § 3-601(J).

69. *Id.* at § 3-602.

70. *Id.* at § 3-603(C), (D), (E).

71. *Id.* at § 3-703(B).

and (3) corporations the original articles of incorporation of which elect, by the same voting margins required for a business combination, to be exempt. The most important exemption is a massive grandfather clause which greatly reduces the immediate significance of the statute. This clause provides that a corporation which, on July 1, 1983, had an existing "interested stockholder" is entirely exempt from the statute, both with respect to transactions with that shareholder and with resect to transactions (*i.e.*, mergers) with any other person that becomes an interested stockholder *after* July 1, 1983. Such a corporation may, however, elect *into* the statute. Conversely, corporations that lacked an "interested stockholder" on July 1, 1983, are subject to the statute unless, prior to September 1, 1983, such companies elected to be exempt from the statute, in whole or in part. This statute does not affect friendly mergers, if such mergers are approved by the board of directors of the Maryland corporation prior to the time that the acquiring company owns 10 percent or more of the Maryland corporation.

If the statute is otherwise applicable, the supermajority approval needed for a "business combination" can be avoided only if a "fair-price" exception is met. While the statutory "fair-price" definition is exceedingly complex,[72] in essence the law requires that shareholders receive the higher of the price paid for any of the stock by the interested stockholder, market value, or the price stockholders would be paid for the stock in the event of liquidation or dissolution of the corporation.[73]

The statutory intent is apparently to protect all shareholders, whether Maryland residents or not, from being "coercively" squeezed out in the second step of a two-step offer for all of the shares of a Maryland corporation. The key legal issue is whether this concern justifies the potentially severe impact of the statute on interstate commerce. The precise effect of this highly complex statute is still unclear—the statute is relatively new, and the grandfather clause reduces its immediate impact.[74]

2. Validity

Any attack on the validity of the Maryland statute would likely be made on Commerce Clause grounds. Such an attack would presumably rely on two theories: (1) that the statute has a chilling effect on nationwide tender offers, because potential bidders will be uncertain of their chances of successfully completing the second step of a two-tier offer, and (2) that, by interfering with the second step of a nationwide tender offer, Maryland is burdening out-of-state transactions with the meaning of *MITE*. This theory

---

72. Md. Corps & Assn's Code Ann. § 3-603(B).

73. The statute is sufficiently complex that the Maryland legislature, immediately after enacting the legislation, appointed a special task force to examine the bill and its effects. *See* Washington Post, June 22, 1983, at C6.

74. Md. Corps. & Assn's Code Ann. 3-603(D).

would involve arguing that, although states have generally been free to regulate freezeout (and other) mergers, including providing for appraisal rights, the Maryland statute violates the Commerce Clause because of the unique impact on out-of-state transactions resulting from state interference with a nationwide tender offer. While the success of these arguments may well depend on the precise context in which the Maryland statute is applied, the state's historic role in merger regulation cannot be ignored. Of the various approaches states have taken to takeover regulation since *MITE*, the Maryland statute seems to have the best chance of surviving judicial challenge.[75]

---

75. At least two other states—Pennsylvania and Wisconsin—have enacted legislation patterned on the Ohio and Maryland statutes.

Amendments to Pennsylvania's Business Corporation Law took effect on December 23, 1983. Provisions of the new statute, similar to the Maryland statute, would make two-tier takeovers more difficult. 1983 Pa. Laws § 409.1(c). Separate provisions of the amended Pennsylvania statute define a "control transaction" as the acquisition of 30% or more of the voting power of the shares of a corporation, with exceptions for certain agents, banks, brokers, and trustees who do not intend to exercise voting power themselves. 1983 Pa. Laws §§ 910, 911. The acquirer of 30% or more of the voting power is defined as a "controlling person." The controlling person must give prompt notice to the remaining shareholders that a control transaction has occurred, and is obligated, upon written demand of shareholders made within a reasonable time after notice is given, to pay a cash amount equal to the fair value of the shareholder's holdings as of the day prior to the date on which the control transaction occurs. In effect, an acquirer of 30% or more of the stock must provide dissenter's rights to the remaining shareholders. The practical result of this "control transaction" statute is that once an offeror acquires 30% or more of the target's stock, whether by tender offer, open market purchase program, or privately negotiated transaction, it must be financially prepared to purchase all of the target's remaining shares. This prospect will, if constitutional, presumably deter partial bids for Pennsylvania coporations. To the extent the costs of acquiring a large Pennsylvania coporation are prohibitive, such companies would tend to be insulated from hostile offers.

Effectively compelling a tender offer after a 30% or more acquisition goes beyond the traditional use of dissenter's rights in the corporate law context. Clearly the Pennsylvania statute's control transaction provisions will affect the interests of stockholders nationwide. The central question would be whether the 30% rule, by making takeover bids substantially more difficult, and potentially depriving nonresident shareholders of substantial profits, burdens interstate commerce. Pennsylvania's approach does, at a minimum, raise serious Commerce Clause questions. *See* Steinberg, *The Pennsylvania Anti-Takeover Legislation*, 12 Sec. Reg. L.J. 184 (1984).

The recently revised Wisconsin takeovers statute adopts significant portions of the Ohio and Maryland statutes discussed above. 1983 Wis. Laws 183.02 *et seq.* It includes the Ohio approach to "control share acquisitions" and the Maryland approach to two-step mergers.

IV. OTHER STATE STATUTES WHICH INHIBIT NATIONWIDE TENDER OFFERS

While the invocation of state authority over the internal affairs of share-holders' rights of domestic corporations is the primary post-*MITE* line of state attack on takeovers, corporation law is not the only weapon in the states' arsenal. Other areas of traditional state police and regulatory power may be pressed into service. Environmental protection, antifraud regulation, and penalties for inadequate disclosure in the takeover context are all examples of potential state attempts to regulate changes in corporate control.

A. The Hawaii Environmental Disclosure Law[76]

1. Description

The Hawaii Environmental Disclosure Law regulates additional purchases of securities or corporate assets by a 10 percent (or greater) shareholder of a Hawaii corporation. Such a 10 percent shareholder cannot "purchase or pay for more than an additional five percent of any such security or . . . assets of such Hawaii corporation during any twelve-month period"[77] unless it has filed a statement with the Office of Environmental Quality Control. This filing must describe the prospective purchaser, any prior proceedings against the purchaser involving any federal or state environmental law or regulation, the prospective purchaser's record of compliance with environmental laws and regulations, and all intentions of the prospective purchaser to influence the issuer to take any action within the next five years which might require the filing of an environmental impact statement under Hawaiian law.[78] There is a fifteen-day waiting period after the statement is filed before shares can be purchased.[79] The Office may extend this period for an additional forty-five days, if it believes a hearing as to the "adequacy, accuracy and completeness of the filing" is necessary.[80] The hearing must be concluded within fifty-five days of the original filing, and the Office has five additional days to issue its opinion.[81] Therefore, a total delay of up to sixty days after filing may occur before shares or assets are purchased. If the prospective purchaser refuses to file, refuses to participate in a hearing, or refuses to produce documents requested by the Office, the Office may recommend to the attorney general that "action be taken to prevent such person from purchasing more than five percent of the voting securities or

---

76. Hawaii Rev. Stat. § 343D-3 *et seq.* (1982).
77. *Id.*
78. *Id.*
79. *Id.*
80. *Id.*
81. *Id.*

the assets which are the subject of the filing within any subsequent 12-month period."[82]

The practical impact of the Hawaii statute is likely to be greatest in the open market purchase context, rather than in the hostile tender offer context. With respect to tender offers, the statute precludes purchase of, or payment for, shares until the filing and hearing requirements are satisfied. This statutory language does not appear to preclude commencement of the tender offer or the tendering of shares into an escrow account. The maximum delay after filing is made is sixty days—exactly the period after commencement of a tender offer when the Williams Act would compel that withdrawal rights be granted if tendered shares have not been purchased.[83] The Office cannot permanently block the purchase if the offeror cooperates by making the required filing, participating in any hearing, and furnishing additional documents as requested.[84] Therefore, the effect of the Hawaii statute on tender offers is to delay their consummation.

With respect to open market purchase programs, however, by requiring filing to be made before any shares are paid for, the statute has the effect of forcing a prospective open market purchaser to "tip his hand" by disclosing his intent to purchase. This is contrary to the federal scheme of postacquisition disclosure for ordinary open market purchases, and the potential sixty-day delay will block trading and disrupt the fairness and orderliness of the market for the security in question.

2. Validity

While Hawaii has a legitimate interest in intrastate environmental protection, *MITE* raises serious questions about the validity of the Hawaii Environmental Disclosure Law. Application of the Hawaii statute to open market purchase programs would block nationwide trading in a security for up to sixty days, thereby substantially burdening interstate commerce. Such a burden violates the Commerce Clause under *MITE*[85] as well as under appellate decisions striking down state regulation of open market purchase programs,[86] unless Hawaii establishes that its interest in protecting the en-

---

82. *Id*. The purchaser can avoid such an action by making a subsequent filing and complying with the statutory procedures. *Id*. Purchase by a majority shareholder and purchases of securities or assets of a corporation with less than 100 stockholders are exempt from the above procedures. Acquisition of securities or assets in violation of the Hawaii statute activates the penalties section of the statute, which provides for civil fines, rescission of unlawful purchases, and other "relief as it [the court] may deem just and proper." Hawaii Rev. Stat. *§ 343D-9, 343D-10 (1982).

83. Section 14(d) (5) of the Securities Exchange Act of 1934.

84. Hawaii Rev. Stat. at §§ 343D-3, D-4, D-6.

85. 457 U.S. at 644.

86. Telvest v. Bradshaw, 697 F.2d 576 (4th Cir. 1983); Esmark, Inc. v. Strode, 639 S.W.2d 768 (Ky. Sup. Ct. 1982).

vironment is akin to the specialized industry regulation, such as of banks, liquor vendors, or utilities, and that such interest outweighs the impact of the statute on interstate commerce. One factor which weakens the argument that Hawaii is engaged in legitimate specialized industry regulation is the fact that the Hawaii statute directly regulates tender offers and does not in any way limit the types of industries it seeks to protect to those uniquely likely to affect the environment. In the open market purchase context, because Hawaii is blocking nationwide trading in a security for up to sixty days, thereby imposing a severe burden on interstate commerce, its statute will be very difficult to sustain under *MITE*'s application of the *Pike v. Bruce Church* balancing test.

B. State Securities Law Antifraud and Disclosure Regulation

1. Antifraud Provisions

State power to prohibit fraud and to require disclosure in connection with intrastate securities transactions is well-established and expressly preserved in the various federal securities statutes.[87] However, this authority has the potential to be stretched beyond its intended realm and impede nationwide tender offers.

The typical state antifraud standard governing takeover bids, like Section 14(e) of the Securities Exchange Act,[88] prohibits fraud, manipulation, and deception in connection with any tender offer. State antifraud enforcement may result in either judicial relief (an injunction against the transaction)

---

87. A typical state statute states that:

> No person shall make any untrue statement of a material fact or omit to state any material fact necessary in order to make the statements made, in the light of the circumstances under which they are made, not misleading, or to engage in any fraudulent, deceptive, or manipulative acts or practices, in connection with any tender offer or request or invitation for tenders, or any solicitation of security holders in opposition to or in favor of any such offer, request, or invitation.

N.Y. Bus. Corp. Law § 1611 (McKinney); Va. Code § 13.1-533.

88. Section 14(e) of the Securities Exchange Act of 1934 provides, in relevant part, that

> [i]t shall be unlawful for any person to make any untrue statement of a material fact or omit to state any material fact necessary in order to make statements made, in the light of circumstances under which they are made, not misleading, or to engage in any fraudulent, deceptive, or manipulative acts or practices, in connection with any tender offer or request or invitation for tenders, or any solicitation of security holders in opposition to or in favor of any such offer, request, or invitation.

or administrative orders issued unilaterally by state officials (*e.g.*, an order requiring curative disclosure). Such a statute may apply only to resident shareholders or may be extraterritorial in its impact. That is, a state may purport to prohibit a nonresident bidder from continuing with a nationwide tender offer, until it has complied with a court order or administrative order,[89] or may only prohibit accceptance of tenders from state residents.[90]

It is difficult to support the proposition that states should be permitted to apply extraterritorially their antifraud prohibitions to transactions that would be tender offers under federal law. In the blue sky context, states clearly lack this power—that is, while a state may forbid a nonresident issuer's offering to state residents, unless the state's disclosure or other requirements are met, it may not block out-of-state transactions. State fraud prosecution in tender offers is likely, by the time hearings are held and appellate review is completed, to cause substantial delays in national transactions, even though the bidder may be in full compliance with federal law.

MITE's broad proscription against extraterritorial state regulation provides a strong argument against such application of a state antifraud statute. When states seek to block nationwide takeover bids, and thereby regulate nonresident shareholders, *MITE* invalidates the state statute. Even if the state review is confined to resident shareholders, the nationwide impact (thereby burdening out-of-state transactions) of removing some shareholders as potential sellers of stock may arguably render the state's action an impermissible burden on interstate commerce.[91] In any event, state antifraud regulations which served only to deprive state residents of the opportunity to tender their shares at a substantial premium over market might well prove politically unsustainable.

2. State "Penalty Box" Disclosure Provisions

Some jurisdictions seek to regulate large open market purchase programs (sometimes known as "creeping tender offers") through statutes that penalize individuals who purchase large amounts of securities without disclos-

---

89. N.Y. Bus. Corp. Law § 1611 *et seq.* (McKinney).

90. Va. Code § 13.1-533 *et seq.*

91. If a state can prohibit a tender offer from being made to its residents, the number of offerees who can sell their shares to the bidder is reduced by a finite number, which may preclude the bidder from obtaining the minimum number of shares that it is seeking and a requisite percentage for control. This effect distinguishes state tender offer regulation from state blue sky regulation since, even if one state prevents an offering subject to its blue sky laws from being made to its residents, the issuer may still sell shares in the offering to residents in 49 other states and presumably raise the amount of funds sought. *See* Martin Marietta Corp. v. Bendix Corp., 690 F.2d 558, 567 (6th Cir. 1982) (Michigan statute, even if applied only to Michigan shareholders, violates the Commerce Clause because it "prevents Michigan shareholders from participating in the nationwide tender offer.").

ing their intention to acquire a controlling position. For example, Section 3 of Chapter 110 of the Massachusetts statute mandates "that a five percent shareholder cannot make a take-over bid if, within the last twelve months, he purchased any shares—even before reaching five percent ownership—without disclosing an intention to gain control if such existed."[92] Any purchase by a 10 percent shareholder falls within the definition of a "takeover bid."[93] Therefore, if such a shareholder is found to have violated Section 3 (by buying additional shares without previously having disclosed an intention to seek control), that shareholder may not make future purchases for one year from the date of the violation.[94] The Massachusetts statute would apply even to a foreign corporation with its principal place of business in Massachusetts.[95] A separate provision of the statute permits the Commonwealth to bar indefinitely a purchaser who has violated the statute from making a takeover bid.[96]

The validity of this latter provision was tested in *Agency Rent-A-Car, Inc. v. Connolly*.[97] This case arose when the Massachusetts securities director concluded that Agency had purchased stock in Spencer Companies, Inc., within twelve months prior to Agency's tender offer for Spencer, without disclosing its intention to acquire control. The Director enjoined Agency from acquiring Spencer common stock for one year and enjoined Agency, for an unspecified time period, from making a takeover bid for Spencer. Agency challenged the director's action, and the district court granted a preliminary injunction against enforcement of the statute on Supremacy Clause grounds.[98] The First Circuit vacated the injunction, without ruling on the merits, and remanded the case to the district court for a determination as to whether a permanent injunction was warranted in light of *MITE*, stating that *MITE* "indicates that the constitutionality of the Massachusetts statute presents very serious and substantial questions, leaving its validity very much in doubt...."[99]

The First Circuit opinion remanding *Agency* did not resolve the constitutional issues. Penalty box provisions presume that federal regulation needs to be supplemented; however, federal regulation already requires the disclosure of control intentions.[100] However, after *MITE*, the automatic penalty

---

92. Agency Rent-A-Car, Inc. v. Connolly, 686 F.2d 1029, 1032 (1st Cir. 1982), quoting Mass. Gen. Laws Ch. 110C, § 3.

93. Mass. Gen. Laws Ch. 110C, § 1.

94. *Id*. at § 3.

95. *Id*. at § 2.

96. *Id*. at § 7.

97. 686 F.2d 1029 (1st Cir. 1982).

98. 542 F. Supp 231 (D. Mass. 1982).

99. 686 F.2d at 1040.

100. Regulation 13D, 17 C.F.R. 240.13d-101, requires that a purchaser, upon holding 5% of the outstanding securities of a public company, must disclose its

provisions of a Massachusetts-type statute are likely invalid. Irrespective of any local interests asserted by the state, the penalty provisions, which constitute an absolute nationwide prohibition on trading, burden transactions occurring outside of the state. Because of its extraterritorial impact, it is unlikely that such a statute would survive a challenge under *MITE*.

V. THE WORK OF THE SEC'S TENDER OFFER ADVISORY COMMITTEE AND RESULTING FEDERAL LEGISLATIVE PROPOSALS

As the foregoing indicates, although *MITE* reflects a strong, constitutionally premised holding against state regulation of securities transactions between nonresidents in the tender offer context, the states have continued to devise tools to subject tender offers to state regulation. Whether or not these provisions survive the inevitable constitutional challenges, there is increasing skepticism at the federal level concerning state regulation of change-of-control share acquisitions. As a result, there are growing indications that Congress may act to preempt state law, to the extent it inhibits such transactions. Both the Report of the Commission's Tender Offer Advisory Committee and pending legislative proposals reflect this possibility.

A. Tender Offer Advisory Committee

The Commission established the Tender Offer Advisory Committee on February 25, 1983, to study changes in acquisition practices since the 1968 adoption of the Williams Act and to formulate recommendations for statutory and administrative action in light of these changes.[101] After a series of public meetings, the Committee members presented their report to the Commission on July 8, 1983.[102] The Commission considered the staff's analysis of the Committee's recommendations at an open meeting on March 13, 1984. Subsequently, Chairman John S. R. Shad testified concerning the Commission's view regarding the Committee's recommendations before the House Subcommittee on Telecommunications, Consumer Protection, and Finance on March 28, 1984.

The recommendations of the Advisory Committee, while acknowledging state regulation of internal corporate affairs, reflect a broad condemnation

---

intentions regarding such purchases. This requirement is enforceable in federal actions either by the Commission or private plaintiffs. *E.g.*, Dan River, Inc. v. Unitex, Ltd., 624 F.2d 1216 (4th Cir. 1980); SEC v. Falstaff Brewing Corp., 629 F.2d 62 (D.C. Cir.), *cert. denied*, Kalmanovitz v. SEC, 449 U.S. 1012 (1980); Kaufman and Broad, Inc. v. Belzberg, [1981 Transfer Binder] Fed. Sec. L. Rep. (CCH) ¶ 97,893 (S.D.N.Y. March 12, 1981).

101. *See* Advisory Committee On Tender Offers, *supra* note 5, at 1-2.

102. *See id.* at 6.

of state law obstacles to national tender offers and a call for federal legislation to preempt such state laws. Three of the Committee's recommendations embody this philosophy:

> *Recommendation 4* states that "[r]egulation of takeovers should recognize that such transactions take place in a national securities market."[103]

> *Recommendation 9* makes clear that the permissible scope of state tender offer regulation extends only to "local companies" and "public interest businesses" such as banks, utilities, and insurance companies. Even in those areas, Recommendation 9 provides that state regulation should only be permitted to the extent that it is justified in relation to the overall objectives of the industry, does not conflict with procedural provisions of federal takeover regulations, and relates to a significant portion of the issuer's business.[104]

> *Recommendation 34* is the heart of the Committee's approach to state takeover regulation. Recommendation 34 provides:

> State laws and regulations, regardless of their form, that restrict the ability of a company to make a tender offer should not be permitted because they constitute an undue burden on interstate commerce. Included in this cateogry should be statutes that prohibit completion of a tender offer without target company shareholder approval[105] and broad policy legislation written so as to impose the ability to transfer corporate control in a manner and time frame consistent with the federal tender offer process.[106]

> Consistent with Recommendation 9, Recommendation 34 recognizes only two exceptions to this broad federal preemption of state takeover statutes—"local companies" and "regulated industries."[107]

When it reviewed the Committee's recommendations, the Commission adopted a somewhat narrower approach than that embodied in these three recommendations. The Commission did agree, consistent with *MITE*, that regulation of takeovers should be federal, since these transactions take place in the national securities market, and regulation by the states would place an undue burden on interstate commerce. The Commission qualified this proposition, however, with the statement, consistent with Committee Recommendation 9(b), that state law should continue preeminent with respect to the internal affairs of a corporation. Exceptions to this principle, the Commission concluded, should be limited to those situations where the

---

103. *Id.* at 15.
104. *Id.* at 17-18.
105. Ohio is an example of such a statute.
106. *See supra* note 5, at 35-36.
107. *Id.*

interests of shareholders are being abused *and* the purposes of the federal regulatory scheme are frustrated.[108] However, the Commission, unlike the Committee, did not endorse the concept of federal legislation to effectuate this philosophy; instead, it expressed its intent to continue to implement its policy on state takeover statutes through its program of *amicus curiae* participation in private litigation challenging state statutes that impede the operation of the federal tender offer process.

B. Pending Legislation

While expressing a general reluctance to intrude upon state corporate law, the Commission determined that federal legislation restricting the ability of target management to invoke defensive measures permissible under state law was necessary in three particular areas. The Commission transmitted to Congress a legislative proposal embodying its suggestions in these areas[109] on May 21, 1984:[110]

---

108. *See generally* Statement of John S. R. Shad, Chairman of the Securities and Exchange Commission, before the House Subcommittee on Telecommunications, Consumer Protection, and Finance (March 28, 1984).

109. The Commission's legislative proposal would also amend Section 13(d) of the Securities Exchange Act of 1934 to permit the Commission to require immediate public announcement of the acquisition of more than 5% of a class of equity securities and to revise the current deadline for filing of the statement of acquisition required by Section 13(d) of the Exchange Act. The legislation also permits the Commission to prohibit purchases of additional shares for a period not to extend beyond the second business day after the filing. The Commission concluded that Section 13(d) requires revision because, at present, its permits acquirers to buy an unlimited number of shares between the time they acquire more than 5% the securities and the filing date, ten days later.

The Commission's proposal also addresses "golden parachutes" by prohibiting a target company from increasing the compensation of officers and directors during tender offers.

H.R. 5694, a proposal drafted by Mr. Martin Lipton, would essentially prevent the acquisition of more than 10% of the outstanding shares of voting stock of a public corporation, unless the acquirer offers to purchase *all* of the shares of common stock in a tender offer. The offer must be (1) for cash at the highest price paid by the acquiring person for any shares of common stock during the preceding twelve months or (2) if no such shares had been acquired, for cash securities, or a combination thereof, so long as "equal value" is offered for each share. This measure, though an innovative response, is troublesome because it could potentially inhibit potential first bidders from acquiring a toehold, thereby potentially diminishing the chances that a contest for control, which often results in significant premiums to shareholders, will ever begin. If this is the measure's effect, it will not achieve its desired purpose of giving all shareholders an opportunity to share in any so-called control premium.

110. *See* letter from SEC Chairman John S. R. Shad to Representative Timothy E.

A target company should be prohibited from acquiring its own securities during the pendency of a third-party tender offer. Defensive
self-tenders almost necessarily preclude the success of the hostile
bidder's offer, since management can draw upon the full assets and
borrowing capacity of the issuer to fund a bid which need only attract
a larger fraction of the shares than does the hostile bidder's offer.
Worse still, management can make its bid contingent on the hostile
bidder's offer. Thus, if the raider is defeated, shareholders may receive
nothing in either offer. This type of management tactic is contrary to
the principle of informed shareholder choice which underlies the
Williams Act.

A target company should be precluded, absent shareholder approval,
from issuing significant amounts of securities during a tender offer or
during a proxy contest. This latter restriction covers, among other
techniques, the issuance of so-called "poison pills." The proposal would
prohibit management from placing voting control in friendly hands
without the necessity of obtaining shareholder approval, thus defeating
a hostile bidder, even if that bidder obtains all of the shares for which
it has bid.[111]

A company should be precluded from paying "greenmail," unless
the same offer is made to all shareholders. Specifically, the Commission's proposal would prohibit an issuer from buying back any of its
securities at a price above the market from any person who holds
more than 3% of the class of securities to be purchased and has held
such securities for less than two years. Such purchases would be
permitted only upon prior security holder approval or if an offer of
at least equal value were made to all holders of such class and any
class into which such securities may be convertible. Greenmail permits
management to pay-off a potential bidder with shareholder assets and
thus deter a tender offer from ever being made.

The Commission's approach is narrow, in that it seeks to curb, only during
certain types of tender offers,[112] specified abuses which generally involve

---

Wirth, dated May 12, 1984, transmitting the Commission's legislative proposal in
the tender offer area.

111. For a discussion of the successful use of such a device, *see, e.g.*, Data Probe
Acquisition Corp. v. Datatab, Inc., 722 F.2d 1 (2d Cir. 1983), *cert. denied*, 104 S.
Ct. 1326 (1984).

112. The restrictions on "golden parachutes" and defensive securities acquisitions
and issuances apply only during tender offers that are unconditional, with respect
to at least 10% of the outstanding class of the securities, and are made at a price
at least 25% greater than the average market price for such securities during the

management's use of shareholders' assets to ward off a takeover. Some legislative proposals now pending in Congress would, however, effect far broader federal intrusion into state law. For example, John Huber, Director of the Commission's Division of Corporation Finance, has recommended that, if challenged, the burden of proof in a contested tender offer situation should be shifted to the directors to justify their actions, where such actions were taken by the board in response to, or in anticipation of, a takeover.[113] Similarly, in the Commission's consideration of Advisory Committee Report Recommendation 33, a recommendation which generally endorsed the business judgment rule, the Commission stated its belief that, in applying the business judgment rule in takeover situations, shareholders would be better served if the courts were more appreciative of the potential conflict of interest between management and shareholders and less willing to presume the regularity of management's conduct.

Consistent with this philosophy, bills have been introduced in both houses of Congress which would deprive management of the presumption normally afforded by the business judgment rule, that management defensive actions in the face of a takeover are proper.[114] For example, H.R. 5972 provides that no registered issuer shall "engage in any transaction in contemplation of effecting, or of defending against, a change in control," unless the issuer can prove, by a preponderance of the evidence, that the transaction is "both prudent for the issuer and fair to the issuer's shareholders." Either the Commission or any shareholder of an issuer would be able to bring a suit in district court to enjoin any such transaction, and attorney's fees could be awarded to shareholders.[115] The proposal would, in the change-of-control context, effectively repeal the business judgment rule via federal legislation. If enacted, such legislation would preempt state corporation law on a broad scale.[116]

---

ten trading days prior to the commencement of the offer. The Commission was concerned that, without these threshold requirements, bidders would have undue power to block or inhibit legitimate corporate actions.

113. *See* Remarks of John J. Huber, Director, Division of Corporation Finance, U.S. Securities and Exchange Commission, to the American Bar Association, Division of Corporation, Banking, and Business Law, Ninth Annual Spring Meeting, April 7, 1984.

114. *See, e.g.*, Panter v. Marshal Field & Co., 646 F.2d 271 (7th Cir.), *cert. denied*, 454 U.S. 1092 (1981).

115. Subjecting "defensive tactics" to prior shareholder approval is another option that has been suggested. A more extreme alternative would place an outright ban on defensive tactics.

116. In addition to the introduction of the Commission's proposal, a variety of measures recently have been introduced in Congress, presenting a wide spectrum of potential solutions to problems associated with the takeover area. For a further

V. CONCLUSION

When the target is a widely held public company, a tender offer is a national transaction, the conduct of which involves the fairness, efficiency, and integrity of our nation's securities markets. While state, rather than federal, regulation of corporate law should continue to be the order of the day, state laws that have the effect of blocking or inhibiting tender offers, or other marketplace transactions, impair the free trading of securities in the national securities markets. Such state regulation, whether cast as tender offer regulation, corporate law, environmental protection, or in any other form, is contrary to the investor protection philosophy underlying the federal securities laws. As *Edgar v. MITE Corp.* illustrates, such regulation may also be contrary to the principles of federal regulation of interstate commerce embodied in the U.S. Constitution.

---

discussion of the principal topics covered by these bills, *see The SEC Advisory Committee on Tender Offers and Its Aftermath—A New Chapter in Change-of-Control Regulation,* by Linda C. Quinn and David B. H. Martin, Jr., in Part I of this volume.

Do the Second-Generation State Takeover Statutes Violate the Commerce Clause? A Preliminary Inquiry

MARK A. SARGENT*

The Securities and Exchange Commission's Advisory Committee on Tender Offers has argued that "[s]tate regulation of takeovers should be confined to local companies."[1] By "state regulation of takeovers" the Advisory Committee meant statutes similar to the Illinois Takeover Offer Disclosure Act[2] declared unconstitutional in 1982 by the Supreme Court in *Edgar v. MITE Corp.*[3] The Illinois statute and others like it had attempted to regulate tender offers *per se*, imposing conditions similar to those applied by the Williams Act. The Advisory Committee specifically distinguished between such "state regulation of takeovers" and aspects of state corporation law, such as the business judgment rule, that also may have an impact on the takeover process.[4] That latter form of state law, the Advisory Committee suggested, should not be preempted or overriden by state corporation law "[e]xcept to the extent necessary to eliminate abuses or interference with the intended functioning of federal takeover regulation."[5]

---

*Mark A. Sargent is associate professor of Law, University of Baltimore School of Law. Copyright © by Mark A. Sargent, 1984. Thanks are extended to Steven Grossman, Cyril Moscow, Charles Rees, and Marc Steinberg for their comments and suggestions.

1. SEC, Advisory Committee on Tender Offers, Report of Recommendations 17 (1983) [hereinafter cited as Report].

2. Ill. Ann. Stat. Ch. 121-1/2, §§ 137.51-.70 (Smith-Hurd Supp. 1982-1983) (repealed 1983).

3. Edgar v. MITE Corp., 102 S. Ct. 2629 (1982).

4. Report, *supra* note 1, at 18,55.

5. *Id.* The Advisory Committee apparently did not have any of the second-generation takeover statutes in mind when it made this distinction. Its distinction between state tender offer regulation and state corporate law thus should not be

The SEC responded to these suggestions by proposing limited changes in the federal regulatory scheme that would have a partially preemptive effect on certain particularly troublesome aspects of state corporate law. These proposed changes, however, would still leave plenty of room for state regulation of the post-tender offer phases of the takeover process.[6]

In short, the Advisory Committee and the SEC have rejected any role for the states in the direct regulation of tender offers, while preserving most of the states' ability to regulate other phases of the takeover process through the substantive internal affairs provisions of their general corporation statutes. The Advisory Committee's recommendation that the states not regulate tender offers reflects, or is at least consistent with, the Supreme Court's decision in *MITE* and the post-*MITE* decisions in the lower federal courts.[7] Whether one agrees with the Advisory Committee's recommendation or not, it is almost certain that the state attempts to regulate the takeover process through Williams Act–type regulation of tender offers are unconstitutional. In other words, the first-generation state takeover statutes are probably dead.

Some of the state legislatures, however, have not allowed the demise of these statutes to divert them from their goal of somehow regulating corporate takeovers. In fact, the repudiation of the first-generation statutes has

---

read as an implied endorsement of these novel forms of state corporate law. These statutes may in fact interfere "with the intended functioning of federal takeover regulation" and, hence, become subject to preemption. This comment, however, will consider only the Commerce Clause status of these laws.

6. *See* Statement of John S. R. Shad, SEC Chairman, before Hearings of the House Subcommittee on Telecommunications, Consumer Protection, and Finance Concerning the Recommendations of the SEC Advisory Committee on Tender Offers. (March 28, 1984), [1983-1984 Transfer Binder] Fed. Sec. L. Rep. (CCH) ¶ 83,511, at 86,678, 86,681-682.

7. Martin Marietta Corp. v. Bendix Corp., 690 F.2d 558 (6th Cir. 1982); National City Lines, Inc. v. LLC Corp., 687 F.2d 1122 (8th Cir. 1982); Telvest, Inc. v. Bradshaw, 697 F.2d 576 (4th Cir. 1982); Occidental Petroleum Corp. v. Cities Serv. Co., [1982 Transfer Binder] Fed. Sec. L. Rep. (CCH) ¶ 99,063 (W.D. Okla. 1982); Bendix Corp. v. Martin Marietta Corp., 547 F. Supp. 522 (D. Md. 1982); Esmark, Inc. v. Strode, 639 S.W.2d 768 (Ky. 1982); *but see* Agency Rent-A-Car, Inc. v. Connolly, 686 F.2d 1029 (1st Cir. 1982). The results in these cases eliminated the theoretical possibility that a state tender offer statute could be drafted in such a way as to avoid the constitutional problems that proved fatal to the Illinois statute in *MITE*. For arguments that such a state tender offer statute could be drafted, *see* Bartell, *State Corporate Takeover Regulation*, 15 Rev. Sec. Reg. 807 (1982); Pozen, *Making State Takeover Statutes Safe from Constitutional Attack*, Nat'l L.J., Aug. 2, 1982, at 18, col. 1; Pitt. *Hostile Tender Offers Now Omnipresent Fact of Life*, Legal Times (Wash.), July 19, 1982, at 16, col. 1.

led to the adoption of some very different forms of takeover regulation.[8] The difference between these second-generation takeover statutes and the unconstitutional first-generation statutes reflects the distinction between state tender offer regulation and traditional state corporation law. That is, the second-generation statutes do not directly condition or restrain the tender offer or the consequent tender of shares; instead, they readjust the target's internal ordering mechanism in a way that will have a substantial impact on what can happen after the tender offer is completed. In essence, the new direction shifts the focus from *securities regulation* to *corporate law*[9]; the new statutes attempt to regulate the takeover process through regulation of the internal affairs of corporations organized under the laws of the state.

In so doing, these statutes have raised new and troublesome questions about the constitutional limits on substantive corporate law. The first intimation of these questions can be found in the *MITE* Court's Commerce Clause analysis. In *MITE*, a majority of the Court agreed that the impact of the Illinois statute's regulation of tender offers on interstate commerce produced a violation of the Commerce Clause.[10] In so holding, the Court rejected an argument that the Illinois statute was an important expression of the state's traditional interest in regulating the internal affairs of its domestic corporations.[11] The Court rejected the argument, because the Illinois statute applied to certain corporations not organized under the laws of Illinois and because Illinois' attempt to regulate transactions between shareholders and offerors did not involve regulation of corporate internal affairs. By deciding that the statute simply did not implicate the state's interest in regulating the internal affairs of its corporations, the Court did not have to consider whether that interest outweighed the statute's burden on interstate

---

8. *Ohio*: 1982 Ohio Legis. Serv. 5-395, 5-402 (Baldwin), to be codified at Ohio Rev. Code §§ 1701.01, 1701.831; *Maryland*: 1983 (Extraordinary Session) Md. Laws 1, to be codified at Md. Corps. & Ass'ns Code Ann. §§ 3-601 - 3-603, 8-301(14); *Pennsylvania*: Pa. Pamphlet Law 395, Act 1983-92, to be codified at Pa. Stat. Ann. §§ 408, 409.1, 910; *Wisconsin*: Wis. 1983, Act 200; *Michigan:* Mich. S. Bill No. 541 (1984). Since the Wisconsin and Michigan statutes are largely dervied from the Maryland and Ohio statutes, this comment will discuss those statutes only incidentally.

9. For explanation of this distinction, *see* Sargent, *On the Validity of State Takeover Regulation: State Responses to* MITE *and* Kidwell, 42 Ohio St. L.J. 689, 722-27 (1981); *see also* Profusek & Gompf, *State Takeover Legislation after* MITE: *Standing Pat, Blue Sky, or Corporation Law Concepts?*, 7 Corp. L. Rev. 3, 24-29 (1983).

10. For summary of the allocation of the justices' votes in this complex set of opinions, *see* Note, *The Unsung Death of State Takeover Statutes:* Edgar v. MITE Corp., 24 B.C.L. Rev. 1017, 1039-44 (1983).

11. *MITE*, 102 S. Ct. at 2643.

commerce.[12] While this distinction between state regulation of tender offers and "true" regulation of internal affairs may be specious,[13] it allowed the Court to deflect the argument that the state's traditional interest in the regulation of corporate internal affairs must be accounted for in the Commerce Clause analysis. This deflection of the internal affairs argument, however, left unanswered the questions that the second-generation statutes are now raising.

That is, suppose a state chooses to regulate the takeover process through altering substantive provisions of the general corporation statute governing the internal affairs of domestic corporations. Those provisions might include the shareholder appraisal remedy, the merger mechanism, the statutory definition of the directors' obligations, or some novel provision regulating control transactions with majority shareholders. In other words, suppose a state chooses to regulate takeovers through a means that indisputably amounts to internal affairs regulation. This is exactly what Ohio, Maryland, Pennsylvania, and other states have done. And suppose that this form of internal affairs regulation has an inhibiting effect on the ability of bidders to launch or successfully complete a hostile takeover bid. Would that effect constitute an impermissible burden on interstate commerce? This is precisely the question raised by the second-generation state takeover statutes.

This question is more complex than it may seem at first glance. It requires consideration of the nature of a state's interest in the application of its corporate law. It requires a distinction between state interests in corporations organized under its laws but not otherwise present in the state and in corporations both organized under its laws *and* substantially present in the state. It requires explanation of how particular forms of corporate internal affairs regulation burden interstate commerce. In short, it requires understanding of how the Commerce Clause limits a state's authority to regulate corporate internal affairs through substantive corporate law. This is apparently a novel question.[14] There has been some consideration of how competing state interests may determine which law shall govern the internal affairs of so-called pseudo-foreign corporations,[15] and there are also well-

---

12. *Id.*

13. For arguments to this effect, *see* Sargent, *supra* note 9, at 724-27; Boehm, *State Interests and Interstate Commerce: A Look at the Theoretical Underpinnings of Takeover Legislation,* 36 Wash. & Lee L. Rev. 733, 743, 756 (1979); Shipman, *Some Thoughts about the Role of State Takeover Legislation: The Ohio Takeover Act,* 21 Case W. Res. L. Rev. 722, 741-45 (1970).

14. The first commentator to emphasize that *MITE* raises this question was Levmore, *Interstate Exploitation and Judicial Intervention,* 69 Va. L. Rev. 563, 619-25 (1983). For a highly conclusory discussion of this issue, *see* Profusek & Gompf, *supra* note 9, at 29; *cf. The Supreme Court, 1981 Term,* 96 Harv. L. Rev. 62, 71 n.56 (1982) [hereinafter cited as *Supreme Court*].

15. *See, e.g.* Oldham, *Regulating the Regulators: Limitations upon a State's Abil-*

organized due process limits on the jurisdiction of state courts under state corporation statutes,[16] but there has been very little analysis of this specific question.

This commentary will not try to provide that analysis in an exhaustive form. Instead, it will use the second-generation statutes to define the need for such analysis and to identify the terms in which such analysis should be made. It will argue that these terms can be found in the convergence of the Commerce Clause issue and the current policy debates over the role of hostile takeovers in the American economy. In other words, this commentary will argue that it is impossible to weigh the burdens on interstate commerce or to define the nature and importance of the state interests without considering the economic arguments raised by Gilson,[17] Easterbrook and Fischel,[18] and others[19] about the structural role of hostile takeovers in the corporate system. In short, by demonstrating the convergence of the Commerce Clause question and the policy question, this commentary

---

ity to Regulate Corporations with Multistate Contacts, 5 Del. J. Corp. L. 181 (1981) [hereinafter cited as Oldham I]; Oldham, *California Regulates Pseudo-foreign Corporations—Trampling upon the Tramp?*, 17 Santa Clara L. Rev. 85 (1977) [hereinafter cited as Oldham II]; Reese & Kaufman, *The Law Governing Corporate Affairs: Choice of Law and the Impact of Full Faith and Credit*, 58 Colum. L. Rev. 1118 (1958); Latty, *Pseudo-foreign Corporations*, 65 Yale L.J. 137 (1955).

16. *See* Shaffer v. Heitner, 433 U.S. 186 (1977); Ratner & Schwartz, *The Impact of Shaffer v. Heitner on the Substantive Law of Corporations*, 45 Brooklyn L. Rev. 641 (1979).

17. Gilson, *Seeking Competitive Bids versus Pure Passivity in Tender Offer Defense*, 35 Stan. L. Rev. 51 (1982); Gilson, *The Case against Shark Repellant Amendments: Structural Limitations on the Enabling Concept*, 34 Stan. L. Rev. 775 (1982); Gilson, *A Structural Approach to Corporations: The Case against Defensive Tactics in Tender Offers*, 33 Stan. L. Rev. 819 (1981).

18. Easterbrook & Fischel, *Antitrust Suits by Targets of Tender Offers*, 80 Mich. L. Rev. 1155 (1982); Easterbrook & Fischel, *Auctions and Sunk Costs in Tender Offers*, 35 Stan. L. Rev. 1 (1982); Easterbrook & Fischel, *Corporate Control Transactions*, 91 Yale L.J. 698 (1982); Easterbrook & Fischel, *Takeover Bids, Defensive Tactics, and Shareholder's Welfare*, 36 Bus. Law. 1733 (1981); Easterbrook & Fischel, *The Proper Role of a Target's Management in Responding to a Tender Offer*, 94 Harv. L. Rev. 1161 (1981); Fischel, *Efficient Capital Market Theory, the Market for Corporate Control, and the Regulation of Cash Tender Offers*, 57 Tex. L. Rev. 1 (1978).

19. *See, e.g.* Bebchuk, *The Case for Facilitating Competing Tender Offers: A Reply and Extension*, 35 Stan. L. Rev. 23 (1982); Bebchuk, *The Case for Facilitating Competing Tender Offers*, 95 Harv. L. Rev. 1028 (1982); Jarrell & Bradley, *The Economic Effects of Federal and State Regulations of Cash Tender Offers*, 23 J.L. & Econ. 371 (1980); Manne, *Cash Tender Offers for Shares: A Reply to Chairman Cohen*, 1967 Duke L.J. 231; Manne, *Mergers and the Market for Corporate Control*, 73 J. Pol. Econ. 110 (1965).

will try to demonstrate that these well-known policy debates have an unexpected constitutional dimension.

Part I of this commentary will briefly describe the three major second-generation statutes and explain how they are intended to work. Part II will examine the need for Commerce Clause analysis of state corporate law and define a point of departure for application of that analysis to these statutes. Part III will then identify the types of questions that must be asked in order for the interstate burdens and state benefits generated by these statutes to be analyzed in Commerce Clause terms. The discussion in Part III will offer only a preliminary inquiry into these novel issues; much fundamental analysis remains to be done.

It is perhaps worth noting what this commentary will not discuss. The second-generation statutes not only may be vulnerable under the Commerce Clause, but also may be subject to preemption by the Williams Act under the Supremacy Clause. This commentary will occasionally suggest that particular aspects of these statutes generate preemption problems, but the overall preemption issue cannot be adequately analyzed in this necessarily brief commentary.

I. AN OVERVIEW OF THE SECOND-GENERATION STATUTES

Complete description and analysis of these statutes is beyond the scope of this commentary. More detailed discussion of them can be found elsewhere,[20] so this commentary will simply summarize the key features of the three major statutes.

A. Ohio

In November 1982, the Ohio legislature enacted a bill requiring all acquisitions of controlling stock interests to be approved by the shareholders.[21] This requirement applies to all control acquisitions, whether

---

20. *Ohio*: Kreider, *Fortress without Foundation? Ohio Takeover Act II*, 52 U. Cinn. L. Rev. 108 (1983); Profusek & Gompf, *supra* note 9, 29-41. *Pennsylvania*: Steinberg, *The Pennsylvania Anti-Takeover Legislation*, 12 Sec. Reg. L.J. 184 (1984). *Maryland*: Hersch & Kako, *New Approach to Takeovers Taken in Maryland*. N.Y.L.J., May 18, 1983, at 1, col. 2.

21. 1982 Ohio Legis. Serv. 5-395, 5-402 (Baldwin), to be codified at Oh. Rev. Code §§ 1701.01, 1701.831. This statute may become a model for other states. The new Wisconsin statute, Wis. 1983, Act 200, is a tripartite statute, containing: (1) a substantially revised version of a first-generation tender offer statute, (2) a version of the Ohio statute, and (3) a substantially revised version of the Maryland statute. A bidder for a Wisconsin corporation subject to this statute thus would have to comply with all three forms of takeover regulation. *See* Malmgren & Pelisek, *Takeovers of Wisconsin Corporations: A New Era of Shareholder Protection Begins*, Wis. B. Bull., May 1984, at 26.

accomplished by tender offer or not, and it applies to all Ohio corporations, unless a corporation's charter excludes the corporation from the coverage of the statute.

Under this statute, the directors of the subject corporation must call a special shareholders' meeting within ten days of receipt of an acquirer's statement of intention to acquire shares sufficient to move the acquirer into a control position or from one level of control to another. At this meeting, which must be held within fifty days of receipt of the acquirer's statement of intention, the shareholders are to vote on the proposed acqusition. In order for the acquisition to proceed, it must be approved by both a majority of the voting power present at the meeting and a majority of the voting power excluding "interested shares" (primarily those owned by the acquirer and its affiliates).

The new Ohio statute thus differs from the first-generation statutes insofar as it does not regulate or otherwise condition either the tender offer itself or the tendering of shares. It shifts the focus of regulation from those phases of the takeover process to the point immediately precedent to any second-step transaction—the actual purchase of the control bloc of shares. The technique of regulation applied at this point is also quite different from those applied under the first-generation statutes to the tender offer; there are no administrative hearings, no proration or withdrawal provisions, no review of the fairness of the offering, indeed no role whatsoever for the state securities administrator. Instead, the Ohio statute draws upon the principle of shareholder approval of organic transactions to regulate this form of control transaction.[22]

The Ohio statute does not represent, however, a complete departure from the first-generation statutes. The new approach is a form of internal affairs regulation, but by imposing conditions upon the offeror's purchase of the tendered shares, the statute will still directly affect transactions between the shareholders and the offeror.[23] The new Maryland statute, in contrast, confines itself to the second-step transaction and has no direct effect on the tender offer. The applicability of the Ohio statute to even this last step in the tender offer phase of the takeover process may make it particularly vulnerable to the Commerce Clause challenge under *MITE*, as the discussion below will suggest.

B. Maryland

The Maryland legislature enacted, in June 1983, a quite different form of takeover statute.[24] This legislation shifted the regulatory focus entirely to

---

22. *Accord*, Kreider, *supra* note 20, at 121.

23. *Id*. at 119-20.

24. 1983 (Extraordinary Session) Md. Laws 1, to be codified at Md. Corps. &

the second-step transaction. It requires the successful tender offeror intending a post-tender offer "business combination" to either obtain supermajority approval from all the shareholders and from the disinterested shareholders or pay a "fair price" to all those nontendering shareholders who are forced to sell in the course of the business combination. In essence, the statute is designed to inhibit front-end–loaded, two-step takeovers, on the ground that such takeover bids are inherently coercive and unfair to nontendering shareholders.[25]

The act is drafted very tightly to cover almost every conceivable form of business combination and to ensure that a truly "fair" price is paid to shareholders bought out in the second-step transaction.[26] The result of this approach is the potential applicability of the fair-price/supermajority provisions to negotiated business combinations and other transactions that have nothing to do with hostile takeovers.[27] The Maryland Act attempts to avoid this problem by granting the board of directors substantial control over when and to whom these provisions will apply. The Act thus operates something like a shark repellant, which the board, rather than the shareholders, has the authority to implement or abandon.

While the Maryland Act represents an abandonment of any attempt to regulate tender offers, it may prevent at least some partial tender offers from being made and may even reduce the aggregate number of takeover bids for Maryland corporations. This raises novel Commerce Clause questions, because these results would be achieved not through a form of securities regulation restraining the tender offeror's acquisition of shares but through corporate internal affairs regulation restricting what can be done with the shares once they have been acquired.[28]

C. Pennsylvania

A Pennsylvania statute enacted in December 1983 represents an even more thorough exploitation of the internal affairs provisions of the general corporation law.[29] First, the Act provides that corporate fiduciaries "may,

Ass'ns Code Ann. 3-601 - 3-603, 8-301(14). Michigan has recently adopted a version of this statute. Mich. S. Bill No. 541 (1984).

25. *See* Dept. of Legis. Ref., Staff Report to the General Assembly of Maryland, Extraordinary Session, June 1983, at 9-10, 14; *Maryland Bill on Takeovers Spurs Fight*, Wall St. J., May 26, 1983, at 33, col. 3; Hersch & Kako, *supra* note 20, at 1.

26. The statute offers three different techniques by which this price should be calculated and requires the highest of those three prices to be paid to the shareholders.

27. *Accord*, Hersch & Kako, *supra* note 20, at 3.

28. *Accord, id.*

29. Pa. Pamphlet Law 395, Act 1983-92, to be codified at Pa. Stat. Ann. §§ 408, 409.1, 910.

in considering the best interests of the corporation, consider the effects of any action upon employers, suppliers and customers of the corporation, communities in which offices and other establishments of the corporation are located and all other pertinent factors." As one commentator has already noted, this language may further expand the presumption of the business judgment rule, making it nearly impossible for a shareholder complaining of management defensive tactics to overcome that presumption.[30] This effect could strengthen management's hand, thereby inhibiting takeover bids for Pennsylvania corporations.

Second, the Act contains provisions similar to the fair-price/supermajority provisions of the Maryland Act and is designed to have similar effects on front-end–loaded, two-step takeovers. The Act also grants the target board substantial leverage over these provisions; second-step transactions are exempted if a majority of the board approves the transactions. Accordingly, these provisions will end up being applied only to hostile takeovers.[31]

Third, the Act requires "controlling shareholders" (persons or groups owning thirty percent of a class of voting stock) to provide notice to the other shareholders that they may obtain an appraisal —"fair" value for their shares—from the controlling shareholder. This provision should seriously inhibit partial bids for the shares of corporations subject to the Act, since it will come into play even if the bidder does not plan a second-step transaction. The board of directors also has substantial leverage over this provision, since timely adoption of an amendment to the bylaws can exempt a particular bidder from its coverage.[32]

II. THE COMMERCE CLAUSE AND STATE CORPORATION LAW: A POINT OF DEPARTURE

The Commerce Clause grants Congress the power "[t]o regulate Commerce . . . among the several states . . . ,"[33] but the Constitution nowhere excludes the states from regulation of interstate commerce. The Constitution's silence on the states' authority to regulate in this area, however, has been read as creating a negative implication that there are some restraints on

---

30. Steinberg, *supra* note 20, at 186-87.

31. *Id.* at 187-88. Wisconsin's version of the Maryland statute, however, provides the target board considerably less control over the applicability of the statute. *See* Wis. 1983, Act 200, § 9.

32. The target board's ability to determine the applicability of both the Maryland and Pennsylvania statutes to individual transactions and bidders may violate the principle of neutrality mandated by the Williams Act, even though these statutes do not directly regulate tender offers.

33. U.S. Const. Art. 1, § 8.

this authority.[34] As a result, many different types of state regulation have succumbed to a judicial finding that the Commerce Clause restrains or prohibits that form of regulation.[35] There is nothing peculiar about the state corporation laws from this perspective. The statutes discussed in Part I of this commentary all affect interstate commerce through conditioning the manner in which hostile takeovers are to be accomplished, raising the cost of such takeovers, and altering the balance between the bidder and target management. They thus do not differ in this regard from the first-generation statutes invalidated on Commerce Clause grounds in *MITE*. Accordingly, they can, indeed must, be analyzed in terms of the negative implications of the Commerce Clause.

It is not entirely clear, however, what the appropriate Commerce Clause analysis is. It is well known that Commerce Clause analysis has been shifting from attempts to distinguish between "indirect" and "direct" regulation of interstate commerce to a more indeterminate, value-laden balancing of interests. In the words of one commentator:

> State regulation affecting interstate commerce will be upheld if (a) the regulation is rationally related to a legitimate state end, and (b) the regulatory burden imposed on interstate commerce, and any discrimination against it, are outweighed by the state interest in enforcing the regulation.[36]

The Supreme Court, however, continues to recognize and give some effect to the distinction between "direct" and "indirect" or "incidental" restraints on interstate commerce.[37] In fact, the leading judicial formulation of the balancing test is phrased in terms of incidental regulation. In *Pike v. Bruce Church, Inc.*,[38] the Court stated:

> Where the statute regulates evenhandedly to effectuate a legitimate local public interest, *and its effects on interstate commerce are only incidental*, it will be upheld unless the burden imposed on such commerce is clearly excessive in relation to the putative local benefits (emphasis added).[39]

MITE itself demonstrates that *Pike*'s distinction between direct and indirect regulation continues to play a role in the Court's decision making.

---

34. L. Tribe, American Constitutional Law § 6-2 320 (1978); Levmore, *supra* note 14, at 566.

35. *See generally* L. Tribe, *supra* note 34, §§ 6-1 - 6-22, at 319-76.

36. L. Tribe, *supra* note 34, § 6-5 at 326.

37. *MITE*, 102 S. Ct. at 2640-41.

38. 397 U.S. 137 (1970).

39. *Pike*, 397 U.S. at 142.

In Part V of his opinion, Justice White stated that "[t]he Commerce Clause ...permits only incidental regulation of interstate commerce by the states; direct regulation is prohibited."[40] In part V-A, he applied this distinction to the Illinois statute, noting that it "directly regulates transactions which take place across state lines, even if wholly outside the State of Illinois."[41] Accordingly, he found that the "sweeping extraterritorial effect" of the Illinois statute constituted a direct restraint on interstate commerce, and he invalidated it without application of the *Pike* balancing test.[42] Justice White failed to command a majority on this issue, so *MITE* does not *hold* that the Illinois statute imposed an unconstitutional direct restraint,[43] but his use of this concept shows the lingering vitality of the direct/indirect distinction. In addition, some of the post-*MITE* decisions have expressly applied the direct restraint analysis and found the statutes before them unconstitutional without any application of the *Pike* balancing test.[44]

While *MITE* and some of its progeny suggest that the old direct/indirect distinction is still alive, it must be emphasized that this distinction has been severely criticized.[45] On one level, it has been criticized because of the difficulty of distinguishing between "direct" and "indirect."[46] The distinction has been described variously as too mechanical, too uncertain in its application, and "misleadingly precise."[47] On a more profound level, it can be criticized as masking the important policy question: To what extent does the state regulation actually impede interstate commerce, and what are the state justifications for so doing? *MITE* and its progeny offer no reformulation of the direct restraint analysis that justifies abandonment of this balancing approach.[48] It may be that the extraterritorial impact of the Illinois statute was very great indeed and that the state interest in its application was meager, but those facts simply dictate a resolution of the balancing test against the state, not an *ex ante* rejection of the test.

---

40. *MITE*, 102 S. Ct. at 2640-41.

41. *Id.*

42. *Id.*

43. Only Justices Burger, Powell, and O'Connor joined in Part V-A of Justice White's opinion.

44. *See, e.g., Occidental Petroleum Corp.*, [1982 Transfer Binder] Fed. Sec. L. Rep. (CCH ¶ 99,063, at 95,042; *Bendix Corp.*, 547 F. Supp. at 532.

45. The Court itself has rejected application of this distinction with respect to Commerce Clause challenges to state taxation. *See* Complete Auto Transit, Inc. v. Brady, 430 U.S. 274, 279-80, 288-89 (1977).

46. *See, e.g.*, DiSanto v. Pennsylvania 273 U.S. 34, 44 (1927) (Stone, J., dissenting); Dowling, *Interstate Commerce and State Power*, 27 Va. L. Rev. 1, 6-8 (1940).

47. L. Tribe, *supra* note 34, § 6-5, at 326. *See also* Maltz, *How Much Regulation is Too Much: An Examination of Commerce Clause Jurisprudence*, 50 Geo. Wash. L. Rev. 47 (1981) (critique of Court applications of balancing test).

48. *Accord, Supreme Court, supra* note 14, at 70-71.

In any event, the second-generation takeover laws may not seem to the federal courts to impose a burden as great as that apparently imposed by the first-generation statutes. The courts thus may be less likely to resuscitate the direct burden analysis in cases involving those statutes.[49] Accordingly, the proper focus of inquiry is the constitutional status of the new direction in state takeover regulation under the *Pike* balancing test.

Application of the *Pike* test in this context, however, will require some fundamental rethinking. It will require that effort because there has been little constitutional analysis of how state corporation laws can burden interstate commerce or of the nature and extent of states' interests in their own corporation laws. Because this kind of analysis is so scarce, we have little, if any, understanding of how the Commerce Clause might restrain the ability of a state to use the internal affairs provisions of its general corporation statute to regulate a particular type of interstate transaction.

A reason why this type of analysis is missing may be that state corporation laws have not created the burdens on interstate commerce likely to trigger Commerce Clause scrutiny, perhaps because they are typically *enabling* rather than *regulatory*.[50] One of the results of the "race to laxity" among state corporation statutes has been that such statutes have tended to increase the ability of corporations and corporation management to accomplish their goals without significant government interference or extensive judicial review. Such statutes are thus unlikely to have had the kind of inhibiting effect on interstate commerce to trigger Commerce Clause challenge.

A perception of burden may also have been lacking because the federal government has not directly regulated in the area of corporate internal affairs. This has helped prevent the kinds of conflicts that could be analyzed in either Commerce Clause or preemption terms. The SEC has occasionally ventured into the area of internal corporate governance, but SEC governance regulation has tended to be "tougher" than the state regulation in the area.[51] If these roles had been reversed and a more stringent form of state regulation had impeded the ability of corporations to do what federal law permitted

---

49. It may also be less likely to do so with respect to those aspects of the second-generation statutes that do not regulate tender offers. The existence of the Williams Act may have had an important, although unarticulated, relation to the *MITE* Court's highly critical Commerce Clause analysis of the Illinois tender offer statute. *See Supreme Court, supra* note 14, at 69-70.

50. On this well-worn point, *see* Cary, *Federalism and Corporate Law: Reflections upon Delaware*, 83 Yale L.J. 663 (1974); Manne, *Our Two Corporation Systems: Law and Economics*, 53 Va. L. Rev. 259 (1967); Latty, *Why Are Business Corporation Laws Largely "Enabling"?* 50 Cornell L.Q. 599 (1965).

51. On the SEC's role in this area during the 1970's *see* J. Seligman, The Transformation of Wall Street: A History of the Securities and Exchange Commission and Modern Corporate Finance 534-51 (1983).

them to do, preemption and Commerce Clause challenges similar to those faced by the first-generation takeover statutes might have surfaced.

Similarly, traditional choice of law rules have dictated that the law of only one state—the state of incorporation—should apply to internal affairs issues. This has prevented the kinds of constitutional problems that can arise when a superimposition of several state requirements creates a pattern of contradictory or at least inconsistent regulation of some aspect of interstate commerce.[52] This last factor may be particularly important. When this strict choice of law rule has been questioned with respect to pseudo-foreign corporations, resulting in a recognition that two states may have legitimate interests in regulating the same corporation, Commerce Clause questions have appeared, and it has become necessary to consider the nature of state interests in their own corporation laws.[53] In general, however, it may be that the enabling character of state corporation laws, when coupled with their relative exclusivity of application, has reduced the possibility that they may be perceived as creating a questionable burden on interstate commerce. As a result, we know very little about how a substantive internal affairs provision of a state corporation law can be said to impose a burden on interstate commerce, and we have very little guidance for defining the nature or weight of a state's interest in its own corporation law.

Perhaps the only real source of guidance is the so-called pseudo-foreign corporation exception to the internal affairs doctrine.[54] That choice of law rule provides a point of departure for Commerce Clause analysis of the second-generation statutes. That point of departure may be simply stated: the variety and weight of a state's interest in corporate internal affairs regulation depend on the local identity of the corporations regulated. A closer look at the evolution of the pseudo-foreign corporation concept will show how emphasis on a corporation's local identity can provide not only a sensible choice of law rule but also a point of departure for Commerce Clause analysis.

The internal affairs doctrine is both familiar and at least apparently simple. First of all, it acknowledges that any number of states may have an interest in applying their laws to transactions between a corporation and the rest of the world. To use one of the simplest cases, if a corporation organized in State A commits a tort in State B injuring residents of State B, the law of State B will govern. In other words, the corporation's *external* affairs are governed by the choice of law rules appropriate to the transaction in ques-

---

52. *See* Horowitz, *The Commerce Clause as a Limitation on State Choice of Law Doctrine*, 84 Harv. L. Rev. 806, 813-14, 819-20 (1971); Ratner & Schwartz, *supra* note 16, at 668; L. Tribe, *supra* note 34, § 6-11, at 338-39.

53. *See, e.g., id.*

54. *See* authorities cited *supra* note 15.

tion. In that context, a corporation is treated much like any other person. Accordingly, choice of law questions concerning the execution of contracts, the commission of torts, the sale of securities, and the conveyance of property by a corporation are not ordinarily governed by an assumption that the law of the chartering state should automatically apply. The corporation's *internal* affairs, on the other hand, are treated much differently. The relations *inter sese* of shareholders, directors, and officers are usually governed by the law of the chartering state. The courts and commentators have disagreed, however, about what constitutes "internal affairs" and have tended to interpret the concept narrowly. The narrowness of this interpretation is reflected in this frequently cited definition:

> [Where] the act complained of affects the complainant solely in his capacity as a member of the corporation, whether it be as a stockholder, director, president, or other officer, and is the act of the corporation, or through its agents, the board of directors, then such action is the management of the internal affairs of the corporation.[55]

Internal affairs cases, thus, typically involve controversies over the duties and liabilities of directors and officers, the proper procedures for holding meetings, electing directors and officers, inspecting records, transferring shares, and so on.

The distinction between external and internal affairs obviously cannot be pressed too hard, since there are gray areas. The distinction has been blurred even further by courts uncomfortable with the results of this choice of law rule and willing to manipulate the definition of internal affairs to produce different results.[56] Good examples of this tendency are cases holding that the inspection rights of shareholders do not involve the internal affairs of a corporation.[57] This commentary will not try to determine, however, whether this distinction is theoretically coherent or practically useful. The internal affairs doctrine will be examined here not for its own sake but because of what the development of this choice of law rule may tell us about the nature and weight of a state's interest in its own corporation law.

It can tell us something about this question, because it has necessitated some thinking about why one state's law should apply as opposed to that of another. This question recurs because a corporation can be incorporated in one state but "located" in one or many other states. The possibility of

---

55. North State Copper & Gold Mining Co. v. Field, 64 Md. 151, 154, 20 A. 1039, 1040 (1885).

56. *See* Oldham II, *supra* note 15, at 93-98.

57. *See, e.g.*, Donna v. Abbot Dairies, Inc., 399 Pa. 497, 161 A.2d 13 (1960); Loveman v. Tutwiler Inv. Co., 240 Ala. 242, 199 So. 854 (1941); McCormick v. Statler Hotels Del. Corp., 55 Ill. App. 2d 21, 203 N.E.2d 697 (1964).

competing state interests thus arises, requiring some explanation of why the law of the chartering state should apply instead of that of some other state. Not all of the justifications used to support this doctrine, however, have turned upon analysis of the state interests at issue.

For example, the oldest justification for the rule depends upon the characterization of the corporation as the "creature" of the chartering state.[58] As one commentator has pointed out, "this quasi-theology gets us nowhere."[59] It tells us nothing about the state's real interests in the application of its corporation laws; it represents a purely formalistic deduction from the basic fact that a state enabling statute is a predicate to incorporation.

Another explanation of the internal affairs doctrine can be found in the vested rights approach to choice of law.[60] In essence, this approach regards rights as vesting in the place where they are created; the law of that state will then be applied to controversies involving those rights, wherever the claim based upon them is brought. This approach seems to reflect the notion that the corporation charter is a kind of contract,[61] with the chartering state the place where the rights of the "parties" to this contract are created and vested. This approach is not as silly as the creature-of-the-state analysis described above, but it shares some similar flaws. For example, the characterization of the charter as a "contract" is really just an analogy, since the state plays a noncontractual role in granting the corporate franchise, and officers and directors of the corporation surely cannot be characterized as parties to a contract, other than in a metaphorical sense. This approach thus operates, at least to some extent, in the realm of fiction. This is not the only similarity to the creature-of-the-state analysis. Like that analysis, the vested rights approach precludes consideration of the interests of other states in the corporate "contract," since it seems to assume that the parties' choice of law should be unquestioned.[62]

Neither the creature-of-the-state analysis nor the vested rights approach,

---

58. *See, e.g.*, Central Transp. Co. v. Pullman's Palace Car Co., 139 U.S. 24, 59-61 (1891); Bank of Augusta v. Earle, 38 U.S. (13 Pet.) 519, 588-89 (1839); Head v. Providence Ins. Co., 6 U.S. (2 Cranch) 127, 167 (1804). *Cf.* Latty, *supra* note 15, at 139; Ratner & Schwartz, *supra* note 16, at 649. Profusek and Gompf pay too much deference to this notion by using it as the main support for their bald assertion "[t]hat the constitutionality of state regulation of the internal affairs of corporations, despite the effect on interstate commerce, cannot be seriously questioned." Profusek & Gompf, *supra* note 9, at 29. The message of *MITE* and its progeny is that such regulation can, and perhaps will, be challenged. *See also* Levmore, *supra* 14, at 619-25.

59. Latty, *supra* note 15, at 139.

60. Oldham II, *supra* note 15, at 91-92.

61. Latty, *supra* note 15, at 138-39.

62. *Id.*

therefore, reflects any consideration of whether the chartering state has an important interest in the application of its corporation law. In fact, their very terms of argument preclude that kind of consideration; the creature-of-the-state analysis depends upon a formalistic deduction, not upon any identification and weighing of real state interests, and the vested rights approach turns exclusively upon the alleged intent of the parties. In short, these justifications of the internal affairs doctrine tell us very little about the state interests in question.

Similarly flawed is the argument that considerations of efficiency and predictability justify the internal affairs doctrine. According to this argument, corporate planners need the certainty of knowing which state's law will apply to the internal affairs of the corporation.[63] Without such certainty, the argument continues, it would be very difficult, or even impossible, for a corporation with interstate operations and ownership to govern itself. The interests of predictability and efficiency, therefore, justify a rule permitting the application of only one state law to internal affairs questions—the law of the chartering state.

An interest in efficiency does suggest that a single law should apply to internal affairs matters.[64] This interest in efficiency may even have a Commerce Clause dimension, since the potential application of a multiplicity of laws to corporate internal affairs might itself create an unconstitutional burden on interstate commerce. The interest in predictability, furthermore, suggests that the rule determining which state's law should apply must be simple and clear. But neither of these interests requires that the law of the chartering state be the single law that applies in every case.[65] There may be another state with an important interest in the application of its corporate laws to the internal affairs of a particular corporation. The interests of efficiency and predictability, as well as the Commerce Clause, may dictate a single law choice of law rule, but they do not dictate *which* states' law should be chosen. Only a direct analysis of the competing state's real interests can fairly determine how that choice is made. As a result of this recognition, the pseudo-foreign corporation concept evolved as an exception to the internal affairs doctrine, an exception built entirely upon comparative analysis of different states' interests.

Under this exception, a pseudo-foreign corporation would be a corporation incorporated in one state but with its primary operations and most of its ownership located in another. The clearest example of a pseudo-foreign corporation might be a small, closely held retail enterprise owned entirely by residents of State A but incorporated in Delaware. A somewhat

---

63. Reese & Kaufman, *supra* note 15, 1126-27.

64. *See* authorities cited *supra* note 52.

65. Latty, *supra* note 15, at 139-40; Reese & Kaufman, *supra* note 15, at 1144-45.

less clear example might be a manufacturing enterprise incorporated in Delaware, with its principal place of business in State A, and financed through a limited offering under Rule 505 of Regulation D.[66] That rule permits securities to be sold to an unlimited number of "accredited investors" and thirty-five nonaccredited investors. Accordingly, this corporation may have a majority of its, say, 100 shareholders residing in the state of its principal place of business and the minority scattered throughout the financial centers of the nation. Another possible example might be a service enterprise incorporated in Delaware, with operations highly localized in State A, with a large number, but not a majority, of shareholders residing in that state, and with a thin over-the-counter public market for its shares. It is, of course, possible to argue over the criteria for determining when a corporation is pseudo-foreign in character, but these examples reflect a general notion that relatively high concentrations of ownership and operations in one state may render a corporation incorporated elsewhere only "pseudo-foreign."

Under a strict application of the internal affairs doctrine, the corporation law of the chartering state would govern the internal affairs of such corporations; their almost complete absence from the chartering state and substantial presence in another state would be irrelevant to the choice of law question. Under the pseudo-foreign corporation exception, a different result might be reached—a court would apply the internal affairs provisions of the corporation's true domiciliary state. This result could be justified on two grounds.

First, the application of the law of the true domiciliary state would not conflict with the need for the application of a single, certain law, because the law of the domiciliary state would not be applied unless the corporation in question had a clear-cut local identity. Accordingly, only one state other than the chartering state would have a substantial interest in the application of its corporation law. A truly national corporation in which no one state has a predominant local interest, however, would continue to be governed by the law of the chartering state in the interests of predictability and efficiency.

Second, the true domiciliary state would have several interests justifying the application of its laws. Because of the local concentration of the corporation's operations and ownership, the state has an interest in maintaining the orderly and equitable operation of the corporation's internal affairs in order to preserve the corporation as a stable component of the state's economy, preserve the jobs of corporate employees resident in the state, and protect the interests of the corporation's creditors located in the state. Because of the in-state concentration of the corporation's shareholders, furthermore, the state would have an interest in protecting those shareholders from unfair or dishonest managerial behavior. By benefiting state

---

66. 17 C.F.R. 230.505 (1985).

residents in that manner, the state would also benefit from increased investor confidence in the securities of its local corporate issuers. These interests are real interests, and they outweigh whatever residual interests the state of incorporation might have.

The pseudo-foreign corporation doctrine has received considerable support from the commentators,[67] and it has been adopted in somewhat different forms by the legislatures of California[68] and New York.[69] This commentary will not, however, attempt to determine whether the doctrine makes sense as a choice of law rule, or whether the existing definitions of pseudo-foreign corporations are coherent or practical, or whether there are unresolved constitutional tensions within this doctrine. These questions can be ignored here, because this commentary is not primarily concerned with the problem of choosing one state's law over another's. The pseudo-foreign corporation doctrine is of interest, because it shows how a state's interest in the application of the internal affairs provisions of its corporation law can be defined and weighed, at least for choice of law purposes. This lesson is quite simple: a state's interest depends on how local the corporation really is. The greater the local concentration of operations and ownership, the more varied and weighty the state interests. If there is no such local concentration, the chartering state's law should be applied because of the interests in predictability and efficiency, not in deference to any important state interest.

This technique of calculating state interests for choice of law purposes thus provides the point of departure needed for Commerce Clause analysis of the second-generation takeover statutes: the variety and weight of a state's interest in corporate internal affairs regulation depend on the local identity of the corporations regulated.

III. A PRELIMINARY COMMERCE CLAUSE INQUIRY

A. Premises

Part II of this commentary attempted to demonstrate that the second-generation takover laws can and should be scrutinized under the Commerce Clause. Part II also emphasized, however, that Commerce Clause analysis of the internal affairs provisions of state corporation laws is highly unusual, largely because such laws have been enabling rather than regulatory and because the the choice of law rules and the lack of concurrent federal regulation have effectively prevented intergovernmental conflict in this area.

---

67. *See* authorities cited *supra* note 15-16.
68. Cal. Corp. Code § 2115 (West Supp. 1984).
69. N.Y. Bus. Corp. Law §§ 1315-20 (McKinney's 1963 & Supp. 1983).

Because state corporation laws have not created, or have not been perceived as creating, a burden on interstate commerce, courts and commentators have not defined conclusively the nature and weight of state interests in their corporation laws. The only important attempt to define those interests arose through the development of the pseudo-foreign corporation exception to the internal affairs choice of law rule. Part II concluded by suggesting that the pseudo-foreign corporation exception provides a point of departure for Commerce Clause analysis of the interstate effects of state corporation law.

That point of departure can be restated as a first premise: *The variety and weight of a state's interests in the internal affairs regulation depend on the local identity of the corporations regulated.* These interests are very similar to those identified above as supporting the pseudo-foreign corporation exception of the internal affairs doctrine. Thus, if a corporation has a predominantly local identity, the state will have several interests in regulating its internal affairs.

First, the state will have an interest in protecting resident shareholders from the disorderly or inequitable operation of corporate governance. This interest actually has two aspects: protection of resident shareholders as such and protection of investor and entrepreneurial confidence in the state's corporate franchise.

Second, the state will have an economic interest in protecting the internal stability of local corporations. This interest also has more than one aspect. For example, the state may be interested in promoting the stability of corporations that provide goods and services for local markets. Similarly, the state has an interest in promoting such stability for the benefit of local creditors of that corporation. Most important, however, may be the state's interest in the local corporation as a stable source of employment for state residents.

Third, the state may have a competitive interest in regulating the internal affairs of the corporation in a manner that eliminates or reduces the incentives for local businesses to incorporate elsewhere. Since out-of-state incorporation may have some effect on franchise tax revenues or the payment of fees to the local bar, this interest may be quite tangible. Accordingly, a state may have several distinct interests in regulating the internal affairs of local corporations. These interests, furthermore, are real interests; they derive from the corporation's reality as an economic entity, not from any formalistic conception of the corporation as a "creature" of the state. The *weight* of these several interests, however, will vary from case to case. The more localized the corporation's ownership and operations, the weightier these state interests will be.

This equation, of course, requires a distinction among different types of corporations. For example, a state will be most interested in a corporation organized under its laws and with almost all of its operations and shareholders located in the state. The state's interests would not be significantly diminished if that type of corporation were incorporated in Delaware. That type of entity would be a pseudo-foreign corporation, and the interests of the true domiciliary state would not only justify application of the state's law but would also be accorded weight under the Commerce Clause. Conversely, Delaware's interests in regulating the internal affairs of another state's pseudo-foreign corporation would seem to be minimal and, perhaps, would be confined to Delaware's interests in securing a flow of corporate franchise taxes and fees for the local bar. A Delaware internal affairs provision that imposed a significant burden on interstate commerce, therefore, would be quite vulnerable under the *Pike* balancing test.

A state would also have weighty interests in a corporation that has substantial local operations but with stock owned by a large number, or even a majority, of nonresident shareholders. The state interests in protection of shareholders may be proportionately less weighty in this context than other interests, but the other state interests will remain important. Of course, the difficult question is determining the necessary ratio of local presence and state interests. That is not, however, an impossible question, and it can be resolved on a case-to-case basis.

In contrast, a truly national corporation, that is, one incorporated in Delaware or State X and with operations and ownership in many states, does not have the kind of local character that would lend special weight to any state's interest in regulating its internal affairs. The interests of predictability and efficiency might justify the *application* of Delaware's or State X's corporate law to the national corporation's internal affairs, but if a particular aspect of that law burdened interstate commerce, those interests would be immaterial to the outcome of the *Pike* balancing test.

In short, the outcome of a *Pike* test in this context may depend not just on the character of the regulation in question, or upon some generalized definition of the state's interests in that form of regulation, but upon the local identity of the corporation whose internal affairs are being regulated. If a court were to apply this approach, the new Ohio, Maryland, and Pennsylvania statutes would be more likely to withstand Commerce Clause challenge when they are applied to corporations with clearly local identities. They are least likely to withstand such challenge when they are applied to truly national corporations that happen to be incorporated in those states.

With this first premise stated, a second premise can be defined: *Different aspects of a state corporation law produce different benefits*. While the state interests in corporate internal affairs can be defined in the broad terms identified above, they must also be analyzed in terms of the specific benefits they provide. Examples of such specific benefits are numerous.

A statute that prohibits a corporate board of directors from making distributions out of stated capital, or in a manner that would render a corporation insolvent, expresses a policy determination that creditors need to be protected from the shareholder's ability to appropriate earnings to the creditor's detriment.[70]

A different benefit is provided by statutory provisions permitting incorporation through filing a simple document at a state office, authorizing the use of general purposes and power clauses in corporate charters, and limiting the shareholder's liability to his equity contribution. These simple provisions eliminating the need for special chartering, reducing the possibility of *ultra vires* problems, and allowing the investor to circumscribe his risk, allow the state to provide a widely available and attractive mechanism for organizing capital and putting it to use.[71]

Some final examples will show how the general state interest in fairness to shareholders can be given specific content. This general state interest is expressed specifically in statutes providing shareholders with a right to vote their shares cumulatively. Because cumulative voting can assure that minority shareholders will secure representation on the board of directors, these mandatory cumulative voting provisions reflect a decision that such minority representation should be encouraged.[72] Similarly, some of the special close corporation statutes contain devices designed to protect minority shareholders from oppression by majority shareholders.[73] These statutes, thus, also give specific expression to the general state interest in fairness to shareholders.

Analysis of the second-generation takover statutes under the *Pike* test, therefore, will require a specific, rather than general, description of the benefits derived by the state from those particular forms of internal affairs regulation. But what are the terms in which those benefits can be described and then balanced against burdens on interstate commerce? This question leads to a third premise: *The burden imposed on interstate commerce and the benefits provided to the state by internal affairs regulation must be defined and balanced in economic terms.*

This premise may, at first glance, appear questionable. It is hornbook law that the "negative implications of the Commerce Clause derive centrally from a political theory of union, not primarily from an economic theory of free trade. The function of the clause is to insure national solidarity, not

---

70. *See generally* B. Manning, Legal Capital (2d ed. 1981).

71. *See generally* L. Friedman, A History of American Law 175-78 (1973).

72. *See* Steadman & Gibson, *Should Cumulative Voting for Directors Be Mandatory,* 11 Bus. Law. 9 (1955); Young, *The Case for Cumulative Voting,* 1950 Wis. L. Rev. 49.

73. *See* Karjala, *A Second Look at Special Close Corporation Legislation,* 58 Tex. L. Rev. 1207 (1981); *cf.* Hall, *The New Maryland Close Corporation Law,* 27 Md. L. Rev. 341 (1967).

national efficiency."[74] This characterization of the purpose of the Commerce Clause is accurate, but it does not contradict the premise just stated. This premise does not suggest that the Commerce Clause expresses a constitutional preference for "free" markets or any other market structure.[75] It suggests, instead, that state attempts to regulate economic enterprise must be analyzed in economic terms. The specific, actual economic effects of that regulation must be understood before a burden on interstate commerce can be identified. Similarly, economic analysis will help determine whether the alleged benefits are substantial enough to be accorded any weight under the Commerce Clause. Economic analysis thus will make possible the balancing of real burdens and real benefits. It will not attempt to transform the Commerce Clause into a constitutional bulwark of "free" markets but will refine the criteria by which Commerce Clause decisions are made.

With these three premises stated, the basic structure of a Commerce Clause analysis of the second-generation takover statutes begins to emerge: (1) these statutes are most likely to withstand Commerce Clause challenge insofar as they are applied to corporations with a local character, (2) the benefits to the state generated by these laws must be identified and weighed with specificity, and (3) both the burdens and the benefits must be analyzed in terms of economic functions and effects.

B. Burdens: Do the Second-Generation Statutes Burden Interstate Commerce?

The post-*MITE* decisions,[76] like most of the pre-*MITE* decisions,[77] held that the state tender offer statutes materially impeded the flow of commerce. Some courts went so far as to say that this effect constituted an unconstitutional direct restraint on commerce.[78] Whether the interstate impact was characterized as direct or indirect, most courts agreed that the sweeping extraterritorial impact of these statutes was the source of the constitutional problem.

According to these courts, the extraterritorial impact derived from the required application of state precommencement waiting periods, filing requirements, lengthy or indefinite postcommencement hearing provisions, and antifraud prohibitions to interstate tender offers. Because these statutes purported to give the state securities administrators the authority to halt tender offers that failed to comply with these statutory requirements, and

---

74. L. Tribe, American Constitutional Law 25 (Supp. 1979) (citing Baldwin v. Seelig, 294 U.S. 511, 522-23 (1935)).

75. L. Tribe, *supra* note 74, at 25.

76. *See* cases cited *supra* note 7.

77. *See* cases cited in Sargent, *supra* note 9, at 692, nn. 17-19.

78. *See* cases cited *supra* note 44.

because completion of the tender offer would be materially delayed even if the bidder complied with those requirements, the statutes were found to have a substantial impact far beyond the borders of the individual states. These courts had little difficulty in identifying these interstate effects as "burdens" on interstate commerce.

The second-generation statutes may present greater difficulties. The extent to which these statutes, especially the Maryland and Pennsylvania statutes, actually "burden" interstate commerce remains to be defined. The Maryland and Pennsylvania statutes, as emphasized above, do not regulate the tender offer phase of the takover process; they regulate what happens after a tender offer has been completed. This is not to suggest that this type of regulation is innocuous. It is merely to point out that these statutes will not directly interfere with the completion of the tender offer once it has commenced. The interstate impact of some of these statutes, then, will be of a different order than that produced by the first-generation statutes. There are several possible effects.

First, the key effects of the Maryland and Pennsylvania statutes may be to: (1) eliminate or significantly reduce the number of partial and two-step takeover bids for corporations subject to those statutes and (2) reduce the total number of hostile tender offers for such corporations. The crucial point to note is that these effects will result from the influence of these statutes on the prospective bidder's decision making. That is, the prospective bidder will have to determine whether the fair-price/supermajority provisions of both of these statutes or the partial bid provision of the Pennsylvania statute would make a two-step or partial bid either impossible or too expensive. Similarly, the potential bidder may decide that the elaborate shareholder approval provisions of the Ohio statute or the expansion of board authority under the Pennsylvania statute would make any type of takeover bid too risky. In short, these statutes might function like legislatively enacted shark repellants, preventing certain kinds of takeovers from being launched at all and, perhaps, reducing the aggregate number of takeovers.

Is this kind of prospective, inhibiting effect a "burden" in Commerce Clause terms? It may very well be that these prospective effects constitute burdens in Commerce Clause terms. The exact nature of the burden, however, remains to be defined. If the net effect of these provisions is to replace certain prospective bidders with bidders willing to incur a greater degree of uncertainty or risk, or to use some novel form of takeover device, then there may not be a burden, because the Commerce Clause does not protect any particular market structure; indeed, it does not even protect the overall efficiency of the market.[79] These provisions may be said to constitute bur-

---

79. *See* L. Tribe, *supra* note 74, at 25, discussing Exxon Corp. v. Governor of Maryland, 98 S. Ct 2207 (1978).

dens only insofar as they materially impede the aggregate flow of takeovers.[80] More needs to be learned about the impact of these statutes on the market for corporate control, however, before it can be assumed that this burden exists.

Second, it could be argued that the actual operation (as distinct from the prospective effect) of the fair-price/supermajority provisions impedes the consummation of the entire takeover process, especially when that process involves two-step transactions. For example, a bidder might obtain a control percentage of the shares of a Maryland corporation, prepare a second-step squeeze-out of the minority shareholders, and launch a "preemptive strike" in federal court against application of the Maryland or Pennsylvania fair-price/supermajority provisions. The argument would be similar to that made in the preemptive strikes against the first-generation tender offer statutes, that is, that the transactions being regulated are inherently interstate because they involve the ownership of public corporations, and the application of these stringent requirements would materially impede their consummation. It should be recognized, however, that this type of internal affairs regulation has never before been characterized as a burden on interstate commerce. In fact, Justice White expressly distinguished between internal affairs regulation and state regulation of transactions between shareholders and third-party tender offerors. This is not to say that the effects of this provision could never be characterized as burdens on interstate commerce but that such a characterization would require some novel rethinking of what such a burden is. The effect of such a characterization, furthermore, on the applicability of other aspects of the state corporate law to the internal affairs of public corporations is potentially enormous.[81]

---

80. *Cf. Exxon Corp.*, 98 S. Ct. at 2215, in which the Court found that Maryland regulation of the retail gasoline market did not materially impede the interstate flow of gasoline and oil into Maryland markets.

81. These provisions of the second-generation statutes may be said to constitute burdens because of their direct impact on a particular type of transaction. But is their extraterritorial effect really any greater than that of the general corporation statute's voting, proxy, merger, appraisal, or "going private" provisions on the nonresident shareholders of public corporations? If the extraterritorial impact is roughly the same, then these provisions could, theoretically, be described as unconstitutional burdens on interstate commerce.

Similarly, the long-established premise (*see* Hall v. Geiger Jones, 242 U.S. 539 (1917)) that the blue sky laws do not violate the Commerce Clause may become subject to challenge. Those state statutes may be said to be valid under the Commerce Clause because: (1) the states have a substantial interest in protecting resident investors from securities fraud or unfair treatment by promoters and (2) a state's blue sky law applies only to securities transactions within the state and thus does not have any direct extraterritorial impact. It is possible, however, that the enforcement of blue sky merit requirements could have a delaying or even a fatal effect on

The Ohio statute, however, may be more easily characterized as burdensome, because its operation is closer to that of the first-generation tender offer statutes. It does not condition or otherwise regulate the bidder's offer or the shareholder's acceptance, but it does restrain the bidder's purchase

---

an interstate offering of securities. This must not happen very often, because the underwriter of the offering will ordinarily "sell around" troublesome states, but it can happen. Accordingly, these statutes can have an *indirect* extraterritorial impact, even though their jurisdiction is limited to transactions within the state's borders. The United States Sixth Circuit Court of Appeal's reasoning in Martin Marietta v. Bendix Corp., 690 F.2d 558 (6th Cir. 1982), suggests that this kind of effect could raise constitutional questions.

In that case, the Michigan Securities Bureau had sought to enforce the antifraud provisions of both the Michigan Takeover Offers Act and the Michigan Uniform Securities Act. The court enjoined enforcement of both of these provisions, finding "that to the extent that the state statutes confer power on state authorities to interfere with the timing of an interstate tender offer made under the Williams Act or compel the revision of the solicitation or tender offer as a condition of the proceeding, they impose an unconstitutional burden on interstate commerce." *Martin Marietta*, 690 F.2d at 656. This finding can, of course, be limited to the application of the blue sky antifraud provisions to tender offers regulated by the Williams Act, but there is nothing in the court's reasoning that mandates a distinction between that context and the context of a public offering registered under the Securities Act of 1933. *Cf.* Levmore, *supra* note 14, at 621-23. As a practical matter, a state securities administrator's action against a tender offer will ordinarily have a more devastating effect than a similar action against a public offering of securities, largely because the bidder cannot "offer around" a recalcitrant state the way an underwriter can "sell around" such states. A state tender offer statute, therefore, might be more vulnerable to Commerce Clause challenge. *See id.* at 623. Under the right circumstances, however, application of the merit standards of a blue sky law might have a damaging effect on a national offering by blocking access to investment capital held by a state's investors, much as a state tender offer statute might block access to the assets of local companies.

Although the blue sky laws have not been seriously challenged on constitutional grounds in recent years (*see* North Star Int'l v. Ariz. Corp. Comm'n, 3 Blue Sky L. Rep. (CCH) ¶ 71,868, at 70,178 (9th Cir. 1983)), language like that quoted below suggests that such challenges are not impossible:

> Even if the [Oklahoma Takeover Bid] Act were construed to apply only to Oklahoma residents, its burden is clearly excessive. Preventing Oklahoma shareholders from participating in a nationwide tender offer burdens interstate Commerce because it may defeat the tender offers of residents from other states where the Oklahoma shares are needed to provide sufficient tendered shares.

Occidental Petroleum Corp., [1982 Transfer Binder] Fed. Sec. L. Rep. (CCH) ¶ 99,063, at 95,043. If this kind of reasoning were applied to blue sky regulation of a national offering of securities, the question would then become whether the state

or "takedown" of the shares. In that way, it, like the first-generation statutes, interferes with transactions between target shareholders and third-party offerors. After *MITE*, the federal courts should have little difficulty in characterizing this as a burden on interstate commerce subject to the *Pike* balancing test; the question would thus become whether the state benefits derived from this form of internal affairs regulation outweigh the burdens.[82]

In sum, the new Ohio approach to takeover regulation may be perceived as burdening interstate commerce, because it is a form of back-end tender offer regulation. The fair-price/supermajority provisions of the Maryland and Pennsylvania statutes and the new statement of target management's rights and obligations in the Pennsylvania statute will present less certain issues. The uncertainty has two sources. First, the key effect of these statutes might be an inhibiting effect on prospective bidders. It will then have to be determined whether these statutes are impeding the flow of takeovers to such an extent as to constitute a burden on interstate commerce. This determination will require both theoretical and empirical analysis of the market for corporate control. Second, the actual operation of these provisions may impede the completion of a given takeover, particularly when it involves a second-step transaction, but a characterization of that effect as a burden on interstate commerce would require reconsideration of the Commerce Clause status of other forms of state internal affairs regulation. The threshold question of whether these new statutes burden interstate commerce is thus quite problematic. The question of defining the benefits derived by the states from this form of regulation, however, is equally problematic.

C. Benefits: Nature and Weight

The legislatures of Ohio, Maryland, Pennsylvania, and other states enacted these statutes with little, if any, debate or controversy.[83] Those bodies, or at least their leaders, must have felt that these statutes offered some important and noncontroversial benefit to their states. The benefit that these

---

interest in protection of resident investors outweighs the burden on interstate commerce created by the denial to a national offering of access to the state's capital markets. Presumably this interest would be accorded great weight, probably much more than that accorded the interests allegedly served by the first-generation takeover statutes and largely because the blue sky laws do not carry the protectionist aroma that those statutes did.

82. For an argument that the Ohio statute would survive such a test, *see* Profusek & Grompf, *supra* note 9, at 36-41; *but see* Kreider, *supra* note 20, at 120-22.

83. For discussion of the background to enactment of the Pennsylvania statute, *see* Steinburg, *supra* note 20, at 184-86. The Maryland bill, to be precise, engendered extensive controversy until it was amended to give corporate boards control over its applicability. *See It's Time for a Veto*, Baltimore Sun, May 31, 1983, at A6, col. 1; Allen, *Maryland Bill on Takeovers Spurs a Fight*, Wall St. J., May 26, 1983, at

legislatures probably had in mind, however, can be accorded little, if any, weight. It is thus necessary to probe below the surface in order to identify and assess the constitutionally legitimate benefits produced by these statutes.

What the state legislatures had in mind, of course, was protection of local companies from hostile takeovers.[84] While this sentiment reflected a concern for protection of local jobs and not target management *per se*, such parochialism remains exactly what the Commerce Clause was designed to prevent.[85] The protectionist impulse that accounts for much of the success of these statutes in the state legislatures thus may prove fatal to them in the courts. The cases involving the first-generation statutes have made clear that this state "benefit" will not outweigh any burdens imposed in interstate commerce.[86]

There are, however, other benefits, at least arguably, derived from these statutes. They are relatively easy to define but also quite difficult to weigh. For example, it may be argued that these statutes:

1. Restrict a form of takeover regarded by some as highly coercive to the target's shareholders: front-end–loaded two-step takeovers;[87]

33, col. 3. Once it was amended, however, all opposition to the bill dissipated. *See* Baltimore Sun, June 22, 1983, at A1, col. 2; Baltimore Sun, June 21, 1983, at B5, col.5.

84. *See, e.g.*, Steinberg, *supra* note 20, at 185 n.9 (statement by Pennsylvania Senator Fumo); *Who's Minding the Store?* Baltimore Evening Sun, June 3, 1983, at A6, col. 1.

85. The drafters and proponents of these acts, at least in Ohio, Maryland, and Wisconsin, had concerns much broader and more legitimate than this kind of protectionism. The Ohio bill, for example, included a finding of fact that tender offers are coercive and stated that it is in the public interest for shareholders to have an opportunity to vote on proposed shifts of control. *See* Ohio Substitute House Bill No. 822, § 3 (A) (3), (4). Similarly, the Maryland bill was designed to respond to the problems faced by nontendering shareholders caught in the second step of a two-step bid. *See* Hersch & Kako, *supra* note 20, at 1. The leading force behind enactment of the Wisconsin statute, furthermore, was the Office of the Commissioner of Securities, which was clearly motivated by its long-standing commitment to investor protection. *See* 12 Wis. Sec. Bull. 1-5 (Jan. 1984); Wis. 1983, Act 200, § 1; Malmgren & Pelisek, *supra* note 21, at 27-28. While the motivations of these proponents were reasonable, indeed laudable, it is fair to assume that the success of these bills in the state legislatures has much more to do with the legislator's instinct for protection of local enterprises from out-of-state bidders.

86. *See, e.g.*, Great Western United Corp. v. Kidwell, 577 F.2d 1256, 1285-86, (1978), *rev'd on other grounds sub nom.* Leroy v. Great Western Corp. 443 U.S. 173 (1979).

87. *See* Lowenstein, *Pruning Deadwood in Hostile Takeovers: A Proposal for Legislation*, 83 Colum. L. Rev. 249, 307-09 (1983); *but see* Comment, *Front-end Loaded Tender Offers: The Application of Federal and State Law to an Innovative Corporate Acquisition Technique*, 131 U. Pa.L. Rev. 389, 403-13 (1982).

2. Allow nontendering shareholders an opportunity to vote on changes in corporate control, thus promoting a particular conception of corporate "democracy";[88]

3. Reduce the aggregate number of, and hence the risk of, hostile takeovers, thereby allowing managers to engage in long-range planning rather than short-sighted profit maximazation designed to prevent their company's stock from appearing undervalued;[89]

4. Allow management a freer hand in determining what, if any, defensive tactics are appropriate response to a hostile tender offer, in effect allowing them to perform a useful bargaining function on behalf of the shareholder;[90]

5. Eliminate so-called greenmail, or partial bids designed to have an *in terrorem* effect on target management, inducing them to repurchase the bidder's shares at a premium.[91]

These arguments of course, are not novel. They have been stated frequently in the policy debates over corporate takeovers. In effect, the second-generation statutes are revisions of the state corporate laws to reflect the beliefs of those critics who regard takeovers as highly questionable from the standpoints of both fairness and economic efficiency. The effect of revising the corporation statutes in this manner, however, is to give a new constitutional dimension to these policy debates and to require the constitutional question to be analyzed in terms of those debates.

The depth of this convergence becomes apparent when we attempt to assess the weight of the benefits allegedly derived from the second-generation statutes. If Gilson, Easterbrook and Fischel, and others are correct in their analysis of the role of hostile takeovers in allocating corporate assets to their most effective use and in disciplining managers to maximize the shareholder's utility rather than their own, then the effects of these statutes will be counterproductive rather than beneficial to shareholder welfare. A summary of this very complex argument is beyond the scope of this commentary, so let it suffice to say that if the market for corporate control

---

88. *See* Profusek & Gompf, *supra* note 9, at 40-41; *but see* Gilson, *The Case against Shark Repellant Amendments: Structural Limitations on the Enabling Concept*, 34 Stan. L. Rev. 775, 818-27 (1982); Manne, *supra* note 19, at 113.

89. *See* Herzel & Schmidt, *Is There Anything Wrong with Hostile Tender Offers?*, 6 Corp. L. Rev. 329, 332-34 (1983); Lowenstein, *supra* note 87, at 310; *but see* Easterbrook & Fischel, *The Proper Role of a Target's Management in Responding to a Tender Offer*, 94 Harv. L. Rev. 1161, 1183-84 (1981).

90. *See* Lipton, *Takeover Bids in the Target's Boardroom*, 35 Bus. Law. 101, 119-20 (1979); Herzel & Schmidt, *supra* note 89, at 336-37; *but see* Gilson, *A Structural Approach to Corporations: The Case against Defensive Tactics in Tender Offers*, 33 Stan. L. Rev. 819, 845-52, 856-59 (1981).

91. *See* Lowenstein, *supra* note 87, at 311; Blustein, *Let Us Now Consider Carl Icahn*, Wall St. J., Dec. 22, 1982, at 14, col. 3.

actually has the positive economic functions defined by these commentators, and if it really does operate fairly with respect to the aggregate universe of shareholders, then these statutes cannot reasonably be said to serve any legitimate state interests. The benefits listed above would thus not really be "benefits" and should be accorded little weight in the *Pike* balancing test.

Recognition of this possibility does not mandate acceptance of the positive view of takeovers. Indeed, this view has been severely criticized from several perspectives,[92] and it certainly cannot be regarded as "proven" in any sense of the word. What is needed, however, is a recognition that the benefits listed above cannot be weighed for Commerce Clause purposes without fundamental consideration of the economic functions of takeovers. That consideration *may* lead to the conclusion that the effects listed above do not really benefit target shareholders, shareholders in general, or state economic interests, but actually injure them. The crucial point, however, is not that this conclusion should be accepted but that Commerce Clause analysis of these statutes should draw upon the insights of economic analysis. If the courts fail to recognize those insights,[93] their constitutional analysis will not penetrate beyond superficial balancing of rhetorical assertions of theoretical state interests.

---

92. Particularly compelling is Lowenstein's attack on the theoretical premises of the thesis propounded by Gilson, Easterbrook and Fischel, and others. *See* Lowenstein, *supra* note 87. *See* also Herzel & Schmidt, *supra* note 89.

93. The court's use of economic analysis to resolve these constitutional questions has been superficial and highly conclusory. *See MITE*, 102 S. Ct. at 2642; *Telvest*, 697 F.2d at 580.

III

SEC TENDER OFFER RULES

During the recent past, the SEC has been fairly active in the tender offer rulemaking setting. The principal provisions of the current SEC rules and regulations were promulgated in November 1979.[1] The rules are quite comprehensive.[2] For example, Rule 14d-9 requires the subject company to file with the Commission a Schedule 14D-9 which calls for the disclosure of specified information. The SEC "believes that the disclosure elicited by the Schedule will assist security holders in making their investment decisions and in evaluating the merits of a solicitation/recommendation."[3] Such information includes, if material, a description of any arrangement or other understanding and conflicts of interest between, among others, the offeror, the subject corporation, and their affiliates.[4] Disclosure is also required in the Schedule of certain negotiations and transactions undertaken by the target company.[5] Moreover, in order to adhere to the disclosure require-

---

1. Securities Exchange Act Release No. 16384, 44 Federal Register 70326 (1979). Generally, the rules are grouped into two regulations, Regulations 14D and 14E. If the tender offer is subject to Section 14(d)(1) of the Williams Act (encompassing securities registered under Section 12 of the Exchange Act as well as securities of certain insurance and investment companies), both regulations apply. If the tender offer is not subject to Section 14(d)(1), only Regulation 14E applies.

2. *See* M. Steinberg, Securities Regulation: Liabilities and Remedies § 11.07 (1984); Bloomenthal, *The New Tender Offer Regimen, State Regulation, and Preemption*, 30 Emory L.J. 35 (1981).

3. 44 Federal Register, *supra* note 1, at 70336.

4. SEC Schedule 14D-9, Item 3(b), 17 C.F.R. § 240.14d-101 (1985).

5. SEC Schedule 14D-9, Item 7. *See* 44 Federal Register, *supra* note 1, at 70336; Rowe, *Tender Offer Regs: Changing the Game Rules*, Legal Times (Wash.), Dec. 21, 1979, at 9 ("Disclosure is required of any negotiations, transactions, board resolu-

ments of Rule 14e-2,[6] the subject company in the Schedule 14D-9[7] must advise shareholders of its position in regard to the tender offer and the reasons therefor.[8] In this respect, "[f]ailure on management's part to abide by this disclosure obligation under Rule 14e-2 may result in antifraud liability under the federal securities laws, even if a valid business purpose defense exists under state law."[9]

The SEC's tender offer rules cover a number of other matters. Rule 14d-6(d), for example, expressly requires an offeror to disclose promptly any material change in the information provided to shareholders.[10] As another example, in an attempt to render invalid many of the state takeover statutes prior to the Supreme Court's decision in *Edgar v. MITE Corp.*,[11] the SEC promulgated Rule 14d-2(b) which defines the commencement of a tender offer.[12]

Since their adoption in 1979, the Commission has periodically revised its tender offer rules. In an effort to deter insider and tippee trading in the tender offer setting in the aftermath of *Chiarella v. United States*,[13] the SEC

---

tions, agreements in principle or signed contracts, undertaken in response to the tender offer which relate to or might result in an extraordinary transaction...").

6. SEC Rule 14e-2, 17 C.F.R. § 240.14e-2 (1985). Rule 14e-2 generally obligates the target company to transmit to its shareholders within ten business days of the commencement of the tender offer a statement of its position in regard thereto. For a more detailed discussion, see M. Steinberg, *supra* note 2, at § 11.07; Gelfond & Sebastian, *Reevaluating the Duties of Target Management in a Hostile Tender Offer*, 60 B.U.L. Rev. 403, 410 (1980); Sommer & Feller, *Takeover Rules: A Cohesive Comprehensive Code*, Legal Times (Wash.), Dec. 17, 1979, at 18.

7. SEC Schedule 14D-9, Item 4, 17 C.F.R. § 240.14d-101 (1985).

8. *See* 44 Federal Register, *supra* note 1, at 70327 ("[T]he statement furnished under Rule 14e-2 [by the subject company]... would under Rule 14d-9 require the filing of Schedule 14D-9 with the Commission..."); sources cited in notes 6-7 *supra*.

9. M. Steinberg, *supra* note 2, at § 11.07.

10. 17 C.F.R. § 240.14d-6(d) (1985). The Commission stated that this rule "comports with current practice and avoids any possible ambiguity, thus ensuring for disclosure of material information during the course of a tender offer." 44 Federal Register, *supra* note 1, at 70333. *See generally* Jacobs v. G. Heileman Brewing Company, Inc., 551 F. Supp. 639, 643-644 (D. Del. 1982).

11. 457 U.S. 624 (1982) (holding the Illinois Business Takeover Act unconstitutional under the Commerce Clause).

12. Rule 14d-2(b) "generally provides that an announcement of an intent to make a tender offer, disclosing the amount of shares sought to be purchased and the price to be offered, triggers the commencement of a tender offer." Steinberg, *supra* note 2, at § 11.07. Subsequent to *MITE*, a number of states have enacted statutes that seek to pass constitutional muster. These developments are discussed in depth herein by Professor Sargent and Messrs. Goelzer and Cohen.

13. 445 U.S. 222 (1980) (holding under Section 10(b) of the Exchange Act and SEC Rule 10b-5 that silence, absent a duty to disclose, does not give rise to liability).

promulgated Rule 14e-3.[14] That rule generally sets forth "disclose or abstain from trading" and "antitipping" mandates under Section 14(e) of the Williams Act.[15] Also, in December 1982, the Commission amended Rule 14d-8 in order to extend the proration period from the previous 10-calendar-day period to the entire period that the offer remains open.[16] More recently, the SEC adopted amendments to Rule 10b-4 to proscribe "hedged" tendering.[17]

The commentary contained in this section by Peter Brennan, Esq., ad-

---

See also Dirks v. SEC, 103 S. Ct. 3255 (1983). Both cases left open the viability of the misappropriation theory. *See* United States v. Newman, 664 F.2d 12 (2d Cir. 1981) (upholding the misappropriation theory to impose liability for violations of Section 10(b) and Rule 10b-5).

14. *See* Securities Exchange Act Release No. 17120, [1980 Transfer Binder] Fed. Sec. L. Rep. (CCH) ¶ 82,646 (S.E.C.).

15. The rule thus far has been upheld. *See* O'Connor & Associates v. Dean Witter Reynolds, Inc., 529 F. Supp. 1179, 1188-1193 (S.D.N.Y. 1981). For further discussion on Rule 14e-3, see M. Steinberg, *supra* note 2, at § 3.06; Gruenbaum, *The New Disclose or Abstain from Trading Rule: Has the SEC Gone Too Far?* 5 Corp. L. Rev. 350 (1981); Note, *Trading on Material, Nonpublic Information under Rule 14e-3*, 49 Geo. Wash. L. Rev. 539 (1981).

The subject of insider trading in the tender offer setting is discussed herein in commentary by Professor Mark Loewenstein.

16. *See* Securities Exchange Act Release No. 19336, 47 Federal Register 57680 (1982).

17. *See* Securities Exchange Act Release No. 20799, 49 Federal Register 13867 (1984). These amendments adopted the recommendations of the SEC's Advisory Committee on Tender Offers. *See* Recommendations 44 and 46 of the SEC Advisory Committee on Tender Offers, Report of Recommendations at 47-50 (1983). Rule 10b-4 was originally adopted by the SEC in 1968 for the purpose of prohibiting "short" tendering. *See* Securities Exchange Act Release No. 8321, 33 Federal Register 8269 (1968). "Short" tendering may be defined as "tendering more shares than a person owns in order to avoid or reduce the risk of *pro rata* acceptance in tender offers for less than all the outstanding securities of a class or series." Securities Exchange Act Release No. 21049, 16 Sec. Reg. & L. Rep. (BNA) 1092, 1093 (1984). The original rule, however, did not proscribe "hedged" tendering, a practice that is closely analogous to "short" tendering. Hence, before the recent amendments to Rule 10b-4, market professionals in oversubscribed tender offers for less than all of the outstanding shares of the target were able to tender all shares owned and then sell in the market that portion of the tendered shares that they estimated would not be accepted by the offeror. The recently adopted amendments to Rule 10b-4 were designed to prevent this practice of "hedged" tendering. To make the prohibition against "short" and "hedged" tendering more effective, the SEC has proposed amendments to Rule 10b-4 which concern guarantees of delivery and the status under the rule of certain short positions in exchange-traded call options. *See* Securities Exchange Act Release No. 21049, 16 Sec. Reg. & L. Rep. (BNA) 1092 (1984).

dresses Rule 14d-8 and two-tier offers. Generally, as amended. Rule 14d-8 obligates a bidder in an oversubscribed partial tender offer "to take up and pay for" shares tendered on a pro rata basis "during the period such offer, request, or invitation remains open."[18] The rule has precipitated comment on the extent of the Commission's rulemaking authority and on the broader question of its effect on the balance between bidder and target in two-tier offers, particularly where the pressure on shareholders to tender is accentuated by a price differential between the tender offer and the proposed subsequent merger.[19]

Although the rule addresses a real problem in terms of individual investors receiving tender offer materials in sufficient time to make informed investment decisions, Mr. Brennan submits that the Commission overstepped its rulemaking authority. He asserts that the rule directly conflicts with the express language of the Williams Act as well as the Act's legislative history. Indeed, the legislative history shows that Congress expressly considered and rejected the time period the Commission enacted by rule. Further, having determined that extending the proration period was of sufficient importance to justify the reach of its rulemaking powers, Mr. Brennan finds it anomalous that the Commission declined to extend the withdrawal period, which would have been clearly within its rulemaking power. According to the author, making the withdrawal period coterminous with the extended proration period would maximize the opportunity for individual shareholders to make informed investment decisions.

The Commission's action, unfortunately, failed to address the substantive fairness of front-end–loaded, two-tier offers. This question, discussed elsewhere in the book,[20] is so central to tender offer regulation that it merits expeditious resolution on either a federal or state level.[21]

---

18. *See* Securities Exchange Act Release No. 19336, 47 Federal Register 57680 (1982).

19. *See, e.g.*, M. Steinberg, *supra* note 2, at § 11.07; Greene and Nathan, *The SEC's New Prorationing Rule Will Change "Partial" Tender Offers*, National Law Journal, Jan. 10, 1983, at 38; Note, *Rulemaking under Section 14 (e) of the Securities Exchange Act: The SEC Exceeds Its Reach in Attempting to Pull the Plug on Multiple Proration Pools*, 36 Vand. L. Rev. 1313 (1983).

20. *See, e.g.*, the commentaries herein by David Martin, Esq., Linda Quinn, Esq., and Professors Fiflis and Steinberg.

21. The SEC has issued a request for public comments on two-tier pricing in tender offers and non-tender offer purchase programs "with a view toward possible rulemaking and legislative proposals." Securities Exchange Act Release No. 21079, 16 Sec. Reg. & L. Rep. (BNA) 1119 (1984).

SEC Rule 14d-8 and Two-Tier Offers

PETER BRENNAN*

INTRODUCTION

Rule 14d-8, promulgated by the Securities and Exchange Commission in December 1982, requires a bidder in an oversubscribed tender offer to accept securities tendered on a pro rata basis during the period such offer remains open.[1] The extension of the proration period thoughout the tender offer more than doubles the minimum proration period, from ten calendar days to at least twenty business days.[2] The rationale articulated by the SEC is grounded in the necessity "to assure security holders the time to consider the merits of a tender offer and to obtain sufficient information upon which

---

*Peter Brennan is an associate of Mason, Griffin & Pierson, Princeton, New Jersey and a member of the District of Columbia, New York, and New Jersey Bars. Formerly, he was deputy attorney general of the White Collar Crime Section of the New Jersey Attorney General's Office; legislative counsel to the National Society of Public Accountants; and legislative assistant to U.S. Senator William V. Roth.

1. Pro Rata Rule, Securities and Exchange Act Release No. 19336, Fed. Sec. L. Rep. (CCH) ¶ 83,306, 47 Federal Register 57680 (December 28, 1982).

> Notwithstanding the pro rata provisions of the section 14(d)(6) of the Act, if any person makes a tender offer or request or invitation for tenders, for less than all of the outstanding equity securities of a class, and if a greater number of securities are deposited pursuant thereto than such person is bound or willing to take up and pay for, the securities taken up and paid for shall be taken up and paid for as nearly as may be pro rata, desregarding fractions, according to the number of securities deposited by each depositor during the period such offer, request or invitation remains open.

2. 47 Federal Register 57680 (December 28, 1982). Rule 14(e)(1) requires that tender offers remain open for a minimum of twenty business days.

to base their investment decisions and to minimize the potential security holder confusion and misunderstanding generated by changing proration periods and multiple proration pools."[3]

This seemingly simple and straightforward rule change raises a number of interesting questions, beginning with the authority of the Commission to promulgate it in light of the fact that the rule contradicts the literal statutory language of Section 14(d)(6) of the Exchange Act. This led two commissioners, including the chairman,[4] to publish dissents. Further, timing has long been recognized as a critical factor in the tender offer process. The Williams Act,[5] enacted in 1968 to curb the "Saturday Night Special," recognized the crucial advantage that surprise brought to bidders and established a mandatory minimum period for a tender offer to remain open to help effect a balance between bidders and targets. Therefore, the rule must be examined not only in terms of its efficacy in achieving its stated purpose but in relation to broader questions, such as its effect on the balance between bidders and targets in the tender offer process, on the structure and pricing of tender offers, and on the number of tender offers made.

I. THE PROBLEMS ADDRESSED BY THE RULE CHANGE

There is no doubt, as the comments to the proposed rule evidence, that the rule change addressed a real and immediate problem for shareholders, particularly individual shareholders, of a target company.[6] The previous rule generally required only that shares tendered during the first ten calendar days of a partial tender offer be accepted pro rata.[7] In some cases, shareholders did not even receive the offering documents during the ten-day period, particularly where the shares were held in street name.[8] It was noted by the Commission that this practical problem at the initiation of the tender offer is perhaps symptomatic of the advantages that professionals and arbitrageurs enjoy throughout the tender offer process, which is enhanced

---

3. 47 Federal Register 24338 (June 4, 1982).

4. 47 Federal Register, *supra* note 1, at 57683. *See also* Note, *Rulemaking under Section 14(e) of the Securities Exchange Act: The SEC Exceeds Its Reach in Attempting to Pull the Plug on Multiple Proration Pools*, 36 Vand. L. Rev. 1313 (1983), in accord with Chairman Shad's dissent that the Commission exceeded its rulemaking authority in promulgating the rule.

5. Publ. L. No. 90-434, 82 stat. 454 (1968).

6. Public Comments Received to Proposed Pro Rata Rule, S.E.C. File No. S7-933. A summary of comments to the proposed rule has been prepared by the Division of Corporate Finance and is part of the file.

7. Prior Rule 14d-8 gave the bidder the option to extend the proration period to cover the life of the tender offer.

8. 47 Federal Register, *supra* note 1, at 57683.

for such investors by extensive use of messengers to pick up offering materials at the initiation of a tender offer and deliver tendered shares at the last moment. Even assuming receipt of materials by public shareholders, it was felt that the ten-day period left individual investors little opportunity to gather information and reach a considered decision whether to tender.[9] Although the tender offer must remain open for twenty days in both a partial tender offer and an "any-and-all" tender offer, and previously tendered shares can be withdrawn up to fifteen days from the commencement of the offer, the prior proration period rule put pressure on a shareholder to tender within ten days. In short, if the offer was fully or oversubscribed in the first ten days, no shares tendered after the first ten days would be accepted for payment.

The problem with the ten-day proration period became accentuated with the widespread use of partial tender offers, a recent phenomenon which can largely be traced to the SEC's 1979 revision of its tender offer rules.[10] The minimum ten-calendar-day proration period was originally set forth in the 1968 Williams Act Amendments to the Securities Exchange Act and was left intact in the 1979 revisions.[11] In the reversal of the conventional wisdom prior to the 1979 revisions, partial bids became strong bids, because they were structured so that the shareholders risked significant loss, as noted above, if their shares were not tendered within the first ten calendar days. The pressure to tender early was increased by structuring the bid as a partial high front-end, low back-end two-tier bid. The bidder offers an initial partial cash tender offer, typically seeking between 45 percent and 55 percent of the stock, and proposes to acquire the remaining stock in a second-step "squeeze-out" merger in which the securities to be offered by the acquiring

---

9. Although no institution admitted such in the comments to the proposed rule, arbitrageurs have noted that even institutional investors were unable to reach a decision and tender with the ten-day period. Interview with Stephen D. Baksa, former Managing General Partner, WGW Associates, New York City, March 18, 1984.

10. Green and Nathan, *The SEC's New Prorationing Rule Will Change "Partial" Tender Offers*, National Law Journal, January 10, 1983, at 38.

11. Section 14(d)(6) of the Williams Act, 15 U.S.C. 78n(d)(6) provides:

> Where any person makes a tender offer, or request or invitation for tenders, for less than all of the outstanding equity securities of a class, and where a greater number of securities is deposited pursuant thereto within ten days after copies of the offer or request or invitation are first published or sent or given to security holders than such person is bound or willing to take up and pay for, the securities taken up shall be taken up as nearly as may be pro rata, disregarding fractions according to the number of securities deposited by each depositor. The provisions of this subsection shall also apply to securities deposited within ten days after notice of an increase in the consideration offered to security holders, as described in paragraph (7), is first published or sent or given to security holders.

corporation have an initial value lower than the cash tender offer price.[12] It has been noted that the bidder may leave the description of the second-step merger somewhat vague, arguably for the purpose of increasing the shareholder's uncertainty as to what he will receive if he does not tender in the first-step offer.[13] The rise in the use of partial tender offers had the effect of undermining the requirement that a tender offer remain open twenty business days as provided in the 1979 revisions. Since many offers were fully or oversubscribed in the initial ten-day period, as a practical matter, this limited the twenty-day requirement to "any-and-all" offers. Although the previous Rule 14d-8 provided that the proration period could be extended voluntarily, it was hardly in the interest of the bidder to do so, since such extention reduced pressure on shareholders to tender.[14]

The short proration period had an additional economic impact in that it sometimes provided a tactical advantage to a partial bid over another bid that might be economically superior. For example, assume a bidder makes a tender offer for 55 percent of Company A at $50 per share, with a ten-calendar-day proration period, and receives shares representing 50 percent of the target company. Therefore, the shareholders who tender are assured that all of the tendered shares will be purchased by the bidder. Such shareholders will have little incentive to withdraw the tendered shares to a second partial bidder, unless the second offer is significantly better than the first. Thus, if a second bidder makes an offer of $54 per share for 51 percent of the target, shareholders who tendered to the first bidder would run the risk of receiving the $54 price for only a portion of their shares.[15]

II. MULTIPLE PRORATION POOLS

One result of the prior proration period was that it led to the formation of the multiple proration pools, thereby increasing shareholder confusion. Multiple proration pools arose from the Williams Act's requirement of an

---

12. The bidder will often make a tender offer for approximately 50% of the outstanding shares, having already accumulated a number of shares in open market or privately negotiated purchases prior to the tender offer. These initial purchases are often termed obtaining a "toehold" in the target.

13. See Greene and Nathan *supra* note 10, at 40. This uncertainty as to the terms of the final third-step squeeze-out merger can only be increased by the recent decision in Osofsky v. J. Ray MacDermott, 725 F.2d 1057 (1984). There, the Second Circuit held that a tender offer did not entail a binding commitment to pay any specific consideration in the event of a subsequent cash-out merger where the price given was qualified by a broad disclaimer that "a variety of factors might affect stock prices [and the final consideration in the third-step merger] may be more or less than $62.50."

14. *See* 17 C.F.R. 240.14d-8 (1983).

15. *See* Comments to Proposed Rule by Morgan Stanley and Co., *supra* note 6.

additional ten-calendar-day proration period whenever a bidder increased its offering price.[16] If a bidder announced a price increase before the original ten-calendar-day proration period expired, such increase would extend the proration period by ten calendar days. An increase announced after the original ten-calendar-day period had expired started a new ten-calendar-day proration period. If the offer had not been oversubscribed during the initial ten-calendar-day period, shares tendered during the initial proration period would be accepted without prorationing. Only the shares tendered into the second pool would be subject to prorationing.[17] Moreover, if there were a gap between the two proration periods, shares tendered during that time would be accepted on a first-come, first-served basis. Multiple proration pools required additional disclosures by the bidder.[18]

As an illustration of the confusion, the Commission noted when new Rule 14d-8 was proposed that in the course of the three-way bidding contest for control of Conoco, Inc., by Seagrams, Du Pont, and Mobil there were nine proration dates and six separate proration pools.[19]

The use of multiple proration pools has been attacked as a manipulative device, a somewhat ironic charge in view of the fact that they were mandated by the prior rule.[20] Multiple proration pools received judicial scrutiny in the Pabst control contest, which arose in the context of bidding for Pabst between Heilman and investor Irwin Jacobs.[21] The court concluded that the use of multiple proration pools was expressly contemplated in the legislative history.[22]

III. RATIONALE OF THE NEW RULE

Clearly, new SEC Rule 14d-8 corrects the mechanical problem of shareholder receipt of the offering materials and also allows sufficient time for an individual shareholder to tender. In this regard, the rule neutralizes the advantage that professionals have vis-à-vis the public shareholder in overcoming the problem of the transmission of offering materials. Beyond this, the rationale for the additional time period is that it will afford the share-

---

16. Securities Exchange Act of 1934 § 14(d)(6), 15 U.S.C. § 78(d)(6) (1976).

17. *See* Rule 14d-7, 17 C.F.R. 240.14d-7 (1983); Proposed Pro Rata Tender Offer Rule, Exchange Act Release No. 18761, Fed. Sec. L. Rep. (CCH) ¶ 83,222 at 85,144 n.17 (May 25, 1982).

18. *Id.* at 85,143-144.

19. 47 Federal Register, *supra* note 3, at 24339. *See also The Bidding for Conoco*, Wall St. J., Aug. 6, 1981, at 8, col. 2; *Seagram Co. to Swap Conoco Stake for 20% of Merged Company*, Wall St. J., Aug. 12, 1981, at 39, col. 3.

20. 47 Federal Register, *supra* note 1, at 57680.

21. Jacobs v. Heileman Brewing Co., 551 F. Supp 639 (D. Del. 1982).

22. *Id.*

holder the opportunity to reach an informed decision with respect to the tender offer. This begs the question, however, of whether informed decisions by stockholders are simply a function of time. Beyond a certain point, does the small shareholder have access to the type of information that is necessary for an informed decision vis-à-vis the arbitrageurs and market professionals, even assuming he has the time in which to do so? Assuming that sophisticated traders will continue to tender at the last possible moment, as was suggested in the comments to the rule,[23] the relative advantage of the professionals may simply be prolonged over the additional proration period.

IV. IMPACT OF THE RULE CHANGE

The questions to be examined in assessing the effects of Rule 14d-8 run the entire gamut of the tender offer process, from what effect the rule may have on the number of tender offers made to the structure of the offers themselves, such as whether the effect of the rule is neutral as between partial and any-and-all offers. This assessment is difficult at best, and it is well to note that the effects may well be unforeseen, as was the strong development of partial tender offers after the 1979 SEC regulations. In assessing the magnitude of any impact, it must be kept in mind that the rule does not prohibit two-tier tender offers which, as noted in the chairman's dissent, irrespective of the proration time period, may be the underlying cause of pressure of shareholders to tender.[24]

The application of the rule may lead to anomalous results in certain circumstances, particularly in view of the problematic relationship between the withdrawal period, which remains at fifteen business days, and the newly expanded proration period. Several commentators suggested that the withdrawal period and the proration period be coterminous, at either fifteeen or twenty business days.[25] Since the proration period will now expire after the withdrawal period ends, a bidder will not be able to purchase the securities tendered at the end of the withdrawal period, which was formerly the case.[26] Moreover, in a protracted series of bids, shares tendered would be committed for a substantial period of time without the security holder knowing what portion would be accepted and without his being able to redeploy those securities not accepted.[27] Thus, in terms of securities being committed for potentially extended periods without payment or withdrawal

---

23. Comments, *supra* note 15.

24. 47 Federal Register, *supra* note 1, at 57680.

25. Greene and Nathan, *supra* note 10, at 39.

26. *See* Rule 14d-7, 17 C.F.R. 240.14d-7 (1983). *See also* Summary of Comments to Proposed Rule, *supra* note 6, at 21.

27. Under Rule 14d-7, the fifteen-day withdrawal period is measured from the

rights, the extra time which the rule provides to investors is not without its costs.

The most significant impact of the rule on security holders may be the result of the indirect impact of the rule on the tender offer process itself, such as the effect on the balance between bidder and target. The passage of time with respect to a tender offer is widely felt to favor the target, allowing more time for defensive tactics.[28] The extension of the proration period would thus seem to favor the target, either by allowing it to fend off the offer or by inducing a competing offeror, a "white knight," to enter the fray. Such an effort would make it correspondingly less attractive to make an initial tender offer bid.[29] To the extent that such bids are impaired, security holders will lose an opportunity to realize a premium.[30]

The lack of empirical data or economic models from which to predict the effect of the rule was noted initially in comments received concerning the rule.[31] One commentator may have proved closest to the truth in noting that the change of this single rule in the total scheme of tender offer regulation "will have no appreciable influence on the volume of tender offers [since] the primary reasons corporations become targets of tender offers are related to economic conditions that are not relevant to tender offer procedures."[32]

Two important tenders in the period immediately following promulgation of the rule, the National Distillers and Chemical Corp. offer for Suburban Propane Gas Corp., in January 1983 and the Esmark offer for Norton Simon in June 1983, were partial offers and illustrative of the continuing widespread use of such offers. The underlying advantages of a two-tier tender offer are too strong to be undercut by a limited procedural change. Any change in the current practice favoring utilization of two-tier tender offers must be directly addressed through substantive regulatory changes, as noted by both Chairman Shad in his dissent and the recommendations of the Securities and Exchange Commission's Advisory Committee on Tender Offers.[33] The arbitrage community, although believing that the prior proration

---

date of commencement of the offer. The rule does not provide for a mandatory renewal of the withdrawal period for a price increase.

28. *See* M. Steinberg, Securities Regulation: Liabilities and Remedies § 11.01 *et seq.* (1984).

29. *See* Comments to Proposed Rule by Professor Frank H. Easterbrook, *supra* note 6.

30. *Id.*

31. *Id.*

32. Comments to Proposed Rule by Morgan Stanley & Co., *supra* note 6.

33. 47 Federal Register, *supra* note 1, at 57683; Securities and Exchange Commission Advisory Committee on Tender Offers, Report of Recommendations (July 8, 1983).

rule was more advantageous in terms of its operations, does not expect that the change will markedly restrict its arbitrage activity.[34]

V. SEC RULEMAKING AUTHORITY

Interestingly, promulgation of Rule 14d-8 raises a question as to the nature and extent of the Commission's rulemaking authority, necessarily invoking an analysis of statutory construction. This question is raised by the apparent contradiction of the rule and the fact that the ten-day period is currently set forth in Section 14(d)(6) of the statute from which the Commission claims to have derived the authority to impose a different proration period.[35] There is the further fact that, in 1968, Congress explicitly rejected a statutory provision requiring proration through a tender offer, which the present rule imposes, as well as a provision that would have given the Commission the rulemaking authority to change the ten-calendar-day period.[36]

This legislative history is relied on by the chairman of the Commission as one of the grounds in his dissent from the adoption of Rule 14d-8.[37] In his brief treatment of the question of the authority of the Commission to issue Rule 14d-8, the chairman finds judicial support for his reading of the import of the legislative history in *Koshland v. Helvering*, where the Supreme Court held that where the provision of an act is unambiguous and its direction specific, there is no power to amend it by regulation.[38] The chairman holds that a change such as Rule 14d-8, with which he disagrees on the merits as well as on the ground of the Commission's lack of authority to promulgate it, must be enacted by Congress, rather than implemented by regulation.[39]

Commissioner James C. Treadway also dissented on the ground that the Commission lacked the authority to adopt the rule in question. He offered a more detailed analysis than Chairman Shad in construing the pertinent statutory provisions. Commissioner Treadway's analysis is premised on the contrast between the lack of any express or implied grant of authority to the Commission to modify the express statutory ten-day proration period on the one hand and the terms of the immediately preceding subsection, Section 14(d)(5), on the other hand. That section expressly confers upon the Commission the authority to modify by rule, regulation, or order the

---

34. Baksa, *supra* note 9.

35. For the text of Section 14(d)(6), see *supra* note 11.

36. *See* Greene and Nathan, *supra* note 10, at 38; S. Rep. No. 550, 90th Cong. 1st Session at 4-5 (1967).

37. 47 Federal Register, *supra* note 1, at 57680.

38. 298 U.S. 441, 447 (1936).

39. *See* 47 Federal Register, *supra* note 1, at 57683.

time period set forth in the provision with respect to withdrawal rights. Commissioner Treadway finds the contrast between the two subsections decisive on the question of Congressional intent in granting authority to modify the expressly stated time frames.[40]

Commissioner Treadway's dissent also calls into question the Commission's reliance on Section 14(e) as authority to promulgate Rule 14d-8.[41] Section 14(e) speaks in terms of the promulgation of rules by the SEC to prevent fraudulent, deceptive, and manipulative acts or practices in connection with tender offers. Commissioner Treadway noted a certain irony in the Commission's deeming compliance with the statutory language of Section 14(d)(6) as conducive to fraudulent, deceptive, or manipulative conduct.[42] The legislative history of Section 14(e), not surprisingly, does not address the effect of that provision on Section 14(d)(6). Commissioner Treadway concluded that activities in connection with tender offers which have been characterized as gamesmanship do not rise to the level of fraudulent, deceptive, or manipulative conduct which Section 14(e) addresses. Therefore, he rejected Section 14(e) as authority for the adoption of new Rule 14d-8.

VI. REGULATION OF TWO-TIER OFFERS

As noted in Chairman Shad's dissent, the question of the regulation of two-tier tender offers cannot be addressed indirectly through procedural rules such as Rule 14d-8.[43] Regulation of a substantive aspect of a control transaction, such as the share price in a second-step merger, would be a profound change from the present federal regulatory framework which aims toward full disclosure rather than substantive regulation. Such regulation,

---

40. *Id.* at 57683-57684.
41. Section 14(e) of the Exchange Act reads:

> It shall be unlawful for any person to make any untrue statement of material fact or omit to state any material fact necessary in order to make the statements made, in light of circumstances under which they are made, not misleading, or to engage in any fraudulent, deceptive, or manipulative acts or practices, in connection with any tender offer or request or invitation for tenders, or any solicitation of security holders in opposition to or in favor of any such offer, request, or invitation. The Commission shall, for the purpose of this subsection, by rules and regulations defined, prescribe means reasonably designed to prevent such acts and practices as are fraudulent, deceptive or manipulative.

Securities Exchange Act of 1934 § 14(e), 15 U.S.C. § 78 n(e) (1976).
42. 47 Federal Register, *supra* note 1, at 57683.
43. *Id.*

however, could be defended under state law as a logical extension of the "best price" rule.[44]

On the federal level, no steps have been taken toward the substantive regulation of the share price in a subsequent merger, but this had been a principal feature of the few state statutes relating to tender offers which have recently been enacted.[45] The Pennsylvania "antitakeover" legislation is the most recent and perhaps broadest of these statutes.[46] Section 409.1 of that Act reaches these "second-step" transactions, providing that, unless the subsequent merger is approved by a majority of disinterested directors or shareholders, the same price must be paid in the "second step" as was paid in the tender offer.[47]

On the other hand, lower prices paid in second-step mergers following a tender offer have survived judicial challenge that such transactions are a breach of fiduciary duty under state law and are "manipulative" under Section 14(e) of the Williams Act.[48] Moreover, state statutes that contain same-price provisions may be subject to attack on constitutional grounds of being violative of the Supremacy Clause and as imposing an under burden on interstate commerce. Thus, governmental regulation of the most coercive element of a two-tier tender offer, the price differential between the tender offer and second-step merger, is at a tentative stage. Similarly, the enforceability of protective corporate provisions, such as those concerning fair-price, mandatory bid, and flip-over preferred stock, have not yet been subject to extensive adjudication.[49]

The SEC's Advisory Committee on Tender Offers in its Report of Recommendations published in July 1983, approximately six months after the promulgation of Rule 14d-8, dealt with the issue of two-tier offers in two of its recommendations. The Committee recommended that the minimum offering period for a partial tender offer should be two weeks longer than that for any-and-all tender offers.[50] The Committee's rationale was that the longer minimum offering period would act as a regulatory disincentive for

---

44. 15 U.S.C. § 78(d)(7) (1976).

45. *See, e.g.*, Md. Bus. & Assoc. Code §§ 3-202, 3-601-03, 8-301(12)-(14); Ohio Rev. Code §§ 1701.01, 1701.831.

46. Pa. Stat. Ann. §§ 409.1.

47. Steinberg, *The Pennsylvania Anti-Takeover Legislation*, 12 Sec. Reg. L.J. 184 (1984).

48. Martin Marietta v. Bendix, 549 F. Supp. 623 (D. Md. 1982); Radol v. Thomas, 534 F. Supp. 1302 (S.D. Ohio 1982).

49. Finkelstein, *Antitakeover Protection against Two-Tier and Partial Tender Offers: The Validity of Fair Price, Mandatory Bid, nd Flip-Over Provisions under Delaware Law*, 11 Sec. Reg. L.J. 291 (1984).

50. Recommendation No. 16, Report of the SEC Advisory Committee on Tender Offers, *supra* note 33, at 25-27.

partial offers and two-tier bids, thereby helping to counterbalance their coercive element and the potential for manipulative practices.[51] The Committee further recommended that the withdrawal period be coterminous with the proration and minimum offering periods, as was suggested by several comments to the proposed rule.[52]

In response to the importance of the problem of pricing in two-tier offers, the Commission has initiated a study and requested comments. This action was taken also as a result of the SEC's concern with several of the Advisory Committee's recommendations.[33] First, the Commission asserted that the question of whether two-tier offers are in fact unduly coercive has not been satisfactorily answered.[54] The Commission futher expressed concern as to whether the two-week extension of the minimum offering for partial offers will be effective in dealing with these coercive pressures and whether it will unduly impinge on partial offers not involving two-tier pricing.[55] Interestingly, the Commission believes there is some indication that Rule 14d-8, which eliminated the use of multiple proration pools, may have contributed to the recent decline in the use of two-tier pricing in tender offers and hopes that the comments received will shed additional light on the empirical effects of the rule change.[56]

CONCLUSION

Rule 14d-8 may be viewed as an unwarranted extension of the Commission's rulemaking authority. Although focusing on helping to ensure informed shareholder decision making and the timely dissemination of tender offer materials, Rule 14d-8 may be seen as provoking comment on the substantive fairness of two-tier offers, particularly where there is a price differential between the tender offer and cash-out merger. Federal regulation of the cash-out price would mark a profound change in the underlying regulatory philosophy, from one premised on disclosure to one based on substantive regulation. Nonetheless, resolution of this important issue, either on a federal or state level, hopefully will be only a matter of time.

---

51. *Id*. at 25.

52. *Id*. Recommendation No. 17, *supra* note 33, at 28. *See also* Comments, *supra* note 6.

53. Two Tier Tender Offer Pricing and Non-Tender Offer Purchase Programs: Advance Notice of Possible Commission Action, Exchange Act Release No. 21079 (June 21, 1984), [1984 Transfer Binder] Fed. Sec. L. Rep. (CCH) ¶ 83, 637 (July 5, 1984).

54. *Id*. at 86,916-917.

55. *Id*. at 86,917.

56. *Id*. at 86,917-18.

IV

TARGET MANAGEMENT'S USE OF DEFENSIVE TACTICS

To fend off hostile tender offers successfully, target mangements have employed a wide variety of defensive tactics. These maneuvers have included, for example, announcing an unprecedented divided increase,[1] issuing stock to a friendly third party,[2] acquiring another corporation to raise antitrust obstacles,[3] finding a white knight to make a competing offer,[4] selling off profitable assets or divisions,[5] or making a tender offer for the original offeror.[6] Indeed, the extent and nature of these antitakeover devices are seemingly unlimited due to the persistent ingenuity of expert counsel and investment bankers.

The propriety of such tactics in general and the application of federal and state regulation to such maneuvers have been widely addressed by both

---

1. *E.g.*, Humana, Inc. v. American Medicorp, Inc., [1977-1978 Transfer Binder] Fed. Sec. L. Rep. (CCH) ¶ 96,286 (S.D.N.Y. 1978).

2. *E.g.*, Applied Digital Data Systems, Inc. v. Milgo Electric Corp., 425 F. Supp. 1145 (S.D.N.Y. 1977). *See also* Data Probe Acquistion Corp. v. Datatab, Inc., 722 F.2d 1 (2d Cir. 1983), *cert. denied*, 104 S. Ct. 1326 (1984).

3. *E.g.*, Panter v. Marshall Field & Co., 646 F.2d 271 (7th Cir.), *cert. denied*, 454 U.S. 1092 (1981); Royal Industries Inc. v. Monogram Industries, Inc., [1976-1977 Transfer Binder] Fed. Sec. L. Rep. (CCH) ¶ 95,863 (C.D. Cal. 1976).

4. *E.g.*, Mobil Corp. v. Marathon Oil Co., 669 F.2d 366 (6th Cir. 1982); Crouse-Hinds Co. v. InterNorth, Inc., 634 F.2d 690 (2d Cir. 1980).

5. *E.g.*, Whittaker Corp. v. Edgar, 535 F. Supp. 933 (N.D. Ill. 1982).

6. *E.g.*, Martin Marietta Corp. v. Bendix Corp., 549 F. Supp. 623 (D. Md. 1983); No. 298, slip op. (Del. Sept. 21, 1982). *See also* Donovan v. Bierworth, 680 F.2d 263 (2d Cir. 1982) (target pension fund trustees purchased target's stock); Mobil Corp. v. Marathon Oil Co., 669 F.2d 366 (6th Cir. 1982) ("lock-up" option granted to "white knight"); Crane Co. v. Harsco Corp., 511 F. Supp. 294 (D. Del. 1984) (target's acquisition of its own shares from abritrageurs).

courts and commentators.[7] In recognition of this fundamental aspect of the tender offer debate, a number of the commentaries contained in other portions of the book, although principally having a different focus, also examine this important subject.[8]

The following commentary by Professor Deborah A. DeMott astutely examines the problems that may follow a counter tender offer defense as a result of provisions of state corporate law and the federal securities laws. The applicability of state statutes that disenfranchise cross-owned shares is examined, as is the effect of state statutes enabling stockholder action by consent in lieu of a meeting. Professor DeMott also analyzes the fiduciary duties of directors of corporations in the aftermath of a counter tender offer and suggests possible legal responses to the dilemmas of the cross-owned enterprise.

---

7. *E.g.*, Data Probe Acqusition Corp. v. Datatab, Inc., 722 F.2d 1 (2d Cir. 1983), *cert. denied*, 104 S. Ct. 1326 (1984); Mobil Corp. v. Marathon Oil Co., 669 F.2d 366 (6th Cir. 1982); Panter v. Marshall Field & Co., 644 F.2d 271 (7th Cir.), *cert. denied*, 454 U.S. 1092 (1981); M. Steinberg, Securities Regulation: Liabilities and Remedies § 11.08 (1984); Easterbrook & Fischel, *The Proper Role of a Target's Management in Responding to a Tender Offer*, 94 Harv. L. Rev. 1161 (1981); Lipton, *Takeover Bids in the Target's Boardroom*, 35 Bus. Law. 101 (1979); Williams, *Role of Directors in Takeover Offers*, 13 Rev. Sec. Reg. 963 (1980). *See also* Advisory Comm. on Tender Offers, U.S. SEC, Report of Recommendations (1983).

8. *See, e.g.* the commentaries herein of Professor Loewenstein, A. A. Sommer, Esq., and Professor Steinberg.

Pac-Man Tender Offers

DEBORAH A. DeMOTT*

INTRODUCTION

The newly developed Pac-Man[1] strategy demonstrates once again the persistence and striking ingenuity of target companies in contested tender offers. In the Pac-Man gambit, the target or object of a tender offer makes a bid for the original offeror. By becoming the aggressor, the target may dissuade the original offeror from pursuing its bid and may even obtain control of the original offeror. However elegant this move from the standpoint of grand corporate strategy, its legal consequences are highly uncer-

---

*Deborah A. DeMott is professor of Law, Duke University School of Law. Gratitude is extended to Lawrence Lederman, Esq., and Professor Elliott J. Weiss for their helpful comments. A slightly different version of this article appeared in the Duke Law Journal, Volume 1983, No. 1. Copyright © 1983 Duke University School of Law.

1. The Pac-Man defense, named for a popular video game, has been used in at least four recent takeover attempts. *See* Martin Marietta Corp. v. Bendix Corp., 549 F. Supp. 623 (D. Md. 1982); American Gen. Corp. v. NLT Corp., [1982 Transfer Binder] Fed. Sec. L. Rep. (CCH) ¶ 98,808, at 94,129-31 (S.D. Tex. July 1, 1982); Cities Serv. Co. v. Mesa Petroleum Co., [1982 Transfer Binder] Fed. Sec. L. Rep. (CCH) ¶ 98,744, at 93,747 (D. Del. June 14, 1982); Wall St. J., Mar. 2, 1982, at 17, col. 1 (takeover battle between General Cinema Corp. and Heublein); *see also* Martin Marietta Corp. v. Bendix Corp., No. 298, slip op. (Del. Sept. 21, 1982); Martin Marietta Corp. v. Bendix Corp., No. 6942, slip op. (Del. Ch. Sept. 19, 1982); Wall St. J., Mar. 3, 1982, at 14, col. 3. For fuller accounts of the Bendix–Martin Marietta imbroglio, *see* H. Lampert, Till Death Do Us Part (1983); A. Sloan, Three Plus One Equals Billions (1983). In addition, Pabst Brewing Co. and Olympia Brewing Co. agreed to make offers for portions of each other's stock to repel a third party's unwanted offer for Pabst. Wall St. J., July 7, 1982, at 8, col. 1; *see infra* text accompanying notes 26-45.

tain. This legal uncertainty may explain why the Pac-Man defense has not been used more extensively. This commentary identifies the legal problems likely to attend the Pac-Man defense and ventures some suggestions for their resolution. Although it eschews much consideration of the economic or societal desirability of such transactions, this commentary also examines possible incentives that might influence the use of Pac-Man strategies.

In the typical case, one party, O, offers to buy all the shares, or at least a majority of the shares, of a target corporation, T. T's management does not welcome O's bid and, to defend against it, makes a bid for all or a majority of O's shares. Assume that T makes its bid for O, while O's bid for T is still outstanding, and that the closing dates of the two offers are relatively close. Assume further that each corporation offers cash rather than its own securities for the other corporation's stock[2] and that both O and T make their purchases after the expiration of the shareholders' right to withdraw the tendered shares.[3] Suppose both offers are successful: a majority of T's stockholders tender their shares to O, and a majority of O's stockholders tender their shares to T. Suppose also that in both corporations, ownership of a simple majority of the stock confers the power to elect all members of the corporation's board of directors.

This outcome, a successful bid followed by a successful Pac-Man defense, raises at least two perplexing questions under state corporate statutes, and the answers may determine the ultimate victor of the takeover battle. First, it is questionable whether the shares that each corporation owns in the other are eligible to vote; second, assuming that these shares are eligible to vote, it is not clear through what mechanisms that voting power may be used. Because these questions concern state corporate law, their resolution is further complicated when O and T are incorporated in states that have corporate statutes that vary somewhat in their relevant provisions.

I. THE APPLICABILITY OF CROSS-OWNERSHIP STATUTES

Most corporate statutes prevent corporations from voting treasury stock and prohibit majority-owned subsidiaries from voting stock they hold in the parent corporation. These cross-ownership provisions may make it illegal for the parties to a Pac-Man defense to vote the stock that they have acquired in each other. The language of Section 160(c) of the Delaware statute is typical:

---

2. This assumption simplifies the analysis. If O and T offer their own voting securities as consideration in the offers, it may be difficult to determine who has voting control of the two companies when the offers are completed.

3. Securities Exchange Act of 1934, § 14(d)(5), 15 U.S.C. § 78n(d)(5) (1976).

Shares of its own capital stock belonging to the corporation or to another corporation, if a majority of the shares entitled to vote in the election of directors of such corporation is held, directly or indirectly, by the corporation, shall neither be entitled to vote nor be counted for quorum purposes. Nothing in this section shall be construed as limiting the right of any corporation to vote stock, including but not limited to its own stock, held by it in a fiduciary capacity.[4]

Because a successful tender offer that provokes a successful Pac-Man defense makes each corporation the owner of a majority of the shares in the other, in reciprocal parent-subsidiary relationships, Section 160(c) and its counterparts in other states may be thought to disenfranchise both control blocks, creating a corporate form of gridlock.

This apparent gridlock is not indissoluble, however. If both O and T are ineligible to vote the shares they hold in each other, the shares eligible to vote will be those held by shareholders who did not tender in response to O's bid for T and T's counterbid for O. Some of these residual shareholders may be the archetypal small shareholder in rural Iowa, who is disabled by the slowness of communications and mail service from promptly learning about tender offers and responding to them within tight deadlines. Other residual shareholders may be sophisticated investors who predicted this complex legal scenario and refrained from tendering in the prospect of exercising voting control. Still others may be shareholders who thought the price offered was to low and who hoped to receive a higher bid from O or T or from other offerors joining in the fray. Considering the acumen and cleverness of those who plan and execute tender offer strategies, it is ironic that the right to vote may ultimately belong to uninformed, uninterested, unpersuaded, or remote shareholders.[5] The statute would disenfranchise

---

4. *See* Del. Code Ann. tit. 8, § 160(c) (1975). The equivalent portion of the Model Business Corporation Act provides:

Neither treasury shares, nor shares held by another corporation if a majority of the shares entitled to vote for the election of directors of such other corporation is held by the corporation, shall be voted at any meeting or counted in determining the total number of outstanding shares at any given time.

Model Business Corp. Act § 33 (1971). Must jurisdictions have adopted identical or comparable language. *Id.* at 633. These statutes do not permit corporations to countermand their effect through charter provisions.

5. Somehow this part of the final dialogue in Eric Ambler's A Coffin for Dimitrios seems apposite: " 'I was thinking,' said Dimitrios, 'that in the end one is always

the shareholder with the greatest investment and the most to protect, while those entitled to vote, although not utterly disinterested, would have much less at stake.[6]

Further, if a cross-ownership statute in a target corporation's state disenfranchises an offeror after a Pac-Man defense, an offeror (either an original offeror or a target using the Pac-Man strategy) is in a stronger position if its target is incorporated in a state with no cross-ownership provision. In the absence of such a provision, the offeror may presumably vote the shares it acquired through the offer. Suppose that O is incorporated in Delaware and that T is incorporated in New Hampshire, which does not have a counterpart to Delaware's Section 160(c), and suppose that O and T each acquire a majority of the other's shares. The statutes of T's home state permit O to vote its shares in T even though the acquired corporation owns a majority of the acquirer's shares. T, however, has acquired shares in a Delaware corporation, and Section 160(c) appears to disqualify T from voting its shares in O because O holds a majority of the shares of T.[7] These possibilities are not among those traditionally taken into account in choosing a situs for incorporation.

However, one ought not to conclude too quickly that cross-ownership provisions unquestionably apply to the parties to a Pac-Man defense. Cross-ownership statutes prevent a subsidiary from voting stock that it owns in its parent.[8] In the aftermath of a Pac-Man defense, each corporation is a subsidiary of the other, but each is also the other's parent. Therefore, application of a cross-ownership statute to such corporations produces the unacceptable result that a parent cannot vote the stock that it owns in its subsidiary. It follows that such statutes ought not apply to the parties to a Pac-Man defense.

This argument has a more formal analogue that stems from the structure of some of the disenfranchisment statutes. Some of the statutes are self-referential and thus self-defeating when applied to the Pac-Man scenario.

---

defeated by stupidity. If it is not one's own, it is the stupidity of others.' " E. Ambler, A Coffin for Dimitrios 208 (1977).

6. Of course, the disenfranchised majority will attempt to exercise its control by soliciting the proxies of the residual shareholders. It seems anomalous that one barred by statute from voting his own shares may vote the shares of others, but a proxy holder need not have an independent right to vote.

7. The argument that Section 160 would disenfranchise the shares an offeror acquires in a Delaware corporation through a Pac-Man defense was apprently persuasive to the chancellor in Martin Marietta Corp. v. Bendix Corp., No. 6942 (Del. Ch. Sept. 22, 1982) (order granting preliminary injunction). Cf. Jacobs v. Pabst, C.A. 82-449, slip op. at 7-8 (D. Del. July 21, 1982) (possibility that § 160 would disenfranchise shares purchased should have been disclosed in acquiring company's proxy statement seeking shareholder approval of merger between the two corporations).

8. See supra text accompanying and preceding note 4.

Section 160(c) prevents a subsidiary from voting stock it owns in its parent "if a majority of the shares entitled to vote in the election of directors of such other [subsidiary] corporation is held, directly or indirectly, by the [parent] corporation."[9] Such a provision disqualifies both O and T, as subsidiaries, from voting the stock each owns in the other. Therefore, neither O nor T owns stock "entitled to vote" in the other, and the statute does not apply.[10] Double disqualification, in short, might mean that neither block of stock is disqualified and that the two disenfranchisements simply cancel each other out; paradoxically, if the statute applies, it does not apply.[11]

This result may be avoided if "entitled to vote" means "entitled to vote but for the effects of this section." But this is a question of interpretation that, like many posed by the Pac-Man scenario, has not been addressed by the case law.[12] Similarly, this particular interpretive problem can be obviated by statutory provisions that are worded somewhat differently. For example, Section 703(b) of California's General Corporation Law provides that "shares of a corporation owned by its subsidiary shall not be entitled to vote on any matter,"[13] and the California statute defines "subsidiary" in terms of "possessing more than a [stated] percent of the voting power."[14] When applied to the Pac-Man scenario, the Delaware statute produces a logical contradiction, because it is triggered by the same "entitlement to vote" that it constrains.[15] The California statute creates no such contradiction, because

---

9. Del. Code Ann. tit. 8, § 160(c) (1975).

10. This result does not occur unless each corporation is both the parent and a subsidiary of the other. As the statute normally operates, it bars a subsidiary from voting its shares in its parent, but there is no effect on the parent's entitlement to vote its shares in the subsidiary. It is the parent's entitlement to vote the majority of the subsidiary's shares that triggers the applicability of Section 160.

11. This derives from the underlying contradiction that if the statute applies, each corporation both is and is not entitled to vote the shares it holds in the other. If O and T, as parents, are entitled to vote their majority shares in their respective subsidiaries T and O, then the statute applies. The statute bars T and O, as subsidiaries, from voting any stock they own in their respective parents O and T. Hence the contradiction: if they are entitled to vote, the statute applies, and if the statute applies, they are not entitled to vote (and the statute does not apply). The initial assumption that the statute applies must be false, because the assumption produces a contradiction. See I. Copi, Symbolic Logic 55 (1954) (indirect proof by *reductio ad absurdum*).

12. As another commentator observed of a related question, "this area of the law is complex and virtually unexplored." Note, *The Voting of Stock Held in Cross Ownership*, 76 Harv. L. Rev. 1642, 1643 (1963), *quoted in* Yoran, *Advance Defensive Tactics against Takeover Bids*, 21 Am. J. Comp. L. 531, 550-51 (1973).

13. Cal. Corp. Code § 703(b) (West 1977).

14. *Id.* § 189(a), (b) (West 1977).

15. *See supra* note 10.

although it too constrains an entitlement to vote, it is triggered by a parent's possession of voting shares rather than by entitlement to vote them.[16]

The most persuasive argument against the application of any cross-ownership statute to the aftermath of a Pac-Man defense is the unlikelihood that the drafters of cross-ownership provisions had such a novel situation in mind. The cross-ownership provisions were preceded by statutory bans on voting treasury stock. Treasury stock, it was thought, ought not be voted because it represents no investment in the corporation, and the function of the franchise is to enable the shareholder to protect his investment.[17] Some courts interpreted the statutory disenfranchisement of treasury stock to apply to stock in the parent corporation held by a subsidiary, reasoning that permitting such stock to vote would enable persons in control of the parent to disenfranchise or at least to dilute the voting rights of the parent's shareholders. For example, the statute at issue in *Italo Petroleum Corp. v. Producers Oil Corp. of America* provided that "shares of its own capital stock belonging to the corporation shall not be voted upon directly or indirectly...,"[18] and the court held that this ban applied to shares in the parent corporation held by a subsidiary in which the parent had a 99 percent interest. As the *Italo Petroleum* court explained, "a subsidiary stockholder wholly owned, controlled, dominated and therefore dictated to" by the parent is a corporate entity insufficiently distinguishable from the parent, so that the shares in question "belong" to the parent.[19]

Of course, not all parents own or control their subsidiaries to the degree present in *Italo Petroleum*; in other cases, it is more difficult to determine whether the parent's control over the subsidiary is sufficient to establish the parent as the true owner of the stock nominally held by the subsidiary.

---

16. It is arguable that to possess voting power is the same as being entitled to vote the shares that one possesses, in which case the California statute is subject to the same logical flaws as is the Delaware statute. This is irrelevant, however, to the possibility of drafting around the logical conundrum.

17. H. Ballantine, Corporations § 176 (Rev. ed. 1946). In contrast, the stock acquired pursuant to a tender offer does represent an investment in the corporation.

18. 20 Del. Ch. 283, 288, 174 A. 276, 278 (Ch. 1934) (interpreting former Gen. Corp. Law § 31).

19. *Id.* at 290, 1974 A. at 279.

The court in Continental-Midwest Corp. v. Hotel Sherman, Inc., 13 Ill. App. 2d 188, 195-96, 141 N.E.2d 400, 403-04 (1957), followed *Italo Petroleum* and held that the Delaware statute would prohibit the voting of "indirect" treasury stock. *Italo Petroleum* was distinguished on its facts in Tennessee *ex rel.* Washington Industries, Inc. v. Shacklett, 512 S.W.2d 284 (Tenn. 1974). In that case the subsidiary held no stock in the parent; rather, the issue was whether the parent could vote stock it held in its subsidiary. The *Shacklett* court held that *Italo Petroleum* was factually inapposite and that to disenfranchise the parent would improperly confer "absolute voting rights" on the small minority interest in the subsidiary. *Id.* at 287.

This is, in effect, a decision whether to disregard the formal separation between the two corporate entities.[20] In *Dal-Tran Service Co. v. Fifth Avenue Coach Lines, Inc.*,[21] the parent corporation owned 68 percent of its subsidiary, which in turn held a sizable minority block in the parent. The trial court in *Dal-Tran* concluded that such a dominated subsidiary could not vote the shares it owns in its parent.[22] The appellate division apparently did not regard the parent's 68 percent ownership as conclusive on the issue of domination; it held that the parent and the subsidiary were "separate corporate entities."[23] The appellate court did not reach the question whether the subsidiary would be entitled to vote its shares in the parent,[24] although this entitlement follows from the court's decision that the two corporations were distinct entities.

Against this case law background statutes like Delaware's Section 160(c) were enacted. These statutes establish a bright-line test for domination based on the parent's percentage ownership of the subsidiary. The statutes may embody a legislative decision to permit a subsidiary to vote stock in the parent when the parent's interest in that subsidiary falls short of the statutory percentage. This interpretation could conflict with prior case law establishing that the court may disenfranchise the subsidiary's holdings in the parent if the parent so dominates its subsidiary that the disputed stock effectively

---

20. In many such cases, the allocation of the burden of proving domination is vigorously contested and outcome determinative. *See* Note, *supra* note 12, at 1646-50.

21. 30 Misc. 2d 236, 217 N.Y.S.2d 193 (Sup. Ct), *rev'd*, 14 A.D.2d 349, 220 N.Y.S.2d 549 (1961).

22. 30 Misc. 2d at 243, 217 N.Y.S.2d at 200.

23. 14 A.D.2d at 355-56, 220 N.Y.S.2d at 556.

24. *Id.* at 352, 220 N.Y.S.2d at 553. The issue in *Dal-Tran* was whether the minority shareholder in the subsidiary could vote its proportionate share of the subsidiary's stock in the parent after the revocation of a provision in a voting trust that purported to confer such a right. The trial court invalidated the trust but invoked equitable considerations to permit the subsidiary's minority shareholder to retain his alleged voting rights in the parent. 30 Misc. 2d at 243, 217 N.Y.S.2d at 200-01. The appellate court held that the parent's grant of voting rights to the minority shareholder was unilaterally revocable for want of consideration, 14 A.D.2d at 356, 220 N.Y.S.2d at 556-57, and that because the parent and the subsidiary were distinct corporations, a shareholder of the subsidiary had no direct right to vote any of the subsidiary's stock in the parent, *id.* at 355-56, 220 N.Y.S.2d at 556. Because the subsidiary had not attempted to vote its stock in the parent, the appellate division declined to decide whether the subsidiary was entitled to vote. *Id.* at 352, 220 N.Y.S.2d at 553. The trial court's extensive discussion of this issue, *see* 30 Misc. 2d at 243, 217 N.Y.S.2d at 200, is perhaps an elaborate dictum, but it indicates the state of the case law in New York at the time of the enactment of that jurisdiction's cross-ownership statute.

belongs to the parent. In the alternative, the statutes may simply place the burden of establishing parental domination and control on the party seeking disenfranchisement when the parent owns less than the statutory percentage of the subsidiary.

Regardless of the statutes' specific effect, it is clear in the light of the cases preceding them that they address the problem of cross-ownership patterns insulating management from the shareholders' effective use of their voting franchise. It strains credulity to suggest that this problem attends Pac-Man defenses. The parties to such tender offers are adversaries, organized into unquestionably separate and independent corporate entities; their relationship is fraught with hostility, not domination or connivance. If the parent had placed some of its shares in the safe hands of its subsidiary as a device to defend against unwanted tender offers, disenfranchisement would be consistent with the policies that cross-ownership statutes represent, but parent-subsidiary relationships that are the product of Pac-Man strategies do not create this kind of insulation.[25]

II. THE TIMING AND MECHANICS OF VOTING

A successful tender offer followed by a successful Pac-Man defense also raises curious legal problems that concern the timing and mechanics of the parties' ability to use the voting power they have acquired in each other. State corporation statutes differ widely on these matters, and these differences may significantly affect the outcome of the takeover battle. Suppose again that both O and T have acquired a majority of each other's shares; assume initially that neither block of shares would be disenfranchised from voting by a cross-ownership statute. It is unlikely that the board of either acquired company would voluntarily cooperate with the acquirer. Therefore, in order for either party to translate its shareholdings into effective control of the other company, it will obviously need to vote its shares to remove the acquired company's incumbent directors (assuming that they have not resigned) and elect new directors to the board. The acquirer must also vote its shares to secure approval of a proposal to merge the two companies, on terms agreeable to the managment of the acquiring company after such a proposal has been duly approved by the newly elected

---

25. *See* Yoran, *supra* note 12, at 551-55. Some commentators advocate passing through the subsidiary's voting rights in the parent to the subsidiary's outside shareholders as a remedy for cross-ownership. *See* Note, *supra* note 12, at 1651-55; Comment, *Voting Rights in the Stock of a Parent Corporation Held by a Subsidiary*, 28 U. Chi. L. Rev. 151, 153-54 (1960). The rationale for pass-through relief does not apply if the two corporations' parent-subsidiary relationship is simply the by-product of a Pac-Man defense. Indeed, the efficacy of the voting franchise may be weakened by reallocating the subsidiary's voting rights in the Pac-Man setting.

directors of the acquired company, or to dissolve the acquired company after the merger and dispose of its shares in the acquiring company in a way that will be attractive to the acquiring company. The nature of these issues makes to clear that the party first to vote its shares scores a preemptive strike. Thus, priority in voting is crucial.

In most states, unless the corporation's shareholders unanimously agree to a given proposition, the majority shareholder may vote its shares only at a shareholders' meeting.[26] Corporation statutes typically require that after the shareholder meeting is duly called,[27] all shareholders of record entitled to vote must receive advance notice of the meeting.[28] Further, if the notice is accompanied by a solicitation of proxies from the shareholders, the SEC's proxy rules require advance filing of the proxy statement with the SEC if

---

26. See, e.g., Model Business Corp. Act § 145 (1971).

27. Unless the corporation has already scheduled an annual meeting that happens to coincide with the takeover struggle, it will be necessary to call a special meeting of shareholders. Section 28 of the Model Business Corporation Act provides that special meetings "may be called by the board of directors, the holders of not less than one-tenth of all the shares entitled to vote at the meeting, or such other persons as may be authorized in the articles of incorporation or the by-laws." Id. § 128. Note that if the cross-ownership statutes disenfranchise the shares held by the new majority shareholder, that shareholder's shares are not "entitled to vote at the meeting" and its ability to call the special meeting is consequently doubtful. In that case, if the incumbent directors and officers resist calling the meeting, the new majority shareholder must patiently await the next annual meeting or must appeal to the unaffiliated shareholders and persuade a sufficient number of them to join in the call. (Query whether this effort at persuasion should be treated as a solicitation of a proxy to which the SEC's proxy rules would apply.) It is also possible to seek judicial intervention to call a meeting. See W. Cary & M. Eisenberg, Corporations 227-29 (5th ed. unabr. 1980).

In contrast, Section 22(d) of the Delaware statute provides that special meetings "may be called by the board of directors or by such person or persons as may be authorized by the certificate of incorporation or by the by-laws." Del. Code Ann. tit. 8, § 211(d) (1975). Unlike the Model Act, the Delaware statute itself does not confer the right to call a special meeting on any stated percentage of stockholders. Unless a court were willing to hold that the power to call a meeting is inherent in the ownership of a majority of a corporation's shares, even a majority shareholder appears to lack the power to call a special meeting under the Delaware statute, unless the corporation itself has language in its certificate or bylaws conferring that power. Thus, a new majority shareholder could be impeded from taking control until the corporation's next annual meeting. This particular difficulty is ameliorated, however, by the latitude of Delaware's consent provision, Section 228. See text accompanying note 36 infra.

28. For example, the Model Business Corporation Act requires that notice of a shareholder meeting be delivered at least ten and no more than fifty days in advance of the meeting. Model Business Corp. Act. § 29 (1971).

the securities to be voted are registered with the SEC pursuant to Section 12 of the Securities Exchange Act of 1934.[29]

In a minority of states, however, the corporation statutes permit shareholders to act with non-unanimous consent and without a meeting, if the number of shares consenting to the action equals the minimum number that would be required to authorize the action at a meeting at which all shares entitled to vote were present and voting.[30] These statutes also permit the corporation to opt out of non-unanimous consent through a provision in its articles of incorporation. (This discussion presupposes that neither party has taken the appropriate steps prior to the tender offer to amend its charter.) Although the consent statutes require that notice be given at some point to the nonconsenting shareholders, a party that acquires a majority of the shares of a corporation organized in a state with a non-unanimous consent provision may more expeditiously exercise its control, because no shareholder meeting is required.

This advantage may be vitiated somewhat if the acquired securities are registered with the SEC. Even in the absence of a proxy solicitation, Section 14(c) of the Securities Exchange Act requires that "prior to any annual or other meeting... information substantially equivalent to the information which would be required to be transmitted if a solicitation were made" be furnished to all stockholders of record.[31] Applying Section 14(c), Rule 14c-2(a) requires that an information statement be furnished to shareholders, "[i]n connection with every annual or other meeting... including the taking of corporate action with the written authorization or consent of the holders of a class of securities...."[32] Rule 14c-2(b) requires that the information statement be sent at least twenty days before either the meeting date or "the earliest date on which the corporate action may be taken."[33] Finally, Rule 14c-5(a) requires that the SEC receive preliminary copies of the information statement at least ten days before the statement is sent to the shareholders, although the Commission may shorten this advance filing period on a showing of good cause.[34] The import of these rules is that if shares are acquired in a corporation within the SEC's ambit under the Exchange Act, an advance information statement must be furnished to share-

---

29. Securities Exchange Act of 1934, § 12(b), (g), 15 U.S.C. § 78l(b), (g) (1976).

30. *See, e.g.*, Del Code Ann. tit. 8, § 228(a), (c) (1975).

31. Securities Exchange Act of 1934, § 14(c), 15 U.S.C. § 78n(c) (1976).

32. 17 C.F.R. § 240.14c-2(a) (1982). The scope of the rule appears to exceed somewhat that of the statute, which on its face is limited to shareholder meetings.

33. 17 C.F.R. § 240.14c-2(b) (1982).

34. *Id.* § 240.14c-5. Indeed, in the Bendix–Martin Marietta transaction, the SEC permitted the information required by Section 14(c) to be included in the tender offer documents.

holders even if proxies are not solicited and even if a shareholder meeting is not held. Nonetheless, if a non-unanimous consent route is available, compliance with the Secion 14(c) requirements may still result in less delay than compliance with the formalities attendant to a shareholder meeting.[35]

The non-unanimous consent statutes themselves differ in some ways that bear on the timing question. Section 228 of the Delaware statute permits shareholder action on non-unanimous consent without prior notice if non-consenting stockholders are given prompt notice of the corporate action taken.[36] Notice given *after* the action has been taken could thus be "prompt" under Section 228. Other statutes, although differing somewhat in their details of mechanics and timing, essentially require that advance notice of the proposed action be given to all stockholders and thereby create the possibility that minority shareholders opposing the action may sue seeking injunctive relief. For example, the California statute requires that notice be given ten days in advance of the action unless the consent of all shareholders has been solicited in writing,[37] and the Florida statute requires that notice be given nonconsenting shareholders within ten days of obtaining non-unanimous consent.[38] New Jersey differentiates between types of actions in its notice requirements: notice must be given twenty days in advance of taking action to merge, consolidate, sell, or exchange assets, but ten days' notice suffices for all other shareholder actions.[39] Although most such statutes permit non-unanimous consent to authorize any action that may be taken by shareholders, Nevada and New Jersey except the election of directors, for which a meeting would be required.[40]

All things considered, then, an offeror is in a strong position if its target is incorporated in Delaware, which is the most permissive jurisdiction in the use of non-unanimous consent for shareholder action. If the target responds with a successful Pac-Man defense, the initial offeror will be in an

---

35. Other aspects of the proxy rules may also be applicable to the solicitation of shareholder consent. In Pabst Brewing Co. v. Jacobs, 549 F. Supp. 1068, 1074-77 (D. Del. 1982), the court held that Rule 14a-4(b)(2), 17 C.F.R. § 240.14a-4(b)(2) (1982), required that shareholders must be given the opportunity to vote selectively to remove directors and elect their successors and cannot be presented with an "all-or-nothing" choice between the incumbents and an insurgent slate.

36. Del. Code Ann. tit. 8, § 228(a), (c) (1975). The omission of a non-unanimous consent provision in the Model Business Corporation Act may explain the substantial variation among statutes.

37. Cal. Corp. Code. § 603(a), (b) (West 1977).

38. 18 Fla. Stat. Ann. § 607.394 (West 1977).

39. N.J. Stat. Ann. § 14A:5-6 (West Supp. 1982-1983).

40. Nev. Rev. Stat. § 78.320(1) (1979); N.J. Stat. Ann. § 14A:5-6 (West Supp. 1982-1983).

even stronger position if it is incorporated in a state requiring that a meeting precede stockholder action[41] or if it has amended its charter to require such a meeting.[42] Even if the initial offeror were incorporated in a state with a non-unanimous consent provision, it could use that route to amend its charter to opt of the statute and to require a shareholders' meeting for some types of corporate action. Obviously, the success of this defensive maneuver will turn on the timing of the proposed amendment, which must be adopted before the target's Pac-Man defense captures a majority of the shares in the initial offeror. Finally, either party's ability to vote the shares

---

41. The court in Martin Marietta Corp. v. Bendix Corp., 549 F. Supp. 623, 633 n.5 (D. Md. 1982), recognized that the law of the original offeror's state of incorporation may determine the efficacy of a Pac-Man defense. Martin Marietta, a Maryland corporation, made a Pac-Man offer for Bendix, a Delaware corporation. Delaware has a non-unanimous consent provision, but Maryland does not. The *Martin Marietta* court observed that Marietta's directors need not assume that their continued tenure in office would be very brief after Bendix acquired a majority of the Marietta shares. The court noted that "due to differences in Maryland and Delaware state law, Marietta's directors 'knew' that if they proceeded with Marietta's offer, they would probably not be displaced by Bendix in a day or even in the foreseeable future." *Id.*

42. *See supra* text following note 30.

It may also be possible for an original offeror to protect itself against some of the discrepancies in voting practices arising from a Pac-Man defense through other kinds of charter amendments. One possibility that has been suggested is that the bidder amend its charter to make the time necessary to convene a meeting of stockholders (to remove directors) the same length as the time necessary to convene a meeting in any company holding a majority of its shares. *Cf.* Securities and Exchange Commission Advisory Committee on Tender Offers, Report of Recommendations 102 n.21 (1983) (Separate Statement of Frank H. Easterbrook & Gregg A. Jarrell) (addressing timing of voting by directors). In effect, the initial offeror would borrow the notice period for a meeting applicable to the countertendering target. But this may not achieve in all instances what the initial offeror desires, namely, an assurance that it will be able to vote its shares in the target *before* the target can vote its shares in the original offeror. This strategy assures the first offeror of the first vote only when its offer closes before that of the target so that it is first actually to purchase shares. The first offeror may be in trouble if the period of its initial offer is longer than the minimum duration or if the offer's duration is extended so that purchases are made later than the target's Pac-Man purchases. This analysis suggests the first offeror would be safer with a charter provision that its shares are not votable until a stated period of time after the original target's shares are votable. A nasty circularity would result if both participants in a Pac-Man contest had such provisions. The original offeror would also be well advised to take any permissible steps under the relevant state statute to make its directors removable only for cause. Under the Delaware statute these would be: excising any certificate provisions making directors removable without cause, and classifying the board. See Del. Code Ann. tit. 8, § 141(k)(i) (1983).

it has acquired is determined in part by the time at which it purchases the shares, which in turn depends on the timing of the offer and the expiration of the shareholders' right under the Williams Act to withdraw shares they have tendered.

The scenario in which the original offeror or its target (turned Pac-Man aggressor) seeks to exercise its newly acquired control grows more complicated if a cross-ownership provision prevents either or both corporations from voting their blocks of stock in the other.[43] If it is disenfranchised, the acquirer can take advantage of a non-unanimous consent statute only by persuading a majority of the residual shareholders to lend their consent. Efforts to persuade these stockholders may well be viewed as the solicitation of proxies, and it may be necessary to comply with the SEC's proxy rules,[44] which will delay the exercise of control on which the outcome of the takeover battle depends. If an acquirer does not or cannot resort to a non-unanimous consent statute, its success depends on the outcome of a shareholder meeting at which the shares voting will be those other than the shares held by the majority stockholder.[45] Realistically, such a shareholder meeting would feature a quite vigorous proxy contest waged by the new majority shareholder against incumbent management.[46]

---

43. *See supra* text accompaying note 4.

44. Rule 14a-1(d) defines "proxy" to include "every proxy, consent, or authorization," including those that take the form of a failure to act. 17 C.F.R. § 240.14a-1(d) (1982).

45. *See supra* text accompanying note 5.

Disenfranchisement of the majority shareholder under a cross-ownership statute would not make it impossible to obtain a quorum for a shareholders' meeting because the calculation of the number of shares outstanding for purposes of determining the quorum number does not include disenfranchised shares. *See, e.g.*, Del. Code Ann. tit. 8, § 160(c) (1975).

The majority stockholder may be in an especially awkward position if the corporation is incorporated in a state that, like Delaware, does not by statute empower stockholders to call special meetings, *see* note 27 *supra*, but that also, unlike Delaware, does not have a non-unanimous consent statute. One possible argument available to the majority stockholder is that, if the corporation statute authorizes *removal* of directors by shareholders, it implicitly empowers shareholders to call a special meeting for that purpose by the same vote required for removal, so that the power to remove is not frustrated by a technical inability to call a meeting. Especially if the corporation statute authorizes removal of directors *without cause*, it arguably empowers the majority stockholder to undertake the preliminaries necessary to exercise the right to remove. The right to remove directors without cause by majority shareholder vote is such a decisive recognition of the residual power of majority stockholders in relation to that of directors that it appears obtuse to frustrate the exercise of the power through the preliminary obstacle of calling a shareholders' meeting.

46. *See supra* note 6.

III. THE FIDUCIARY DUTIES OF THE TWO BOARDS OF DIRECTORS

In the aftermath of a successful Pac-Man defense, the new majority share-holders will be in an especially awkward position with respect to the incumbent directors. Conflict between new owners and old directors is not unusual in the wake of a takeover; the problem is exacerbated here by the prolongation of the struggle for control. Until one corporation succeeds in exercising its newly acquired control over the other, it is not clear which is in control, and in each corporation the interests of the new majority and the current directors are directly opposed. The problem arises even before the Pac-Man defense begins. Once O acquires a majority of the shares in T, T's directors are conceivably bound by their fiduciary duty to do nothing inconsistent with O's wishes, which presumably do not encompass a Pac-Man offer for O's shares. Similarly, if T undertakes a Pac-Man defense and acquires a majority of the shares in O, O's directors may be bound to abide by T's desires. If T must act in accordance with O's wishes while O is bound to obey T, the situation is not only awkward, it is viciously circular.

Again, an appeal to the residual shareholders solves the conundrum. T's directors owe their fiduciary duty to all of the shareholders of T, not simply to the majority shareholder. Indeed, the interests and wishes of O as the majority stockholder may be so inconsistent with the interests of T's minority stockholders that it would be improper for T's directors to pursue the majority's goals exclusively. Furthermore, to the extent that T's directors owe deference to O as a majority stockholder, they owe this deference to O's shareholders, not simply its management, because O's shareholders are the beneficial owners of O's majority holding in T. O's principal shareholder is T, but there will also be minority shareholders in O, to whom T's directors now owe a fiduciary duty. In the mirror-image world of the Pac-Man defense, what is true of T is equally true of O. Therefore, the directors of each corporation owe their fiduciary duty to the same set of shareholders: the minority shareholders of T and O. This is no surprise; in effect, there is now only one corporation, not two, and its shareholders are those shareholders of T and of O who did not sell their stock in the tender offer and Pac-Man defense.[47] The only question is which board of directors will control the merged entities.[48]

The Delaware Supreme Court in *Martin Marietta Corp. v. Bendix Corp.*[49]

---

47. Although after a successful Pac-Man defense there is one corporation for purposes of analyzing the fiduciary duties of the two boards, there are still two corporations for purposes of holding shareholder meetings and electing directors.

48. In the alternative, a white knight may appear and acquire both corporations. *See infra* note 59.

49. No. 298, slip op. (Del. Sept. 21, 1982).

ventured a very different analysis of the directors' duties in the aftermath of a Pac-Man defense. The court opined that once Bendix became the majority shareholder of Martin Marietta, Martin Marietta would violate "a moral duty to its majority shareholder, Bendix," if it were to acquire a majority of Bendix's shares and use them under Delaware's non-unanimous consent statute to gain control of the Bendix board.[50] According to the *Martin Marietta* court, this moral transgression might warrant legal or equitable intervention.[51]

No doubt the Bendix managment was outraged and surprised by Martin Marietta's Pac-Man defense. The Delaware court, however, exaggerated the magnitude of this outrage when it suggested that Bendix would be entitled to legal or equitable relief. It is also possible that the Delaware court perceived the irony of a foreign corporation, such as Martin Marietta, being able to use Delaware's non-unanimous consent statute to capture a Delaware corporation, such as Bendix, while Bendix, the original offeror, was crippled by the lack of a non-unanimous consent statute in Maryland, Martin Marietta's state of incorporation. At any rate, the Delaware Supreme Court's analysis in *Martin Marietta* ignored the fact that a target corporation's board of directors owes its fiduciary duty to all its shareholders, not simply to the majority shareholders.

Futhermore, the decision of a target's board to retaliate with a Pac-Man defense ought to receive the deference that is customarily management's due. If the decision is made in good faith and in pursuit of what is reasonably believed to be a good corporate purpose, it ought to be protected by the business judgment rule from judicial scrutiny of its correctness.[52] While in the fray of battle, the target's directors are not psychologically disinterested in its outcome, but courts thus far have required a more palpable conflict of interest before they will disqualify the directors' decisions from the protection of the business judgment rule.[53] The directors of the original

---

50. *Id.* at 2. Oddly enough, the court's articulation of the Marietta directors' moral duties conflicts sharply with the view of those duties expressed by one Marietta director. He argued at a Marietta board meeting that, having made its tender offer for Bendix, Marietta was under a "moral obligation" to buy the shares tendered. American Lawyer, Feb. 1983, at 35, 39, col. 2.

51. No. 298, slip op. at 2-3.

52. This analysis follows the reasoning in Martin Marietta Corp. v. Bendix Corp. 549 F. Supp. at 633-34. The court expressly rejected the Sixth Circuit's interpretation of Section 14(e) of the Williams Act in Mobil Corp. v. Marathon Oil Co., 669 F. 2d 366 (6th Cir. 1981), that some tender offer defenses, albeit not deceptive, are manipulative interferences with market forces. *Id.* at 630.

53. *See, e.g.*, Panter v. Marshall Field & Co., 646 F.2d 271 (7th Cir.), *cert. denied*, 454 U.S. 1092 (1981); Treadway Cos. v. Care Corp., 638 F.2d 357 (2d Cir. 1980). Some courts have intimated that directors, despite their formal disinterest in a transaction, nonetheless may have strong ties of loyalty to the corporation's man-

offeror may well disagree with the target's directors about the best interests of the companies and their shareholders, but this kind of difference in judgment is perfectly consistent with deference to the decisions of both boards under the business judgment standard.

IV. CONCLUSION

Several aspects of the Pac-Man defense present troubling legal questions. Although variations among state corporation statutes sometimes determine the outcome of takeover battles, the applicability of cross-ownership statutes and non-unanimous shareholder consent statutes is not among the factors that traditionally influence the choice of a legal locale for incorporation or the choice of a tender offer target. In advising on incorporation decisions, corporate counsel takes into account considerations such as the level of the state's franchise tax and the overall certainty and flexibility of the state's corporate law. Perhaps counsel will expand its list of relevant state law considerations to include those that bear on the Pac-Man defense, or perhaps it will take care that the corporation's articles are originally drafted or subsequently amended to minimize some of the difficulties identified in this commentary. These peculiarities of state corporate law may also become significant in the choice of takeover targets and defensive planning.

It is equally likely, however, that any state law barriers to the use of the Pac-Man defense will simply contribute to the growth of a strong disenchantment with the determinative effect of such statutes on the outcome of takeover contests. While the success of a disputed tender offer may turn on many factors, including the relative financial strengths and strategic acumen of the bidders, differences among state corporation statutes should not be crucial to the outcome. Having the good fortune to be an offeror incorporated in Maryland or New Jersey who chooses a target incorporated in New Hampshire is not the kind of quirk on which corporate control should turn, other things being equal. Because variations in state corporation statutes can arbitrarily determine the winner of a takeover battle, corpo-

---

agers. *See* Joy v. North, 692 F.2d 880, 888 (2d Cir. 1982); Zapata Corp. v. Maldonado, 430 A.2d 779, 787 (Del. 1981). *See generally* Cox, *Searching for the Corporation's Voice in Derivative Suit Litigation: A Critique of* Zapata *and the ALI Project,* 1982 Duke L.J. 959. In *Joy* and *Zapata,* however, the question of director independence arises in the context of the nominally independent directors' ability to use a special litigation commission to cause the dismissal of derivative suits brought against corporate officers and other directors. This context may somewhat limit the courts' misgivings about director independence, because the courts may view themselves as possessing a special aptitude to evaluate the probable merits of corporate litigation whereas they would be more reluctant to review the merits of more typical business decisions. *See* Joy v. North, 692 F.2d at 888.

rations may become the surprising new advocates of statutory uniformity.[54] Uniformity could be most directly achieved by a federal incorporation statute or by federal statutory provisions that supervene the states' treatment of questions crucial to contested tender offers. Less directly, and short of congressional action, the SEC could attempt to use its rulemaking authority under Section 14(c) of the Securities Exchange Act of 1934[55] and under the Williams Act[56] to achieve greater uniformity, subject to the risk of a successful challenge to such rules as beyond Congress's intention in the Exchange Act.

As the law now stands, courts may mistakenly use cross-ownership statutes to disenfranchise one or both of the parties to a Pac-Man defense, and variations among state corporation statutes with respect to the timing and mechanics of voting may arbitrarily determine the outcome of a takeover battle. The resolution of these problems, however, would not answer the more fundamental question of how the legal system is to decide who will win control of two offer-entangled enterprises. The current means of determining the winner is as arbitrary as a coin toss, but if the coin toss is abolished, a new decision-making procedure must take its place. The Delaware Supreme Court's confused and moralistic analysis of fiduciary duty in the aftermath of a Pac-Man defense[57] suggests that courts may find it difficult to resolve the battle for control by recourse to traditional legal principles. Furthermore, this commentary's conclusion that the board of directors of each of the entangled corporations owes its fiduciary duty to the same set of shareholders[58] suggests that traditional principles will fail to guide courts through the mirror-image world of the Pac-Man defense.

This legal infirmity may be tolerable as long as the Pac-Man defense is only a threat. But if tender offer targets continue to make offers for control of the original offeror and to purchase the shares tendered, the legal confusion will become intolerable. At present, only the timely arrival of a white knight to purchase both adversaries[59] can redeem the parties from the chaos

---

54. Corporations have generally disfavored statutory uniformity, which would preclude the creation of corporate havens.

55. *See* 15 U.S.C. § 78n(c) (1976).

56. *See* Securities Exchange Act of 1934, § 14(d)(1), (d)(4), 15 U.S.C. § 78n(d)(1), (d)(4) (1976).

57. *See supra* text accompanying notes 59-51 and text following note 51.

58. *See supra* text preceding note 47.

59. The deal through which the white knight resolves the confusion may not result in the white knight's control of both adversaries. For example, in the denouement of the Martin Marietta–Bendix offers, Allied Corporation agreed to merge with Bendix by buying Martin Marietta's block of Bendix along with the Bendix shares that had not been tendered. To pay for Marietta's block of Bendix shares, Allied relinquished part of Bendix's block of Marietta; Allied retained 39% interest

they have created. In some cases, however, the rival offerors' balance sheets will be so depleted of cash and so laden with debt after their contest that they will confound the mettle of even the most valiant white knight. The extremity of the situation would then warrant a novel, and perhaps even an audacious, legal response to the general problem of Pac-Man defenses.

There are a number of different avenues that such a legal response might follow. Although this commentary describes them only briefly and in the broadest of terms, it will be apparent that each has its own attractions and drawbacks. Perhaps the simplest to execute is a legislative or administrative prohibition against Pac-Man defenses or, more generally, against a range of tender offer defenses. Such a prohibition, however, would deny shareholders of target companies the benefits of larger-offer premiums that the threat of a counteroffer may engender. The prohibition would also preclude the possible success of the threat as a deterrent to the original offeror or as a cry for a white knight to come to the rescue.

Another possible legal response would be to give some judicial or administrative body the power to review the merits of each board of directors' claim to control the corporations. The reviewing authority would also determine the capital and management structure that would best serve the interests of the companies' remaining stockholders and would be most likely to further the effective operation of their businesses. As these inquiries are necessarily empirical and complex, an administrative and regulatory agency would be better suited than the courts for this purpose. An analogy of some force is the mandate given to the SEC by Section 11 of the Public Utility Holding Company Act of 1935[60] to "examine the corporate structure" of registered holding companies to determine whether that structure might be simplified to further a fair and equitable distribution of voting rights among holders of securities and to achieve the limitation of the companies' properties and business "to those necessary or appropriate to the operations of an integrated public utility system."[61] Surely a comparable mandate, of equivalent breadth, could be designed for the SEC to execute in the aftermath of a successful Pac-Man maneuver.

Of course, the risk of falling under the SEC's aegis could discourage ambitious Pac-Man offers, but this might be a desirable side effect. This solution does, however, assume that these situations are so extraordinary that the customary governmental deference to private business decisions should be suspended. As an alternative to such radical governmental interference, legislation could require the SEC to select independent directors

---

in Marietta but agreed to vote it as the Marietta board directed. *See* Rowan & Moore, *Behind the Lines in the Bendix War*, Fortune, Oct. 18, 1982, at 157.

60. 15 U.S.C. § 79k (1976).

61. *Id.* § 79k(a).

in the wake of a Pac-Man debacle, directors whose term in office might well be limited but whose mandate would include the choice of an appropriate management structure for the cross-owned enterprise. This solution minimizes governmental intrusion into decisions about private business corporations, while providing some device lacking at present to resolve rationally the impasse that marks the success of a Pac-Man defense.

V

A VIEW FROM INSIDE COUNSEL

The role of inside counsel in today's complex and ever-changing corporate world is challenging. Today, inside counsel plays an active role in shaping corporate events as they occur, in assessing and helping to determine corporate policies, and in establishing the tone and standard for what may be called "the conduct of corporations." Undoubtedly, the responsibility and prestige of inside counsel have increased dramatically in recent years.[1]

Given the opportunities that exist to help mold corporate policies, practices, and standards, it is somewhat surprising that inside counsel has not been more vocal in the tender offer debate. In the ensuing commentary, James J. Harrison, Esq., the inside general counsel of a company that was the subject of an unsuccessful takeover bid, presents his views on hostile

---

1. *See* M. Steinberg, Corporate Internal Affairs: A Corporate and Securities Law Perspective 251–268 (1983); Ferrara & Steinberg, *The Role of Inside Counsel in the Corporate Accountability Process*, 4 Corp. L. Rev. 3 (1981); Williams, *The Role of Inside Counsel in Corporate Accountability*, [1979–1980 Transfer Binder] Fed. Sec. L. Rep. (CCH) ¶ 82,318 (1979). *See generally* Creedon, *Lawyer and Executive: The Role of the General Counsel*, 39 Bus. Law. 25 (1983); Forrow, *The Corporate Law Department Lawyer: Counsel to the Entity*, 34 Bus. Law. 1797 (1979); Gruenbaum, *Clients' Frauds and Their Lawyers' Obligations*, 68 Geo. L. J. 197 (1979); Gruner, *Improving the Effectiveness of Corporate Counsel: An Information Processing Analysis*, 9 J. Corp. L. 217 (1984); Hershman, *Special Problems of Inside Counsel for Financial Institutions*, 33 Bus. Law. 1435 (1978); Sommer, *The Emerging Responsibilities of the Securities Lawyer*, [1974–1975 Transfer Binder] Fed. Sec. L. Rep. (CCH) ¶ 79,631 (1974); Taylor, *The Role of Corporate Counsel*, 32 Rutgers L. Rev. 237 (1979); Williams, *Corporate Accountability and the Lawyer's Role*, 34 Bus. Law. 7 (1978).

tender offers.[2] Mr. Harrison asserts that such offers frequently make little sense from an economic viewpoint. Although shareholders of the target corporation may receive a substantial premium on the shares tendered, in many cases neither company ultimately benefits. Moreover, takeover bids divert needed capital from more productive opportunities and impair the performance of both bidder and target managements. Calling hostile tender offers "the corporate-world version of war," the author concludes that the massive amounts of human talent and dollars expended in these battles for corporate control ordinarily cannot be justified.

---

2. The views expressed herein are those of Mr. Harrison and not necessarily those held by McCormick & Company.

View from Inside Counsel

JAMES J. HARRISON, JR.*

These are a series of thoughts on the often-discussed subject of tender offers—the not-so-tender wars fought by businesses—domestically and internationally. There seem to be a number of common denominators—many of them negative—to these battles.

First, if the raider is successful, it acquires a business or company where the new combination usually does not make any readily identifiable additional contribution to the economic betterment of society or, in many cases, even to the raider's own betterment other than magnifying its assets through the purchase. The raider becomes larger and often more unwieldy from an organizational point of view. The argument has been made that the threat of tender offers keeps management of potential targets on its toes and inclined to be more efficient and effective, but what of the management of raiders who seek to enlarge their companies through hostile tender offers without displaying or expending the type of management expertise so often sought in target companies and without any ascertainable real benefits to their shareholders?

Were the senior managements of the Standard Oil Company of California and Allied and Bendix (et al.) effectively running their own companies while expending great lumps of top management time in trying to acquire others? It could be, but there is justifiable concern that the acquiring companies survive the acquisition process in spite of the process and resulting acquisitions and not because of them.

A corollary concern is the increasing practice of some companies of taking stock positions in potential targets with the targets then buying back the

*James J. Harrison, Jr., is vice president, secretary, general counsel, and a member of the board of directors of McCormick & Company, Inc.

stock at a premium to eliminate the threat of takeover. This would not seem to serve the best interests of the stockholders of the target, although it may well be in their long-term financial best interests to have the company stay independent. However, once again the benefit to the economy and American business in general is not apparent; it is true that the coffers of the potential raider are enriched at the expense of the potential target, but to what overall benefit for American business?

In the case of the large oil company mergers, such as the $13.2 billion merger of Gulf into Standard Oil of California, where is the net benefit to American society, American business, the oil business, and our oil and gas exploration efforts? Giant amounts of credit were used to finance the acquisition (credit that might have otherwise been used for useful purposes, such as financing long-range oil and gas exploration), the stockholders of Gulf did see the value of their investment double from roughly $40 to $80 per share, and Standard absorbed all of Gulf's oil and gas reserves and service stations. Where or what is the benefit other than the dramatic increase in value of Gulf stock? And even there, it is safe to assume that a buyer is going to want to pay something less than the full, fair value of the acquired stock (how one would ever determine "full, fair value" is another very difficult question).

Keeping in mind that the nature of tender offers is such that offers are made almost solely on the basis of whatever public information is available on the company and without the benefit of any representations or warranties that the acquirer is getting what it thinks it paid for, it is small wonder that so many acquisitions made via the tender offer route are at best disappointments to the raider and the raider's shareholders. Who, then, are the beneficiaries of the successful tender offer?

Despite the often-heard rhetoric that management of the target resists the tender offer in order to protect its jobs or its "entrenched management position," the facts usually are that the senior management of the acquired company would become instant millionaires or better after a successful tender offer, by reason of the dramatic increase in value of its stock holdings in the acquired company and, often more important, by the cash payoff it receives for its stock options. So, what becomes of the "entrenched management" after the acquisition? A few may lose their jobs—especially if they were part of the key management team resisting a hostile takeover—but they usually leave with financial resources far greater than they would have had for many years had the takeover not occurred (this ignores the possibility of their having had "golden parachutes," which would have further parlayed their gains from the acquisition).

However, many more stay than leave, and the more typical story seems to be one of ascendency within the combined company—after all, one of the often-expressed reasons for an acquisition is to acquire new or greater depth of management talent. Why then do company managements resist tender offers?

If one accepts that the top "entrenched management" will be substantially enriched by a successful takeover attempt, then it follows that its motives in resisting the takeover are not selfish, at least from a financial viewpoint. This is still America, a place of dreams and opportunity to fulfill them. One reason, then, is the desire to continue doing well what has been done well without interference from people who do not know the target's business as well as the target's management.

There are often a substantial number of shareholders who have had close relationships with the target, who have grown with the target as long-term successful investors in it, and who have no desire to cash in their holdings for the "fast buck." The better-managed growth companies (and hence the most attractive companies to raiders) have rewarded their investors hand-somely over the long pull. It is upsetting or worse for an attractive man-agement team and its loyal, long-term shareholders to see their successful company sold out quickly to the highest bidder for no apparent purpose other than realizing the "fast buck" of special interest to speculators (and arbitrageurs). Obviously, there is, and always will be, at least two diverse groups of shareholders in a company: the loyal long-term growers of the company and the short-term speculators.

What does a "hostile" takeover attempt do to the target company? In-herent in this is the word "hostile." First, the attempt is disruptive to the management of the company. Instead of being able to devote the normal time to managing and developing the company, key members of the man-agement company—usually including the chairman and chief executive officer, president and chief operating officer, chief financial officer, and chief legal officer—are partially or totally involved in defending the company from the attack. Other support personnel throughout the target company are involved. The interruption in management attention to normal business matters is usually aggravated by litigation, filed by or against the raider, which often involves management depositions and document discovery. Endless document preparation and press releases are generated as part of the battle. Strategy planning and its implementation are always urgent and ongoing—around the clock some days and weeks—and the toll on people is evident emotionally. Inside and outside, members of the company team must be available at all times; dates and times must be set and met, and if people and events don't move quickly, the players can get caught up in the emotional roller coaster of what is about to happen. It is necessary to keep the key inside management group together as much as possible, so the group hears the same information at the same time. The board of directors has tremendous pressure on it, and usually none of the members has ever experienced a takeover attempt before. It is a pressure-filled experience in which the directors earn their Ph.D.'s in the responsibilities of directors.

Second is the financial expense. The horde of outside advisors—partic-ularly special counsel, investment bankers, and public relations firms—does not come cheap. Yet when one is in such a battle, it seems important to have the best advisors money can buy (although, in the final analysis, dedication, common sense, and "street smarts" are the most valuable attributes).

It is important to preserve the target company's "culture" as it anticipates or goes through such a battle. By culture is meant the basic values, organization, and management philosophy of the company. Many articles have been written on so-called shark repellants and other changes to a company and its structure to enable it better to rebuff unwanted takeover attempts. Most of these involve fundamental changes to the company, many or most of which would not have been made except for the hostile tender offer or the threat thereof. If such changes are of long-term benefit to the company, then by all means they should be made. But if such changes adversely affect the structure or the basic reasons for the success of the company, then any such changes are, at best, questionable.

It is difficult, if not impossible, to gauge the long-term impact of most "shark repellants" or other changes one could put in place for a target company. If the sole reason is takeover protection, any such potential changes should be carefully analyzed from the viewpoint of their long-term impact on the target company. The "bottom line" of any takeover attempt is the price offered, and the protection afforded by most shark repellants or other changes to a target company is inversely proportional to the price.

So, what is the viewpoint of inside counsel on tender offers? Tender offers, particularly the "hostile" ones, are the corporate-world version of war. It is a game that has winners and losers; uniquely, for the reasons given, the raider and its shareholders usually pay a dear price, the "entrenched management" of the target, as well as the target's shareholders, is usually dramatically enriched, and American business generally has not benefited. If the acquisition affects competition directly and adversely, there will be antitrust implications to the acquisition that may thwart it. But aside from that issue, the other aspects of importance to American business generally do not seem to be considered. Some of these aspects are the use of credit to finance such acquisitions, credit that might otherwise be available for the true growth of American business, and the effect on the people involved—the employees, the community, the suppliers, the customers, and last, but certainly not least, the investors (particularly the long-term loyal investor).

It cannot be said that all acquisitions as a result of tender offers are bad, but there are precious few reasons or situations to support affirmatively most of such activities. The expenditure of massive amounts of human talent and dollars in the making and defense of tender offers does not appear justified, at least not in any way important to the successful growth of American business.

VI

TENDER OFFER
LITIGATION

The abundance of federal and state litigation in the tender offer context is well documented. The business judgment rule and the fiduciary duties of care and loyalty,[1] state blue sky and tender offer statutes,[2] the Williams Act,[3] Section 10(b) of the Exchange Act, and SEC Rule 10b-5 promulgated thereunder,[4] the Hart-Scott-Rodino Antitrust Improvements Act,[5] and the Racketeer Influenced and Corrupt Organizations Act (RICO)[6] all serve as examples

---

1. See the commentaries herein of A. A. Sommer, Esq., and Professor Steinberg for discussion of these principles.

2. See the commentaries herein by Messrs. Goelzer and Cohen and by Professor Sargent addressing the pertinent statutes.

3. The Williams Act amended the Exchange Act by adding Sections 13(d), (e) and 14(d), (e), and (f), 15 U.S.C. §§ 78m(d), (e), 78n(d), (e), (f). The Act is discussed at length in several of the commentaries contained herein.

4. These antifraud provisions generally apply to the tender offer setting, providing there is a "purchase" or "sale" of a security. See generally Blue Chip Stamps v. Manor Drug Stores, 421 U.S. 723 (1975). See also M. Steinberg, Securities Regulation: Liabilities and Remedies § 7.01 et seq. (1984).

5. Generally, the Hart-Scott-Rodino Antitrust Improvements Act of 1976 and regulations issued thereunder provide for significant preacquisition notification and informational requirements for certain tender offerors. See 15 U.S.C. § 18a. For commentary on the Act, see, e.g., Axinn, Fogg & Stoll, Acquisitions under the Hart-Scott-Rodino Antitrust Improvements Act (1979); Kintner, Griffin & Goldston, The Hart-Scott-Rodino Antitrust Improvements Act of 1976: An Analysis, 46 Geo. Wash. L. Rev. 1 (1976); Lesser, Pre-Merger Notification Revisited, 17 Rev. Sec. Reg. 937 (1984); Scher, Emerging Issues under the Antitrust Improvements Act of 1976, 77 Colum. L. Rev. 679 (1979).

6. Congress enacted RICO as Title IX of the Organized Crime Control Act of 1970 (OCCA), Pub. L. No. 91-452, 84 Stat. 92 (1970). It is codified at 18 U.S.C. §§

of the tenacity displayed by the participants, counsel, and other affected parties in these struggles for corporate control.[7] While a number of the foregoing statutes and judicial principles are discussed at length elsewhere in the book,[8] this section contains three commentaries that address specifically litigation developments in the hostile takeover setting.

In the first article, Professor Mark Loewenstein analyzes Section 14(e) of the Securities Exchange Act, the antifraud component of the Williams Act, and the development of decisional law under this provision. Assuming the propriety of implying a private cause of action under Section 14(e),[9] Professor Loewenstein asserts that the judiciary's reliance on Rule 10b-5 precedents to set the parameters of the Section 14(e) right of action is unwarranted. He concludes that scienter should not be an element of the Section 14(e) cause of action, that plaintiffs invoking Section 14(e) should be required to prove reliance only if it is necessary to show causation, that a tender offeror should have standing to seek equitable relief if target management breaches its fiduciary duties to the shareholders and the breach interferes with the tender offer, and that the SEC did not exceed its rulemaking authority in promulgating Rule 14e-3.

The second commentary by Messrs. Levine, Lykos, and Chafetz addresses the recent federal court decisions construing the term "manipulation" under Section 14(e) of the Williams Act. The authors assert that those decisions holding Section 14(e) to be solely a disclosure provision are erroneous. They contend that the statute's proscription against manipulation encompasses acts that artificially impair the tender offer market for the target corporation's stock, irrespective of whether such conduct may be viewed as "fraudulent" or "deceptive." Thereafter, Messrs. Levine, Lykos, and Chafetz turn to state regulation of defensive tactics. They argue that entrenched

---

1961–1968. Professor Tyson's and Mr. Ain's commentary in this section discusses RICO's applicability in the tender offer setting.

7. *See* Electronic Specialty Co. v. International Controls Corp., 409 F.2d 937, 948 (2d Cir. 1969) (Friendly, J.) (Because tender offer contestants must "act quickly, sometimes impulsively, often in angry response to what they consider whether rightly or wrongly, to be low blows by the other side, [there will] probably . . . no more be a perfect tender offer than a perfect trial.").

8. *See, e.g.*, notes 1–3 *supra.*

9. *See* Mobil Corp. v. Marathon Oil Co., 669 F.2d 366 (6th Cir. 1981); Weeks Dredging & Contracting, Inc. v. American Dredging Co., 451 F. Supp. 468 (E.D. Pa. 1978); Humana, Inc. v. American Medicorp, Inc., 445 F. Supp. 613 (S.D.N.Y. 1977). *But see* Liberty National Insurance Holding Co. v. Charter Co., [1984 Transfer Binder] Fed. Sec. L. Rep. ¶ 91, 539 (11th Cir.) (no implied right of action for an issuer seeking injunctive relief mandating divestiture under Sections 10(b), 13(d), 14(d), and 14(e) of the Exchange Act). For an excellent treatment of this issue, see Loewenstein, *Section 14(e) of the Williams Act and the Rule 10b-5 Comparisons*, 71 Geo. L.J. 1311, 1313–1330 (1983).

management's insulation from meritorious shareholder claims based on breach of fiduciary duty is largely due to the expansive interpretation given by the courts to the business judgment rule. The authors submit that such an unduly solicitous approach ignores the conflicts of interest, legitimate shareholder needs, and practical realities that exist in the tender offer context. Accordingly, they advance a proposed framework to correct this asserted inadequacy in state law.

In the third commentary, Professor William Tyson and Mr. Anthony Ain examine the use of the Racketeer Influenced and Corrupt Organizations Act (RICO) in litigation involving tender offers. Relevant cases in which RICO has been used in takeover litigation are evaluated to corroborate the hypothesis that RICO can have a significant impact in this setting. The authors conclude that such an effect was not intended by Congress and, hence, that Congress should amend RICO to curtail its use in corporate takeover litigation.

As noted above, the last portion of Professor Loewenstein's commentary discusses SEC Rule 14e-3 and insider trading in the tender offer context. Undoubtedly, this area during the past half-decade has been the subject of increased judicial scrutiny, vigorous SEC enforcement, and Congressional attention. Since 1980, the Supreme Court has decided two cases in this area. In *Chiarella v. United States*,[10] the Court held that silence, absent a duty to disclose, will not give rise to liability under Section 10(b) of the Securities Exchange Act and Rule 10b-5 promulgated thereunder by the SEC.[11] In *Dirks v. SEC*,[12] the Court held that the duty of tippees to disclose or abstain from trading under Section 10(b) and Rule 10b-5 depends on "whether the insider personally will benefit [e.g., by receipt of pecuniary gain or reputational enhancement that will translate into future earnings], directly, or indirectly, from his disclosure. Absent some personal gain, there has been no breach of duty to stockholders. And absent a breach by the insider, there is no derivative breach [by the tippee]."[13]

---

10. 445 U.S. 222 (1980).

11. *Id*. at 226–235.

12. 103 S. Ct. 3255 (1983).

13. *Id*. at 3265–3266. For more discussion on *Chiarella, Dirks*, and their implications, *see* M. Steinberg, Securities Regulation: Liabilities and Remedies § 3.01 *et seq*. (1984); Branson, *Discourse on the Supreme Court Approach to SEC Rule 10b-5 and Insider Trading*, 30 Emory L.J. 263 (1981); Hiler, Dirks v. SEC: *A Study in Cause and Effect*, 43 Md. L. Rev. 292 (1984); Langevoort, *Insider Trading and the Fiduciary Principle: A Post-*Chiarella *Restatement*, 70 Calif. L. Rev. 1 (1982); Levmore, *Securities and Secrets: Insider Trading and the Law of Contracts*, 68 Va. L. Rev. 117 (1982); Phillips, *Insider Trading Liability After* Dirks, 16 Rev. Sec. Reg. 841 (1983); Wang, *Trading on Material, Nonpublic Information on Impersonal Stock Markets: Who Is Harmed and Who Can Sue Whom under SEC Rule 10b-5?*, 54 S. Calif. L. Rev. 1217 (1981).

The decisions in *Chiarella* and *Dirks*, although embracing certain traditional principles that had been adopted by the lower courts and the SEC,[14] will render it more difficult for the SEC and private claimants to emerge victorious. Thus far, the SEC generally has met this challenge. In both *Chiarella* and *Dirks*, for example, the Court left unresolved the viability of the misappropriation theory.[15] After *Chiarella*, the SEC and the Justice Department successfully invoked this rationale. In *United States v. Newman*,[16] the Second Circuit upheld an indictment on the grounds that the defendants had allegedly misappropriated valuable nonpublic information entrusted to them in the utmost secrecy. The court found that the defendants had "sullied the reputations" of their employers, investment banks, "as safe repositories of client confidences" and had deceived the clients of these investment banks "whose takeover plans were keyed to target company stock prices fixed by market forces, not artificially inflated through purchases by purloiners of confidential information."[17] Investors trading contemporaneously in the securities markets in such misappropriation cases, however, may be left without a remedy. In *Moss v. Morgan Stanley*,[18] the Second Circuit, in affirming the dismissal of an action seeking monetary damages for violations of Section 10(b), held that the plaintiffs in order to recover must prove that the defendants breached a duty owed to them.[19]

Another example of the SEC's response to *Chiarella* was its promulgation, pursuant to Section 14(e) of the Williams Act, of Rule 14e-3 which seeks to deter, *inter alia*, insider and tippee trading in the tender offer setting.[20] Generally, the rule, with certain exceptions, contains broad "disclose or abstain from trading" as well as "antitipping" provisions.[21] In the release

---

14. *See, e.g.*, SEC v. Texas Gulf Sulphur Co., 401 F.2d 833 (2d Cir. 1968) (en banc), *cert. denied*, 394 U.S. 976 (1969) (imposing a fiduciary duty on corporate officers and directors to refrain from trading on material nonpublic information); *In re* Cady, Roberts & Co., 40 S.E.C. 907 (1961) (same).

15. 103 S. Ct. at 3255; 445 U.S. at 235–237.

16. 664 F.2d 12 (2d Cir. 1981).

17. *Id.* at 17–18.

18. [1983–1984 Transfer Binder] Fed. Sec. L. Rep. (CCH) ¶ 99,478 (2d Cir. 1983).

19. *Id.* at 94,975–76. *But see* O'Connor & Associates v. Dean Witter Reynolds, Inc., 529 F. Supp. 1179, 1187 (S.D.N.Y. 1981). For further discussion of these cases, see M. Steinberg, *supra* note 4, at § 3.04.

20. Securities Exchange Act Release No. 17120, 17 C.F.R. § 240.14e-3 (1985), [1980 Transfer Binder] Fed. Sec. L. Rep. (CCH) ¶ 82,646 (S.E.C.).

21. *Id.*, [1980 Transfer Binder] Fed. Sec. L. Rep. (CCH) ¶ 82,646, at 83,461–62. See M. Steinberg, *supra* note 4, at § 3.06 ("As adopted, with certain exceptions, Rule 14e-3 applies this disclose-or-abstain provision to the possession of material information relating to a tender offer where the person knows or has reason to know that the information is nonpublic and was received directly or indirectly from

adopting the rule, the Commission asserted that *Chiarella* did not limit its authority under Section 14(e) to prescribe such a mandate regulating insider trading in the tender offer context.[22]

The Commission has also responded tenaciously to the apparent limitations of *Dirks*. One route has been to embrace the quasi-insider principle[23] that received approbation in *Dirks*. Under this rationale, individuals enjoying a special relationship with the corporation—such as accountants, attorneys, consultants, and underwriters—may be viewed as insiders when they trade on material, nonpublic information that they legitimately received during the course of that relationship. As stated by the *Dirks* Court, "[t]he basis for recognizing this fiduciary duty is not simply that such persons acquired nonpublic corporate information, but rather that they have entered into a special confidential relationship in the conduct of the business of the enterprise and are given access to information solely for corporate purposes."[24] Another approach invoked by the Commission has been to make the showing of "benefit," required by *Dirks*, by proving that the insider made a "gift" of material nonpublic information to the tippee.[25] Relying upon language contained in *Dirks*, the SEC argues that "[t]he tip [by the insider] and [subsequent] trade [by the tippee] resemble trading by the insider himself followed by a gift of the profits to the recipient."[26]

Congress has also been active in this area by recently enacting the Insider Trading Sanctions Act.[27] Due to the difficulty in comprehensively defining

---

the offeror, the subject corporation, any of their affiliated persons, or any person acting on behalf of either company.").

22. [1980 Transfer Binder] Fed. Sec. L. Rep. (CCH) ¶ 82,646, at 83,456. The Commission in the release also asserted the continued viability of the misappropriation rationale under Section 10(b). *Id.* Rule 14e-3 has thus far been upheld by the courts. *See* O'Connor & Associates v. Dean Witter Reynolds, Inc., 529 F. Supp. 1179, 1188–1193 (S.D.N.Y. 1981). For commentary on Rule 14e-3, see M. Steinberg, *supra* note 4, at § 3.06; Gruenbaum, *The New Disclose or Abstain from Trading Rule: Has the SEC Gone Too Far?*, 5 Corp. L. Rev. 350 (1981); Heller, Chiarella, *SEC Rule 14e-3 and* Dirks: *"Fairness" versus Economic Theory*, 37 Bus. Law. 517 (1982); Note, *Private Causes of Action under SEC Rule 14e-3*, 51 Geo. Wash. L. Rev. 290 (1983); Note, *Trading on Material Nonpublic Information under Rule 14e-3*, 49 Geo. Wash. L. Rev. 539 (1981).

23. *See, e.g.*, SEC v. Lund, [1983–1984 Transfer Binder] Fed. Sec. L. Rep. (CCH) ¶ 99,495 (C.D. Cal. 1983).

24. 103 S. Ct. at 3261 n.14.

25. *See e.g.*, SEC v. Platt, [1984 Transfer Binder] Fed. Sec. L. Rep. (CCH) ¶ 91,420 (W.D. Okla.); SEC v. Thayer, 84 Civ. 0066 (S.D.N.Y. complaint filed Jan. 5, 1984).

26. 103 S. Ct. at 3266. The principles are discussed at length in M. Steinberg, *supra* note 4, at §§ 3.02-3.03.

27. See 16 Sec. Reg. & L. Rep. (BNA) 1243 (1984).

"insider trading," Congress elected to leave the further development of this concept to judicial interpretation. Among other provisions, the Act amends Section 21(d) of the Exchange Act to authorize the SEC to seek the imposition of a civil monetary penalty amounting to three times the profit received or loss avoided due to the violative conduct.[28]

---

28. *Id.* For further discussion, see M. Steinberg, Securities Regulation: Liabilities and Remedies § 3.05 (1984); Levine, *Insider Trading Act Broadens Enforcement Scope*, Legal Times (Wash.), September 10, 1984, at 17.

Private Litigation under Section 14(e) of the Williams Act

MARK J. LOEWENSTEIN*

I. INTRODUCTION

When Congress enacted the Williams Act[1] in 1968 to regulate tender offers, it included a broad antifraud provision, codified as Section 14(e)[2] of the Securities Exchange Act of 1934.[3] The courts have interpreted Section 14(e) with reference to Section 10(b),[4] the general antifraud provision of the

---

*Mark J. Loewenstein is associate professor of Law, University of Colorado School of Law. This chapter is reprinted with the permission of the publisher, © 1983 The Georgetown Law Journal Association, which published a somewhat different version of this article, Volume 71, No. 5 (June 1983).

1. 15 U.S.C. §§ 78m(d)-(e), 78n(d)-(f) (1976). The Williams Act is the popular name of Pub. L. No. 90-439, 82 Stat. 454 (1968), originally entitled: Full Disclosure of Corporate Equity Ownership and in Corporate Takeover Bids. The Act was passed in response to an increasing number of cash tender offers and the abuses perceived in those transactions. *See* S. Rep. No. 550, 90th Cong., 2d Sess. 2–3 [hereinafter cited as Senate Report], *reprinted in* 1968 U.S. Code Cong. & Ad. News 2811, 2812. The Act added a new Section 13(d) to the Securities Exchange Act of 1934, requiring certain disclosures by persons who acquire more than 10% (later amended to 5%) of any registered equity security, and a new Section 14(d) requiring that certain disclosures be made in connection with a tender offer. In addition, the Act added a new Section 13(e) to regulate purchases by an issuer of its own securities; a new Section 14(f) to require certain disclosures of specified changes in the board of directors of an acquired company; and Section 14(e), a broad antifraud rule applicable to all tender offers.

2. 15 U.S.C. § 78n(e) (1976).

3. 15 U.S.C. §§ 78a–78kk (1976) [hereinafter cited as Exchange Act].

4. Securities Exchange Act of 1934, § 10(b), 15 U.S.C. § 78j (1976). The federal courts have long recognized the existence of a private cause of action to enforce the proscriptions of Rule 10b-5. *See* Herman & MacLean v. Huddleston, 103 S. Ct.

Exchange Act, and they have relied on case law developed under Section 10(b) and Rule 10b-5[5] to establish the elements of a cause of action under 14(e).[6] Indeed, the courts have held that a private cause of action exists under Section 14(e), even though the statute does not expressly provide

---

683, 686–87 (1983). Kardon v. National Gypsum Co., 69 F. Supp. 512 (E.D. Pa. 1946), was the first case holding that a private remedy exists under Rule 10b-5. *Id.* at 514. In the years since *Kardon*, a considerable body of law has developed around Rule 10b-5. *See generally* A. Jacobs, The Impact of Rule 10b-5 (rev. ed. 1980); A. Bromberg & L. Lowenfels, Securities Fraud & Commodities Fraud (1982).

5. *See* 17 C.F.R. § 240.10b-5 (1983) which provides:

> It shall be unlawful for any person, directly or indirectly, by the use of any means or instrumentality of interstate commerce, or of the mails or of any facility of any national securities exchange, (1) to employ any device, scheme, or artifice to defraud, (2) to make any untrue statement of a material fact or to omit to state a material fact necessary in order to make the statements made, in the light of the circumstances under which they were made, not misleading, or (3) to engage in any act, practice, or course of business which operates or would operate as a fraud or deceit upon any person in connection with the purchase or sale of any security.

17 C.F.R. § 240.10b-5 (1985).

Section 14(e) provides:

> It shall be unlawful for any person to make any untrue statement of a material fact or omit to state any material fact necessary in order to make the statements made, in the light of the circumstances under which they are made, not misleading, or to engage in any fraudulent, deceptive, or manipulative acts or practices, in connection with any tender offer or request or invitation for tenders, or any solicitation of security holders in opposition to or in favor of any such offer, request, or invitation. The Commission shall, for the purposes of this subsection, by rules and regulations define, and prescribe means reasonably designed to prevent, such acts and practices as are fraudulent, deceptive, or manipulative.

Securities Exchange Act of 1934, § 14(e), 15 U.S.C. § 78n(e) (1976). The last sentence of Section 14(e) was added by the 1970 amendments to the Williams Act. Pub. L. No. 91-567, § 5, 84 Stat. 1497–98 (1970).

6. *See, e.g.*, Bell v. Cameron Meadows Land Co., 669 F.2d 1278, 1281 n.7 (9th Cir. 1982); H. K. Porter Co., Inc. v. Nicholson File Co., 482 F.2d 421, 425–26 (1st Cir. 1973); Electronic Specialty Co. v. International Controls Corp., 409 F.2d 937, 940-41 (2d Cir. 1969); Berman v. Gerber Prods. Co., 454 F. Supp. 1310, 1318, 1323–24 (W.D. Mich. 1978); Dyer v. Eastern Trust and Banking Co., 336 F. Supp. 890, 913-14 (D. Me. 1971). In *Dyer*, an early and influential decision in this area, the court wrote that "[a] sensible and coherent interpretation of the provisions of the two statutes mandates implication of a damage remedy under Section 14(e) corresponding to that available under Section 10(b). There is every reason to believe that Congress intended the remedies to be similar." 336 F. Supp. at 914. The court

for one, largely because a private cause of action has been recognized under Rule 10b-5.[7] Judicial developments under Rule 10b-5 occurring after the enactment of the Williams Act have influenced the way Section 14(e) is interpreted.

II. PRIVATE LITIGATION UNDER SECTION 14(e):
RULE 10b-5 COMPARED

The years since 1975 have seen several Supreme Court decisions restricting private damage actions under Rule 10b-5. The Court has held that scienter is a necessary element of a Section 10(b) violation,[8] that mere breaches of fiduciary duty are not contemplated within the section,[9] that silence in connection with the purchase or sale of a security cannot constitute a violation of Rule 10b-5 unless the defendant has some independent duty to disclose,[10] and that only purchasers and sellers of securities have standing to maintain private damage actions under Section 10(b) and Rule 10b-5.[11] These decisions rest primarily on an analysis of the language of

---

cited no authority for its observation that Congress intended the remedies to be similar, as, indeed, there is none.

7. *See generally* Loewenstein, *Section 14(e) of the Williams Act and the Rule 10-b(5) Comparisons*, 71 Geo. L.J. 1311, 1313–32 (1983). In Piper v. Chris-Craft Indus., Inc., 430 U.S. 1 (1977), the Supreme Court held that a defeated tender offeror did not have standing to maintain an implied cause of action for damages under Section 14(e). The Court reserved judgment on whether shareholder-offerees of the target corporation would have standing, *id*. at 42 n.28, or whether a suit in equity for injunctive relief would lie in favor of a tender offeror under Section 14(e). *Id*. at 47, n.33. The lower federal courts have held "that private damage actions may be inferred from Section 14(e) in favor of both tendering," *see* Bell v. Cameron Meadows Land Co., 669 F.2d 1278, 1281 n.7 (9th Cir. 1982), and nontendering shareholder-offerees, *see* Hurwitz v. R. B. Jones Corp., 76 F.R.D. 149, 160 (W.D. Mo. 1977), as well as option-traders, *see* O'Connor & Assoc. v. Dean Witter Reynolds, Inc., 529 F. Supp. 1179, 1193 (S.D.N.Y. 1982). The courts have also found an implied private action for injunctive relief in favor of target companies, Camelot Indus. Corp. v. Vista Resources, Inc., 535 F. Supp. 1174, 1181 (S.D.N.Y. 1982), and tender offerors, *see* Mobil Corp. v. Marathon Oil Co., 669 F.2d 366, 372 (6th Cir. 1981), *cert. denied*, 102 S. Ct. 1490 (1982).

8. Ernst & Ernst v. Hochfelder, 425 U.S. 185, 201 (1976).

9. Santa Fe Indus., Inc. v. Green, 430 U.S. 462, 479–80 (1977).

10. Chiarella v. United States, 445 U.S. 222, 233–34 (1980).

11. Blue Chip Stamps v. Manor Drug Stores, 421 U.S. 723, 754–55 (1974). The Court departed from a restrictive approach of interpreting the federal securities laws in its more recent decision in Herman & MacLean v. Huddleston, 103 S. Ct. 683 (1983). The Court held that an action may be maintained under Rule 10b-5 even if the conduct giving rise to the action would also support an action under

Section 10(b) and its legislative history.[12] But the message from the Supreme
Court is clear: the federal securities laws are not a panacea for all wrongdoing
in which securities are involved.[13] The lower federal courts have, for the
most part, heeded this message and reduced the importance of Rule 10b-
5 as a principal litigating weapon.[14] More important for present purposes,
the lower federal courts have applied this philosophy to other sections of
the federal securities laws, including Section 14(e), limiting the impact of
these sections as well.[15]

Section 11 of the Securities Act and that persons seeking to recover under Section
10(b) must prove their cause of action by a preponderance of the evidence only,
not by clear and convincing evidence. *Id.* at 690–93.

The Court's decision in United States v. Naftalin, 441 U.S. 768 (1979), might also
be viewed as a departure from its restrictive approach. In *Naftalin*, the Court held
that the proscriptions of Section 17(a) (1) of the Securities Act were applicable to
frauds perpetrated on brokers as well as "investors." *Id.* at 771-79. To the extent,
however, that the Court reached its conclusion by close attention to the language
and legislative history of Section 17(a), its opinion is entirely consistent with its
Section 10(b) decisions. *See* Steinberg, *Section 17(a) of the Securities Act of 1933
after* Naftalin *and* Redington, 68 Geo. L.J. 163 (1979).

    12. *Chiarella*, 445 U.S. at 233–34; *Santa Fe*, 430 U.S. at 477-80; *Ernst & Ernst*,
425 U.S. at 733–36.

    13. *See Santa Fe*, 430 U.S. at 478. The Court's reluctance to extend the use of
the federal securities laws is most evident in its cases deciding what is a "security"
for purposes of the federal securities laws. *See* Marine Bank v. Weaver, 455 U.S. 551,
555–61 (1982) (bank certificate of deposit and private profit-sharing agreement not
securities within meaning of Exchange Act); International Bhd. of Teamsters v.
Daniel, 439 U.S. 551, 558–70 (1979) (noncontributory, compulsory pension plan
was not a security); United Housing Found., Inc. v. Forman, 421 U.S. 837, 847–58
(1975) (shares issued by a nonprofit cooperative housing corporation not securities).

    14. *See, e.g.*, Feldman v. Simkins Indus., Inc., 679 F.2d 1229, 1303-04 (9th Cir.
1982) (minority shareholder without controlling interest or access to confidential
information not an "insider"); O'Brien v. Continental Ill. Nat'l Bank and Trust, 593
F.2d 54, 62–63 (7th Cir. 1979) (termination of trust or agency agreement not a
securities transaction); Hundahl v. United Benefit Life Ins. Co., 465 F. Supp. 1349,
1357 (N.D. Tex. 1979) (minority shareholders who did not respond to parent
corporation's tender offer not "sellers" within meaning of Rule 10b-5). *But cf.*
Goldberg v. Meridor, 567 F.2d 209, 220-21 (2d Cir. 1977), (corporation may sue
its directors and controlling stockholder under Section 10(b) for causing corporation to enter disadvantageous transaction without disclosing material facts), *cert.
denied*, 434 U.S. 1069 (1978). For a thoughtful treatment of the impact of the *Santa
Fe* decision, *see* Ferrara & Steinberg, *A Reappraisal of* Santa Fe: *Rule 10b-5 and the
New Federalism*, 129 U. Pa. L. Rev. 263 (1980).

    15. *See, e.g.*, Billard v. Rockwell Int'l Corp., 683 F.2d 51, 56 (2d Cir. 1982)
(applying *Santa Fe* definition of manipulation in tender offer context); Panter v.
Marshall Field & Co., 646 F.2d 271, 287–88 (7th Cir. 1981) (applying *Santa Fe*
treatment of breach of fiduciary duty in tender offer context); *cert. denied*, 454 U.S.

Consistent with this philosophy, the federal courts have held that scienter is a necessary element in a Section 14(e) action[16] and that a mere breach of fiduciary duty may not be a basis for an action under that section.[17] Based on principles established in other Rule 10b-5 litigation, the courts have also held that reliance is a necessary element of claims brought under Section 14(e).[18] These decisions analogize Section 14(e) to Rule 10b-5 in ways that may conflict with Congressional intent and sound jurisprudence, as an examination of each of these areas will demonstrate.

1092 (1981); Radol v. Thomas, 534 F. Supp. 1302, 1311 (S.D. Ohio 1982) (applying *Santa Fe* definition of manipulation in tender offer context). *See also* Abella v. Universal Leaf Tobacco, 546 F. Supp. 795, 803 (E.D. Va. 1982) (mere claim of breach of fiduciary duty does not lie under Section 14(e)); Hundahl v. United Benefit Life Ins. Co., 465 F. Supp. 1349, 1370 (N.D. Tex. 1979) (plaintiff's claim for damages under Section 14(e) dismissed on basis of Supreme Court decisions under federal antifraud laws); Bucher v. Shumway, [1979–1980 Transfer Binder] Fed. Sec. L. Rep. (CCH) ¶ 97,142 at 96,303 (S.D.N.Y. 1979) (allegation that defendant failed to disclose brech of fiduciary duty does not transform common law breach into basis for federal cause of action), *aff'd*, 622 F.2d 572 (2d Cir.), *cert. denied*, 449 U.S. 841 (1980); Altman v. Knight, 431 F. Supp. 309, 314 (S.D.N.Y. 1977) (*Santa Fe* dictates that claims amounting only to breaches of fiduciary duty should be decided under state law); Schreiber v. Burlington Northern, Inc., 568 F. Supp. 197 (D. Del. 1983), *aff'd*, [1984 Transfer Binder] Fed. Sec. L. Rep. (CCH) ¶ 91,407 (3d Cir. 1984) (attempt to characterize state law claims as violation of federal securities laws is a "ploy" foreclosed since *Santa Fe*).

16. *E.g.*, Bell v. Cameron Meadows Land Co., 669 F.2d 1278, 1281 (9th Cir. 1982); Lowenschuss v. Kane, 520 F.2d 255, 268 n.10 (2d Cir. 1975); Smallwood v. Pearl Brewing Co., 489 F.2d 579, 605–06 (5th Cir.), *cert. denied*, 419 U.S. 873 (1974); Chris-Craft Indus., Inc. v. Piper Aircraft Corp., 480 F.2d 341, 363–64 (2d Cir.), *cert. denied*, 414 U.S. 910 (1973); Broder v. Dane, 384 F. Supp. 1312, 1321 (S.D.N.Y. 1974); see E. Aranow, H. Einhorn & G. Berlstein, Developments in Tender Offers for Corporate Control 118-22 (1977).

17. *See supra* note 15.

18. *E.g.*, Panter v. Marshall Field & Co., 646 F.2d 271, 283–84 (7th Cir.), *cert. denied*, 454 U.S. 1092 (1981); Lewis v. McGraw, 619 F.2d 192, 195 (2d Cir.), *cert. denied*, 449 U.S. 951 (1980); Chris-Craft Indus., Inc. v. Piper Aircraft Corp., 480 F.2d 341, 373–75 (2d Cir.), *cert. denied*, 480 U.S. 341 (1973); Atchley v. Qonaar Corp., [1982 Transfer Binder] Fed. Sec. L. Rep. (CCH) ¶ 98,725 at 93,643 (N.D. Ill. 1982), *rev'd on other grounds*, 704 F.2d 355 (7th Cir. 1983); Hundahl v. United Benefit Life Ins. Co., 465 F. Supp. 1349, 1368–69 (N.D. Tex. 1979); Berman v. Gerber Prod. Co., 454 F. Supp. 1310, 1324–25 (W.D. Mich. 1978); Neuman v. Electronic Specialty Co., [1969–1970 Transfer Binder] Fed. Sec. L. Rep. (CCH) ¶ 92,591 at 92,748 (N.D. Ill. 1969). *But see* Bell v. Cameron Meadows Land Co., 669 F.2d 1278 (9th Cir. 1982); Clayton v. Skelley Oil Co., [1977–1978 Transfer Binder] Fed. Sec. L. Rep. (CCH) ¶ 96,269 at 92,747 (S.D.N.Y. 1977); McCloskey v. Epko Shoes, Inc., 391 F. Supp. 1279, 1283–84 (E.D. Pa. 1975); Petersen v. Federated Dev. Co., 387 F. Supp. 355, 359–60 (S.D.N.Y. 1974).

A. Scienter

In *Ernst & Ernst v. Hochfelder*,[19] the Supreme Court held that a private cause of action for damages under Section 10(b) and Rule 10b-5 will not lie in the absence of an allegation of scienter—that is, an intent to deceive, manipulate, or defraud.[20] This holding was based primarily on the language of Section 10(b): the words "manipulative or deceptive" are used in conjunction with "device or contrivance," suggesting that the section was intended to proscribe knowing or intentional misconduct. The Court attached particular significance to the word "manipulative," which, the Court said, "connotes intentional or willful conduct designed to deceive or defraud investors by controlling or artificially affecting the price of securities."[21] The Court found some support for its conclusion in the scant legislative history of Section 10(b)[22] and greater support in the overall scheme of the federal securities law.[23]

With respect to the securities laws in general, the Court in *Ernst v. Ernst* noted, for instance, that the language of Section 11 of the Securities Act, which permits recovery for negligent acts, differs considerably from the language of Section 10(b), suggesting that Section 10(b) cannot also cover negligent conduct.[24] Furthermore, the Court recognized that under the express civil remedy provisions of the Securities Act, which allow recovery for negligent conduct,[25] Congress imposed significant procedural safeguards

---

19. 425 U.S. 185 (1976).

20. *Id.* at 193. The Court has extended the holding of *Ernst & Ernst* to injunctive actions brought by the SEC. Aaron v. SEC, 446 U.S. 680, 687–95 (1980).

In *Ernst & Ernst*, the Court defined "scienter" as "a mental state embracing intent to deceive, manipulate or defraud." 425 U.S. at 193 n.12. The Court expressly left undecided the question of whether reckless behavior is sufficient to impose civil liability under Section 10(b) and Rule 10b-5. *Id.* The federal circuit courts that have ruled on this question have decided that recklessness satisfies the scienter requirement of *Ernst & Ernst. E.g.*, Hackbart v. Holmes, 675 F.2d 1114, 1117–18 (10th Cir. 1982); G. A. Thompson & Co. v. Partridge, 636 F.2d 945, 959 (5th Cir. 1981); Nelson v. Serwold, 576 F.2d 1332, 1337 (9th Cir.), *cert. denied*, 439 U.S. 970 (1978); Rolf v. Blyth, Eastman Dillon & Co., 570 F.2d 38, 44 (2d Cir.), *cert. denied*, 439 U.S. 1039 (1978). Given its narrowest reading, *Ernst & Ernst* holds that a defendant who is merely negligent does not have the mental state required to violate Section 10(b) and Rule 10b-5. This article uses scienter in that sense, i.e., a mental state embracing something more than simple negligence. *See generally* Bucklo, *Scienter and Rule 10b-5*, 67 Nw. U.L. Rev. 562 (1972).

21. *Ernst & Ernst*, 425 U.S. at 199.

22. *Id.* at 202–03.

23. *Id.* at 206–11.

24. *Id.*

25. *Id.* at 209–10.

but that similar procedural limitations do not exist for the judicially created private damage remedy under Section 10(b).[26] From this the Court concluded that extending Section 10(b) to cover negligent conduct would conflict with Congressional intent, because plaintiffs could bring causes of action under 10(b), rather than under the express liability provisions of the Securities Act, and thereby avoid the carefully drawn procedural limitations of the express liability provisions.[27]

In the course of the *Ernst & Ernst* decision, the Court conceded that, "[v]iewed in isolation, the language of subsection [(2) of Rule 10b-5] and arguably that of subsection [(3)] could be read as proscribing, respectively, any type of material misstatement or omission, and any course of conduct, that has the effect of defrauding investors, whether the wrongdoing was intentional or not."[28] This reading of the rule, advocated by the SEC in an amicus brief,[29] would have made the rule broader than the Court's reading of Section 10(b) and, therefore, would have exceeded the SEC's rulemaking authority under Section 10(b). For this reason, the Court could not accept the SEC's argument.[30]

The factors that convinced the Court that Section 10(b) requires an allegation of scienter are not present with respect to Section 14(e). The language of the first clause of Section 14(e), which provides that it is unlawful "to make any untrue statement of material fact or omit to state any material fact necessary in order to make the statements made, in the light of the circumstances under which they are made, not misleading," is not patterned after Section 10(b). Instead, this language of Section 14(e) is identical to that of Subsection (2) of Rule 10b-5, which the Court conceded in *Ernst & Ernst* could be read as covering unintentional wrongdoing,[31] and which the Court essentially read as covering negligent conduct when it construed very similar language in Section 17(a)(2) of the Securities Act.[32]

Based on the statutory language alone, a case might even be made for imposing absolute liability for misstatements and omissions in connection with tender offers. Language in the Securities Act's Section 11(a),[33] which is identical to Section 14(e), imposes absolute liability on the issuers of registered securities for misstatements and omissions in a registration state-

---

26. *Id.*
27. *Id.* at 210.
28. *Id.* at 212.
29. *Id.* at 187, 212.
30. *Id.* at 212–14. The Court also felt that the history of Rule 10b-5 indicated that it was intended to apply only when intentional misconduct was involved, *Id.* at 212 n.32.
31. *See supra* note 28 and accompanying text.
32. Aaron v. SEC, 446 U.S. 680 (1980).
33. 15 U.S.C. § 77k(a) (1976).

ment, subject to the limitations of Section 11(e).[34] Experts and certain others connected with a registration statement may also be liable for misstatements and omissions contained therein. Section 11(b)[35] provides a "due diligence" defense, indicating that the draftsmen of Section 11 believed that in the absence of some qualifying language, the language concerning misstatements and omissions, standing alone, imposes absolute liability.

The language of the first clause of Section 14(e) might also be compared to the second clause, which prohibits "fraudulent, deceptive, or manipulative acts or practices." If by Section 14(e)'s first clause Congress intended to prohibit only those misstatements or omissions that were accompanied by an intent to deceive, or scienter, then the section is redundant, because the acts and practices prohibited by the second clause include fraudulent misstatements and omissions. Traditional statutory interpretation would reject such a reading because the first clause would be rendered meaningless.[36] To give the two clauses independent significance, scienter cannot be a necessary element in the first clause. Thus, there is no basis for concluding that the language of Section 14(e) requires an allegation of scienter, if the plaintiff's cause of action is based on misstatements or omissions.

Just as the language of 10(b) and 14(e) differs, so does the legislative histories of them. The *Ernst & Ernst* Court noted that the legislative history of the Exchange Act was bereft of any explicit explanation of Congress's intent with respect to Section 10(b), but the Court was apparently persuaded by the few bits of relevant legislative history brought to its attention suggesting that Section 10(b) contemplated a scienter standard, not merely negligence.[37] Although the legislative history of Section 14(e) is not extensive, there is evidence that the first clause of Section 14(e) was not intended as a scienter provision. For instance, in explaining Section 14(e), the Senate Report of the bill said:

> Proposed subsection (e) would prohibit any misstatement or omission of material fact, or any fraudulent or manipulative acts or practices, in connection with any tender offer.... This provision would affirm the fact that persons engaged in making or opposing tender offers... are under an obligation to make full disclosure of material information to those with whom they deal.[38]

---

34. 15 U.S.C. § 77k(e) (1976) sets forth the measure of damages in actions based on Section 11(a). Under Section 11(a) a person who knew of the untruth or omission at the time he acquired a security may not maintain a suit. 15 U.S.C. § 77k(a) (1976).

35. 15 U.S.C. § 77k(b) (1976).

36. *See* Hart v. McLucas, 535 F.2d 516, 519 (9th Cir. 1976).

37. 425 U.S. at 201–06.

38. *See* Senate Report, *supra* note 1, at 10, 11. There is no indication that Section

The Senate Report, like the language of Section 14(e) itself, separates the prohibition against misstatements and omissions from the prohibition against fraudulent or manipulative acts or practices, and gives no indication that

---

14(e) was patterned after Rule 10b-5 or that Rule 10b-5 jurisprudence should govern the interpretation of Section 14(e).

Indeed the legislative history of the Williams Act, which is rather extensive because substantial hearings were held in both the Senate and the House, contains few references to Section 14(e). One interesting reference can be found in the written statement submitted to the Senate committee by William H. Painter, then professor of law at the University of Missouri at Kansas City. He pointed out the similarities and differences among the various antifraud provisions of the federal securities laws and noted, on the basis of that analysis, that the precise meaning of Section 14(e) was unclear. Full Disclosure of Corporate Equity Ownership and in Corporate Take-over Bids: Hearings on S. 510 before the Subcomm. on Securities of the Senate Comm. on Banking and Currency, 90th Cong., 1st Sess. 140–41 (1967) [hereinafter cited as 1967 Senate Hearings].

The notion that Congress intended Section 14(e) to be construed with reference to Rule 10b-5 is traceable, at least in part, to Judge Gignoux's opinion in Dyer v. Eastern Trust & Banking Co., 336 F. Supp. 890 (D. Me. 1971), which sets forth that conclusion.

In *Dyer*, an early and influential decision in this area, the court wrote that "[a] sensible and coherent interpretation of the provisions of the two statutes mandates implication of a damage remedy under Section 14(e) corresponding to that available under Section 10(b). There is every reason to believe that Congress intended the remedies to be similar." 336 F. Supp. at 914. The court cited no authority for its observation that Congress intended the remedies to be similar, as, indeed, there is none.

Judge Gignoux cited two district court opinions, Fabrikant v. Jacobellis, [1969–1970 Transfer Binder] Fed. Sec. L. Rep. (CCH) ¶ 92,686 (E.D.N.Y. 1970) and Neuman v. Electronic Specialty Co., [1969–1970 Transfer Binder] Fed. Sec. L. Rep. (CCH) ¶ 92,591 (N.D. Ill. 1969) as support for his decision. 336 F. Supp. at 914. *Fabrikant* was a decision on a motion to dismiss in which the court seemed to assume, without so stating, that a cause of action for damages existed under Section 14(e). ¶ 92,686 at 99,017–18. The court did not discuss the relationship between Section 14(e) and Rule 10b-5.

The *Neuman* court did, however, discuss that relationship and, based on the following language quoted from the House and Senate Reports describing Section 14(e), concluded that the provisions were to have the same interpretation:

> This provision would affirm the fact that persons engaged in making or op-posing tender offers or otherwise seeking to influence the decision of investors of the outcome of the tender offer are under an obligation to make full disclosure of material information to those with whom they deal.

¶ 92,591 at 98,705 (quoting Senate Report, *supra* note 1, and H.R. Rep. No. 1711, 90th Cong., 2nd Sess. 11 (1968). The court read this to mean that Congress intended "to 'affirm' the applicability to tender offers of the standards of disclosure in Rule

the misstatements or omissions had to be made knowingly, or with an intent to deceive, or with any other specific mental state.[39]

The legislation, when viewed as a whole, together with relevant statements made during the Senate hearings,[40] does not support the conclusion

---

10b-5." ¶ 92,591 at 98,705. *Neuman* may have ascribed a greater meaning to the word "affirm" than it can reasonably bear, since nowhere do the House or Senate Reports mention Rule 10b-5. A more plausible reading of the Reports is that Congress was relating Section 14(e) to the rest of the Williams Act, "affirming" that a failure to disclose under Section 14(d), for instance, has consequence, *viz.*, such failure is also made unlawful under Section 14(e). *See also* Judge Friendly's opinion in Electronic Specialty Co. v. International Controls Corp., 409 F.2d 937, 940–41 (2d Cir. 1969), which asserted that Section 14(e) in effect applies Rule 10b-5 to tender offers and which has been influential in the development of the notion that Congress intended Section 14(e) to be construed with reference to Rule 10b-5. *See generally* Loewenstein, *Section 14(e) of the Williams Act and the Rule 10b-5 Comparisons,* 71 Geo. L.J. 1311 (1983).

39. *Id.*

40. During the course of the Senate hearings, a panel of securities law experts, consisting of Arthur Fleischer, Jr., and Professors Stanley A. Kaplan, Robert H. Mundheim, and William H. Painter, appeared before the subcommittee. At one point, Professor Kaplan commented on what he perceived to be a significant problem: the "increasing tendency on the part of management in office to feel that it is able to engage almost on its own in a series of efforts to continue its own control arrangements." 1967 Senate Hearings, *supra* note 78, at 125. Professor Mundheim then commented: "I would say in that connection that I would certainly favor [Section 14(e)]. I think that [it] is very salutary and gets to the kind of problem you are talking about." *Id.* This suggests that, at least for Professor Mundheim, Section 14(e) represented something more than a garden-variety antifraud provision. *See also id.* at 131 (statement of Arthur Fleischer, Jr.).

Professor Painter's prepared remarks pointed out the differing language among the various antifraud provisions of the securities laws and asked whether the language of these various provisions meant the same thing. *Id.* at 140–41. Nothing in the legislative history suggests an answer to Professor Painter's query.

Finally, references can be found in the legislative history suggesting that the Williams Act was patterned after the laws and rules governing proxy solicitation. During the Senate debate, for instance, Senator Javitz remarked: "The Senator [Williams] represents to the Senate, and I accept his representation fully, that this [bill] is analogous to the proxy rules, so that very much the same principles obtain as to what the British call a takeover, as to a proxy fight by a group of stockholders." 113 Cong. Rec. 24,665 (1967). Senator Williams responded: "This legislation is patterned on the present law and the regulations which govern proxy contests." *Id. See also* Senate Report, *supra* note 1, at 2811–13; 1967 Senate Hearings, *supra* note 78, at 16 (remarks of SEC Chairman Manuel F. Cohen).

These references, together with the remarkable absence of any affirmative indication in the legislative history that Section 14(e) was intended to incorporate Rule 10b-5 jurisprudence into the Williams Act, suggest that Section 14(e) should be construed independently of Rule 10b-5.

reached by several lower courts that Section 14(e) was intended to incorporate the proscriptions of Rule 10b-5 into tender offer law. The Williams Act is not simply another piece of antifraud legislation. Rather, the Act seeks to regulate tender offer contests by positive means: the accumulation of more than 5 percent of a class of registered securities must be disclosed;[41] a tender offer may not be made unless certain disclosures are filed with the SEC;[42] shareholders who tender pursuant to a tender offer are afforded certain withdrawal and proration rights;[43] and if a tender offeror increases the consideration offered to shareholders, the increased consideration must be paid to those who tendered prior to the announced increase.[44] By prohibiting material misstatements and omissions, Section 14(e) serves as more than an antifraud provision; it gives meaning to the disclosure provisions in the same way that a prohibition against material misstatements and omissions in Section 11(a) of the Securities Act gives meaning to the disclosure requirements of Section 7.[45] Like the disclosure provisions of the Securities Act, the disclosure provisions of the Williams Act are intended to do more than merely prohibit fraud.

If anything, the legislative history indicates that the Williams Act should be construed with reference to the proxy rules. Several statements made during the hearings support this view,[46] as do statements made by Senator Harrison Williams (D-N.J.), the Act's principal sponsor, on the floor of the Senate during debates on the Act. For example, Senator Williams stated: "What this bill would do is to provide the same kind of disclosure requirements which now exist, for example, in contests through proxies for controlling ownership in a company.... This legislation is patterned on the present law and the regulations which govern proxy contests."[47] Moreover, reference to the proxy rules is logical as proxy contests are, of course, another means by which one might gain control of a company. Materially false or misleading proxy statements violate Rule 14a-9(a)[48] of the rules

---

41. 15 U.S.C. § 78m(d) (1976).

42. 15 U.S.C. § 78n(d) (1976).

43. 15 U.S.C. § 78n(d)(5), (6) (1976).

44. 15 U.S.C. § 78n(d)(7) (1976).

45. 15 U.S.C. § 77(g) (1976). *See supra* note 38.

46. *See supra* note 40.

47. 113 Cong. Rec. 24665 (1967). *See also supra* note 40 and Judge Friendly's observation comparing tender offers and proxy contests in Electronic Specialty Co. v. International Controls Corp., 409 F.2d 937, 948 (1969).

48. Rule 14a-9(a) provides:

> No solicitation subject to this regulation shall be made by means of any proxy statement, form of proxy, notice of meeting or other communication, written or oral, containing any statement which, at the time and in the light of the circumstances under which it is made, is false or misleading with respect to any material fact necessary in order to make the statements therein not false

adopted by the SEC under Section 14(a) of the Exchange Act and may form the basis of a private damage action. The courts generally have not insisted that plaintiffs allege and prove that defendants acted with scienter in actions based on Rule 14a-9.[49]

The leading case discussing whether scienter is a necessary element in a private damage action based on Rule 14a-9 is *Gerstle v. Gamble-Skogmo, Inc.*,[50] a 1973 opinion of the Second Circuit authored by Judge Friendly. The court concluded that scienter was not required under Rule 14a-9, noting as support several differences between Section 14(a), on the one hand, and Section 10(b) and Rule 10b-5 on the other hand—differences that are equally applicable to a comparison of Section 14(e) and Rule 10b-5. For instance, the *Gerstle* court first concluded that the statutory language of Section 14(a), unlike that of Section 10(b), does not emphasize the prohibition of fraudulent conduct but rather indicates a Congressional concern with "protection of the outsider whose proxy is being solicited."[51] Similarly, at least with respect to material misstatements and omissions, Section 14(e) is not concerned with fraudulent conduct, but with protecting shareholders confronted with a tender offer.[52]

Second, the court noted in *Gerstle* that although a negligence standard in Rule 10b-5 would undercut the express civil liability provisions of the securities laws,[53] reading Rule 14a-9 as not requiring scienter is completely compatible with the statutory scheme.[54] The express civil liability provision that concerned the court was Section 18[55] of the Exchange Act, which provides a private right of action to persons who purchase or sell a security in reliance upon a material misstatement or omission contained in a document filed with the SEC. A defense is provided under Section 18 if the defendant "acted in good faith and had no knowledge that such statement was false or misleading."[56] Arguably, a negligence standard under Rule 14a-

---

> or misleading or necessary to correct any statement in any earlier communication with respect to the solicitation of a proxy for the same meeting or subject matter which has become false or misleading.

17 C.F.R. § 240.14a-9 (1983).

49. Gould v. American-Hawaiian S. S. Co., 535 F.2d 761, 777–78 (3d Cir. 1976); Gerstle v. Gamble-Skogmo, Inc., 478 F.2d 1281, 1298–1301 (2d Cir. 1973). *But see* Adams v. Standard Knitting Mills, Inc., 623 F.2d 422, 428–31 (6th Cir.), *cert. denied*, 449 U.S. 1067 (1980) (scienter should be an element of liability in private suits under the proxy rules as they apply to outside accountants).

50. 478 F.2d 1281 (2d Cir. 1973).

51. *Id.* at 1299.

52. *Piper*, 430 U.S. at 35.

53. 478 F.2d at 1299. *See also Ernst & Ernst*, 425 U.S. at 210.

54. 478 F.2d at 1299 n.18.

55. 15 U.S.C. § 78r (1976).

56. *Id.*

9 would be inconsistent with the Congressional intent, expressed in Section 18, of providing a good faith defense.[57] Nevertheless, the court found no incompatibility, because Section 18 applies to any document filed with the SEC, while Section 14(a) was specifically directed at proxy regulation, and because most of the documents filed pursuant to Section 18 are not distributed to stockholders for the purpose of inducing action.[58] These distinctions apply with equal force to Section 14(e). Applying a negligence standard to the first clause of Section 14(e) in the face of the higher standard under Section 18 can be rationalized on another basis as well: Section 14(e) may be violated in the absence of a purchase or sale of a security, which is a necessary prerequisite to an action based on Section 18.[59]

Finally, the court in *Gerstle* assessed the effect of permitting a negligence standard under Section 14(a), again comparing it to Rule 10b-5. In concluding that negligence was the appropriate standard for actions based on Section 14(a), the court said:

> [A] broad standard of culpability here will serve to reinforce the high duty of care owed by a controlling corporation to minority shareholders in the preparation of a proxy statement seeking their acquiescence in this sort of transaction, a consideration which is particularly relevant since liability in this case is limited to the stockholders whose proxies were solicited. While "privity" is not required for most actions under the securities laws, its existence may bear heavily on the appropriate standard of culpability.[60]

The court contrasted this assessment with the effect of allowing a negligence standard under Rule 10b-5, which, the court surmised, would deter the laudable corporate policy of publicly disclosing important business and financial developments. Although the court's conjecture regarding Rule 10b-5 may be questioned,[61] its conclusion with respect to Section 14(a) seems sound and equally applicable to Section 14(e).

---

57. It is not clear that Section 18(a) is a scienter provision. Professor Loss has referred to plaintiff's burden of proof under Section 18(a) as "a first cousin to *scienter*." 3 L. Loss, Securities Regulation 1752 (2d ed. 1961). In any event, it clearly requires something more than negligence. *Ernst & Ernst*, 425 U.S. at 209 n.28 ("Each of the provisions of the 1934 Act that expressly create civil liability [other than Section 16(b)] . . . contains a state-of-mind condition requiring something more than negligence.").

58. 478 F.2d at 1299, n.18.

59. The same may, of course, be said with respect to proxy solicitations.

60. 478 F.2d at 1300 (footnote omitted).

61. The New York Stock Exchange rules require listed companies to promptly release to the public material information. New York Stock Exchange Company Manual, § A-6. Thus, for listed companies, the incentive to release information is

Providing a negligence standard under the first clause of Section 14(e) is particularly appropriate since an obvious use of this provision would be in suits by target stockholders against target management claiming that a tender offer was defeated as a result of management's allegedly false statements.[62] In such a suit, a number of factors justify a strict standard of liability: requiring a high duty of care is not unreasonable because management owes a fiduciary duty to its stockholders;[63] individuals in management would gain personally if the tender offer is defeated, and, therefore, they should proceed cautiously when advising stockholders,[64] and management is under no obligation to express any opinion with respect to a tender offer, so that when it undertakes to do so it should exercise care.[65]

---

unaffected by the standard of culpability in a subsequent fraud action. *See generally* Industrial Fund, Inc. v. McDonnell Douglas Corp., 474 F.2d 514, 521–22 (10th Cir. 1973) (recognizing corporate duty to disclose, but holding that timing of disclosure is subject to the business judgment rule); Vaughan, *Timing of Disclosure*, 13 Rev. Sec. Reg. 911 (1980); Bauman, *Rule 10b-5 and the Corporation's Affirmative Duty to Disclose,* 67 Geo. L.J. 935 (1979); Allen, *The Disclosure Obligation of Publicly Held Corporations in the Absence of Insider Trading*, 25 Mercer L. Rev. 479 (1974).

62. As a result of the decision in Panter v. Marshall Field & Co., 646 F.2d 271, 286 (7th Cir. 1981), the shareholders' cause of action is contingent upon an offer actually being made.

63. *See* Chris-Craft Indus. Inc. v. Piper Aircraft Corp., 480 F.2d 341, 363 (2d Cir.); Swanson v. American Consumer Indus., Inc., 415 F.2d 1326, 1331–32 (7th Cir. 1969).

64. The personal gain is the retention of a corporate office, which is of value even to directors who are not otherwise employed by the company. *See* Panter v. Marshall Field & Co., 646 F.2d 271, 300 (7th Cir. 1981) (Cudahy, C. J., dissenting). The courts have held that this personal interest does not create a conflict of interest that would shift the burden of proof to management to justify its actions. Treadway Companies, Inc. v. Care Corp., 638 F.2d 357, 382 (2d Cir. 1980). *See generally* Lipton, *Takeover Bids in the Target's Boardroom*, 35 Bus. Law. 101 (1979); Lipton, *Takeover Bids in the Target's Boardroom: An Update after One Year*, 36 Bus. Law. 1017 (1981). However, given the delicate situation in which management finds itself, it is entirely appropriate to require management to proceed with due care and to hold management responsible if it acts negligently.

65. Rule 14e-2 provides:

(a) *Position of subject company.* As a means reasonably designed to prevent fraudulent, deceptive or manipulative practices within the meaning of the Act, the subject company, no later than 10 business days from the date the tender offer is first published or sent or given, shall publish, send or give to security holders a statement disclosing that the subject company:

(1) Recommends acceptance or rejection of the bidder's tender offer;

(2) Expresses no opinion and is remaining neutral toward the bidder's tender offer; or

Damage actions might also be brought by target stockholders against the bidder alleging material misstatements or omissions. These actions may include allegations that the bidder sought to discourage stockholders from tendering to a rival bidder or, for some reason, to itself,[66] or that the bidder made a misrepresentation in its tender offer materials regarding the value of the deal to the stockholders.[67] In any of these situations, liability should be imposed even if the misstatment or omission was only negligent, since a bidder who seeks to discourage tenders to a rival bidder is, in some respects, like target management seeking to discourage its stockholders from tendering to a bidder. Like management, the dissuading bidder stands to gain from successful influence, and, like management, the dissuading bidder is under no obligation to make any statements regarding its rival. Although the bidder may not owe a fiduciary duty to the stockholder-offerees, these other factors suggest that, like management, a tender offeror should be held to a high standard of care in its communications with target stockholders. If the bidder seeks to discourage certain stockholders from tendering to itself, as might happen when the bidder has arranged to purchase a sufficient number of shares from a select group of insiders,[68] the bidder must have acted intentionally, and thus the question of the appropriate standard is mooted.

Finally, if the offering materials include a material misrepresentation, a case can be made that liability ought to be imposed without regard to fault, at least with respect to those matters within the knowledge or control of the bidder. If, for instance, the bidder misrepresents the value of securities to be delivered to stockholders in a post-offer merger, the effect of such a misrepresentation is analogous to a misrepresentation by an issuer in a registration statement. In both cases, the investor is asked to make an in-

---

(3) Is unable to take a position with respect to the bidder's tender offer.

Such statement shall also include the reason(s) for the position (including the inability to take a position) disclosed therein.

17 C.F.R. § 240.14e-2 (1985).

66. Petersen v. Federated Dev. Co., 387 F. Supp. 355, 358–60 (S.D.N.Y. 1974) (nontendering shareholder may maintain action against successful bidder who allegedly discouraged him from tendering because bidder wanted only stock from specific group of shareholders with a controlling interest).

67. Osofsky v. Zipf, 645 F.2d 107, 115 (2d Cir. 1981) (tendering shareholders may maintain an action against successful bidder who misrepresented value of preferred stock to be issued in merger); McCloskey v. Epko Shoes, Inc., 391 F. Supp. 1279, 1282 (E.D. Pa. 1975) (nontendering shareholders may maintain suit against bidder who allegedly overstated the value of securities being exchanged and understated consideration received by insiders in prior block purchase).

68. See supra note 66.

vestment decision based on inaccurate or incomplete information furnished by a party who seeks a certain response from the investor. Section 11(a) of the Securities Act imposes virtually absolute liability on the issuer for deficiencies in the registration statement, presumably because some party must be responsible for the contents of a registration statement.[69] This same rationale would apply to tender offer materials prepared by the bidder.

B. Reliance

As a general proposition, proof of reliance is a necessary element of a private damage action under Rule 10b-5. This requirement arose because Rule 10b-5 jurisprudence has been shaped with reference to the common law action of deceit.[70] The common law insists that the plaintiff prove reliance to establish a causal connection between the wrongful conduct and the resulting damage, a requirement typical in the law of torts.[71]

Many Rule 10b-5 actions would have failed, however, if the courts had not recognized the difficulties inherent in a strict adherence to the common law reliance requirement. Thus, when the Rule 10b-5 cause of action is based on a failure to disclose or on an omission, as opposed to a misrepresentation, the Supreme Court has said "positive proof" of reliance is not necessary.[72] Rather, a plaintiff need only prove that the facts withheld would be material to a reasonable investor.[73] The obligation to disclose combined with materiality establishes the necessary causation in fact.[74]

Similarly, the courts have been troubled by the reliance requirement when the suit is a class action[75] or when the plaintiff alleges that he "relied" on the integrity of the marketplace in making his investment decision.[76] In each of these instances, the courts have also been willing to find exceptions to the traditional reliance requirement.[77] The rationale for these exceptions

---

69. *See supra* note 34.

70. L. Loss, *supra* note 57, at 1430–44; A. Jacobs, Litigation and Practice under Rule 10b-5 1–6 (1981).

71. *See* W. Prosser, Law of Torts 714-20 (4th ed. 1971).

72. Affiliated Ute Citizens v. United States, 406 U.S. 128, 152–53 (1972).

73. *Id.* at 153–54.

74. *Id.* at 154. The Fifth Circuit has interpreted *Affiliated Ute* as holding that a material nondisclosure creates a presumption of reliance that may be rebutted by the defendant. Shores v. Sklar, 647 F.2d 462, 468 (5th Cir. 1981), *cert. denied*, 103 S. Ct. 722 (1983); Rifkin v. Crow, 574 F.2d 256, 261 (5th Cir. 1978).

75. Shores v. Sklar, 647 F.2d 462, 464 (5th Cir. 1981); Blackie v. Barrack, 524 F.2d 891, 906 (9th Cir. 1975), *cert. denied*, 429 U.S. 816 (1976).

76. Shores v. Sklar, 647 F.2d 462, 464 (5th Cir. 1981). *See generally* Note, *The-Fraud-on-the-Market Theory*, 95 Harv. L. Rev. 1143 (1982).

77. *See* cases cited *supra* note 75 and *infra* note 78.

has generally proceeded from a perceived need to simplify the proof of reliance in the given action.[78]

Because early Section 14(e) cases analogized the private damage action thereunder to Rule 10b-5 actions, proof of reliance was assumed to be an element of the Section 14(e) plaintiff's cause of action.[79] The courts have not been unanimous in requiring proof of reliance, and some courts have carved out exceptions to the rule.[80] A few prominent decisions, however, such as *Lewis v. McGraw*[81] and *Panter v. Marshall Field & Co.*,[82] have turned on the absence of reliance. To the extent that the courts in these cases failed to explain *why* reliance must be shown, the opinions may be criticized. Therefore, they provide a framework for discussing the applicability of reliance in Section 14(e) actions.

Lewis v. McGraw arose out of the aborted effort of American Express to take over McGraw-Hill.[83] After the McGraw-Hill board rejected as "reckless," "illegal," and "improper" an American Express merger offer, American Express announced its intention to make a cash tender offer for any and all McGraw-Hill stock.[84] This tender offer was never made, however, and was replaced with a new proposal, submitted to the McGraw-Hill board.[85] The new offer, which was to take the form of a tender offer to McGraw-Hill stockholders, provided for a substantially higher price than the first offer rejected by the McGraw-Hill board but would not become effective unless McGraw-Hill's management agreed not to oppose it by "propaganda, lobbying or litigation."[86] This offer, too, was resisted by the McGraw-Hill board and subsequently expired by its own terms.[87] The plaintiffs' action, brought on behalf of McGraw-Hill stockholders, alleged that public statements by the McGraw-Hill board were false and misleading and resulted in American Express failing to consummate the tender offer.[88] This, in turn, allegedly

---

78. *See* Panter v. Marshall Field & Co., 646 F.2d 271, 284 (7th Cir. 1981); Kohn v. American Metal Climax, Inc., 458 F.2d 255, 290 (3d Cir.) (Adams, J., concurring in part, dissenting in part), *cert. denied*, 409 U.S. 874 (1972); Fischer v. Wolfinbarger, 55 F.R.D. 129, 132 (W.D. Ky. 1971); R. Jennings & H. Marsh, Jr., Securities Regulation 1049–53 (5th ed. 1982). *See also* Mills v. Electric Auto-Lite Co., 396 U.S. 375, 384–85 (1970).

79. *See supra* note 18 and accompanying text.

80. *See supra* note 18.

81. 619 F.2d 192 (2d Cir.), *cert. denied*, 449 U.S. 951 (1980).

82. 646 F.2d 271 (7th Cir. 1981).

83. *Lewis*, 619 F.2d at 193.

84. *Id.* at 194.

85. *Id.*

86. *Id.*

87. *Id.*

88. *Id.*

damaged the plaintiff class, because it denied the class the opportunity to tender at a price substantially above the market price.[89]

The district court in *Lewis* dismissed the plaintiffs' action because the complaint failed to allege that the plaintiffs relied on the defendants' misstatements and omissions.[90] The Second Circuit affirmed, reasoning that since a tender offer was never made for McGraw-Hill stock, the plaintiffs could not have relied on the defendants' misstatements in deciding whether to tender.[91] Therefore, because reliance could not be demonstrated, no cause of action could be stated under Section 14(e).

Although the outcome in *Lewis* may have been correct, the court painted with too broad a brush. The opinion seems to require that any damage a Section 14(e) plaintiff suffers must arise in connection with his decision to tender. Section 14(e) is, however, broader than the common law action of deceit.[92] For instance, the section prohibits fraudulent and manipulative acts—that is, acts which might damage target stockholders whether or not the decision to tender is influenced.

Furthermore, the court's decision in *Lewis* makes proof of reliance the *sine qua non* in Section 14(e) actions, failing to recognize that reliance is important only to establish causation. If a link between the plaintiff's loss and the defendant's violation of the statute can be shown, it should not matter if reliance is present. In *Lewis*, causation of a sort was alleged. The defendants' resistance to the final American Express offer prevented the offer from going forward and denied stockholders the opportunity to tender at an attractive price. The real problem with the plaintiffs' complaint was the lack of any causal link between the defendants' alleged misstatements and the plaintiffs' loss. The tender offer failed to materialize not because the defendants made false and misleading statements but simply because

---

89. *Id.*

90. Lewis v. McGraw, 495 F. Supp. 27, 32 (S.D.N.Y. 1979).

91. 619 F.2d at 195.

92. The Supreme Court recently made a similar observation with respect to Rule 10b-5. In Herman & MacLean v. Huddleston, 103 S. Ct. 683 (1983), the Court held that the common law rule that fraud must be proved by clear and convincing evidence would not govern actions under Rule 10b-5. *Id.* at 690-92. In rejecting the common law rule, the Court reasoned:

> [T]he antifraud provisions of the securities laws are not coextensive with common law doctrines of fraud. Indeed, an important purpose of the federal securities statutes was to rectify perceived deficiencies in the available common law protections by establishing higher standards of conduct in the securities industry.

Id. at 691.

the defendants resisted it. Management's resistance of a hostile tender offer, standing alone, does not violate Section 14(e).[93]

Panter v. Marshall Field & Co.[94] presented facts similar to *Lewis*: an announced tender offer was withdrawn before it became effective as a result of vigorous resistance by target management.[95] As in *Lewis*, the disappointed shareholders filed a class action against the target company and its directors, alleging that the defendants' actions deprived the plaintiffs of the opportunity to tender their shares.[96] In *Panter*, however, the plaintiffs also alleged that they would have sold their shares in the market but for their reliance on the defendants' false and misleading statements, which caused them to retain their shares.[97] Nevertheless, the plaintiffs' action failed.

Relying heavily on *Lewis*, the Seventh Circuit disposed of the lost tender offer opportunity claim, stating that the requisite element of reliance was lacking.[98] The *Panter* court also rejected the plaintiffs' claim that they were unlawfully persuaded not to sell into the market, holding simply that Section 14(e) does not provide a damage remedy for misrepresentations or omissions if the proposed tender offer never becomes effective.[99] Although this holding would appear to make the decision one in which reliance was not a pivotal issue, the reasoning of the opinion has a significant impact on the reliance issue. To reach its conclusion that Section 14(e) does not apply if a tender offer does not become effective, the court reasoned that the proscriptions of Section 14(e), at least in private damage actions, are limited to protecting a shareholder faced with a decision to tender or retain his shares.[100] This narrow reading of the purpose of the Williams Act, Section

---

93. *See* Panter v. Marshall Field & Co., 646 F.2d 271, 300 (7th Cir. 1981). *See generally* Lipton, *Takeover Bids in the Target's Boardroom*, 35 Bus. Law. 101 (1979); Lipton, *Takeover Bids in the Target's Boardroom: An Update after One Year*, 36 Bus. Law. 1017 (1981).

94. 646 F.2d 271 (7th Cir. 1981).

95. *Id.* at 281.

96. *Id.* at 277.

97. *Id.* at 285.

98. *Id.* at 283–85.

99. *Id.* at 285.

100. The court reasoned first that the language of Section 14(e), which applies to conduct "in connection with any tender offer or request or invitation for tenders, or any solicitation of security holders in opposition to or in favor of any such offer, request or invitation," suggests that an effective offer must come into existence. Second, the legislative history indicates that the intent of Congress was to afford a measure of protection to shareholders faced with a tender offer decision. Finally, the court noted the trend of Supreme Court cases that have "continually limited the federal remedy in private federal securities actions." For these reasons, the court denied relief when the offer does not become effective. *Id.* at 285–86.

14(e) in particular, has an impact on the reliance issue because, if the court was correct, the type of damage a shareholder can suffer as a result of a violation of Section 14(e) is limited to the loss he may suffer as a result of an incorrect investment decision under the pressure of a tender offer. This type of loss would naturally be caused by some type of reliance. But if, on the other hand, the purposes of the Williams Act are broader and include protection of shareholders from the effects of false and misleading statements in the absence of reliance, then reliance is not necessarily the sole causal link between the violation and the loss.

In *Panter*, the Seventh Circuit cited legislative history to support its narrow reading of the purposes of the Williams Act.[101] None of the legislative history cited by the court related directly to Section 14(e); rather, it was directed to the disclosure provisions of the Act.[102] Congress was apparently concerned with more than disclosure, however, as the substantive provisions of the Act noted above demonstrate.[103] Section 14(e), which prohibits any fradulent, manipulative, or deceptive act or practice is also concerned with more than disclosure.[104] In short, Congress was concerned with the "industrial warfare" that results when a tender offer is announced and the damage to shareholders that may ensue.[105] Surely management's misleading statements made to resist a hostile tender offer are part of that "industrial warfare" whether or not the tender offer becomes effective. To the extent shareholders act on those statements, surely they may be damaged.[106]

---

101. *Id.*

102. *Id.* at 286.

103. *See supra* notes 41–48 and accompanying text.

104. During hearings on the 1970 amendments to the Williams Act, Senator Williams asked the SEC to submit a memorandum describing the problem areas it would address if granted rulemaking authority under Section 14(e). The problems delineated by the Commission included areas other than disclosure problems and thus demonstrate that the Commission has long held the view that Section 14(e) deals with more than misrepresentations and omissions. Additional Consumer Protection in Corporate Takeovers and Increasing the Securities Act Exemptions for Small Businessmen: Hearings before the Subcommittee on Securities of the Senate Committee on Banking and Currency, 91st Cong., 2d Sess. 12 (1970) [hereinafter cited as 1970 Senate Hearings].

105. The use of the term "industrial warfare" to describe tender offer battles appears from time to time in the course of the legislative history of the Williams Act. *See, e.g.,* 1967 Senate Hearings, *supra* note 38, at 178.

106. *See* Berman v. Gerber Prods. Co., 454 F. Supp. 1310, 1320 (W.D. Mich. 1978). Shareholders as a whole are disadvantaged by a rule which exempts pre-offer statements from the antifraud provisions of Section 14(e). As Judge Cudahy, dissenting in *Panter*, pointed out:

> The type of rule which the majority advocates is simply an invitation to incumbent management to make whatever claims and assertions may be ex-

Another difficulty with *Panter* is that while shareholders may still have a claim for damages against their management for misleading statements made during a preeffective period if an offer is subsequently made,[107] a damage claim will not be available to the defeated bidder.[108] Thus, the decision in *Panter* favors management vis-à-vis the potential bidder and runs contrary to the neutrality principle that Congress sought to achieve in the legislation.[109]

The proper approach to the reliance issue must recognize two principles. First, Section 14(e) is broader than the common law deceit action; second, reliance is relevant only insofar as it is needed to establish causation—if causation can otherwise be established, lack of reliance ought not dispose of a claim under Section 14(e). The judicial decisions supporting these principles are sound because they further shareholder protection in a way that favors neither management nor bidders.[110] Under these principles, management is not inhibited from resisting a tender offer but is prohibited from resisting by improper means only. Bidders are not liable for every material misstatement or omission, only those that cause damage to shareholder-offerees. Finally, reliance remains an element of the plaintiff's cause of action if the plaintiff alleges that the misstatement or omission affected his investment decision.

C. Breach of Fiduciary Duty

Since the Supreme Court's 1977 decision in *Sante Fe Industries, Inc. v. Green*,[111] a cause of action under Rule 10b-5 must allege conduct that "can

---

pedient to force withdrawal of an offer. Management could speak without restraint knowing that once withdrawal is forced there is no Securities Act liability for deception practiced before withdrawal took place. Such a rule provides a major loophole for escaping the provisions of Section 14(e) and obviously frustrates the remedial purpose of the Act.

646 F.2d at 310 (Cudahy, J., dissenting).

107. 646 F.2d at 285; *see* Lewis v. McGraw, 619 F.2d 192, 195 (2d Cir. 1980).

108. Piper v. Chris-Craft Indus., Inc., 430 U.S. 1, 41–42 (1977).

109. At several points in the legislative history, Senator Williams and others made it clear that the intent of the Act is to favor neither incumbent management nor the bidder. *See, e.g.*, 113 Cong. Rec. 24,664 (1967) (remarks of Senator Williams); Senate Report, *supra* note 1, at 2813 ("The bill avoids tipping the balance of regulation either in favor of management or in favor of the person making the takeover bid.").

110. *See, e.g.*, Bell v. Cameron Meadows Land Co., 669 F.2d 1278, 1283–84 (9th Cir. 1982); Clayton v. Skelly Oil Co., [1977–1978 Transfer Binder] Fed. Sec. L. Rep. (CCH) ¶ 96,269 at 92,747–48 (S.D.N.Y. 1977); McCloskey v. Epko Shoes, Inc., 391 F. Supp. 1279, 1281–83 (E.D. Pa. 1975); Petersen v. Federated Dev. Co., 387 F. Supp. 355, 359 (S.D.N.Y. 1974).

111. 430 U.S. 462 (1977).

be fairly viewed as 'manipulative or deceptive' within the meaning of the statute."[112] In *Santa Fe*, the Court rejected the Second Circuit's conclusion that a complaint alleges a claim under Rule 10b-5 when it alleges a breach of fiduciary duty by a majority shareholder in effecting a short-form merger under Delaware law without justifiable business purpose.[113] The appellate court based its conclusion on Clause (3) of Rule 10b-5,[114] which prohibits "an act, practice, or course of business which operates or would operate as fraud," reasoning that such conduct by the majority shareholder constitutes fraud.

Significantly, the Supreme Court did not hold that a breach of fiduciary duty is not a fraud; rather, the Court held, in an opinion paralleling its decision in *Ernst & Ernst v. Hochfelder*,[115] that the language of Section 10(b) contemplates only manipulative or deceptive conduct.[116] Because the complaint in *Santa Fe* alleged neither, it did not state a claim under Section 10(b). The Court recognized that the appellate court was relying on the language of Rule 10b-5, but, citing *Ernst & Ernst*, noted that such reliance was inappropriate:

> To the extent that the Court of Appeals would rely on the use of the term "fraud" in Rule 10b-5 to bring within the ambit of the Rule all breaches of fiduciary duty in connection with a securities transaction, its interpretation would, like the interpretation rejected by the Court in *Ernst & Ernst*, "add a gloss to the operative language of the *statute* quite different from its commonly accepted meaning."[117]

Based on *Santa Fe*, numerous lower federal courts have held that shareholder actions under Section 14(e) alleging breach of fiduciary duty fail to state a claim under that section.[118] The language of Section 14(e), however, specifically prohibits "fraudulent . . . acts or practices." Therefore, if conduct that constitutes a breach of fiduciary duty is "fraudulent," it is presumably

---

112. *Id.* at 474.

113. Green v. Santa Fe Indus., Inc., 533 F.2d 1283, 1291 (2d Cir. 1976), *rev'd*, 430 U.S. 462, 471 (1977).

114. *Id.* at 1287.

115. 425 U.S. 185 (1976).

116. *Santa Fe*, 430 U.S. at 471–72.

117. *Id.* at 472 (quoting *Ernst & Ernst*, 425 U.S. at 199) (emphasis added).

118. *E.g.*, Panter v. Marshall Field & Co., 646 F.2d 271, 283-87 (7th Cir. 1981); Lewis v. McGraw, 619 F.2d 192, 195 (2d Cir. 1980); Oklahoma Publishing Co. v. Standard Metals Co., 541 F. Supp. 1109, 1112-13 (W.D. Okla. 1982); *In re* Sunshine Mining Co. Sec. Litig., 496 F. Supp. 9, 11 (S.D.N.Y. 1979); Hundahl v. United Benefit Life Ins. Co., 465 F. Supp. 1349, 1370 (N.D. Tex. 1979); Altman v. Knight, 431 F. Supp. 309, 313–14 (S.D.N.Y. 1977).

violative of Section 14(e).[119] The appellate court decision in *Santa Fe* is arguably still good law to the extent it determined that a breach of fiduciary duty by the controlling shareholder was a fraud on the minority shareholders, and the court's reasoning, or lack thereof, is worth examining.

The appellate court decision in *Santa Fe* relied on three things: earlier Second Circuit decisions which minimized the importance of deception as a necessary element in a Rule 10b-5 action;[120] the Supreme Court's observation in *Superintendent of Insurance v. Bankers Life and Casualty Co.*[121] that "[S]ection 10b must be read flexibly, not technically and restrictively,"[122] and a statement in the Court's 1963 decision in *SEC v. Capital Gains Research Bureau, Inc.*[123] that fraud, in the sense of a court of equity, properly includes "all acts, omissions and concealments which involve a breach of legal or equitable duty, trust, or confidence...and are injurious to another, or by which an undue and unconscientious advantage is taken of another."[124] The appellate court opinion, however, failed to address why a breach of fiduciary duty, standing alone, is a fraud and, more broadly, whether fraud can exist in the absence of a deception. The majority avoided these questions by reading Rule 10b-5 as a proscription against unfairness.[125] Judge Mansfield's concurring opinion[126] also failed to discuss why a breach of fiduciary duty is a fraud.

This shortcoming in the majority and concurring opinions did not go unnoticed in Judge Moore's vigorous dissent. He wrote: "It states the obvious to say that the essence of fraud is deliberate *deception or concealment* which is calculated to deprive the victim of some right or to obtain, by some *deceptive means*, an impermissible advantage over him."[127] Judge Moore cited only Black's and Ballentine's law dictionaries to support this proposition[128] but went on to demonstrate that each of the earlier Second Circuit cases upon which the majority relied involved an element of deception.[129] Although Judge Moore concluded that the defendant did not

---

119. The notion that a breach of fiduciary duty may be fraudulent within the meaning of Section 14(e) has not met with judicial approval. *In re* Sunshine Mining Co. Sec. Litig., 496 F. Supp. 9, 11 (S.D.N.Y. 1979).

120. 533 F.2d at 1290–92.

121. 404 U.S. 6 (1971).

122. *Id.* at 12. The Court reaffirmed this statement in Herman & MacLean v. Huddleston, 103 S. Ct. 683, 690 (1983).

123. 375 U.S. 180 (1963).

124. *Id.* at 194 (quoting from Moore v. Crawford, 130 U.S. 122, 128 (1888)).

125. 533 F.2d at 1291.

126. *Id.* at 1294 (Mansfield, J., concurring).

127. *Id.* at 1301 (Moore, J., dissenting) (footnote omitted) (emphasis added).

128. *Id.*

129. *Id.* at 1301-04. In *Santa Fe*, the Supreme Court disposed of these cases in

breach its fiduciary duty, he also argued, in contrast to the majority opinion, that breach of fiduciary duty and fraud "are wholly different from one another."[130]

The court of appeals opinions in *Santa Fe* thus join issue on whether fraud can exist in the absence of deception. Judge Moore's observation that the answer is obvious is not borne out by a review of judicial decisions or the literature concerning the meaning of the term "fraud." Fraud is used in a variety of contexts, only some of which involve deception.[131] The meaning

---

a lengthy footnote, demonstrating that each involved an element of deception. 430 U.S. at 475, n.15.

130. 533 F.2d at 1304.

131. *Compare* Hart v. McLucas, 535 F.2d 516, 519 (9th Cir. 1976) (construing a prohibition against fraudulent entries in flight logbook as requiring proof of "(1) false representation (2) in reference to a material fact (3) made with knowledge of its falsity (4) with the intent to deceive and (5) with action taken in reliance upon the representation") *and* People v. Federated Radio Corp., 244 N.Y. 33, 38–39, 154 N.E. 655, 657 (1926) (construing fraud in context of New York blue sky statute as including "all deceitful practices contrary to the plain rules of common honesty") *with* Arlington Trust Co. v. Hawkeye-Security Ins. Co., 301 F. Supp. 854, 857–58 (E.D. Va. 1969) (construing fraudulent acts within coverage of fidelity bond as including acts "which show a want of integrity or breach of trust") *and* Kugler v. Koscot Interplanetary, Inc., 120 N.J. Super. 216, 228, 293 A.2d 682, 688 (1972) (stating in dictum that consumer fraud statute may be violated "even though one has not in fact been misled or deceived by an unlawful act or practice").

A number of cases finding fraud under various sections of the securities laws speak in terms of deception, but in reality turn on findings of unfairness or breach of fiduciary duty. Typical are the cases brought against brokers and dealers alleging a violation of the antifraud rules because of excessive markups, Charles Hughes & Co. v. SEC, 139 F.2d 434, 435 (2d Cir.) *cert. denied*, 321 U.S. 786 (1944), or excessive trading (churning), Hecht v. Harris, Upham & Co., 283 F. Supp. 417, 425 (N.D. Cal. 1968), *modified*, 430 F.2d 1202, 1207 (9th Cir. 1970). Language from the court's opinion in *Charles Hughes & Co.* is telling:

> Even considering petitioner [the broker-dealer] as a principal in a simple vendor-purchaser transaction . . . it was still under a special duty, in view of its expert knowledge and proffered advice, not to take advantage of its customers' ignorance of market conditions. The key to the success of all of petitioner's dealings was the confidence in itself which it managed to instill in the customers. Once that confidence was established, the failure to reveal the mark-up pocketed by the firm was both an omission to state a material fact and a fraudulent device.

139 F.2d at 437. The evil in excessive markup and churning cases is not the failure to disclose but the unfairness of what the broker-dealer has done to its customers. Consequently, bringing churning within the proscription of Rule 10b-5 has proved somewhat difficult. S. Goldberg, Fraudulent Broker-Dealer Practices 12–13 (1978) ("A rather technical chain must be forged through the Securities Exchange Act, and the various rules adopted thereunder, in order to prove churning a violation of

of "fraud" is elusive and has prompted many writers to observe that "fraud" is a vague term with numerous definitions.[132] By carefully choosing one's authorities and relying on selected quotations, a persuasive case can be made on either side of the issue.[133]

---

section 10(b) and rule 10b-5."). *See also* Dirks v. SEC, 681 F.2d 824, 840 (D.C. Cir.) (noting that the Second Circuit has applied Rule 10b-5 to nondeceptive breaches of fiduciary duty by broker-dealer), *rev'd on other grounds*, 103 S. Ct. 3255 (1983).

The Second Circuit has also held that an indictment charging a defendant with aiding others in violating their fiduciary duties of honesty, loyalty, and silence was sufficient to allege a criminal violation of Section 10(b) and Rule 10b-5. United States v. Newman, 664 F.2d 12, 15–16 (2d Cir. 1981).

This broad concept of fraud is consistent, however, with the definition set forth in the seventh edition of William Kerr's 19th-century treatise on fraud:

> The Courts have always avoided hampering themselves by defining or laying down as a general proposition what shall be held to constitute fraud. Fraud is infinite in variety. The fertility of man's invention in devising new schemes of fraud is so great, that the Courts have always declined to define it, or to define undue influence, which is one of its many varieties, reserving to themselves the liberty to deal with it under whatever form it may present itself. Fraud, in the contemplation of a Civil Court of Justice, may be said to include properly all acts, omissions, and concealments which involve a breach of legal or equitable duty, trust or confidence, justly reposed, and are injurious to another, or by which an undue or unconscientious advantage is taken of another. All surprise, trick, cunning, dissembling and other unfair way that is used to cheat any one is considered as fraud.

W. Kerr, Fraud and Mistake 1 (7th ed. 1952) (quoted in Kugler v. Romain, 58 N.J. 522, 543 n.4, 279 A.2d 640, 651–52 n.4 (1971)).

132. Pomeroy, writing in 1882, observed:

> It is utterly impossible to formulate any single statement which shall accurately define the equitable conception of fraud, and which shall contain all of the elements which enter into that conception; these elements are so various, so different under the different circumstances of equitable cognizance, so destitute of any common bond of unity, that they cannot be brought within any general formula. To attempt such a definition would therefore be not only useless but actually misleading.

3 J. Pomeroy, Equity Jurisprudence II 420–21 § 873 (5th ed. 1941). Professor Prosser, writing many years later, noted that the term fraud was "so vague that it requires definition in nearly every case." W. Prosser, *supra* note 237, at 684. The courts have been similarly mystified by the term fraud.

133. *See* authorities cited *supra* note 131. *Compare* Old Dominion Copper Mining & Smelting Co. v. Lewisohn, 210 U.S. 206, 216 (1908) (promoter's duty was to corporation as it then existed, not as it was contemplated) *with* Old Dominion Copper Mining & Smelting Co. v. Bigelow, 203 Mass. 159, 196, 89 N.E. 193, 209 (1909) (promoter's disclosure must extend beyond current shareholders to extent of promoted plan), *aff'd on other grounds*, 225 U.S. 111 (1912).

One might argue that the language of Section 14(e), prohibiting "fraudulent, deceptive, or manipulative acts or practices," supports the conclusion that fraud can exist in the absence of deception, because, unless fraud and deception are different acts, the section would be redundant, a result that courts seek to avoid in construing legislation.[134] Furthermore, in light of the meticulous attention the Court has paid to statutory language in its recent securities laws decisions,[135] one can easily imagine the Court saying that if Congress wanted Section 14(e) to be construed identically to Section 10(b), it could have easily done so by utilizing identical language. Failing to do this, and purposefully having used the ambiguous term "fraudulent," Congress "intended" the courts to give broader meaning to Section 14(e) than to Section 10(b).

Although this argument has some surface appeal, it presumes too much regarding Congressional intent. The language of Section 14(e) is typical of the antifraud provisions of the securities laws and probably was not drafted with the care that the above analysis implicitly assumes. Little of the rather long legislative history of the Williams Act is devoted to the meaning of the language of Section 14(e). Indeed, only Professor Painter commented on it and then only in passing.[136] The reports of the Senate and House committees that held hearings on the Williams Act contained identical, cryptic comments as to the purpose of the section.[137] It does not appear that the Congressional committees considered the precise wording of the statute significant; if they had, a more extensive explanation of the language would likely have been provided. In sum, one must go beyond the language of the statute and historical precedent to determine its meaning.

Another approach utilized to determine meaning is that of *Cort v. Ash.*[138]

---

134. *See* Hart v. McLucas, 535 F.2d 516, 519 (9th Cir. 1976).

135. *See, e.g.*, Aaron v. SEC, 446 U.S. 680, 687–702 (1980); Ernst & Ernst v. Hochfelder, 425 U.S. 185, 195–215 (1976); Blue Chip Stamps v. Manor Drug Stores, 421 U.S. 723, 727–55 (1975). *See also* John Nuveen & Co., Inc. v. Sanders, 450 U.S. 1005 (1981), *denying cert. to* 619 F.2d 1222 (7th Cir. 1980) (Powell, J., dissenting) (arguing that the term "reasonable care" in Section 12(2) of the Securities Act should be interpreted differently than the term "reasonable investigation" in Section 11(b) of the Act.)

136. *See supra* notes 38 and 40.

137. *See supra* note 38.

138. 422 U.S. 66 (1975). In this landmark case, four factors were identified as crucial for determining whether a private right of action can be recognized:

> First, is the plaintiff "one of the class for whose *especial* benefit the statute was enacted,"—that is, does the statute create a federal right in favor of the plaintiff? Second, is there any indication of legislative intent, explicit or implicit, either to create such a remedy or to deny one? Third, is it consistent with the underlying purposes of the legislative scheme to imply such a remedy

In *Santa Fe*, the Supreme Court applied *Cort* as an alternative basis in deciding that Section 10(b) did not cover breaches of fiduciary duty.[139] The Court first identified the fundamental purpose of the Exchange Act as the implementation of a philosophy of full disclosure.[140] The Court then concluded that recognizing a cause of action for breach of fiduciary duty would at best serve a "subsidiary purpose" of the federal legislation.[141] As another reason to deny a federal remedy, the Court noted that the action it was being asked to recognize in *Santa Fe* was one "traditionally relegated to state law."[142]

Although a similar analysis might be applied with respect to Section 14(e), some differences are noteworthy. First, although Congress was primarily concerned with disclosure in adopting the Williams Act,[143] it also expressed a concern for the fair treatment of shareholders.[144] The resulting presence in the Act of substantive protections for shareholders shows that this was something more than a subsidiary Congressional concern.

The second factor of importance to the Court in *Santa Fe*, the existence of state law on the subject,[145] provides a basis for resolving the question of whether a breach of fiduciary duty ought to be actionable under Section 14(e). Shareholders claiming that management's actions in resisting an attractive tender offer were motivated by a desire to maintain itself in office may state a claim recognizable under state law.[146] That shareholders may not fare terribly well in such litigation[147] is no reason to federalize the cause of action. So long as management does not issue false or misleading statements or otherwise engage in deceptive or manipulative conduct, the tender offer process can proceed as contemplated in the Williams Act. Thus, claims

---

for the plaintiff? And finally, is the cause of action one traditionally relegated to state law, in an area basically the concern of the States, so that it would be inappropriate to infer a cause of action based solely on federal law?

139. 430 U.S. at 477-80 (1977). Justices Blackmun and Stevens dissented from this portion of the Court's opinion. *Id.* at 480 (Blackmun, J., concurring in part); *id.* at 480–81 (Stevens, J., concurring in part).

140. *Id.* at 477–78.

141. *Id.* at 478.

142. *Id.* at 478–9.

143. *See supra* note 1.

144. *Id. See also* Proposed Amendments to Tender Offer Rules, [1978–1979 Transfer Binder] Fed. Sec. L. Rep. (CCH) ¶ 82,374 at 82,610 (1979) ("The congressional purpose underlying the Williams Act was to require fair and equal treatment of all holders of the class of security which is the subject of the tender offer.").

145. 430 U.S. at 478.

146. *See* Panter v. Marshall Field & Co., 646 F.2d 271, 293 (7th Cir. 1981).

147. *See* Easterbrook & Fischel, *The Proper Role of Target's Management in Responding to a Tender Offer*, 98 Harv. L. Rev. 1161, 1163 (1981).

of unfairness that shareholders might have can be left to the state courts.

When management's actions, or proposed actions, in the face of a hostile tender offer would effectively terminate the offer, however, and would breach management's fiduciary duty to the shareholders imposed by state law, the bidder ought to be able to obtain equitable relief against such actions in federal court. Legislative history, administrative necessity, and historical precedents all favor this conclusion. The recent Sixth Circuit decision in *Mobil Corp. v. Marathon Oil Co.*[148] illustrates a factual context in which breach of fiduciary duty might have been utilized to give the plaintiff the relief it was seeking. Instead the court chose a novel, and questionable, interpretation of the statute to reach an equitable result.

Mobil arose out of the contest between Mobil and U.S. Steel for Marathon.[149] After an uninvited bid by Mobil for 40 million shares of Marathon at $85 per share, Marathon sought a "white knight" and eventually reached an agreement with U.S. Steel, pursuant to which U.S. Steel agreed to make a tender offer through a subsidiary for 30 million shares of Marathon stock at $125 per share.[150] To help assure the success of the U.S. Steel offer, Marathon granted it two options: first, an irrevocable option to purchase 10 million authorized but unissued shares of Marathon common stock for $90 per share and, second, an option to purchase Marathon's 48 percent interest in oil and mineral rights in the Yates Field[151] for $2.8 billion.[152] This latter option, giving U.S. Steel the right to acquire the "crown jewel" of Marathon's assets, was exercisable only if the U.S. Steel offer failed and another offer succeeded.[153]

Mobil filed suit to enjoin the exercise of the options, arguing that Marathon failed to disclose to its shareholders material information regarding the purpose of the options, that the options were "manipulative" in violation of Section 14(e), and that the grant of the options violated the corporate law of Ohio, the state of Marathon's incorporation.[154] Underlying these arguments was the reality that the options had damaging effects on Mobil's attempt to acquire Marathon. The effect of U.S. Steel's Yates Field option was to decrease the interest Mobil, or any other bidder, might have in Marathon.[155] As to the stock option, because the exercise price was below the tender offer price and related to authorized but unissued shares, the

---

148. 669 F.2d 366 (6th Cir. 1981).

149. *Id*. at 367.

150. *Id*.

151. Yates Field, in West Texas, has been one of the largest producing oil fields in the world. *See id*. at 368–69.

152. *Id*. at 367.

153. *Id.*

154. *Id.* at 368.

155. *Id.* at 375.

stock option had the effect of increasing the cost to any bidder competing with U.S. Steel. For instance, Marathon's investment banker calculated that it would cost Mobil an additional $1.1–1.2 billion to match U.S. Steel's tender offer.[156] Thus, the two options effectively "locked up" Marathon for U.S. Steel by deterring rival bids.

The Sixth Circuit first held that Mobil had standing to seek injunctive relief under Section 14(e) as a tender offeror.[157] It then found this "lock-up" effect "manipulative" within the meaning of Section 14(e) and thus granted Mobil's plea for equitable relief.[158] The court's analysis of the manipulation issue began with a citation to the Supreme Court's definitions of the term "manipulative" in *Ernst & Ernst* and *Santa Fe*. In *Ernst & Ernst*, the Court said: "It is and was virtually a term of art when used in connection with securities markets. It connotes intentional or willful conduct designed to deceive or defraud investors by controlling or artificially affecting the price of securities."[159] In *Santa Fe*, the Court offered this illustration of the term "manipulation": "The term refers generally to practices, such as wash sales, matched orders, or rigged prices, that are intended to mislead investors by artificially affecting market activity."[160] The appellate court in *Mobil* reasoned that the options had the effect of creating an artificial price ceiling in the tender offer market for Marathon stock and therefore fell within the Supreme Court's definition of manipulation.[161]

The Sixth Circuit's conclusion in *Mobil* that the options constituted manipulation is at odds with the traditional meaning of the term and the spirit of the Supreme Court's decisions from which the court quoted.[162] Professor Loss's discussion of the term "manipulation,"[163] cited with approval by the Supreme Court,[164] demonstrates that the term generally refers to undisclosed stock transactions intended to mislead investors. Although the effect of the Marathon–U.S. Steel options may have been to place an artificial ceiling on the price of Marathon stock, that alone cannot render the options ma-

---

156. *Id*. at 375–76.

157. *Id*. at 372.

158. The court effectively voided the two options, required that the shareholders be notified and given an opportunity to withdraw their shares, and ordered that the tender offer be extended for a reasonable time. *Id*. at 377–78.

159. 425 U.S. at 199 (quoted in *Mobil*, 669 F.2d at 374).

160. 430 U.S. at 476 (quoted in *Mobil*, 669 F.2d at 374).

161. 669 F.2d at 375.

162. The court's conclusion has also been judicially questioned. Data Probe Acquisition Corp. v. Datatab, Inc., 721 F.2d 1 (2d Cir. 1983), *cert. denied* 104 S. Ct. 1326 (1984); Marshall Field & Co. v. Icahn, 537 F. Supp. 413, 422 (S.D.N.Y. 1982). *See also* Trane Co. v. O'Connor Securities, 561 F. Supp. 301 (D. N.Y. 1983).

163. 3 L. Loss, *supra* note 57, at 1529–30.

164. *Santa Fe*, 430 U.S. at 476.

nipulative, because manipulation relates to manner as well as effect.[165] Therefore, although an announcement by a corporation that it will repurchase its own shares at a given price creates a floor below which the share price will not fall, it cannot be seriously argued that such an announcement is manipulative. By comparison, wash sales or matched orders or other schemes which might have the same effect would be deemed manipulative. The difference is that, in the latter case, investors are misled as to the truth, while in the former they are not. The prohibition against manipulation was intended to deal only with the latter case. Moreover, the significance of the Marathon–U.S. Steel options was not their impact on the price of Marathon's stock but their effective foreclosure of rival bids.

The real issue in the *Mobil* case, therefore, was whether target management violated Section 14(e) when it undertook a course of conduct that did not involve misstatements, omissions, or manipulative or deceptive conduct but that had the effect of eliminating the plaintiff as a tender offeror. The resolution of this issue should turn on whether management violated its fiduciary duty. If management's actions were consistent with its fiduciary duty, no basis exists for judicial interference. If, however, management's actions violated a fiduciary duty, then the Williams Act ought to afford a measure of protection, at least to the extent of providing a cause of action for injunctive relief for the tender offeror.[166] Unlike the shareholders of the target company, the offeror may not have a state remedy: it may lack standing to maintain an action for breach of fiduciary duty,[167] and an action alleging interference with prospective commercial advantage may not be ade-

---

165. The court conceded that nondisclosure is "usually essential to the success of a manipulative scheme," 669 F.2d at 376 (quoting from *Santa Fe*, 430 U.S. at 477), but, focusing on the effect of the options, the court concluded that the fact of disclosure in this case would not render the options nonmanipulative. The court said, "To find compliance with section 14(e) solely by the full disclosure of manipulative acts as a *fait accompli* would be to read the 'manipulative acts and practices' language completely out of the Williams Act." 669 F.2d at 377.

166. *Cf.* United States v. Newman, 664 F.2d 12, 16–17 (2d Cir. 1981) (indicating that an employee's breach of his fiduciary duty to his employer may give rise to a cause of action under Section 10(b) and Rule 10b-5 in favor of third parties who might have been injured thereby). *See* Marshall Field & Co. v. Icahn, 537 F. Supp. 413 (D. N.Y. 1982).

167. Under state law, only shareholders would have standing to allege a breach of fiduciary duty by corporate management. The tender offeror may be, but need not be, a shareholder of the target. Even if the offeror is a shareholder, however, it is conceivable that a state court could deny it relief on the grounds that it is seeking relief not in its capacity as a shareholder but in its capacity as a tender offeror. *Cf.* Piper v. Chris-Craft Indus., Inc., 430 U.S. 1, 35–36 (1977). *See also* A & K R. R. Materials, Inc. v. Green Bay and W.R.R. Co., 437 F. Supp. 636, 644 (E.D. Wis. 1977) (tender offeror has no standing under state law to challenge target management's breach of fiduciary duty). In *Piper*, the Court noted that plaintiff-tender offeror was

quate.[168] In addition, the argument that a breach of fiduciary duty is a fraud is strongest when the complaining party seeks only an equitable remedy.[169] Finally, this result is consistent with the purpose and legislative history of the Williams Act: shareholder protection is enhanced when the tender offeror can obtain injunctive relief to help assure that the offer will become effective. Thus, Section 14(e) should be construed as providing a cause of action to a tender offeror to seek injunctive relief against target management when management breaches its fiduciary duty to its shareholders and the effect of that breach is to thwart the offeror's efforts.[170]

D. Trading on Nonpublic Information: *Chiarella* and Rule 14e-3

Relying on Rule 10b-5 jurisprudence, some commentators have criticized Commission Rule 14e-3[171] because that rule prohibits certain conduct that

---

a shareholder of the target company. Nevertheless, the Court analyzed the standing issue as though the plaintiff was suing solely as a disappointed tender offeror, because the damages it was seeking were those it suffered in its capacity as a defeated tender offeror, not as a target shareholder. *Id.*

168. The *Mobil* court referred to dictum in *Piper* suggesting that a defeated tender offeror may have a common law cause of action for damages under principles of interference with a prospective commercial advantage. *Mobil*, 669 F.2d at 372. *See Piper*, 430 U.S. at 40–41. The *Mobil* court went on to observe: "While such an action may be an effective common law alternative for a damage action, we do not believe that the common law has traditionally provided an injunctive remedy that would effectively protect Marathon shareholders from nondisclosure or manipulation by the parties in the bidding." 669 F.2d at 372. *See also* Belden Corp. v. InterNorth, Inc., 90 Ill. App.3d 547, 413 N.E.2d 98 (1980), in which the court vacated a preliminary injunction in favor of Belden enjoining InterNorth's tender offer for Crouse-Hinds. Belden had argued that the tender offer interfered with its proposed merger with Crouse. *Id.* at 553, 413 N.E.2d at 103. The appellate court rejected this contention, setting forth a test for obtaining relief under the theory of interference with prospective advantage: "Belden cannot meet the requirements for interference with prospective advantage unless it makes a showing of unfair competition on the part of InterNorth." *Id.*

169. *See* SEC v. Capital Gains Research, 375 U.S. 180, 193 (1963) ("Fraud has a broader meaning in equity [than at law] and intention to defraud or to misrepresent is not a necessary element") (quoting W. DeFuniak, Handbook of Modern Equity 235 (2d ed. 1956)).

170. Naturally, the traditional grounds for equitable relief must also be established. *See* Otis Elevator Co. v. United Technologies Corp., 405 F. Supp. 960, 965 (S.D.N.Y. 1975). *See generally* Note, *Preliminary Injunctive Relief and Tender Offers: An Analysis under the Williams Act,* 49 Geo. Wash. L. Rev. 563, 593–94 (1981).

171. *See* Heller, Chiarella, *SEC Rule 14e-3, and* Dirks: *Fairness versus Economic*

the Supreme Court found unobjectionable under Rule 10b-5 in *Chiarella v. United States*.[172] Rule 14e-3, which was adopted by the Commission pursuant to the rulemaking authority granted it in Section 14(e), generally prohibits anyone other than the offeror from trading in target company securities on the basis of nonpublic information relating to a proposed tender offer until the information is made public.[173] By comparison, in *Chiarella*, the Court reversed the criminal conviction of an employee of a financial printer who, in the course of his employment, deciphered the names of target companies and traded the securities of those companies at a profit, without disclosing to the target shareholders his knowledge of the proposed takeover.[174] The Court held that the printer had not violated Section 10(b), because he had no duty to the target shareholders to disclose the information he deciphered.[175]

In *Chiarella*, the Court grappled with the issue of who, under Section 10(b), has a duty to disclose material, nonpublic market information before trading on that information.[176] Although the language of the statute and its legislative history are silent on the question, the Court found support for its narrow holding in previous administrative and judicial decisions[177] and in the notion that Congress, not the courts, should mandate the broad expansion of liability that the government was seeking in that case.[178] The administrative and judicial decisions the Court cited established that silence in connection with the purchase or sale of a security may be fraudulent when there is a "duty to disclose arising from a relationship of trust and confidence between the parties to a transaction."[179] In the absence of a duty to disclose, the Court said, the defendant's actions could not violate Section

---

Theory, 37 Bus. Law. 517, 541–46 (1982); Peloso & Krause, *Trading on Inside Information*, 14 Rev. Sec. Reg. 941, 947–48 (1981).

172. 445 U.S. 222 (1980). Moreover, since Rule 14e-3 contains a "should have known" or negligence standard, one might speculate that it is inconsistent with the scienter standard of *Ernst & Ernst*. *See* Peloso & Krause, *supra* note 171, at 945.

173. 17 C.F.R. 240.14e-3 (1983).

174. 445 U.S. at 224–25.

175. *Id.*

176. The Court distinguished "inside information" from "market information." In the context of this case, inside information would concern the earning power or operations of the target company, while market information would relate to the plans of the acquiring company. *Chiarella*, 445 U.S. at 231. *See generally* Fleischer, Mundheim & Murphy, *An Initial Inquiry into the Responsibility to Disclose Market Information*, 121 U. Pa. L. Rev. 798 (1973). *But see* Dirks v. SEC, 103 S. Ct. 3255 (1983).

177. 445 U.S. at 230.

178. *Id.* at 235.

179. 445 U.S. at 230.

10(b), despite the unfairness inherent in his actions.[180] Citing *Santa Fe*, the Court noted that not all unfairness is fraudulent.[181]

In a footnote, the *Chiarella* Court dealt with the liability of "tippees." The Court noted that a person who receives material, nonpublic information from an insider should refrain from trading on that information or risk being cast as "a participant after the fact in the insider's breach of fiduciary duty."[182] Presumably, persons tipped by noninsiders are free, under Section 10(b), to trade on the information.

Two issues were left open by the Court in *Chiarella*.[183] The first, and more important, was whether the petitioner might have been convicted on the theory that trading on misappropriated nonpublic information violates Section 10(b) and Rule 10b-5 because the misappropriation involves a breach by the defendant of his fiduciary duty to his employer. This issue was not clearly before the Court, because the jury was not instructed that a breach of a defendant's duty to his employer may form the basis of liability under Rule 10b-5.[184] Subsequent federal courts that have faced this issue have decided it in the affirmative.[185]

The second issue left open in *Chiarella* was whether possession of "inside information" creates different duties than possession of "market information." Inside information is information about and emanating from the target company, generally concerning its earning power or operations. Market information is information external to the company, such as information about plans of another to acquire the company.[186] Obviously, market information often comes from a source other than the target company. By specifically noting that this case involved market information,[187] the opinion implied that the two types of information might be subject to different

---

180. *Id*. at 232.

181. *Id.*

182. *Id*. at 239 n.12. *See* Dirks v. SEC, 103 S. Ct. 3255 (1983).

183. The first issue was explicitly left open by the Court. 445 U.S. at 221. The second issue is impliedly left open by the Court's specific distinction between market information and insider information. *Id*. at 231, 233. *But see* Dirks v. SEC, 103 S. Ct. 3255 (1983).

184. *Id*. at 235–37. Chief Justice Burger, dissenting, thought that the jury instructions covered the misappropriation theory and, even if the instructions were deficient in failing to charge misappropriation with sufficient precision, any error was harmless beyond a reasonable doubt. *Id*. at 243–45.

185. United States v. Newman, 664 F.2d 12, 16 (2d Cir. 1981); O'Connor & Assoc. v. Dean Witter Reynolds, Inc., 529 F. Supp. 1179, 1185 (S.D.N.Y. 1982).

186. *See* Dirks v. SEC, 681 F.2d 824, 834 (D.C. Cir.) (defining market information as information relating "solely to the market for the securities" rather than their intrinsic value), *rev'd on other grounds*, 103 S. Ct. 3255 (1983).

187. 445 U.S. at 231, 233.

treatment. A rationale for treating the two types of information differently may be that private disclosure of inside information would likely involve an insider who breached his fiduciary duty. A person who trades on that information then becomes "a participant after the fact in the insider's breach of fiduciary duty."[188] It is also possible, however, for a person to obtain inside information in a way that does not involve a breach of fiduciary duty by an insider, and it is difficult to see why such a person should be treated differently than the petitioner in *Chiarella*.[189]

The Commission seized upon the first of these open issues as a basis for supporting its Rule 14e-3: "The Commission continues to believe that such conduct undermines the integrity of, and investor confidence in, the securities markets, and that *persons who unlawfully obtain or misappropriate* material, nonpublic information violate Rule 10b-5 when they trade on such information.[190]

Implicit in this position is a suggestion that even if Section 10(b) and Rule 10b-5 create the parameters for Section 14(e), Rule 14e-3 can still be justified because *Chiarella* did not reach or question the rationale for Rule 14e-3. The only problem with the Commission's position is that its rule covers a larger class of persons than those who "unlawfully obtain or misappropriate nonpublic information." For instance, the rule prohibits a tippee from trading on the nonpublic information if he knows or has reason to know that the information has been acquired directly or indirectly from the offeror, the target, or any officer, director, partner, employee, or any other person acting on behalf of the offeror or the target.[191] Since a tippee is, in the normal case, simply told the information, he may not be involved in a misappropriation but would be in violation of the rule if he had reason to know its source was the target or offeror.

One might argue that the tippee has unlawfully obtained the information simply by receiving it. This argument, however, assumes its conclusion. It would mean, for instance, that if *A* overheard *B* and *C* discussing a proposed takeover of XYZ, Inc., *A* could not trade on that information if the other requirements of the rule were satisfied, because the information was un-

---

188. *Id* at 230 n.12.

189. Assume, for instance, Chiarella had, as a printer, worked on a press release that disclosed material, nonpublic information about the company that was issuing the release. If he traded on the "inside" information before it was made public, it could not be said that he was participating in "an insider's breach of fiduciary duty." *See also* Dirks v. SEC, 103 S. Ct. 3255 (1983); ALI Fed. Sec. Code § 1603 (Comment (2)(s)) (Proposed Official Draft) (suggesting there is no reason to distinguish an "insider's" use of "market information" from "inside information").

190. Securities Act Rel. No. 6239, Fed. Sec. L. Rep. (CCH) ¶ 82,646 at 83,456 (1980) (emphasis added).

191. 17 C.F.R. 240.14e-3(a) (1985).

lawfully obtained. Although this result is no doubt what the Commission intended in promulgating Rule 14e-3, it is a far cry from the undecided issue in *Chiarella* and is difficult to sustain on the basis of any existing precedent.

A stronger basis of support for Rule 14e-3 lies in the language and legislative history of the Williams Act. Under the original bill, no tender offer could be made unless notice thereof was filed with the SEC at least five days prior to the commencement of the offer.[192] Because of the potential impact of disclosure of an impending offer, the SEC would have been required to keep the filing confidential. Commentators objected to this provision because it increased the likelihood that trading might occur to the disadvantage "of those innocent stockholders who sell their shares unaware of the impending offer."[193] Deletion of this provision by Congress suggests that Congress agreed with the objectors and was concerned about pre-offer trading by those who knew of the impending offer.[194]

Further support for the rule is found in the 1970 amendments to the Williams Act that, among other things, granted the SEC broad rulemaking authority to implement Section 14(e).[195] In the course of the Senate hearings on the proposed amendments, Senator Williams asked the Commission to give his committee some examples of fraudulent, deceptive, or manipulative practices used in tender offers that the proposed rulemaking powers would prevent.[196] The Commission's memorandum in response included the following example of a "problem area" that might be dealt with by rulemaking:

> The person who has become aware that a tender bid is to be made, or has reason to believe that such a bid will be made, may fail to disclose material facts with respect thereto to persons who sell to him securities for which the tender bid is to be made.[197]

The Commission did not limit its concern to insiders or persons who misappropriated or illegally obtained the information. This memorandum was a part of the public record and received no adverse comment.

It also might be argued that the rulemaking authority granted to the Commission in Section 14(e) is sufficiently broad to sustain Rule 14e-3. Under Section 14(e), the Commission is empowered to promulgate rules

---

192. S. 510, 90th Cong., 1st Sess. § 2 (1967).

193. 1967 Senate Hearings, *supra* note 38, at 73 (statement of Donald L. Calvin, Vice President, New York Stock Exchange).

194. Senator Bennett, a member of the subcommittee, also expressed concern about trading on nonpublic information about a tender offer. *Id.* at 74.

195. Pub. L. No. 91-567, § 5, 84 Stat. 1497, 1498 (1970).

196. 1970 Senate Hearings, *supra* note 104, at 11.

197. *Id.* at 12.

and regulations to "define, and prescribe means reasonably designed to prevent, such acts and practices as are fraudulent, deceptive, or manipulative."[198] By comparison, the Commission's rulemaking authority under Section 10(b) does not include the power to define manipulative or deceptive devices or contrivances, nor does it include the power to adopt prophylactic measures. Under Section 10(b), the Commission is simply empowered to adopt rules and regulations to prohibit manipulative or deceptive devices or contrivances, consistent with the public interest and the protection of investors. That the Commission views the powers to "define" and "prevent" as particularly broad powers is apparent from the rules it adopted under Section 15(c)(1) and (2) of the Exchange Act, where similar rulemaking authority is granted.[199] It is difficult to see why Congress would grant such broad powers to the SEC if the SEC was not expected to have some leeway in utilizing its powers. The practices the Commission has prohibited in Rule 14e-3 are, at least arguably, fraudulent practices, and it would appear to be within the broad rulemaking authority of Section 14(e) for the Commission to prohibit them.

The validity of Rule 14e-3 ought not be judged as though it were promulgated pursuant to Section 10(b). As in the other areas of comparison noted above, the language, legislative history, and spirit of the Williams Act support a contrary conclusion.

III. CONCLUSION

Early decisions from the lower federal courts that simply assume a correspondence between Section 14(e) and Rule 10b-5 are questionable. From the very existence of a private cause of action to the elements of that cause of action, the courts have depended on developing Rule 10b-5 decisions. If Rule 10b-5 was the model for Section 14(e), and if Congress intended to incorporate Rule 10b-5 decisional law into the meaning of Section 14(e), one might argue that Rule 10b-5 cases decided after 1968, when the Williams Act was passed, should not be binding on the interpretation of Section 14(e) if those post-1968 decisions mark a departure from prior case law. No court has so held, because the fortunes of Rule 10b-5 and Section 14(e) have become so intertwined as to obliterate any distinction between them. Indeed, in many decisions that involve both provisions, it is often unclear which one the court is discussing.

---

198. 15 U.S.C. § 78n(e) (1976).

199. 24 C.F.R. c1-1 to c1-11 (1985). Congressional legislation against the background of the Commission's Section 15(c) rules suggests that its rulemaking authority under Section 14(e) should be similarly broad.

The courts ought to look anew at Section 14(e) and redetermine its parameters. In such a fresh look, a court might reasonably conclude that no basis exists for recognizing a private damage action under Section 14(e). However, if private actions are sanctioned, the courts should be alert to the differences between Rule 10b-5 and Section 14(e) and shape the contours of each with reference to those differences. Those differences justify the conclusions discussed above:

1. Scienter ought not be a necessary element in an action based on the first clause of Section 14(e). Negligent misstatements or omissions may form the basis for a damage action under Section 14(e) and, if a bidder makes a misrepresentation in its offering materials, it should be held liable without regard to fault.

2. The plaintiff in a Section 14(e) damage action should not be required to prove reliance unless proof of reliance is needed to prove causation.

3. A tender offeror should have standing to seek equitable relief against target management that breaches its fiduciary duty to its shareholders when that breach unduly interferes with the tender offeror's offer.

4. SEC Rule 14e-3 is not subject to criticism on the grounds that the rule exceeds the SEC's rulemaking authority. Such criticisms are based on judicial decisions construing Rule 10b-5 and the SEC's rulemaking authority under Section 10(b). Section 14(e) is, however, broader than Section 10(b), as is the SEC's rulemaking power under Section 14(e). These factors validate a rule that might not withstand scrutiny under Section 10(b).

Application of the Federal Securities Laws to Defensive Tactics in Control Contests

THEODORE A. LEVINE,
THOMAS J. LYKOS, JR.,
and MARC EDWARD CHAFETZ*

I. INTRODUCTION

Contests for corporate control have become ever more frequent phenomena on the American business scene. Waged with the intensity of military campaigns and the weaponry of seemingly bottomless bankrolls, these battles determine the destinies of large and small corporations alike. Elaborate strategies and ingenious tactics have been developed both to facilitate takeover attempts and to defend against them. Skirmishes are fought in company boardrooms, in shareholders' meetings, and with increasing regularity, in the courts.[1]

Once the private domain of investment bankers, lawyers, and corporate executives, control contests have become an increasingly popular spectator sport. The publicity surrounding several recent multibillion-dollar acquisitions has familiarized the public with the glossary of new terms including,

---

*Mr. Levine is a partner with the firm of Wilmer, Cutler & Pickering, Washington, D.C. B.A., 1966, Rutgers University; J.D., 1969, George Washington University.

Mr. Lykos is associate minority counsel to the United States House of Representatives Committee on Energy and Commerce. B.A., 1978, Harvard University; J.D., 1981, University of Texas.

Mr. Chafetz is an attorney at the Washington, D.C., office of Ballard Spahr Andrews & Ingersoll. B.A., 1975, Oberlin College; J.D., 1979, University of Virginia.

1. *See* Norlin Corporation v. Rooney Pace Inc., [1984 Transfer Binder] Fed. Sec. L. Rep. (CCH) ¶ 91,564 (2d Cir. 1984).

among others: golden parachutes, greenmail, shark repellants, poison pills, Pac-Man defense, scorched-earth defense, lock-up, leg-ups, crown jewels, silver wheel chairs, and white knights. These terms have been used to describe the various offensive and defensive tactics which may be employed to execute or prevent a successful change in control.

The increasing use of defensive tactics to thwart hostile takeover attempts has been the recent subject of a great deal of scrutiny by Congress, the SEC, corporate executives, the legal community, and academicians.[2] Questions have been raised about the propriety of the defensive tactics being employed[3] and the motives of those employing such tactics.[4]

The judiciary should play an active role in addressing the legal controversies which are generated by the control contests. As Judge Kaufman correctly described such a role in the *Norlin* case:

> [T]he judicial role is neither to displace the judgment of the partici-
> pants nor to predetermine the outcome. Rather, the responsibility of
> the court is to insure that rules designed to safeguard the fairness of
> the takeover process be enforced. Our most important duty is to
> protect the fundamental structure of corporate governance.[5]

Congress has already provided the judiciary with the tools to carry out that responsibility—Section 14(e) of the Securities Exchange Act of 1934.[6]

Section 14(e) should be applied, in the authors' views, to prohibit defensive tactics which threaten the fairness of the takeover process. Fairness during a tender offer requires, at a minimum, that no action be taken that

---

2. The SEC commissioned an Advisory Committee to study the effects of various takeover tactics on corporate acquisitions and to offer recommendations in response to concerns about the use of these tactics. On July 8, 1983, the Advisory Committee issued a report containing 50 recommendations, some of which would require administrative or legislative action to implement. Congress is also contemplating legislative proposals in an attempt to mitigate the costs and pressures which some of the more questionable tactics impose upon shareholders.

3. Congress has recently considered various proposals to curb the perceived abuses of certain defensive tactics. The proposals have ranged from a modified version of the British rule to a piecemeal approach designed to remedy certain specific tactics. (*See* House Committee on Energy and Commerce, Subcommittee on Telecommunications, Consumer Protection, and Finance, Hearings on Takeover Tactics, March 23, 1984, and May 28, 1984.)

4. *See* Norlin Corporation v. Rooney Pace Inc., [1984 Transfer Binder] Fed. Sec. L. Rep. (CCH) ¶91,564 (2d Cir. 1984).

5. *Id.* at 98,868.

6. 15 U.S.C. § 78n(e) (1982). Section 14(e) in pertinent part provides: "It shall be unlawful for any person ... to engage in any fraudulent, deceptive, or manipulative acts or practices, in connection with any tender offer...."

impedes the operation of an auction market. Shareholders are the ultimate beneficiaries of an unfettered auction market, because they can receive the highest possible price for their shares. Such an application would require the courts to construe Section 14(e) in a substantive manner to determine the validity of the challenged conduct.

II. CRITIQUES OF A SUBSTANTIVE APPLICATION OF SECTION 14(e)

Generally, the courts have been unwilling to apply Section 14(e) substantively.[7] Although exceptions exist,[8] curative disclosure is the remedy applied to bidders found to have violated that section.[9]

The courts have viewed Section 14(e) as merely mandating accurate and complete disclosure.[10] The courts have required some form of deceit as a necessary element to prove a violation of Section 14(e). Such an interpretation has resulted in decisions holding that defensive tactics, regardless of their effect on the transaction or the market price of the stock, cannot be fraudulent or manipulative under Section 14(e), because the use of these tactics and the terms relevant to them have been disclosed.[11]

The legislative intent of the Williams Act and the Supreme Court's holding in *Santa Fe Industries v. Green*[12] are cited as support for the proposition that Section 14(e) is only a reporting requirement and that nondisclosure

---

7. *See e.g.*, Whittaker Corp. v. Edgar, [1981–1982 Transfer Binder] Fed. Sec. L. Rep. (CCH) ¶ 98,483 (N.D. Ill. Jan. 25), *aff'd mem.*, Nos. 1305 and 1307 (7th Cir. Mar. 5, 1982); Marshall Field & Co. v. Icahn, 537 F. Supp. 413 (S.D.N.Y. 1982); Swanson v. Wabash, Inc., [1983–1984 Transfer Binder] Fed. Sec. L. Rep. (CCH) ¶ 99,725 (N.D. Ill. Dec. 16, 1983).

But see Mobil Corp. v. Marathon Oil Co., 669 F.2d 366 (6th Cir. 1981) and Data Probe Acquisition Corp. v. Datatab, Inc., 568 F. Supp. 1538 (S.D.N.Y.), *rev'd*, 722 F.2d 1 (2d Cir. 1983), *cert. denied*, 104 S. Ct. 1326 (1984).

8. This is usually the case where the defendant's conduct is willful or gives it a significant advantage over the target or competing bidders. *See, e.g.,* General Steel Industries, Inc. v. Walco National Corp., [1981–1982 Transfer Binder] Fed. Sec. L. Rep. (CCH) ¶ 98,402 (E.D. Mo. Nov. 24, 1981).

9. *E.g.,* Treadway Cos. v. Care Corp., 638 F.2d 357, 380 (2d Cir. 1980); Chromalloy American Corp. v. Sun Chemical Corp., 611 F.2d 240, 249 (8th Cir. 1979); General Aircraft Corp. v. Lampert, 556 F.2d 90, 97 (1st Cir. 1977); Raybestos-Manhattan, Inc. v. Hi-Shear Industries, Inc., 503 F. Supp. 1122 (S.D.N.Y. 1980); Standard Metals Corp. v. Tomlin, 503 F. Supp. 586 (S.D.N.Y. 1980); Avnet, Inc. v. Scope Industries, 499 F. Supp. 1121 (S.D.N.Y. 1980); Brascan Ltd. v. Edper Equities Ltd., 477 F. Supp. 773 (S.D.N.Y. 1979).

10. *See* note 7 *supra*.

11. *Id.*

12. 430 U.S. 462 (1977).

or misrepresentation are essential elements of a cause of action under Section 14(e).[13] In an apparently even more restrictive view of the purpose of Section 14(e), at least one court has found that "the sole purpose of the Williams Act is to provide information to the investor so that he may make a rational decision whether or not to tender all or part of his shares."[14]

In *Santa Fe*, the Court held that to establish a violation of Section 10(b) and Rule 10b-5, an element of deception must be present. Since the language of Rule 10b-5 and Section 14(e) of the Williams Act is identical except as to their respective "in connection with" clauses,[15] it has been argued that a similar interpretation should be applied to Section 14(e).

The reliance on the *Santa Fe* decision to construe Section 14(e) is neither warranted nor properly placed. Using the Court's interpretation of Section 10(b) as a precedent for applying Section 14(e) fails to consider the different contexts in which these statutes are invoked. Although the Williams Act and the Securities Exchange Act of 1934 share the goal of investor protection, Section 10(b) is part of a statutory scheme for the regulation of securities trading while Section 14(e) of the Williams Act is directed specifically at the regulation of tender offers and securities transactions executed during the pendency of such offers.[16] To advance the purposes of the Williams Act, Section 14(e)'s prohibition against fraudulent, deceptive, or manipulative

---

13. The Williams Act was designed to close "a significant gap in investor protection under the federal securities laws by requiring the disclosure of pertinent information to stockholders when persons seek to obtain control of a corporation by a cash tender offer or through open market or privately negotiated purchases of securities." 113 Cong. Rec. 854 (1967) (Statement of Senator Williams).

14. Bucher v. Shumway, 452 F. Supp. 1288, 1294 (S.D.N.Y. 1978). *But see* Piper v. Chris-Craft Industries, Inc., where the Court stated: "The legislative history thus shows that the sole purpose of the Williams Act was the protection of investors who are confronted with a tender offer." 430 U.S. 1, 35 (1977).

15. Rule 10b-5, 17 C.F.R. § 240.10b-5 (1983), applies "in connection with" purchases and sales of securities while Section 14(e) applies "in connection with" a tender offer.

16. The 1934 Act protects investors by regulating trading markets, requiring disclosure, and prohibiting deception and classic kinds of market manipulation. The Williams Act protects investors by requiring offerors to make extensive disclosures about themselves, the source of their financing, and their plans for the target company. The Williams Act provides specific substantive benefits to tendering shareholders, including rights to withdraw tendered shares, to participate pro rata in offers for less than all of a company's shares, and to receive the highest price that a tender offeror pays for a target company's shares. Finally, the Williams Act proscribes all "fraudulent, deceptive, or manipulative acts or practices in connection with any tender offer or request or invitation for tenders, or any solicitation of security holders in opposition to or in favor of any such offer, request or invitation" even though no specific guidance is offered as to what acts are deceptive or manipulative. 15 U.S.C. § 78n(e) (1982).

acts or practices must be viewed in this context.[17] While Section 14(e) was not designed to govern the day-to-day running of corporate affairs, it was specifically designed to assure investor protection in the high-pressure, high-stakes environment which typically surrounds takeovers.

The Williams Act was painstakingly drafted to strike a delicate balance between targets and bidders. Neither target nor bidder was to receive advantage over the other under the Act as originally promulgated. Maintaining this delicate balance has been viewed by the SEC, the Tender Offer Advisory Committee, and Congress as critical to ensure the effective operation of the Act.

In striking a balance between bidders and targets, the protections of the Williams Act were enacted to benefit shareholders through the full and fair disclosure of all material information and through proscriptions against fraudulent, deceptive, and manipulative practices. An interpretation of Section 14(e) that provides substantive and procedural protections in the context of a takeover is consistent with the Congressional intent[18] and will ultimately inure to the benefit of such security holders.[19]

---

17. Another related argument urging a more restrictive application of Section 14(e) suggests that by reading substantive rights into the statute to thwart defensive tactics the balance between the bidder and defending management, which the Williams Act sought to preserve, would be tipped in favor of the bidder. It is further contended that bidders are not the intended beneficiaries, because they have the resources and arsenal of moves to adequately protect their interests.

This factor influenced the Supreme Court's conclusion in Piper v. Chris-Craft Industries, Inc. that a defeated bidder lacks standing to sue for damages under Section 14(e). 430 U.S. 1 (1977). The Court noted that tender offerors were not the intended beneficiaries of the Williams Act. *Id.* at 28. The Court reasoned that the Williams Act's "express policy of neutrality scarcely suggests an intent to confer highly important, new rights upon the class of participants whose activities prompted the legislation in the first instance." *Id.* at 30.

Reliance upon the Court's holding in *Piper* is misplaced. First, the *Piper* decision centered on implying a private damages remedy under Section 14(e) on behalf of a defeated tender offeror. Second, the use of Section 14(e) to enjoin the use of such techniques does not tip the balance in favor of the bidder. Rather, it seeks to restore the balance originally contemplated by the Williams Act, because at the time of the Act's passage its authors could not have contemplated the plethora of defensive techniques that have arguably tipped the balance in the target's favor. Finally, substantive application of Section 14(e) benefits shareholders by enabling an auction market to be preserved. A substantive approach is entirely consistent with the legislative intent of the Williams Act, because it is the shareholders who stand to reap the greatest benefit from the restoration of a true auction market through a limitation or elimination of defensive tactics the courts deem manipulative under Section 14(e).

18. *See* notes 22–30 *infra.*

19. *See* text accompanying notes 27 and 72 *infra.*

Further, the statements concerning manipulation in *Santa Fe* should not be controlling on the issue of what constitutes manipulation under Section 14(e). Although the language of Section 10(b) and Rule 10b-5 and Section 14(e) are in part the same, this fact alone should not preclude a different interpretation of manipulation under Section 14(e). Specifically, with regard to the application of sections of the Act that contain similar or identical words, the Supreme Court has found that such language in different federal securities statutes may be interpreted differently where a different interpretation is justified by the history and the statutory context of the legislation.[20]

III. A PROPER APPLICATION OF SECTION 14(e)

Prior to the Sixth Circuit's decision in *Mobil Corp. v. Marathon Oil Co.,*[21] the courts demonstrated a reluctance to apply Section 14(e) to bar conduct that was beyond the scope of traditional market manipulations regarding the sale and purchase of securities.[22] In the context of a takeover battle, the court in *Marathon* included within the scope of manipulation those practices, specifically target granted lock-ups, which target companies utilize to fend off unwelcome takeover bids.

---

20. *See, e.g.*, Kern County Land Co. v. Occidental Petroleum Corp., 411 U.S. 582 (1973), where the Court found that an exchange of stock pursuant to a merger agreement did not constitute a sale under Section 16(b) while such an exchange was previously found to be a sale under Section 10(b) of the 1934 Act. SEC v. National Securities, Inc., 393 U.S. 453 (1969).

See also the Court's different requirements regarding the element of scienter in cases alleging violations of Section 10(b) and Section 206(2) of the Investment Advisors Act of 1940, 15 U.S.C. § 80b-6 (1982). In requiring proof of scienter in Section 10(b) cases and not in Section 206(e), the Court reasoned that this variance was permissible because the different statutory schemes served different purposes. Aaron v. SEC, 446 U.S. 680, 695 (1980); SEC v. Capital Gains Research Bureau, Inc., 375 U.S. 180 (1963).

21. 669 F.2d 366 (6th Cir. 1981). *See also* Hanna Mining Co. v. Norcen Energy Resources Ltd., [1982 Transfer Binder] Fed. Sec. L. Rep. (CCH) ¶ 98,878, at 94,569 (N.D. Ohio, June 11, 1982), where the court found that Norcen's repeated misrepresentations of its intentions to acquire control of Hannah stock prior to the announcement of a tender offer were manipulative violations of Sections 10(b) and 14(e) and Rule 10b-5. The court further held that curative disclosure was not enough to remedy the manipulation and rejected the contention that misrepresentation and deception were essential elements of a Section 14(e) manipulation. *Id.* at 94,586-596.

22. *See, e.g.,* Santa Fe Industries v. Green, 430 U.S. 462 (1977). The Court concluded: "The term [manipulation] refers generally to practices, such as wash sales, matched orders, or rigged prices that are intended to mislead investors by artificially affecting market activity." *Id.* at 476.

The critical issue that courts must address is whether the defensive tactics that have come under SEC and Congressional scrutiny are "fraudulent, deceptive, or manipulative acts or practices" within the meaning of Section 14(e). The initial inquiry must therefore center upon: (1) an analysis of the effect such defensive tactics have on the tender offer market for the target company's shares; and (2) the ability of shareholders, who so desire, to participate in the tender offer. Arguably, any action taken by the company as a defense against an unwelcome tender offer has a potentially artificial impact on market activity and limits the ability of shareholders to participate in an offer. However, the Supreme Court has previously construed manipulation in the Section 10(b) context to connote "intentional or willful conduct designed to deceive or defraud investors by controlling or artificially affecting the price of securities."[23]

An argument can be set forth that where defensive tactics have an artificial impact on the market, they can be found to be a manipulative practice, within the meaning of Section 14(e), without being viewed as perpetrating a fraud upon shareholders. Moreover, defensive tactics can perpetrate a fraud upon investors, even absent a manipulation, by denying shareholders the opportunity to participate in a tender offer, thereby precluding them from realizing a premium above the market price of the stock. In short, by the courts construing Section 14(e) as only a disclosure statute, shareholders are denied substantive protections.

The determination of whether an act or practice in the context of a tender offer constitutes a manipulative practice should be centered upon whether the conduct was intentional, the motive for employing the tactics at issue, and whether the conduct at issue distorts the stock's price as compared with the stock's expected value in a true auction market. Thus, the essential inquiry centers on whether the defensive tactic has an artificial impact upon market activity.

Such an interpretation suggests a distinction between deceptive acts and manipulative acts. Congress's use of the disjunctive in Section 14(e), which bars "fraudulent, deceptive, *or* manipulative acts or practices" supports such an interpretation.[24] Further support for the position that manipulative schemes need not necessarily involve deception can be found by implication in the Supreme Court's statement that "nondisclosure is *usually* essential to the success of a manipulative scheme."[25]

Such an interpretation of Section 14(e) is not particularly radical when viewed in the context of implementing the Congressional intent of the Williams Act. The Williams Act was designed to protect shareholders through its extensive reporting requirements, its grant of substantive rights to ten-

---

23. Ernst & Ernst v. Hochfelder, 425 U.S. 185, 199 (1976).
24. 15 U.S.C. § 78n(e) (1982) (emphasis added).
25. Santa Fe Industries v. Green, 430 U.S. at 477.

dering shareholders, and its prohibition against all fraudulent, deceptive, or manipulative acts "in connection with any tender offer or request or initiation for tenders, or any solicitation of security holders in opposition to or in favor of any such offer, request or invitation."[26]

Although there are no specific provisions of the Act that identify or define fraudulent or deceptive or manipulative acts or practices, the language of Section 14(e) and an examination of its legislative history support an interpretation that Section 14(e)'s ban includes any manipulative act, regardless of its origin, that artificially impairs the tender offer market for a company's shares.[27]

IV. A CASE EXAMPLE: A LOOK AT *DATA PROBE*

An interpretation of Section 14(e) that more nearly satisfies the legislative intent of the Williams Act was articulated by Judge Sofar in *Data Probe Acquisition Corp. v. Datatab, Inc.*[28] Although reversed by the Second Circuit,[29] United States District Court Judge Sofar's well-reasoned opinion in *Data Probe* found that the proscriptions of Section 14(e) of the Securities Exchange Act of 1934 include a prohibition against fraudulent and manipulative activities. The significance of Judge Sofar's decision is the finding that the language of Section 14(e) has greater breadth than the analogous language found in Rule 10b-5.[30] In *Data Probe*, Judge Sofar ruled that unlike

---

26. 15 U.S.C. § 78n(e) (1982).

27. *See, e.g.*, Justice White's plurality opinion in Edgar v. MITE Corp., 457 U.S. 624 (1982). Justice White noted:

> [I]t is ... crystal clear that a major aspect of the [Williams Act's] effort to protect the investor was to avoid favoring either management or the takeover bidder. ... We, therefore, agree with the Court of Appeals that Congress sought to protect the investor not only by furnishing him with the necessary information but also by withholding from management or the bidder any undue advantage that could frustrate the exercise of an informed choice.

Id. at 633-34. *See also* Full Disclosure of Corporate Equity Ownership and in Corporate Takeover Bids: Hearings on S. 510 before the Subcomm. on Securities of the Senate Comm. on Banking and Currency, 90th Cong., 1st Sess. 15 (1967); House Comm. on Foreign Commerce, Disclosure of Corporate Equity Ownership, H.R. Rep. No. 1711, 90th Cong. 2d Sess. 5 (1968); Senate Comm. on Banking & Currency, Full Disclosure of Corporate Equity Ownership and in Corporate Takeover Bids, S. Rep. No. 550, 90th Cong., 2d Sess. 3 (1967); 113 Cong. Rec. 854–855 (1967) (remarks of Sen. Williams).

28. 568 F. Supp. 1528 (S.D.N.Y. 1983).

29. 722 F.2d 1 (2d Cir. 1983), *cert. denied*, 104 S. Ct. 1326 (1984) ("Justice Powell would grant certiorari").

30. 430 U.S. 462 (1977). *Santa Fe* involved the merger of a partially owned

Section 10(b) of the Exchange Act, the definition of manipulative acts or practices under Section 14(e) is not limited simply to the question of the adequacy of disclosure; the enactment into law in 1968 of Section 14(e) with the passage of the Williams Act regulated more than the adequacy of disclosure or the lack thereof.

Judge Sofar justified this interpretation of Section 14(e) upon a finding that the purpose of the Williams Act, as reflected in its legislative history, contemplated that additional protection was necessary for investors because of the nature of tender offers. Judge Sofar explained as follows:

> Merely requiring disclosure of material facts does not assure share-holders a fair opportunity actually to tender their shares. To achieve the [Williams] Act's objectives most effectively, it should be construed to require that shareholders also be protected from those devices that unduly interfere with informed tenders.[31]

Judge Sofar's holding is logical from both a philosophical and policy perspective of the Williams Act's intended protections. In short, Section 14(e)—unlike Section 10(b)—was designed to do more than regulate disclosures; it was enacted to proscribe certain kinds of substantive fraud in connection with tender offers.

A. Facts

The *Data Probe* case arose out of a hostile tender offer; the target company's response effectively precluded the tender offeror from possible success. The target company, Datatab, Inc., and CRC Information Systems, Inc., had entered into successful discussions about a possible merger between the two companies. On May 26, 1983, proxy materials were sent to Datatab's shareholders explaining and recommending the merger offer made by CRC.

---

subsidiary into its parent corporation. Because only 5% of the subsidiary's stock was not owned by the parent, the parent company was able to use a simplified procedure under Delaware law known as a "short-form" merger. This simplified procedure provided for a merger to be consummated without approval from either companies' shareholders when the parent owns at least 90% of the subsidiary. A shareholder of the subsidiary brought suit under Rule 10b-5 alleging that the cash offer for purchase of the shares pursuant to the merger was grossly inadequate and therefore constituted a fraud under the rule. The Supreme Court held that the plaintiff's remedy was to sue in state court; Rule 10b-5 did not proscribe a mere breach of duty. "[T]he transaction...was neither deceptive nor manipulative and therefore did not violate either § 10(b) of the [Exchange] Act or Rule 10b-5." *Id.* at 474.

31. 568 F. Supp. at 1547.

Among other things, the proxy materials stated that Datatab's Board of Directors felt the offer of $1.00 per share of Datatab was a fair price and that a special shareholders' meeting to discuss and vote on the proposed merger was announced to be held on June 23, 1983.[32]

On June 21, 1983, Data Probe, Inc., announced a cash tender offer for all outstanding common stock of Datatab. On June 23, 1983, Datatab's special shareholders' meeting to discuss and vote on the merger offer by CRC was cancelled and rescheduled for a later time.

In response to Data Probe's offer, CRC increased the per share offer price for Datatab to $1.40. CRC, however, made its $1.40 per share offer conditional: Datatab's management would have to grant CRC a one-year option whereby CRC could purchase the 1,407,674 voting shares of Datatab's authorized but unissued stock[33] for CRC to make the $1.40 per share offer. Datatab's authorized but unissued stock was double the amount of its stock then outstanding.

On July 1, 1983, Datatab's management agreed to grant CRC a one-year option to purchase all of Datatab's authorized but unissued stock in connection with management's decision to accept the new merger offer. The same day, a notice was sent to Datatab shareholders recommending acceptance of CRC's new merger offer, explaining management's decision to grant CRC an irrevocable option to purchase Datatab's authorized but unissued stock and scheduling a meeting in August for shareholders to have the opportunity to vote on CRC's amended merger agreement. Datatab did not explicitly inform its shareholders, however, that the irrevocable one-year option that management granted CRC effectively rendered nugatory the shareholder vote on CRC's amended merger offer. Moreover, Datatab did not inform its shareholders that the grant of the option to CRC effectively ended the possibility of future increased bids for the company by Data Probe or any other entity. This resulted from CRC's ability to force Datatab into a merger.

The irrevocable option granted CRC by Datatab's management—a decision which was not reviewable by Datatab's shareholders—had the effect of ensuring that Datatab's proposed merger with CRC would occur regardless of what action Datatab's shareholders took at the special meeting that had been called to discuss and vote on CRC's proposed merger offer. CRC's option to purchase Datatab's authorized but unissued stock meant that CRC alone—if it exercised its option granted by Datatab's management—could

---

32. In addition, the proxy materials disclosed that if the merger plan were successful, the principal officers of Datatab, who then only had month-to-month employment agreements, would receive three-year employment contracts at increased salaries.

33. The price per share for Datatab's authorized but unissued shares was also $1.40.

force approval of its own merger offer. Moreover, Data Probe or any other entity was effectively precluded from increasing the price offered for Datatab stock; with its option to purchase Datatab's authorized but unissued stock, CRC was in a position to force the merger at $1.40 per share. Datatab's grant of this option to CRC effectively nullified any potentially successful competing bids for Datatab stock. If the option was valid, the highest price per share that Datatab shareholders would be able to receive would be $1.40.

Datatab subsequently made a second tender offer for all Datatab shares outstanding on July 14, 1983; its per share bid was increased to $1.55. At the same time, Data Probe filed suit in federal district court in the Southern District of New York claiming, among other things, that the irrevocable option granted to CRC by Datatab—or "lock-up agreement"—constituted a manipulative act or practice in connection with a tender offer and therefore violated Section 14(e).[34]

B. Holding and Analysis

Judge Sofar found that Datatab's grant of an irrevocable option to CRC to purchase 200 percent of Datatab's authorized but unissued stock effectively invalidated Datatab's shareholders' opportunity to vote on the merger offer, halted the auction market for Datatab stock that would otherwise have continued to function, and therefore constituted a manipulative act or practice in connection with a tender offer as prohibited by Section 14(e). As a result, Judge Sofar granted Data Probe's request that an injunction issue in order to bar the merger between Datatab and CRC.

An important issue raised in *Data Probe* is "whether the Williams Act is anything more than a disclosure statute."[35] After a lengthy review of the Act's legislative history as well as judicial interpretations thereof, Judge Sofar concluded that Section 14(e) regulated more than simply the adequacy of disclosure.

> A different form of protection is necessary under the Williams Act, because tender offer battles, even in a context of full disclosure, create extreme pressures and may involve tactics which distort or even abort the investment decision. Furthermore, whereas available state court remedies might be sufficient to warrant refusing to recognize a federal claim for "unfairness" under Section 10(b), a federal, injunctive rem-

---

34. The plaintiffs also claimed that Datatab's July 1, 1983, letter to its shareholders constituted a proxy solicitation in violation of Section 14(a) of the Exchange Act because, among other things, of its failure to disclose material information. Judge Sofar determined that the Section 14(a) claim was not sufficient for injunctive relief.

35. 568 F. Supp. at 1543.

edy is a necessary adjunct to the Williams Act goal of preventing abuses of the tender offer procedure *before* they damage shareholders by undermining or aborting the tender offer process.[36]

The Act's purpose was not to provide for qualitative fairness; it was designed to provide shareholders with the information necessary to have an informed judgment as well as an opportunity to exercise that judgment. Judge Sofar explained as follows: "Congress therefore imposed in the Act not one, but two duties on tender-offer participants: first, to provide shareholders the required information; and second, to refrain from any conduct that unduly impedes the shareholders' exercise of the decision-making prerogative guaranteed to them by Congress."[37] The logic and simplicity of Judge Sofar's essential premise is unassailable: of what value is the disclosure of information necessary to make an investment decision if an opportunity to use the information received and exercise an investment decision is denied? The Williams Act "concerned not only the provision of information, but the guarantee of a fair opportunity to use it."[38]

In a cursory rejection of Judge Sofar's analysis, the Second Circuit in an opinion authored by Judge Winter reversed the district court's holding.[39] Judge Winter concluded that Datatab's grant to CRC of an irrevocable option to purchase 300 percent of Datatab's authorized but unissued stock was neither manipulative nor made in a misleading manner so as to violate Section 14(e). The Second Circuit determined that Datatab's violation—if one existed—should be redressed in state court for management's breach of its fiduciary duty.

Judge Winter framed narrowly the question to be decided as follows: "whether Section 14(e) authorizes federal courts to review the substantive validity of corporate actions undertaken during the course of a tender offer."[40] The federal securities laws, held the Second Circuit citing *Santa Fe*, provide no relief for instances of corporate mismanagement that amount merely to a breach of a fiduciary duty. Judge Winter stated that "[a] complaint which alleges only that management has for self-serving reasons acted so as to deprive shareholders of a favorable financial opportunity does not state a valid claim under Section 14(e)...."[41]

The Second Circuit concluded that "[m]isrepresentation is thus an essential element of a cause of action under Section 14(e)."[42] With respect

---

36. *Id.* at 1544 (emphasis in original).

37. *Id.* at 1545.

38. *Id.* at 1547.

39. Data Probe v. Datatab, [1983–1984 Transfer Binder] Fed. Sec. L. Rep. (CCH) ¶ 99,569 at 97,240 (2d Cir. Nov. 22, 1983).

40. *Id.* at 97,240.

41. *Id.* at 97,241.

42. *Id.*

to Datatab's failure to inform its shareholders that management's grant of an option effectively deprived its shareholders of a meaningful opportunity to participate in the merger decision, the court found such failure to be inconsequential:

> As for the failure to state that the option, if valid, brought the takeover contest to an end, that conclusion is obvious to anyone conversant with elementary mathematics. We are also not inclined to subject every tender offer to nitpicking judicial scrutiny which will in the long run injure shareholders by preventing them from taking advantage of favorable offers.[43]

It is astonishing that judicial scrutiny of the actions taken by Datatab's management—with undisclosed effect—that halted the auction market for Datatab stock during the pendency of a tender offer, thereby injuring shareholders, could be viewed as "nitpicking." The essence of Judge Winter's holding is to deprive shareholders of the right to participate in an ongoing tender offer—an intended objective with the passage of the Williams Act. A hostile tender offer is a fierce battle fought between two entities. Under such circumstances, time is of the essence and information is often communicated to shareholders under hurried circumstances.

The Williams Act was passed not only to compel tender offerors and subject companies to provide certain information to the public so that shareholders could make a reasoned investment decision but also to insure such shareholders an opportunity to use such information. Obviously, there is no value in requiring that information be provided shareholders if the opportunity to use such information to make an investment decision is precluded.

Judge Sofar's decision upheld the self-evident and legislatively proclaimed intent of the Williams Act—in addition to the disclosure of required information during a tender offer, there must also be no impediment to the meaningful use of that information. Such an impediment constitutes a violation of Section 14(e). In *Data Probe*, the shareholders of Datatab were deprived by the company's management of further opportunity to participate in the tender offer process.

V. STATE REGULATION OF DEFENSIVE TACTICS

By construing Section 14(e) as merely prohibiting deceit, the federal courts have abrogated to the states the responsibility of protecting the substantive rights of shareholders confronted by tender offers and defensive

---

43. *Id.* at 97,242.

tactics.[44] Such an abrogation of authority presents problems because the states have been ineffective in protecting the rights of shareholders in such situations.

The state statutes provide the regulatory framework which defines the relationships among a company's directors, corporate managers, and shareholders.[45] The directors of a corporation are permitted to have a great deal of discretion in the operation of corporate affairs. This discretion is limited by the fiduciary duties of loyalty and care to shareholders imposed by state statutes and case law. The fiduciary duties management owes to shareholders, however, were not conceived as a method of regulating corporate conduct during battles for corporate control. Moreover, when invoked as a basis for challenging the conduct of corporate management in the midst of tender offers, arguments based on breach of fiduciary duty have met with little, if any, success.[46]

---

44. The application by the ill-conceived progeny of *Santa Fe* to Section 14(e) emphasizes that challenges to the use of defensive techniques are "precisely the kind of claim the Supreme Court in *Santa Fe* felt should be decided under state corporate law." Altman v. Knight, 431 F. Supp. 309, 314 (S.D.N.Y. 1977). The logical conclusion of such an interpretation of Section 14(e) is reflected by that court's statement: "[I]t is clear that [the target's defensive acquisition,] even if for no valid business purpose, does not alone constitute a manipulative or deceptive device, as is necessary to state a claim under § 14(e) of the Act." *Id.* at 313–14. Such a pronouncement reveals the court's failure to consider the impact on the price of shareholders' stock of a corporate action that has no economic justification other than to defeat a tender offer. This is the type of corporate conduct a broader application of Section 14(e) would prohibit.

45. Traditionally, state corporate law has governed the internal formation and operation of corporations. However, state law has proven to be inadequate, and the remedies afforded shareholders under state law would appear to have diminished since the Commission announced its going-private rules in 1979.

In deferring the decision as to whether its going-private rules should include a fairness requirement, the SEC noted that "developments in the remedies provided by state law for unfairness in going private transactions will also be important" in deciding whether there should be a fairness requirement in the Commission's going-private rules. Securities Exchange Act Release No. 16075.

One reason for the inadequacy of state remedies is that appraisal may be held to be an exclusive remedy, thereby blocking a shareholder from seeking a remedy for breach of fiduciary duty in a state court. *See* Weinberger v. UOP, Inc., 457 A.2d 701, 714–715 (Del. 1983).

Even if an appraisal remedy is not exclusive, the effectiveness of a state law remedy is uncertain because of confusion in the law as to whether a state court suit brought as a class action on behalf of all shareholders binds class members who are not residents of the state where the lawsuit is brought. Since the ability to bring an action as a class action is critical in determining whether it makes economic sense to pursue the litigation, the uncertainty of state law is therefore important.

46. *See, e.g.,* Panter v. Marshall Field & Co., 646 F.2d 271 (7th Cir.), *cert. denied,*

In the last decade, several states enacted legislation designed to regulate directly tender offers. These regulations typically took the form of antitakeover statutes which protected incumbent corporate management.[47] Until the Supreme Court's decision in *Edgar v. MITE Corp.*, state takeover legislation was an important aspect of the structuring of almost any nationwide tender offer.[48] In *Edgar v. MITE Corp.*, the Court held that the Illinois antitakeover statute was unconstitutional because it imposed an impermissible burden on interstate commerce.[49] Corporate management has responded to this decision by developing and deploying defensive tactics, often without shareholder consent, to restore the competitive advantage that it previously enjoyed under state antitakeover provisions.

An important reason why state law has been ineffective in this area is the application of the business judgment rule which virtually insulates management from liability. When the legality of defensive tactics has been challenged under state corporation law, the courts have rejected these challenges holding that the business judgment rule[50] gives target directors virtually

---

454 U.S. 1092 (1981); Johnson v. Trueblood, 629 F.2d 287 (3d Cir. 1980), *cert. denied*, 450 U.S. 999 (1981); Crouse-Hinds Co. v. InterNorth, Inc., 634 F.2d 690, 702–03 (2d Cir. 1980); Heit v. Baird, 567 F.2d 1157, 1161 (1st Cir. 1977); Lynch & Steinberg, *The Legitimacy of Defensive Tactics in Tender Offers*, 64 Cornell L. Rev. 901, 926 (1979); Rosenzweig, *The Legality of "Lock-Ups" and Other Responses of Directors to Hostile Takeover Bids or Stock Aggregations*, 10 Sec. Reg. L.J. 291, 294 (1983). *See also* Pogo Producing Co. v. Northwest Industries, Civil No. H-83-2667 (S.D. Tex. May 24, 1983); Conoco, Inc. v. Seagram Co., 517 F. Supp. 1299 (S.D.N.Y. 1981).

47. *See generally*, Langevoort, *State Tender Offer Legislation: Interests, Effects and Political Competency*, 62 Cornell L. Rev. 213, 217–218 (1977).

48. *See generally* Shapiro, *State Takeover Laws*, 12 Inst. on Sec. Reg. 401 (1980).

49. 457 U.S. at 634. For example, the Sixth Circuit relied on *MITE* to invalidate the application of the antifraud provisions of the Michigan blue sky statute to national tender offers, even though the state limited its role to the protection of local shareholders. *See* Martin Marietta Corp. v. Bendix Corp., 690 F.2d 558, 567 (6th Cir. 1982). Similarly, the Maryland district court applied *MITE* in striking down the Maryland takeover statute in Bendix Corp. v. Martin Marietta Corp., 547 F. Supp. 522 (D. Md. 1982). Also, the Second Circuit applied *MITE* to strike down provisions of the Connecticut Liquor Control Act in United States Brewers Association v. Healy, 692 F.2d 275 (2d Cir. 1982).

50. The business judgment rule provides that:

> a court will not interfere with the judgment of a board of directors unless there is a showing of gross and palpable overreaching. A board of directors enjoys a presumption of sound business judgment, and its decisions will not be disturbed if they can be attributed to any rational business purpose. A court under such circumstances will not substitute its own notions of what is or is not sound business judgment.

Sinclair Oil Corp. v. Levien, 280 A.2d 717, 720 (Del. 1971) (citations omitted).

unassailable discretion in countering tender offers.[51] As a practical matter, officers and directors are always able to come up with some alleged reason why the actions they have taken are in the best interests of the shareholders and are not designed simply to benefit themselves. In addition, in the overwhelming preponderance of cases, the so-called outside directors rally behind management to protect the insiders from shareholder attack. It is very difficult to overcome the seeming independence of these outside directors, many of whom have local or national prestige. Since the burden is on the shareholder to demonstrate affirmatively lack of any reasonable business judgment, the shareholder has an almost impossible task if the issue is resolved under the business judgment rule.

Historically, the protections afforded management by the business judgment rule do not apply in a conflict-of-interest situation. However, the courts have been reluctant to define takeover situations as conflict-of-interest situations and have applied the business judgment rule unless it can be shown conclusively that protection of management jobs was management's *sole* or *primary* purpose. The courts have generally applied a presumption of good faith on management's part and placed the burden on the shareholders to demonstrate affirmatively the opposite.[52] The burden on shareholders has been unreasonable and represents a judicial blindness to the practical realities of takeover situations.[53]

As previously noted, actions by directors are frequently insulated from judicial scrutiny under the business judgment rule because of the participation in the decision by so-called independent directors.[54] However, empirical studies have demonstrated that so-called disinterested directors are likely to be influenced by loyalty to existing management and cannot be trusted to be truly disinterested.[55]

---

51. *See* note 47 *supra.*

52. *See, e.g.*, Aronson v. Lewis, 473 A.2d 805, (Del. 1984). Panter v. Marshall Field & Co., 646 F.2d 271 (7th Cir. 1981), and cases cited in the *Panter* opinion at 295.

53. *See* the dissenting opinion by Judge Cudahy in *Panter*, 646 F.2d at 299.

54. The courts have also applied undue deference to the opinions of investment bankers, who are strongly motivated to cultivate good relationships with management, and "special committees" established by the board.

55. *See* Note, *The Business Judgment Rule in Derivative Suits against Directors*, 65 Cornell L. Rev. 600 (1980):

> Numerous empirical studies have demonstrated the extent to which directors are economically or psychologically dependent upon or tied to the corporation's executives, particularly its chief executive.... Additionally, outside directors on a typical board who are lawyers, bankers, or major customers of the corporation are likely to be responsive to subtle pressure to support the incumbent management with whom [they hope] to have future dealings.

The significant structural biases which typically prevent outside directors from being truly independent have been recognized by several courts.[56] Despite such decisions, most courts, including the court which decided *Zapata v. Maldanado*, have remained extremely deferential in situations where future benefits to management are involved.[57] Even the courts in jurisdictions which have recognized the danger of director bias have typically failed to examine the actual fairness to shareholders of management activities and have severely limited their review to an inquiry regarding management's apparent independence and good faith.

Therefore, absent a federal check in the form of either judicial review or legislation, defensive actions by target management might, as a practical matter, go unregulated because of the applicability of the business judgment rule in actions predicated on state law.[58] This sentiment was expressed by Judge Cudahy in *Panter v. Marshall Field & Co.*:

> I emphatically disagree that the business judgment rule should clothe directors, battling blindly to fend off a threat to their control, with an almost irrebuttable presumption of sound business judgment, prevailing over everything but the elusive hobgoblins of fraud, bad faith or abuse of discretion.[59]

To limit the ability of target managements to entrench themselves with impunity by hiding behind the business judgment rule, the courts should apply the rule differently to defensive actions which were prompted by the

---

Id. at 619–621, and the studies cited therein.

See also M. Eisenberg, The Structure of the Corporation 147 (1976):

> The retired chairman of a medium-sized company in the midwest stated: "In the companies I know, the outside directors always agree with management. That's why they are there. I have one friend that's just the greatest agreer that ever was, and he is on a dozen boards...."

56. *E.g.,* Hasan v. CleveTrust Realty Investors, [1983–84 Transfer Binder] Fed. Sec. L. Rep. (CCH) ¶ 99,704 (6th Cir. 1984); Joy v. North, [1982 Transfer Binder] Fed. Sec. L. Rep. (CCH) ¶ 98,860 (2d Cir. 1982); Zapata Corp. v. Maldanado, 430 A.2d 779, 787 (Del. 1981).

57. *E.g.,* Aronson v. Lewis, 473 A.2d 805 (Del. 1984).

58. The Second, Third, and Seventh Circuits have rejected state law challenges to the utilization by target companies of various defensive tactics to thwart unwelcome takeover bids. Treadway Cos. v. Care Corp., 638 F.2d 357 (2d Cir. 1980); Crouse-Hinds Co. v. InterNorth, Inc., 634 F.2d 690 (2d Cir. 1980); Johnson v. Trueblood, 629 F.2d 287 (3d Cir. 1980); Panter v. Marshall Field & Co., 646 F.2d 271 (7th Cir.), *cert. denied,* 454 U.S. 1092 (1981).

59. Panter v. Marshall Field & Co., 646 F.2d 271, 299 (7th Cir.), *cert. denied,* 454 U.S. 1092 (1981).

initiation of a tender offer. Unless the business judgment is construed differently, it may also become the paramount obstacle to any allegation that a particular defensive tactic is violative of Section 14(e).[60] The business judgment rule has been effectively asserted as an affirmative defense, because courts have been reluctant to enter the boardroom and tamper with the conduct of corporate affairs. The courts have reasoned that corporate management, rather than the judiciary, is particularly well qualified to make business judgments.[61]

Management's opposition to an unwelcome tender offer is justified where, for example, the takeover bid was financially inadequate or would harm the corporate enterprise.[62] In fact, management may have an affirmative obligation to oppose inadequate or illegal offers, and any action taken to satisfy this obligation is properly protected.[63] However, the protections of the business judgment rule should not be so willingly extended by the courts reviewing the propriety of a defensive tactic in the absence of a showing that management acted reasonably and in the best interests of the shareholders.

The decisions which have applied the business judgment rule to uphold the validity of various defensive tactics employed by target management have applied the business judgment rule in a traditional manner. Such an application of the business judgment rule in the context of tender offers is inappropriate due to the nature of the transaction itself and the economic interests of those affected by the offer.[64] In the context of a tender offer,

---

60. Mobil Corp. v. Marathon Oil Co., [1981–1982 Transfer Binder] Fed. Sec. L. Rep. (CCH) ¶ 98,375 at 92,285 (S.D. Ohio, Dec 7), rev'd, 669 F.2d 366 (6th Cir. 1981).

61. For example, in Crouse-Hinds Co. v. InterNorth, Inc., the court observed "the prudent recognition that courts are ill equipped and infrequently called on to evaluate what are and must be essentially business judgments." 634 F.2d 690, 702 (2d Cir. 1980) (quoting Auerbach v. Bennett, 47 N.Y.2d 619, 629–31, 419 N.Y.S.2d 920, 926–27, 393 N.E. 2d 994 (1979)).

62. See, e.g., Heit v. Baird, 567 F.2d 1157, 1161 (1st Cir. 1977). See also Panter v. Marshall Field & Co., 646 F.2d 271, 297 (7th Cir.), cert. denied, 454 U.S. 1092 (1981); Treadway Cos. v. Care Corp., 638 F.2d 357, 382–83 (2d Cir. 1980); Crouse-Hinds Co. v. InterNorth, Inc., 634 F.2d 690, 702 (2d Cir. 1980); Conoco, Inc. v. Mobil Oil Corp., No. 4787 (S.D.N.Y. Aug. 4, 1981); GM Sub Corp. v. Liggett Group, Inc., No. 6155 (Del. Ch. Apr. 25, 1981).

63. See, e.g., Crouse-Hinds Co. v. InterNorth, Inc., 634 F.2d 690, 701 (2d Cir. 1980) ("The starting point for analysis of an attack by a shareholder on a transaction of the corporation is the business judgment rule.").

64. See, e.g., Note, The Misapplication of the Business Judgment Rule in Contests for Corporate Control, 76 Nw. U.L. Rev. 980 (1982); Klein, Takeover Abuses Demand Congressional Reform, Legal Times (Wash.), June 25, 1984, at 12.

the courts must apply the business judgment rule in a manner that distinguishes those actions which are undertaken for the benefit of the corporation and its shareholders from those that are directed primarily at protecting corporate control.

A departure from the traditional application of the business judgment rule,[65] which protects management's actions, is justified where corporate conduct is motivated by a hostile tender offer.[66] Where decisions involve the daily operation of the company, the interests of a majority of the company's shareholders and its management usually coincide. Courts must recognize that this is not the case in hostile tender offers. In applying the business judgment rule to a hostile tender offer, the interests of shareholders would be better served if the courts gave greater recognition to potential conflicts of interest between shareholders and the board. Unlike the ordinary business decisions made by directors, decisions to defend against hostile tender offers are often in part motivated by self-interest. Position, perquisites, and prestige can understandably compel the target's board to defend against a hostile tender offer where the best interests of the shareholders dictate otherwise.[67] In sum, because of the exigencies created by the belligerent environment surrounding tender offers, the rule cannot be applied in the same manner as it applies to other major business decisions.

This is not to say that courts should abandon the business judgment rule

---

65. The business judgment rule provides protection for informed business decisions that are honestly and rationally undertaken in good faith by a properly informed board of directors. Absent proof of self-dealing, improper purpose, or other fiduciary breach, the decisions of the board generally will be sustained. Challengers must first establish a breach of duty before substantive judicial review can occur. *See generally* Arsht, *The Business Judgment Rule Revisited*, 8 Hofstra L. Rev. 93 (1979); Fischel, *Efficient Capital Market Theory, the Market for Corporate Control, and the Regulation of Cash Tender Offers*, 57 Tex. L. Rev. 1 (1979); Huber, *Hostile Tender Offers and the Business Judgment Rule: Another Prospective*, Remarks to the American Bar Association, Section of Corporation, Banking, and Business Law, Ninth Annual Spring Meeting, April 7, 1984.

66. In advancing this application of the business judgment rule, the authors depart from the Advisory Committee Report which recommended that "the business judgment rule should be the principal governor of decisions made by corporate management including decisions that may alter the likelihood of takeovers."

67. The dissenting opinions in several recent cases also question the applicability of the rule in the traditional manner where the directors' actions were undertaken in the face of a challenge to their control. *See* Treadway Cos. v. Care Corp., 638 F.2d 357 (2d Cir. 1980, J. Feinberg dissent); Johnson v. Trueblood, 629 F.2d 287 (3rd Cir. 1980) (J. Rosenn dissent), *cert. denied*, 450 U.S. 999 (1981); Panter v. Marshall Field & Co., 646 F.2d 271 (7th Cir.) (J. Cudahy dissent), *cert. denied*, 454 U.S. 1092 (1981).

altogether in the context of tender offers. The rule's protection of decisions that are made in good faith, all due care, and total loyalty need not be abandoned. However, in determining the applicability of the rule to tender offer contests, the courts should shift the burden of proof from those challenging target management's conduct. In such contested tender offers, the burden should be placed upon the target's directors and officers to justify their actions both prior to and in the "heat" of a hostile tender offer.[68] For example, the burden should be shifted in situations involving anticipated takeover activity, existing takeover fights, freezeouts, leveraged buy-outs, and situations where management or an affiliate takes steps that may injure shareholders by eliminating or materially impairing the public market for trading in the shares of the company.

This approach, when contrasted with other recent federal legislative proposals in the takeover area, provides a potentially broad solution to many abusive policies. An application of the business judgment rule as proposed is not limited to an effort to identify and proscribe each specific form of activity that is considered undesirable. Certain activities may be reasonable under one set of facts and highly unfair to shareholders in a different situation. Furthermore, one is not always confronted with the "garden-variety" wrong in the takeover area. Managements of large corporations have the resources to pay for the most sophisticated and imaginative advisors, and those advisors are expert in developing new techniques to protect management or to effectuate a coercive takeover without clearly violating the letter of a statute or regulation addressed to a specific form of wrongful activity. A shifting of the burden for breach of fiduciary duty is necessary to enable shareholders to seek relief against whatever types of coercive and unfair tactics may yet be developed.

Moreover, management will sometimes engage in activity that, while it may or may not be a response to a clearly anticipated takeover threat, is aimed at insuring that control will not ultimately pass to "unfriendly" hands (in such circumstances, one may well ask whether the "unfriendly" hands

---

68. The application of the business judgment rule in this manner is not a novel concept. The Delaware courts, for example, have recognized that the burden of proof shifts where the directors' self-interest is shown. In Bennett v. Propp, 187 A.2d 405 (Del. 1962), the Supreme Court of Delaware held that the use of corporate funds to repurchase shares when a threat to control is involved poses an "inherent danger." Said the court: "[T]he directors are of necessity confronted with a conflict of interest and an objective decision is difficult. . . . Hence, in our opinion, the burden should be on the directors to justify such a purchase as one primarily in the corporate interest." 187 A.2d at 409. That holding was subsequently reaffirmed in Cheff v. Mathes, 199 A.2d 548 (Del. 1964). See also Condec Corp. v. Lunkenheimer Co., 230 A.2d 769 (Del. Ch. 1967); Petty v. Penntech Papers, Inc., 347 A.2d 140 (Del. Ch. 1975).

would actually be unfriendly to the shareholders or only to existing management). It is simple realism to question whether management's basic
motivation is not to protect its own position when it engages in tactics such
as placing a controlling block in friendly hands, passing porcupine or "shark"
repellant amendments, utilizing scorched-earth or "Pac-Man" defenses, providing themselves "golden parachutes," or passing supermajority provisions.
The steps taken may eliminate or materially reduce the likelihood that an
outside party will subsequently pay fair value to the shareholders in order
to obtain control (or to obtain all) of the corporation. These steps may also
materially impair the public trading market for the issuer's securities (for
example, by a self-tender for so many shares that the public float is drastically
reduced,[69] creating an extremely thin market) and a delisting of the shares
from a public stock exchange might even result. In such situations, the
shareholders would be seriously injured. Consequently, shifting the burden
requires the corporation and its officers and directors in takeover situations
to demonstrate affirmatively that any action taken was in fact fair to the
shareholders.

Rather than demonstrate that the directors engaged in self-dealing, improper conduct, or a breach of their fiduciary duties, shareholders should
only need make a *prima facie* showing of a likelihood that the board's
response to a hostile tender offer will result in its entrenchment or the
conferral of benefits at the expense of shareholders' interests. The burden
would then shift to the directors to prove, by a preponderance of the
evidence, that their conduct was undertaken in good faith and with due
care to promote the best interests of the shareholders and the corporation
rather than their own.[70] Judicial reluctance to apply the rule as described
above will result in a continued disregard of shareholder interests and a
frustration of the federal regulatory scheme.[71]

---

69. An example of a large self-tender is found in Carter Hawley Hale's efforts to
fend off The Limited, in part through massive stock repurchases.

70. *See, e.g.*, Klein, *Takeover Abuses Demand Congressional Reform, supra* note
64, at 14. The creation of a federal cause of action that would shift the burden upon
management to justify its actions during the pendency of a tender offer has prompted
a legislative proposal which is presently under consideration by the Telecommunications, Consumer Protection, and Finance Subcommittee of the House Committee
on Energy and Commerce. *See* Hearings, *supra* note 27.

71. During Senate hearings on the Williams Act, former Commission Chairman
Manuel F. Cohen observed that one of the principal purposes of the Williams Act
was to provide protection against

> management efforts designed to resist bids when the information furnished
> may be given in the context in which the desire to obtain and retain existing
> emoluments may make difficult impartial and complete disclosure of relevant
> factors. . . .

VI. CONCLUSION

Section 14(e) of the Williams Act can be applied by the courts in a substantive manner to examine the legality of various defensive tactics employed by the directors of a target company. The legislative history and purpose support an application of Section 14(e) that results in a finding that certain defensive tactics are violative of the statute's proscription against manipulation.

Absent judicial construction of Section 14(e) in a substantive manner, the remaining recourse to challenge the validity of defensive tactics lies in state common law causes of action. To date, actions based upon state law have met with little success because of the traditional application of the business judgment rule in the context of tender offers. The traditional application of the business judgment rule is not warranted in this context. Unlike the ordinary business decisions made by directors, tender offers create an environment where the best interests of the company and its shareholders and those of the directors do not coincide. Therefore, the courts should be reluctant to employ a traditional application of the business judgment rule where the decisions of directors are influenced by forces tending to create conflicts of interests.

It would be naive to assume that tender offers are not, at times opposed by managements motivated by their own interests in staving off a change in control.

Full Disclosure of Corporate Equity Ownership and in Corporate Takeover Bids: Hearings on S. 510 before the Subcomm. on Securities of the Senate Comm. on Banking and Currency, 90th Cong., 1st Sess. 19 (1967). *See also id.* at 35, 178, 183, 196, 204–205; Senate Report, *supra*, at 3; Takeover Bids: Hearings on H.R. 14475, S. 510 before the Subcomm. on Comm. and Finance of the House Comm. on Interstate and Foreign Comm., 90th Cong., 2d Sess. 18 (1968); 113 Cong. Rec. 24664 (1967) (Remarks of Sen. Williams).

RICO: The Newest Litigation Gambit in Corporate Takeover Battles

WILLIAM C. TYSON and ANTHONY AIN*

I. INTRODUCTION

Hostile corporate takeovers are synonymous with litigation. Indeed, almost whenever an unfriendly corporate takeover is launched, the corporation targeted for takeover dashes to the courthouse, intent on charging the raiding corporation with every impropriety that counsel can muster.[1] The

*William C. Tyson is assistant professor, The Wharton School, University of Pennsylvania. A.B., 1967, Princeton University; J.D., 1970, Harvard University. Anthony Ain is an associate of Fried, Frank, Harris, Shriver & Jacobson, Washington, D.C. A.B., 1980, Cornell University; J.D., 1984, University of Pennsylvania. This chapter was originally published as an article in 6 J. Comp. Bus. & Cap. Mkt. L. 355 (1984) by North-Holland Publishing Company, which holds copyright on the article. All rights reserved.

1. *See, e.g.*, E. Aranow, H. Einhorn & G. Berlstein, Developments in Tender Offers for Corporate Control 193–206 (1977); Easterbrook & Fischel, *The Proper Role of a Target's Management in Responding to a Tender Offer,* 94 Harv. L. Rev. 1161 (1981). Judge Friendly described the inevitable stream of litigation from a hostile tender offer in this way:

> Drawing Excalibur from a scabbard where it would doubtless have remained sheathed in the face of a friendly tender offer, the target typically hopes to obtain a temporary injunction which may frustrate the acquisition since the offering company may well decline the expensive gambit of a trial or, if it persists, the long lapse of time could so change conditions that the offer will fail even if, after a full trial and appeal, it should be determined that no ... violation has been shown.

Missouri Portland Cement Co. v. Cargill, Inc., 498 F.2d 851, 854 (2d Cir.), *cert. denied*, 419 U.S. 883 (1974). *See also* 1 A. Fleischer, Tender Offers: Defenses,

newest gambit that targets' counsel have stumbled upon, which seems to have escaped their ingenuity for over a decade,[2] is a suit based on the Racketeer Influenced and Corrupt Organizations Act (RICO),[3] a federal statute enacted in 1970.

In this chapter, at the outset, we set forth the basic structure of the RICO statute and illustrate how target management has utilized RICO in its mission to thwart a hostile, and allegedly unlawful, takeover attempt. We then review the cases in which targets have embarked on such a litigation course in order to examine the mixed judicial endorsement and resistance that they have encountered and inspect some of the vexing questions that have arisen. In the next section of the chapter, we suggest the framework and the likely underpinnings for an as yet untested RICO suit, one instituted by a bidder for corporate control. Last, we make an overall assessment of RICO's use in takeover battles. In subscribing to the notion—which underlies the decisions of many courts that have heard RICO cases—that it is the function of Congress, not the courts, to impose restrictions on RICO's use, we conclude (1) that in the absence of such restrictions, RICO is a potent and significant litigation strategy and (2) that if Congress, when it drafted RICO, had been aware of the effect RICO could have, it would have formulated a statute that substantially curtailed the use of RICO in corporate takeover battles. Accordingly, we recommend that Congress act with all due speed to solve what could prove to be an intractable problem.

II. THE RICO ACT AND HOW TARGETS HAVE USED IT

RICO, enacted as Title IX of the Organized Crime Control Act of 1970,[4] seeks to halt organized crime's infiltration of the American economy by creating sanctions and remedies against those who engage in racketeering activity to operate or gain control-of-business enterprises.[5] For example, RICO's Section 1964(c) grants a private right of action for treble damages,

---

Responses, and Planning 299 (2d ed. 1983) ("A well-prepared raider has been advised to anticipate and is ready to defend against aggressive litigation.").

Targets, however, are not the only parties who can bring suit. Especially of late, "bidders have been using the courts offensively" to block a target's defensive tactics. *Id.* at 290.

2. *See, e.g.,* Morrison, *Old Bottle—Not So New Wine: Treble Damages in Actions under the Federal Securities Laws*, 10 Sec. Reg. L.J. 67, 68 (1982); Note, *RICO and Securities Fraud*, 83 Colum. L. Rev. 1513, 1517 (1983).

3. 18 U.S.C. §§ 1961–68 (1982).

4. Pub. L. No. 91-452, § 902–904, 84 Stat. 922, 941–47 (1970) (codified as amended in scattered sections of 18 & 28 U.S.C. (1982)).

5. The Congressional Statement of Findings and Purpose of the Organized Crime Control Act stated that:

a reasonable attorney's fee, and arguably a private right of action for equitable relief, to "any person injured in his business or property by reason of a violation of [RICO's] Section 1962."[6] Section 1962 enumerates three principal violations: Section 1962(a) makes it unlawful to invest funds derived from a pattern of racketeering activity in an enterprise[7] engaged in interstate or foreign commerce,[8] Section 1962(b) makes it unlawful to operate or acquire an interest in any such enterprise through a pattern of racketeering activity,[9] and Section 1962(c) makes it unlawful to conduct the affairs of any such enterprise through a pattern of racketeering activity.[10] Finally, RICO's Section 1961 defines a "pattern of racketeering activity" as at least two occurrences (within ten years) of any of several predicate criminal offenses,[11] including "any offense involving...fraud in the sale of securities ...punishable under any law of the United States"[12] and indictable violations of the federal mail[13] and wire fraud[14] statutes.

Counsel representing target management whose tenure has been threatened by a takeover bid have ostensibly been able to tailor the syntax and substance of the RICO statute to their clients' purposes. They have filed complaints that on their face amply seem to support a RICO suit for damages and equitable relief alleging, for instance, (1) that the raider intentionally effected two fraudulent transactions that violated the federal securities laws or the federal mail and wire fraud statutes, (2) that these criminal transgres-

---

It is the purpose of this Act...to seek the eradication of organized crime in the United States by strengthening the evidence-gathering process, *by establishing new penal prohibitions, and by providing enhanced sanctions and new remedies* to deal with the unlawful activities of those engaged in organized crime.

Id. § 1, 84 Stat. at 923 (reproduced but not codified following 18 U.S.C. § 1961 (1982)) (annotation entitled "Congressional Statement of Findings and Purpose") (emphasis added).

6. 18 U.S.C. § 1964(c) (1982). Section 1964(c) also provides for recovery of "the cost of the suit." *Id.* The issue of the propriety of private injunctive relief under RICO will be discussed *infra* notes 113–17 and accompanying text.

7. An enterprise is defined in § 1961 to include "any individual, partnership, corporation, association, or other legal entity, and any union or group of individuals associated in fact although not a legal entity." *Id.* § 1961(4) (1982).

8. *Id.* § 1962(a). The section also applies to income derived "through collection of an unlawful debt," as do all the other subsections.

9. *Id.* § 1962(b).

10. *Id.* § 1962(c). In addition, § 1962(d) makes it unlawful to conspire to violate any of the three previous subsections. *Id.* § 1962(d).

11. *Id.* § 1961(1), (5).

12. *Id.* § 1961(1) (D).

13. *Id.* § 1961 (1)(B). Mail fraud is indictable under 18 U.S.C. § 1341 (1982).

14. *Id.* § 1961(1)(B). Wire fraud is indictable under 18 U.S.C. § 1343 (1982).

sions facilitated the raider's acquisition of the target's stock, and (3) that the acquisition caused injury to the target's business or property. The threat of a massive RICO award can deter the raider from proceeding with the takeover, and the RICO claim for equitable relief can serve as an engine of delay that could stymie the takeover indefinitely. The initiation of RICO litigation, therefore, can have the seemingly unintended effect of saving target management from displacement.[15]

III. THE JUDICIAL RESPONSE TO RICO IN TAKEOVER BATTLES

RICO claims similar to the ones described above have been brought by target management in five litigated takeover attempts.[16] In each case, the RICO count was based on a violation of one or more of the three major subsections of Section 1962, and in each case the pattern of racketeering activity on which these violations were predicated derived from alleged violations of the federal securities laws, the federal mail and wire fraud statutes, or both. Each RICO claim, which sought damages or equitable relief (or in some instances both remedies), was accompanied by claims seeking like remedies for violations either of the underlying predicate offenses themselves or of other statutory provisions. None of these five RICO cases ever reached trial. In two of the cases, the RICO decisions arose on motions to dismiss, and the RICO charges survived the defendants' motions, but the cases were thereafter settled.[17] In the other three, the RICO decisions arose on motions for equitable relief, and, in each, the RICO allegations were unsuccessful in affording the target the relief it had sought.[18]

---

15. *But cf.* 1 A. Fleischer, *supra* note 1, at 299 ("A well-prepared raider...is not likely to be thwarted merely by the burden, expense, or potential delay which litigation may cause. Unless the bidder has seriously underestimated its legal exposure or overestimated its steadfastness, a target cannot necessarily expect a vigorous litigation campaign to cause the bidder to abandon its offer.").

16. *See* Dan River, Inc. v. Icahn, 701 F.2d 278 (4th Cir. 1983); Bayly Corp. v. Marantette, [1982 Transfer Binder] Fed. Sec. L. Rep. (CCH) ¶ 98,834 (D.D.C. Oct. 19, 1982); Hanna Mining Co. v. Norcen Energy Resources Ltd., [1982 Transfer Binder] Fed. Sec. L. Rep. (CCH) ¶ 98,742 (N.D. Ohio June 11, 1982); Marshall Field & Co. v. Icahn, 537 F. Supp. 413 (S.D.N.Y. 1982); Spencer Cos. v. Agency Rent-A-Car, Inc., [1981–1982 Transfer Binder] Fed. Sec. L. Rep. ¶ 98,361 (D. Mass. Nov. 17, 1981).

17. Hanna Mining Co. v. Norcen Energy Resources Ltd., [1982 Transfer Binder] Fed. Sec. L. Rep. (CCH) ¶ 98,742 (N.D. Ohio June 11, 1982); Spencer Cos. v. Agency Rent-A-Car, Inc., [1981–1982 Transfer Binder] Fed. Sec. L. Rep. (CCH) ¶ 98,361 (D. Mass. Nov. 17, 1981).

18. Dan River, Inc. v. Icahn, 701 F.2d 278 (4th Cir. 1983); Bayly Corp. v. Marantette, [1982 Transfer Binder] Fed. Sec. L. Rep. (CCH) ¶ 98,834 (D.D.C. Oct. 19, 1982); Marshall Field & Co. v. Icahn, 537 F. Supp. 413 (S.D.N.Y. 1982).

One caveat is in order before we turn to a discussion of these five cases. Our narrative of the two suits, in which the RICO charges were successful, encompasses the entire history of the case from complaint to settlement and not only explores the RICO aspects of the litigation but touches on the other claims as well. The purpose of this extended discussion is to provide an overview of the RICO claim in the context of the entire lawsuit so as to facilitate our analysis of the effect of the RICO claim both on the outcome of the litigation and on the takeover battle itself. Our discussion of the three cases in which the RICO counts were unsuccessful, on the other hand, is comparatively brief and focuses instead on the salient features of each court's treatment of the RICO cause of action.

A. The Successful RICO Suits

1. An Overview of the Suits

Spencer Cos. v. Agency Rent-A-Car, Inc.[19] and *Hanna Mining Co. v. Norcen Energy Resources Ltd.*[20] are the two cases in which courts have tacitly

---

19. The litigation in *Spencer* comprises numerous decisions and a variety of issues. The reported decisions, in chronological order, address the following: the major non-RICO counts, Spencer Cos. v. Agency Rent-A-Car, Inc., [1981–1982 Transfer Binder] Fed. Sec. L. Rep. (CCH) ¶ 98,301 (D. Mass. Sept. 21, 1981) [hereinafter cited as *Spencer I*]; the RICO count, Spencer Cos. v. Agency Rent-A-Car, Inc., [1981–1982 Transfer Binder] Fed. Sec. L. Rep. (CCH) ¶ 98,361 (D. Mass. Nov. 17, 1981) [hereinafter cited as *Spencer II*]; Agency's motion for a preliminary injunction enjoining enforcement of the Massachusetts takeover statute, Agency Rent-A-Car, Inc. v. Connolly, 542 F. Supp. 231 (D. Mass.) (preliminary injunction issued; takeover statute preempted by the Williams Act), *rev'd*, 686 F.2d 1029 (1st Cir. 1982); and Spencer's motion for a preliminary injunction based on a non-RICO count, Spencer Cos. v. Agency Rent-A-Car, Inc., 542 F. Supp. 237 (D. Mass. 1982) [hereinafter cited as *Spencer III*].

There are four unreported opinions: Spencer Cos. v. Agency Rent-A-Car, Inc., No. 81-2097-S, slip op. (D. Mass. Jan. 4, 1982) (available June 1, 1982, on LEXIS, Genfed library, Dist file); Spencer Cos. v. Agency Rent-A-Car, Inc., No. 2097-S, slip op. (D. Mass. Dec. 7, 1981) (available June 1, 1982, on LEXIS, Genfed library, Dist file); Agency Rent-A-Car, Inc. v. Spencer Cos., No. 81-2542-S, slip op. (D. Mass. Oct. 15, 1981) (available June 1, 1982, on LEXIS, Genfed library, Dist file); Spencer Cos. v. Agency Rent-A-Car, Inc., No. 81-2097-S, slip op. (D. Mass. Oct. 7, 1981) (available June 1, 1982, on LEXIS, Genfed library, Dist file).

20. There are two reported decisions in the *Hanna* litigation which address the following: the major non-RICO counts, Hanna Mining Co. v. Norcen Energy Resources Ltd., [1982 Transfer Binder] Fed. Sec. L. Rep. (CCH) ¶ 98,878 (N.D. Ohio June 11, 1982) [hereinafter cited as *Hanna I*]; and the RICO count, Hanna Mining Co. v. Norcen Energy Resources Ltd., [1982 Transfer Binder] Fed. Sec. L. Rep. (CCH) ¶ 98,742 (N.D. Ohio June 11, 1982) [hereinafter cited as *Hanna II*]. There is one unreported decision: Hanna Mining Co. v. Norcen Energy Resources Ltd., No. C82-959 (N.D. Ohio June 11, 1982). *See infra* note 50 and accompanying text.

approved of a target's invocation of the RICO statute to fend off a hostile takeover. The takeovers involved in *Spencer* and *Hanna* followed a common pattern: relatively sizeable open market purchases of the target's stock by the raider followed by an announcement of a cash tender offer to acquire a majority interest in the target.

In *Spencer*, the target (Spencer) brought suit, long before the tender offer was launched, against Agency, its chairman of the board, and its president, alleging that Agency's open market purchases of Spencer stock were made in contravention of Sections 9(a)(2)[21] and 13(d)[22] of the Securities Exchange Act of 1934[23] and of RICO.[24] Spencer sought a preliminary injunction and permanent equitable relief for the Exchange Act violations and treble damages for the RICO claim.[25] Agency, for its part, moved to dismiss all counts.[26] The court granted Agency's motion to dismiss the Section 9(a)(2) count[27] but denied its motion as to the Section 13(d) allegation, stating that, contrary to the grounds asserted by Agency for dismissal, a target does have standing to seek an injunction under Section 13(d).[28] With the Section 13(d) count still alive, the court, in a separate opinion, denied Agency's motion to dismiss the RICO count, holding that Spencer's complaint was sufficient to state a civil RICO claim for treble damages,[29] but stayed all discovery proceedings until Spencer could demonstrate that the defendants' alleged RICO violation had caused Spencer "legally compensable injury."[30]

---

21. 15 U.S.C. § 78i(a)(2) (1982).

22. *Id.* at § 78m(d) (1982).

23. *Id.* at § 78a-78kk (1982).

24. *Spencer I*, [1981–1982 Transfer Binder] Fed. Sec. L. Rep. (CCH) ¶ 98,301, at 91,894. Spencer also alleged a violation of § 14(d) of the Exchange Act, 15 U.S.C. § 78n(d) (1982), which the court mentioned but did not discuss. *Spencer I*, [1981–1982 Transfer Binder] Fed. Sec. L. Rep. (CCH) ¶ 98,301, at 91,894. Finally, Spencer alleged that Agency had violated § 14(e) of the Exchange Act, 15 U.S.C. § 78n(e) (1982), but the court did not mention this allegation. First Amended Complaint at 1 & 11, *Spencer I*, [1981–1982 Transfer Binder] Fed. Sec. L. Rep. (CCH) ¶ 98,301.

25. First Amended Complaint at 12–14, *Spencer I*, [1981–1982 Transfer Binder] Fed. Sec. L. Rep. (CCH) ¶ 98,301, at 91,894.

26. *Spencer I*, [1981–1982 Transfer Binder] Fed. Sec. L. Rep. (CCH) ¶ 98,301, at 91,894. Actually, the defendant's motion to dismiss only encompassed the allegations under §§ 9(a)(2) and 13(d) and under RICO. *Id.*; *see also supra* note 24 (pointing out that Spencer alleged violations of §§ 14(d) and 14(e) of the Exchange Act as well).

27. *Spencer I*, [1981–1982 Transfer Binder] Fed. Sec. L. Rep. (CCH) ¶ 98,301, at 91,896.

28. *Id.* at 91,895 ("an issuer's standing to seek injunctive relief under § 13(d) is the settled practice in this circuit.").

29. *Spencer II*, [1981–1982 Transfer Binder] Fed. Sec. L. Rep. (CCH) ¶ 98,361, at 92,216–17.

30. *Id.* at 92,217.

While Spencer's motion for a preliminary injunction to redress the Section 13(d) violations was under consideration, Agency made the tender offer, and some shares were tendered. At that point, Spencer filed an action to enjoin preliminarily and permanently the tender offer itself, alleging that Agency's tender offer had been effected in violation of Exchange Act Sections 14(d)[31] and 14(e).[32] Several months later, the court ruled on both of Spencer's motions for preliminary injunctive relief.[33] Applying one of the traditional federal standards for granting a preliminary injunction,[34] the court

---

31. 15 U.S.C. § 78n(d) (1982).

32. *Id*. at § 78n(e) (1982); *see Spencer III*, 542 F. Supp. at 237–38.

33. *Spencer III*, 542 F. Supp. at 237–38.

34. The Supreme Court has noted that at least two factors are relevant in determining whether to grant a preliminary injunction: "first, the [plaintiff's] possibilities of success on the merits; and second, the possibility that irreparable injury would have resulted, absent interlocutory relief." Brown v. Chote, 411 U.S. 452, 456 (1973). The courts of appeals, however, at different times have applied seemingly different, although perhaps overlapping, standards for granting a preliminary injunction. The Court of Appeals for the Ninth Circuit, for example, has admitted that this confusion exists:

> [T]his court has announced two legal standards applicable to the grant or denial of preliminary injunctions. At first glance these standards may appear entirely different; nonetheless "they are merely extremes of a single continuum." On the one end of the scale we require the moving party to show (1) probable success, and (2) the possibility of irreparable injury. On the other end, the moving party is required to demonstrate (1) that serious questions are raised, and (2) that the balance of hardships are tipped sharply in his favor.

Miss Universe, Inc. v. Flesher, 605 F.2d 1130, 1134 (9th Cir. 1979) (quoting Benda v. Grand Lodge of the Int'l Ass'n of Machinists & Aerospace Workers, 584 F.2d 308, 314 (9th Cir. 1978)) (citations omitted). The Court of Appeals for the Ninth Circuit proceeded to compound this confusion by later asserting that "[t]he *traditional* equitable criteria for granting preliminary injunctive relief are (1) a strong likelihood of success on the merits, (2) the possibility of irreparable injury to plaintiff if the preliminary relief is not granted, (3) a balance of hardships favoring the plaintiff, and (4) advancement of the public interest (in certain cases)." Los Angeles Memorial Coliseum Comm'n v. National Football League, 634 F.2d 1197, 1200 (9th Cir. 1980) (emphasis added). *See also In re* Permanent Surface Mining Regulation Litig., 617 F.2d 807, 808 (D.C. Cir. 1980) (adding to the list of factors "the harm caused to others by granting the injunction"); Omega Satellite Prods. Co. v. City of Indianapolis, 694 F.2d 119, 123 (7th Cir. 1982) (opinion by Posner, J.) (stating that "[t]he decision to grant or deny a preliminary injunction involves a comparison of the probabilities, and consequences (public as well as private), of two types of error: granting an injunction to an undeserving plaintiff, that is, one who will not be able to establish a legal right to an injunction when the case is tried in full rather than in the necessarily hasty and incomplete hearing on the motion for preliminary injunction; and denying

found both that Spencer had a reasonable likelihood of establishing violations of Sections 13(d), 14(d), and 14(e) and that Spencer and its shareholders would be likely to suffer irreparable harm if Agency were permitted to gain control of Spencer through the tender offer.[35] Accordingly, the court ordered disenfranchisement of the shares Agency had purchased allegedly in violation of Section 13(d) and enjoined Agency from accepting stock tenders unless the tenderors were individually served with supplementary information remedying the alleged violations of Sections 14(d) and 14(e).[36]

Before the litigation proceeded to a trial on the merits for a determination of the appropriate permanent equitable relief for the Exchange Act claims, Spencer was able to revive its RICO damage claim by demonstrating to the court's satisfaction that the defendants' alleged RICO violations had caused it "legally compensable injury."[37] Shortly thereafter, the litigants entered into an all-encompassing settlement agreement in which the defendants represented that they had sold all their Spencer stock to an investment banking firm; Spencer additionally required the defendants to agree that they would not acquire or hold directly or indirectly any Spencer stock for ten years.[38] The tender offer had indeed been unsuccessful.

In *Hanna*, the target (Hanna) instituted suit against Norcen, two members of its board, and its president, within an hour of the tender offer announcement, to enjoin Norcen's proposed tender offer on the grounds that Norcen's open market acquisition of Hanna stock and proposed tender offer violated Sections 10(b) (and Rule 10b-5 thereunder),[39] 13(d), and 14(e), of the Exchange Act, and the Ohio takeover statute.[40] Hanna requested a temporary restraining order, preliminary and permanent injunctions, and divestiture of the shares Norcen had acquired on the open market.[41] The same day, the court issued the requested temporary restraining order which was extended by stipulation until a decision was reached on Hanna's motion for

---

an injunction to a deserving plaintiff."). Despite all the various constructions of the standard, however, the traditional four factors are those cited in *Los Angeles Memorial Coliseum Comm'n. See* 11 C. Wright & A. Miller, Federal Practice and Procedure § 2948 (1973).

35. *Spencer III*, 542 F. Supp. at 237–38.

36. *Id.* at 238.

37. No record of the court order was made on the docket sheet. This information was obtained from written communications with counsel for the litigants (on file with the Journal of Comparative Business and Capital Market Law).

38. Joint Motion for Voluntary Dismissal with Prejudice, *Spencer III*, 542 F. Supp. 237.

39. 15 U.S.C. § 78j(b) (1982); 17 C.F.R. § 240.10b-5 (1984). *See infra* note 73.

40. *See Hanna I*, [1982 Transfer Binder] Fed. Sec. L. Rep. (CCH) ¶ 98,878, at 94,570.

41. Verified Complaint at 13–14, *Hanna I*, [1982 Transfer Binder] Fed. Sec. L. Rep. (CCH) ¶ 98,878 (N.D. Ohio June 11, 1982).

a preliminary injunction.[42] Hanna filed an amended complaint soon thereafter, seeking additional injunctive relief for alleged violations of the Hart-
Scott-Rodino Antitrust Improvements Act of 1976 and damages and injunctive relief for alleged violations of the RICO statute.[43]

The court's initial dispositions of Hanna's various claims are contained in
three separate decisions.[44] In the opinion relating to Hanna's allegations
under the Exchange Act, the court held, as the *Spencer* court had, that a
target corporation has standing to maintain a private right of action for
equitable relief under Section 13(d);[45] the court also noted that private
rights of action under Sections 14(e) and 10(b) and Rule 10b-5 are unquestioned.[46] Further, the court concluded that Hanna had demonstrated a
substantial probability of success on the merits of its Exchange Act claims[47]
and had shown it would suffer irreparable injury in the absence of a preliminary injunction.[48] Accordingly, the court issued the requested preliminary injunction restraining the defendants from carrying out their proposed
tender offer and indicated that, although the formulation of an appropriate
remedy would have to await a final hearing on a permanent injunction,
Hanna's preliminary evidence supported the requested remedy of divestiture.[49] With respect to Hanna's claim under the Ohio takeover statute, the
court, in an unreported opinion, held that the statute was unconstitutional.[50]
In the third opinion, the court granted the defendants' motion to dismiss
Hanna's claim under the Hart-Scott-Rodino Act holding that the statute did
not create a private right of action in favor of anyone.[51] The court refused
to dismiss Hanna's RICO claim, however, finding unsound and unpersuasive
the several contentions Norcen had advanced in support of its motion to
dismiss.[52] The court reserved further ruling on the RICO claim and permitted discovery to proceed.

---

42. *Hanna I*, [1982 Transfer Binder] Fed. Sec. L. Rep. (CCH) ¶ 98,878, at 94,583.

43. Supplemental and Amended Complaint at 18–20, 22–23, *Hanna II*, [1982
Transfer Binder] Fed. Sec. L. Rep. (CCH) ¶ 98,742. Although the complaint reflects
various requests for injunctive relief, the target (Hanna) never *moved* for an injunction.

44. *See supra* note 20.

45. *Hanna I*, [1982 Transfer Binder] Fed. Sec. L. Rep. (CCH) ¶ 98,878, at 94,588.

46. *Id.*

47. *Id.* at 94,589.

48. *Id.* at 94,591. The court also considered "whether issuance of a preliminary
injunction would cause substantial harm to others" and "whether the public interest
would be served by issuing a temporary injunction." *Id.* at 94,588, 94,591.

49. *Id.* at 94,596.

50. *See supra* note 20. The decision is on file with the Journal of Comparative
Business and Capital Market Law.

51. *Hanna II*, [1982 Transfer Binder] Fed. Sec. L. Rep. (CCH) ¶ 98,742, at
93,739–40.

52. *Id.* at 93,739.

Norcen promptly responded to the court's rulings by requesting an appeal, on an expedited basis, of the preliminary injunction restraining the tender offer.[53] The court allowed this appeal, but Hanna and Norcen settled the litigation before the appeal was heard.[54] Under the terms of the settlement agreement, Norcen was able to increase its holdings of Hanna common stock to 20 percent but agreed not to acquire directly or indirectly any additional shares for eight years.[55] Although the settlement agreement did not restore the *status quo ante* as completely as it had done in *Spencer*, Norcen's tender offer nonetheless was withdrawn.

2. The RICO Counts: The Violations

The RICO count in *Spencer* is paradigmatic, because it involves properly alleged violations of the three major subsections of 1962. First, Spencer claimed that Agency had violated Section 1962(a) by acquiring an interest in Spencer with funds derived from a pattern of racketeering activity.[56] The pattern alleged by Spencer consisted of intentional violations of Section 13(d) of the Exchange Act and the federal mail and wire fraud statutes.[57]

---

53. *Hanna I*, [1982 Transfer Binder] Fed. Sec. L. Rep. (CCH) ¶ 98,878, *appeal docketed*, No. 82-3386 (6th Cir. June 28, 1982), *dismissed per stipulation*.

54. Agreement among Norcen Energy Resources Limited, the Hanna Mining Company, Conrad M. Black, and G. Montegu Black (July 7, 1982) (on file with the Journal of Comparative Business and Capital Market Law).

55. *Id.* at 7. This covenant was binding, however, only if Hanna allowed three Norcen representatives to be seated on Hanna's board of directors. *Id.* at 8.

56. *Spencer II*, [1981–1982 Transfer Binder] Fed. Sec. L. Rep. (CCH) ¶ 98,361, at 92,215.

57. First Amended Complaint at 8, *Spencer II*, [1981–1982 Transfer Binder] Fed. Sec. L. Rep. (CCH) ¶ 98,361. The definition of a "pattern of racketeering activity" has troubled some courts, perhaps because "[t]he critical statutory word—pattern—'is relatively new to the legislative criminal lexicon.'" United States v. Dean, 647 F.2d 779, 788 (8th Cir. 1981), *rev'd en banc on other grounds*, 667 F.2d 729 (8th Cir.), *cert. denied*, 456 U.S. 1006 (1982) (quoting United States v. Stofsky, 409 F. Supp. 609, 613 (S.D.N.Y. 1973), *aff'd*, 527 F.2d 237 (2d Cir. 1975), *cert. denied*, 429 U.S. 819 (1976). One element of doubt has been whether two or more predicate acts committed during the course of a single transaction can constitute a "pattern of racketeering activity" under RICO. Most courts that have addressed this issue seem to have concluded that acts that are separately chargeable or punishable are separate predicate offenses and that when two separate predicate offenses have occurred a "pattern of racketeering activity" has been established. *See, e.g.,* United States v. McManigal, 708 F.2d 276, 282 (7th Cir.) *vacated and remanded on other grounds*, 104 S. Ct. 419 (1983); United States v. Weatherspoon, 581 F.2d 595, 601–02 (7th Cir. 1978); United States v. Parness, 503 F.2d 430, 438 (2d Cir. 1974), *cert. denied*, 419 U.S. 1105 (1975). *But see* United States v. Weisman, 624 F.2d 1118, 1120–21 (2d Cir.), *cert. denied*, 449 U.S. 871 (1980).

These violations, according to Spencer, stemmed from a series of misleading public statements (Schedules 13D) filed with the Securities and Exchange Commission (SEC) in connection with the purchase of stock in another company, the sale of which, a year later, provided the funds for the acquisition of the Spencer stock.[58] Second, Spencer alleged that Agency had violated Section 1962(b) by acquiring an interest in Spencer through a pattern of racketeering activity that consisted of Agency's intentional filing of misleading Schedules 13D with the SEC in connection with the open market acquisition of the Spencer stock, in violation of Section 13(d) and the federal mail and wire fraud statutes.[59] Spencer claimed that the allegedly improper Schedules 13D were deliberately filed with misleading statements to permit Agency to continue its systematic acquisition of Spencer stock.[60] These misleading Schedules 13D were the basis for Spencer's concurrent claim under Section 13(d).[61] Finally, Spencer contended that the individual defendants had contravened Section 1962(c) by conducting Agency's affairs through these two alleged patterns of racketeering activity.[62] Although the RICO count was successful, the court disregarded Spencer's allegation under Section 10(b) and the mail and wire fraud statutes, finding them conclusory and without sufficient averment of supporting facts.[63] The Section 13(d) violations thus stood as the sole foundation for the alleged pattern of racketeering activity.

The RICO claim in *Hanna* is similar to the Section 1962(b) claim in *Spencer*. Hanna alleged that Norcen and the individual defendants had violated Section 1962(b) by acquiring and maintaining an interest in Hanna through a pattern of racketeering activity consisting of intentional violations of Sections 10(b), 13(d), and 14(e) and Rule 10b-5 of the Exchange Act and the federal mail and wire fraud statutes.[64] The alleged Section 13(d) predicate offense was the defendants' intentional filing with the SEC, in

---

58. *Spencer II*, [1981–1982 Transfer Binder] Fed. Sec. L. Rep. (CCH) ¶ 98,361, at 92,215.

59. *Id.* at 92,216.

60. *Id.*

61. *See supra* text accompanying notes 21–38.

62. *Spencer II*, [1981–1982 Transfer Binder] Fed. Sec. L. Rep. (CCH) ¶ 98,361, at 92,216.

63. *Id.* at 92,214 n.2. Spencer did not allege that its claims under §§ 14(d) and 14(e) constituted racketeering activity under RICO. *Id.* at 92,215 n.3.

64. *See Hanna II*, [1982 Transfer Binder] Fed. Sec. L. Rep. (CCH) ¶ 98,742, at 93,733. The case itself made no mention of the mail and wire fraud allegations. Reference to these allegations can be found in Memorandum of Plaintiffs in Opposition to Defendant's Motion to Dismiss Counts Four and Five of the Supplemental and Amended Complaint at 10–13, *Hanna II*, [1982 Transfer Binder] Fed. Sec. L. Rep. (CCH) ¶ 98,742.

connection with the open market purchases of Hanna stock, of Schedules 13D that were materially false, misleading, and deceptive.[65] The alleged predicate offenses under Sections 10(b) and 14(e) and Rule 10b-5 were based on the defendants' intentional ongoing unlawful conduct from the inception of its acquisition plan up to its announcement of the tender offer, namely, a willful failure to disclose material facts and intentional manipulation of the trading market in Hanna's stock.[66] The alleged predicate offenses supporting the RICO claim were the gravamen of Hanna's Sections 13(d) and 14(e) claims discussed above.[67] The court never even mentioned the predicate offense bottomed on the mail and wire fraud statutes; therefore, the Sections 10(b), 13(d), and 14(e) and Rule 10b-5 claims remained as the basis of Hanna's successful RICO count.

3. *The RICO Counts: The Issues*

Civil RICO litigation in the last few years has raised many thorny issues regarding the proper application and scope of the RICO statute. Some of the issues have been eschewed entirely by the federal courts; others have generated a mounting controversy among the lower courts, which the Supreme Court has not yet had occasion to mediate. As a consequence, it seems fair to say that most of the troublesome issues remain essentially unresolved. The RICO portions of the *Spencer* and *Hanna* litigations provide fertile ground for a discussion of three such issues which are particularly relevant in tender offer litigation. Stated briefly, the three issues—which shade into each other at the edges—are: (1) what is meant by RICO's predicate offense of "fraud in the sale of securities . . . punishable under any law of the United States" and how does it interrelate with the other RICO predicate fraud offenses, indictable federal mail and wire fraud; (2) is RICO limited to activities involving organized crime; and (3) what type of injury is cognizable under RICO?

a. *RICO Fraud and RICO Mail and Wire Fraud*

The drafters of RICO failed to supply either a definition of "fraud" or a reference to other federal laws contemplated by the predicate offense of "fraud in the sale of securities . . . punishable under any law of the United States." Furthermore, the legislative documents do not evince any unequivocal Congressional intent, and the federal courts deciding RICO cases have not explicitly delineated a definition. The Court of Appeals for the Second Circuit recently voiced concern about this lack of legislative and

---

65. Supplemental and Amended Complaint at 15–16, *Hanna II*, [1982 Transfer Binder] Fed. Sec. L. Rep. (CCH) ¶ 98,742.

66. *Id.* at 14-15.

67. *See supra* notes 39–55 and accompanying text.

judicial guidance but acknowledged that defining RICO fraud is a "complex and far-reaching" problem.[68]

By and large, the federal court decisions fall into two camps. The majority of the courts have simply assumed that the offense takes its coloration, in large measure, from the federal securities laws and that a RICO claim can thus be predicated on traditional securities fraud.[69] Other courts, however, have rejected this approach in an attempt to filter out many RICO claims, maintaining that the statute does not embrace ordinary violations of the federal securities laws.[70] As we shall demonstrate below, this latter view is more a manifestation of the conviction that RICO should be limited to organized crime activities or that RICO should only compensate certain types of injury than it is an attempt to grapple with the statute's notion of fraud.

Spencer and *Hanna* are typical of the former approach. Both courts held *sub silentio* that the alleged intentional violations of the Exchange Act were RICO fraud. Regarding the RICO claims, grounded on violations of Section 13(d), the court's quiescent analysis most likely took the following path: Section 13(d) requires a corporation, whenever it becomes the beneficial owner of more than 5 percent of a class of equity securities of another corporation, to file a Schedule 13D with the SEC disclosing, among other things, the purpose of the acquisition.[71] And because Spencer and Hanna had alleged that each of the Schedules 13D filed by Agency and Norcen,

---

68. Moss v. Morgan Stanley, Inc., 719 F.2d 5, 18 n.14 (2d Cir. 1983).

69. Most of these cases seem to accept implicitly the notion that "garden-variety" securities fraud will serve as a RICO predicate offense. *See, e.g.,* Schact v. Brown, 711 F.2d 1343, 1353–57 (7th Cir.), *cert. denied,* 104 S. Ct. 508 (1983); Katz v. David W. Katz & Co., [1983–1984 Transfer Binder] Fed. Sec. L. Rep. (CCH) ¶ 99,669, at 97,690 (S.D.N.Y. Feb. 14, 1984); *In re* Catnella & E. F. Hutton & Co. Sec. Litig., M.D.L. No. 546, slip op. (E.D. Pa. Apr. 9, 1984) (available May 1, 1984, on LEXIS, Genfed library, Dist file); Gilbert v. Bagley, [1983–1984 Transfer Binder] Fed. Sec. L. Rep. (CCH) ¶ 99,483, at 96,795 (M.D.N.C. Sept. 17, 1983); Mauriber v. Shearson/ American Express, Inc., 567 F. Supp. 1231 (S.D.N.Y. 1983); Gunther v. Dinger, 547 F. Supp. 25 (S.D.N.Y. 1982); Engl v. Berg, 511 F. Supp. 1146 (E.D. Pa. 1981).

70. *See, e.g.,* Mon-Shore Management, Inc. v. Family Media, Inc., No. 83 Civ. 2013-CLB, slip op. (S.D.N.Y. Mar. 29, 1984) (available May 1, 1984, on LEXIS, Genfed library, Dist file); Moss v. Morgan Stanley, Inc., 553 F. Supp. 1347, 1358–64 (S.D.N.Y.), *aff'd on other grounds,* 719 F.2d 5 (2d Cir. 1983); Noonan v. Granville-Smith, 537 F. Supp. 23, 29 (S.D.N.Y. 1981).

71. Under § 13(d), a purchaser or beneficial owner of more than 5% of a corporation's stock must file with the SEC a report indicating, *inter alia,* the purpose of the acquisition "if the purpose of the purchases . . . is to acquire control of the business of the issuer." 15 U.S.C. § 78m(d)(1)(C) (1982). The specific items that must be disclosed are governed by Schedule 13D, 17 C.F.R. § 240.13d-101 (1984).

respectively, did not disclose that they were contemplating a takeover, not only had Spencer and Hanna adequately alleged a violation of Section 13(d), but at the same time they had also adequately alleged fraud. Furthermore, since it was alleged that Agency and Norcen had intentionally filed fraudulent Schedules 13D, their conduct would support a finding of scienter and therefore would be punishable under Section 32(a) of the Exchange Act.[72] Accordingly, this conduct of Agency and Norcen constituted fraud under RICO. With respect to the RICO claims based on Sections 10(b) and 14(e) and Rule 10b-5 in *Hanna*, the logic ran in a similar vein. Both Section 10(b) (and Rule 10b-5) and Section 14(e) outlaw fraud. Specifically, Section 10(b) and Rule 10b-5 prohibit false or misleading statements and deceptive or manipulative acts, in connection with the purchase or sale of a security;[73] Section 14(e) proscribes the same conduct in connection with a tender

---

72. Section 32(a) provides that "[a]ny person who *willfully* violates any provision of [the Exchange Act]..., or any rule or regulation thereunder..., or ... who *willfully and knowingly* makes, or causes to be made, any statement in any [required report that is]... false or misleading with respect to any material fact" is subject to criminal fines and/or imprisonment. 15 U.S.C. § 78ff(a) (1982) (emphasis added). Thus, a violation of the Exchange Act is criminally punishable—and hence a potential RICO predicate offense—only if it is willful. This clearly corresponds to the definition of scienter, a "term [that] is frequently used to signify the defendant's guilty knowledge." Black's Law Dictionary 12.7 (rev. 5th ed. 1979). In the context of the securities laws—specifically, in reference to § 10(b) and Rule 10b-5 of the Exchange Act—the Supreme Court has defined scienter as "a mental state embracing intent to deceive, manipulate, or defraud." Ernst & Ernst v. Hochfelder, 425 U.S. 185, 194 n.12 (1976). Although an allegation of scienter is necessary to base a RICO claim on a violation of the federal securities laws, a prior criminal conviction for the securities law violation should not be necessary. Two new cases in the Court of Appeals for the Second Circuit, however, have sparked a debate over whether a criminal conviction is in fact necessary to support a private civil RICO action. *See* Sedima, S.P.R.L., v. Imrex Co., [Current Binder] Fed. Sec. L. Rep. (CCH) ¶ 91,599 (2d Cir. July 25, 1984); Bankers Trust Co. v. Rhoades, [Current Dinder] Fed. Sec. L. Rep. (CCH) ¶ 91,600 (2d Cir. July 26, 1984). These cases held that a private civil RICO action may be pursued only after the defendant has been convicted of the predicate criminal offenses. After rehearing en banc was denied, Judge Cardamone, who had dissented in each of the two opinions, joined a unanimous panel in reluctantly following the two precedents. Furman v. Cirrito, [Current Binder] Fed. Sec. L. Rep. (CCH) ¶ 91,633 (2d Cir. July 27, 1984). The panel in *Furman* did, however, issue an opinion expressing strongly its disagreement with the earlier results in *Sedima* and *Bankers Trust*. The *Furman* analysis (although not the result) follows what had been thought to be the correct position—that no criminal conviction is necessary. *See* USACO Coal Co. v. Carbonium Energy, Inc., 689 F.2d 94, 95 n.1 (6th Cir. 1982) (citing cases).

73. Section 10(b) proscribes the use of "any manipulative or deceptive device

offer.[74] And since Hanna's complaint alleged that Norcen had disguised its true intentions in acquiring Hanna stock, so that it could pursue its strategy to obtain control of Hanna for less than the free market price, the complaint adequately described conduct violative of Sections 10(b) and 14(e) and Rule 10b-5; the alleged conduct was therefore fraud. Finally, because Hanna had alleged that this conduct was willful, and involved scienter, it was likewise punishable under Section 32(a) and once again fraud under RICO.

Because ordinary securities fraud under the federal securities laws falls within the letter of the RICO statute, we suggest that the definition of fraud that underlies the *Spencer* and *Hanna* decisions should and will be adopted uniformly by the federal courts, once it is fully developed. With the benefit of such an expansive definition, a target alleging either a Section 1962(a) or Section 1962(c) violation should be able to employ as predicate offenses virtually every securities transaction that violates an antifraud or reporting-disclosure provision of the federal securities laws. For a Section 1962(b) violation, however, the array of possible predicate offenses available to a target will necessarily be limited by the facts. Indeed, Hanna seems to have utilized the principal candidates, alleging, as we have seen, a pattern of

---

or contrivance in contravention of such rules and regulations as the Commission may prescribe," if the device or contrivance was "in connection with the purchase or sale of any security." 15 U.S.C. § 78j(b) (1982). Under the rulemaking authority in that section, the SEC adopted Rule 10b-5, which states somewhat more broadly that it shall be unlawful, in connection with the purchase or sale of any security,

(1) to employ any device, scheme, or artifice to defraud,

(2) to make any untrue statement of a material fact or to omit to state a material fact necessary in order to make the statements made, in light of the circumstances under which they were made, not misleading, or

(3) to engage in any act, practice, or course of business which operates or would operate as a fraud or deceit upon any person.

17 C.F.R. § 240.10b-5 (1984).

Nevertheless, the Supreme Court has held that the scope of Rule 10b-5 "cannot exceed the power granted the Commission by Congress under § 10(b)." Ernst & Ernst v. Hochfelder, 425 U.S. 185, 214 (1976).

74. Section 14(e) (which was enacted as part of the Williams Act in 1968) tracks the language of § 10(b) (which was enacted in 1934) and Rule 10b-5 very closely, but contains some important differences. Section 14(e) makes it unlawful "for any person to make any untrue statement of a material fact or [to] omit to state any material fact necessary in order to make the statements made, in the light of the circumstances under which they are made, not misleading, or to engage in any fraudulent, deceptive, or manipulative acts or practices, in connection with any tender offer...." 15 U.S.C. § 78n(e) (1982).

racketeering activity based on violations of Sections 10(b), 13(d), and 14(e) and Rule 10b-5.[75]

One terminological difficulty remains. Since the phrase "fraud in the sale of securities" employs only the word "sale," the question naturally arises whether a fraudulent purchase of securities falls within RICO's coverage. Indeed, the issue cropped up in both *Spencer* and *Hanna*, since Agency and Norcen were purchasers, and not sellers, of securities. Unable to marshal a judicial precedent interpreting the phrase, the *Spencer* court relied on Congress's declaration that RICO's provisions should be "liberally construed to effectuate its remedial purposes" and concluded that the statute "would appear to encompass fraud committed by the purchaser of securities, as well as by the seller."[76] The *Hanna* court found that reasoning persuasive and adopted the *Spencer* court's analysis.[77]

The results in *Spencer* and *Hanna* on this issue seem sound. Although the phrase appears to be limited expressly by its terms to fraudulent acts in connection with the sale of securities, it is common sense that every sale involves a corresponding purchase. Moreover, even though there is no telling piece of legislative history on this point, it would appear that RICO's pervasive concern with deterring certain acquisitions by "racketeers" is inconsistent with any cramped construction of the phrase "fraud in the sale of securities" that excludes purchases. Such a construction would seriously restrict the scope of Section 1962(b)'s prohibition of the *acquisition* of an interest in an enterprise through a pattern of racketeering activity. Indeed, it is by the purchase, not by the sale, of securities that an interest in an enterprise is customarily acquired.

Congress was more explicit in defining the other major RICO predicate offenses involving fraud. Mail and wire fraud are defined as indictable violations of the federal mail and wire fraud statutes, respectively, and specific references to the United States Code sections are provided.[78] Despite all this explicitness, a handful of federal courts seem inclined to limit the use of mail and wire fraud in civil RICO cases. These courts note that private rights of action have never been implied under the federal mail and wire

---

75. A target might also allege that the raider intentionally violated § 14(d) of the Exchange Act and the rules thereunder, which prescribe the procedural requirements for a tender offer. *See* 15 U.S.C. § 78n(d) (1982). *See also* note 63.

76. *Spencer II*, [1981 Transfer Binder] Fed. Sec. L. Rep. (CCH) ¶ 98,361, at 92,215.

77. *Hanna II*, [1982 Transfer Binder] Fed. Sec. L. Rep. (CCH) ¶ 98,742, at 93,738. *See also In re* Catanella & E. F. Hutton & Co. Sec. Litig., M.D.L. No. 546, slip op. at n.56 (E.D. Pa. Apr. 9, 1984) (available May 1, 1984, on LEXIS, Genfed library, Dist file).

78. *See* 18 U.S.C. § 1971(1)(B) (1982).

fraud statutes and, therefore, feel that the inclusion of mail and wire fraud in RICO has the potential to federalize common law fraud—a result Congress could never have intended.[79] Other courts, however, have been hospitable to the seemingly plain inclusion of mail and wire fraud in RICO.[80]

---

79. "The sweep of the statute does not embrace ordinary violators charged in common law fraud actions or federal securities law violations as the predicate offenses for RICO relief.... The supporting civil remedies of the statute were designed against organized criminals and terrorists as an additional weapon in the crime fighters' arsenal." Moss v. Morgan Stanley, Inc., 553 F. Supp. 1347, 1361 (S.D.N.Y.), *aff'd on other grounds*, 719 F.2d (2d Cir. 1983). The district court in *Moss* felt that the judiciary should "filter[ ] out many RICO claims that are just efforts to claim treble damages for ordinary violations of criminal or tort laws." *Id.* at 1360. To accomplish this, the court suggested that "plaintiff's injury to be cognizable under RICO must be caused by a RICO violation and not simply by the commission of a predicate offense, such as mail fraud or federal securities fraud." *Id.* at 1361. The Court of Appeals for the Second Circuit noted that "[t]he district court's opinion [was] replete with expressions of concern about the broad scope of civil RICO," 719 F.2d at 20, and "sympathize[d] with [these]...concerns," but in dicta declared that courts must apply RICO as it is written and not as they would wish that it had been written. 719 F.2d at 21. *See also* Furman v. Cirrito, 578 F. Supp. 1535 (S.D.N.Y. 1984); Haroco v. American Nat'l Bank & Trust Co., 577 F. Supp. 111 (N.D. Ill. 1983); County of Cook v. Midcon Corp., 574 F. Supp. 902 (N.D. Ill. 1983); Guerrero v. Katzen, 571 F. Supp. 714 (D.D.C. 1983).

80. One example is Schact v. Brown, 711 F.2d 1343 (7th Cir.), *cert denied*, 104 S. Ct. 508 (1983), in which the RICO count was based solely on the predicate offense of mail fraud. The court noted the defendants' argument that a broad reading of RICO would "unreasonably federalize the common law of 'garden variety' business fraud, and eclipse the federal securities laws, providing treble damage actions for all securities-related mail fraud." *Id.* at 1353. The court felt, however, that the "defendants' profession of alarm at the expansion of federal jurisdiction over business fraud through RICO amounts to nothing less than a dispute with the very design, and not the mere application, of the statute." *Id.* at 1355. The court agreed:

> that the civil sanctions provided under RICO are dramatic, and will have a vast impact upon the federal-state division of substantive responsibility for redressing illegal conduct, but, like most courts who have considered the issue, we believe that such dramatic consequences are necessary incidents of the deliberately broad swath Congress chose to cut in order to reach the evil it sought; we are therefore without authority to restrict the application of the statute.

Id. at 1353. The court thus affirmed the district court's denial of a motion to dismiss the RICO count. *See also* United States v. Greenleaf, 692 F.2d 182 (1st Cir. 1982), *cert. denied*, 103 S. Ct. 1522 (1983) (allowing consecutive sentences for criminal violations of mail fraud and RICO, where mail fraud constituted the RICO predicate offense).

In tender offer litigation, targets have predicated RICO suits on mail or wire fraud, but no court has squarely passed on the claim.[81] Further, the receptiveness of the *Spencer* and *Hanna* courts to the plaintiffs' mail and wire fraud charges is not really discernable. The allegations of mail and wire fraud found in these cases were skeletal at best, and had the complaints laid out—in sufficient detail with sufficient supporting facts the scheme to defraud that had been devised, the various occasions on which the mails or the telephones had been utilized to further the scheme, and an allegation of scienter—the mail and wire fraud claims might not have been disregarded.[82]

It would seem, however, that if a plaintiff has a viable RICO claim based on securities fraud, an analogous RICO claim based on mail or wire fraud would be superfluous. But, if there has been a series of fraudulent purchases, but no sales, and a court interprets "fraud in the sale of securities" to exclude purchases, or if fraud can be alleged, but there has been no sale or purchase of securities with which to connect the fraud, the mail and wire fraud claims under RICO may be the only way for the plaintiff to sidestep the absence of a "sale."

b. Organized Crime

A large quantity of ink has been spilled, albeit neatly, in discussing whether a RICO count must be premised on proof or allegations of a connection with organized crime. From the courts' deft pens, two points of view have emerged. For a time, many courts scoffed at the use of RICO in cases far removed from the context that Congress had envisioned when it enacted the statute. Such courts, for example, were inclined to screen out most civil RICO claims based on federal securities law violations and common law fraud by requiring the plaintiff to point to a factual basis that the defendant had some tie to a structured criminal organization or organized criminal activity.[83] This trend, though, seems to have been effectively checkmated

---

81. *See, e.g.*, First Amended Complaint at 8, *Spencer I*; Complaint for Violation of the Securities Exchange Act of 1934 and Racketeer Influenced and Corrupt Organizations Act at 20-21, Bayly Corp. v. Marantette, [1982 Transfer Binder] Fed. Sec. L. Rep. (CCH) ¶ 98,834 (D.D.C. Oct. 19, 1982); Complaint at 27, Dan River, Inc. v. Icahn, 701 F.2d 278 (4th Cir. 1983).

82. *See supra* note 63 and accompanying text. *See also* Eisenberg v. Gagnon, 564 F. Supp. 1347, 1352–53 (E.D. Pa. 1983) ("repeated acts of mail fraud and wire fraud would constitute a pattern of racketeering activity under the statute, and the plaintiffs have alleged at least that much.").

83. One court stated that

> Congress did not intend that RICO encompass garden variety securities fraud, without any alleged nexus to organized criminal activity as that term is used and understood, for which investors and others might seek ample recourse pursuant to a pervasive statutory and regulatory scheme that was in place

by what is now a virtual consensus among the courts of appeals that have considered the issue that such a requirement of organized crime involvement is neither warranted by the facial terms of the statute nor supported by RICO's legislative history.[84]

Spencer and *Hanna* were two of the early federal district court decisions espousing this latter and preferable view. Although the *Spencer* court failed to justify adequately its conclusion that "RICO's sanctions were not limited to members of organized crime,"[85] the decision in *Hanna* examines the problem of RICO's intended scope fairly thoroughly. In brief, the court observed that even though the overriding purpose of Congress in enacting RICO was to combat organized crime, the legislative history conclusively demonstrated that Congress intentionally refused to limit RICO to organized crime because such a restriction could raise doubts as to the statute's con-

---

long before Congress decided to add a new weapon to the fight against organized crime.

Wagner v. Bear, Stearns & Co., [1982–1983 Transfer Binder] Fed. Sec. L. Rep. (CCH) ¶ 99,032, at 94,913 (N.D. Ill. Sept. 17, 1982). It has also been suggested that "Congress [when it enacted RICO] had no intention of enacting a new substantive securities law." Divco Constr. & Realty Corp. v. Merrill Lynch, Pierce, Fenner & Smith, Inc., 575 F. Supp. 712, 714 (S.D. Fla. 1983). Using these arguments, then, these courts have required plaintiffs "to muster an allegation of involvement in organized crime." *Id.* at 715. *Accord*, Gilbert v. Prudential-Bache Sec., Inc., No. 83-1513, slip op. at 4 (E.D. Pa. Jan. 10, 1984) (available May 1, 1984, on LEXIS, Genfed library, Dist file); Hokama v. E. F. Hutton & Co., 566 F. Supp. 636, 643 (C.D. Cal. 1983); Noonan v. Granville-Smith, 537 F. Supp. 23, 29 (S.D.N.Y. 1981); Waterman Steamship Corp. v. Avondale Shipyards, Inc., 527 F. Supp. 256, 260 (E.D. La. 1981); Adair v. Hunt Int'l Resources Corp., 526 F. Supp. 736, 747–48 (N.D. Ill. 1981); Kleiner v. First Nat'l Bank, 526 F. Supp. 1019, 1022 (N.D. Ga. 1981).

84. "[T]he overwhelming majority of cases have rejected the organized crime limitation." *In re* Catanella & E. F. Hutton & Co. Sec. Litig., M.D.L. No. 546, slip op. (E.D. Pa. Apr. 9, 1984) (available May 1, 1984, on LEXIS, Genfed library, dist file). As the text indicates, the courts of appeals have uniformly agreed that the organized crime limitation does not accord with the statutory language, legislative history, or Congressional intent. *See, e.g.,* Sutliff, Inc. v. Donvon Co., No. 83-1308, slip op. at 7 (7th Cir. Feb. 9, 1984) (available May 1, 1984, on LEXIS, Genfed library, Dist file); Moss v. Morgan Stanley, Inc.,719 F.2d 5, 21 (2d Cir. 1983); Schact v. Brown, 711 F.2d 1343, 1353 (7th Cir.), *cert. denied,* 104 S. Ct. 508 (1983); Bennett v. Berg, 685 F.2d 1053, 1063 (8th Cir. 1982), *rev'd in part, aff'd in part on rehearing en banc,* 710 F.2d 1361, 1364 (8th Cir.), *cert. denied sub nom.* Prudential Ins. Co. v. Bennett, 104 S. Ct. 527 (1983). *See also In re* Catanella & E. F. Hutton & Co. Sec. Litig., M.D.L. No. 546, slip op. (E.D. Pa. Apr. 9, 1984) (available May 1, 1984, on LEXIS, Genfed library, Dist file) (citing an exhaustive list of cases on this point).

85. *Spencer II,* [1981 Transfer Binder] Fed. Sec. L. Rep. (CCH) ¶ 98,361, at 92,214.

stitutional validity and would permit some organized crime members to evade the statute's sanctions by suppressing evidence of their unlawful associations.[86]

Evaluated against this backdrop, RICO takeover litigation should not founder for lack of proof or allegations of the raider's ties to organized crime. Although Congress set out to attack the problems of organized crime and not those of corporate control, when it drafted RICO it was forced to cut a wide swathe, one that could envelop not only organized crime but securities fraud and other white-collar crime as well.

c. Type of Injury Cognizable under RICO

RICO's 1964(c) civil remedies provision grants recovery to those injured by "reason of a violation of 1962."[87] The federal courts, in interpreting this provision, have construed it in two diametrically opposite ways. Some courts, based on their own view of the plain language of the provision, have imposed a standing or causation requirement by requiring plaintiffs to show that they seek relief for an injury that resulted from a violation of Section 1962 and not simply from Section 1961 racketeering activity.[88] By positing that Congress did not intend to preempt or supplement the remedies already provided by the statutes that define the predicate offenses,[89] these courts accordingly insist on a demonstration of competitive injury or infiltration,

---

86. *Hanna II*, [1982 Transfer Binder] Fed. Sec. L. Rep. (CCH) ¶ 98,742, at 93,734-36.

87. 18 U.S.C. § 1964(c) (1982).

88. *See, e.g.*, Furman v. Cirrito, 578 F. Supp. 1535 (S.D.N.Y. 1984); Haroco v. American Nat'l Bank & Trust Co., 577 F. Supp. 111 (N.D. Ill. 1983); Dakis v. Chapman, 574 F. Supp. 757 (N.D. Cal. 1983); Richardson v. Shearson/American Express Co., 573 F. Supp. 133 (S.D.N.Y. 1983); Bankers Trust Co. v. Feldesman, 566 F. Supp. 1235 (S.D.N.Y. 1983); Erlbaum v. Erlbaum, [1982 Transfer Binder] Fed. Sec. L. Rep. (CCH) ¶ 98,772 (E.D. Pa. July 13, 1982), *dismissed*, 709 F.2d 1491 (3d Cir.), *cert. denied*, 104 S. Ct. 486 (1983).

89. A violation of a provision of the federal securities laws involving fraud in the sale of a security, however, will not *ipso facto* constitute a "pattern of racketeering activity." First, under RICO there must be at least two violations of the federal securities laws. Second, RICO requires scienter even when the securities laws (such as Exchange Act §§ 13(d) and 14(e) (first prong)) do not. Furthermore, the measure of recovery in a RICO damages suit—notwithstanding the treble damages feature of § 1964(c)—should be different from the measure of recovery under the securities laws. For example, in an action for damages for securities fraud, the measure of recovery would be based on either the so-called loss-of-bargain rule or out-of-pocket rule. On the other hand, in a § 1964(c) suit, the measure of recovery would be based on the damages to plaintiff's business stemming from the § 1962 activity—a measure similar to that utilized in awarding damages in a suit brought under the antitrust laws.

whether it be genuine or metaphysical.[90] The alternative approach permits a plaintiff to recover under Section 1964(c) for injury resulting from the Section 1961 racketeering activity alone.[91] Courts advocating this approach contend that the more restrictive view is contrary to the language of the statute and does not comport with the legislative history.[92]

Under either view, a target should confront no barriers in stating a claim under Section 1964(c), because the target will ordinarily be the victim of the alleged Section 1962 violation. Indeed, in both *Spencer* and *Hanna*, the targets were allegedly victims under Section 1962. Nonetheless, both the *Spencer* and *Hanna* courts wrestled with the intended meaning of Section 1964(c). *Spencer* ostensibly implemented the restrictive construction, whereas *Hanna* strenuously adopted the broader approach. In *Spencer*, the court found that since Agency had infiltrated Spencer through an alleged pattern of racketeering activity, Spencer's alleged injury—to its business relationships with present and future suppliers, contractors, and customers—stemmed from the proscribed Section 1962 violations and was sufficient to state a claim under Section 1964(c).[93] Couched in this manner, the court's holding seems to suggest that had the claimed injury been caused solely by the racketeering activities, Spencer's RICO claim would not have been viable. In *Hanna*, the court declined to follow *Spencer* at least to the extent that it could be read as imposing any infiltration requirement as a restriction on standing.[94] Rather, the court authorized Hanna's RICO suit under Section 1964(c) based on the alleged predicate acts of securities fraud alone.[95]

---

90. *See, e.g.*, Bankers Trust Co. v. Feldesman, 566 F. Supp. 1235, 1241 (S.D.N.Y. 1983) ("it seems appropriate to limit the extraordinary private remedy of § 1964 to the class of plaintiffs who have suffered a competitive injury by reason of the defendant's racketeering activities.").

91. *See, e.g.*, Bunker Ramo Corp. v. United Business Forms, Inc., 713 F.2d 1272 (7th Cir. 1983); Schact v. Brown, 711 F.2d 1343 (7th Cir.), *cert. denied*, 104 S. Ct. 508 (1983); Bennett v. Berg, 685 F.2d 1053, 1059 (8th Cir. 1982), *rev'd in part, aff'd in part on rehearing en banc*, 710 F.2d 1361 (8th Cir.), *cert. denied sub nom.* Prudential Ins. Co. v. Bennett, 104 S. Ct. 527 (1983); *In re* Catanella & E. F. Hutton Sec. Litig. M.D.L. 546, slip op. (E.D. Pa. Apr. 9, 1984) (available May 1, 1984, on LEXIS, Genfed library, Dist file); *In re* Longhorn Sec. Litig., 573 F. Supp. 255 (W.D. Okla. 1983); Ralston v. Capper, 569 F. Supp. 1575 (E.D. Mich. 1983).

92. *See, e.g.*, Bunker Ramo Corp. v. United Business Forms, Inc., 713 F.2d 1272, 1288 (7th Cir. 1983).

93. *Spencer II*, [1981–1982 Transfer Binder] Fed. Sec. L. Rep. (CCH) ¶ 98,361, at 92,216.

94. *Hanna II*, [1982 Transfer Binder] Fed. Sec. L. Rep. (CCH) ¶ 98,742, at 93,737-38.

95. *Id.* at 93,739.

B. The Unsuccessful RICO Suits

In the three cases in which the RICO counts were unsuccessful, the target requested treble damages and preliminary and permanent injunctions. Moreover, the target *moved* for the requested injunctive relief.[96] Hence, each of these decisions, arising on a motion for a preliminary injunction, had a procedural posture different from that found in *Spencer* and *Hanna*. *Spencer* and *Hanna*, it should be recalled, arose in the context of a motion to dismiss by the defendant, and, thus, the courts were required to determine only whether the allegations, as matter of law, were sufficient to state a claim under RICO. In the three unsuccessful RICO cases, however, the court, in accordance with the traditional standard for granting equitable relief, was obliged to consider not only the relevant law but also the target's proof of the likelihood of success on the merits at the trial for the permanent injunction. Under this more stringent standard for procedural success, the motions for injunctive relief under RICO were denied—for want of sufficient proof. In one of the cases, however, the court expressed substantial doubt whether RICO grants private parties a cause of action for equitable relief.

In *Marshall Field & Co. v. Icahn*,[97] the court addressed a Section 1962(a) RICO claim brought by Marshall Field, a company targeted for takeover by Carl Icahn. The complaint alleged that Icahn had acquired an interest in Marshall Field with money derived from fraudulent sales of securities.[98] As proof of the fraud, Marshall Field relied first on civil settlements and stipulations entered into by Icahn with the SEC in earlier administrative proceedings unrelated to the litigation under discussion and second on evidence adduced in those proceedings.[99] The court assumed without discussion that private injunctive relief was available under RICO but found that the settlements and stipulations themselves revealed no violations, were not admissible, and that the evidence adduced was not sufficient to show a likelihood of success on the merits with respect to establishing a pattern of fraudulent sales of securities.[100]

---

96. In *Hanna*, the plaintiff (Hanna) *requested* injunctive relief, *see* Supplemental and Amended Complaint, *Hanna II*, [1982 Transfer Binder] Fed. Sec. L. Rep. (CCH) ¶ 98,742, but never *moved* for injunctive relief.

97. 537 F. Supp. 413 (S.D.N.Y. 1982).

98. Complaint, Marshall Field & Co. v. Icahn, 537 F. Supp. 413 (S.D.N.Y. 1982).

99. 537 F. Supp. at 420.

100. *Id.* Marshall Field had alleged that Icahn violated Exchange Act § 13(d) and that these violations constituted RICO predicate offenses. The court did not discuss this claim, however, because the court had already found that there had not yet been a conclusive determination that Icahn had violated § 13(d) and that Marshall Field would have difficulty in proving these violations. 537 F. Supp. at 418–19.

The litigation in *Bayly Corp. v. Marantette*[101] involved an alleged attempt to seize control of Bayly by a group of individuals headed by David Marantette. Bayly claimed that the Marantette group had violated RICO Section 1962(b) in connection with this attempted takeover by acquiring and maintaining an interest in Bayly through a pattern of violations of Exchange Act section 13(d), the proxy rules under Exchange Act Section 14(a), and the mail and wire fraud statutes.[102] As in *Marshall Field,* the court assumed the availability of injunctive relief but found that the evidence did not support violations of any of the predicate offenses.[103] The court expressed its reservations about the use of RICO in this context, however, and, speaking *obiter,* stated that even if it had found violations of the predicate offenses "the RICO provisions have no application as an alternative or cumulative remedy for private plaintiffs alleging securities fraud."[104]

In *Dan River, Inc. v. Icahn,*[105] Carl Icahn was greeted with another attempt by target management to enjoin one of his takeovers. Dan River's RICO count, which was quite in vogue by the time of the lawsuit, undoubtedly did not startle Icahn or his counsel. The court focused on Dan River's Section 1962(a) RICO claim: Icahn's acquisition of Dan River shares, prior to the announcement of a tender offer, with proceeds that could be traced to earlier Icahn takeovers in which Icahn had used funds from one of his companies that had failed to register as an "investment company" as required by the Investment Company Act of 1940.[106] Dan River contended that Icahn's use of the funds amounted to a pattern of securities and mail fraud, because his company had been unregistered.[107] At the outset, the court

---

101. [1982–1983 Transfer Binder] Fed. Sec. L. Rep. (CCH) ¶ 98,834 (D.D.C. Oct. 19, 1982).

102. Complaint for Violations of the Securities Exchange Act of 1934 and the Racketeer Influenced and Corrupt Organization Act at 20–22, Bayly Corp. v. Marantette, [1982 Transfer Binder] Fed. Sec. L. Rep. (CCH) ¶ 98,834 (D.D.C. Oct. 19, 1982).

103. Bayly Corp. v. Marantette, [1982 Transfer Binder] Fed. Sec. L. Rep. (CCH) ¶ 98,834, at 94,291–92 (D.D.C. Oct. 19, 1982).

104. *Id.* at 94,291. In addition, the court found that Bayly had not made the showing of irreparable injury necessary to secure injunctive relief and thus that corrective disclosure would be the only relief to which Bayly would be entitled. *Id.*

105. 701 F.2d 278 (4th Cir. 1983). The issue on appeal in *Dan River* was the propriety of the district court's Solomon-like ruling, sterilizing Icahn's shares in Dan River but permitting Icahn to proceed with his tender offer for additional Dan River stock. *See id.* at 282.

106. *Id.* at 289–90.

107. *Id.* at 290.

considered whether private injunctive relief was available under Section 1964(c). Pointing to the contradistinction between Section 1964(c), which mentions a private right of action for treble damages but says nothing explicitly about private equitable relief, and Section 1964(b), which authorizes governmental equitable proceedings, the court concluded that an express right of action for injunctive relief was doubtful and an implied right of action uncertain.[108] Assuming *arguendo* that RICO does afford private equitable relief, however, the court turned to the merits of the RICO claim and held that Dan River was unlikely to succeed on the merits.[109] First, the court found that the "investment company" status of the company under consideration was not clear and hinged on sophisticated questions of real estate valuations.[110] Second, the court raised the difficulty confronting Dan River in proving scienter with regard to Icahn's failure to register the company, a necessary ingredient, as we have indicated, of both RICO securities fraud and mail fraud.[111] And last, the court noted the controversy in the federal courts over the use of RICO in cases not involving organized crime, a fray the court chose not to enter.[112]

The question that the courts in *Marshall Field, Bayly*, and *Dan River* did not really reach—whether private party injunctive relief is available under RICO—is another of the many perplexing questions that surfaces throughout the statute. Although several courts, such as *Marshall Field* and *Bayly*, have assumed that private injunctive relief might be available under RICO, while other courts, such as *Dan River*, have expressed uncertainty,[113] only three

---

108. *Id.*

109. *Id.* at 290–91.

110. *Id.* at 291.

111. "Criminal intent is, of course, necessary to either mail fraud or securities fraud . . . [and] it appears that Carl C. Icahn acted pursuant to bona fide legal opinions. . . . In the face of such evidence, it would seem extremely unlikely that Dan River will be able to prove the predicate acts of mail or securities fraud." *Id.*

112. "Finally, we note the mounting controversy in the federal courts over the proper limits, if any, upon the use of RICO in cases far removed from the context which Congress had in mind when it enacted the statute. . . . We do not propose to enter the fray. We only note that the reach of RICO is itself a troubling issue. . . . " *Id.* In dissent, Judge Butzner asserted that Dan River had indeed proven that Icahn had violated the federal securities laws and suggested that the court should have affirmed the district court's order because it struck an equitable balance. *Id.* at 291–95 (Butzner, J., dissenting).

113. *Compare* Vietnamese Fishermen's Ass'n v. Knights of the Ku Klux Klan, 518 F. Supp. 993, 1014 (S.D. Tex. 1981) (assuming, without discussion, that preliminary injunctive relief would be available to private plaintiffs under RICO but refusing to issue a preliminary injunction because plaintiff failed to show a substantial likelihood it would succeed on the merits), *with* Trane v. O'Connor Sec., 718 F.2d 26, 28–29

courts have directly ruled on the issue. One court granted injunctive relief without providing any analysis.[114] Another court flatly held that there was no express or implied right of action for injunctive relief in the RICO statute; and although conceding that the language of the statute was "arguably ambiguous," the court found that the legislative history militated against

---

(2d Cir. 1983) (expresing doubt "as to the propriety of private party injunctive relief, especially in a case of this nature alleging at most . . . garden-variety securities law violations as predicates for the RICO violation"). In a very recent case, however, the Court of Appeals for the Second Circuit, which decided *Trane*, seemed to accept a district court's award of injunctive relief to a private party under RICO. *See* Aetna Casualty & Sur. Co. v. Liebowitz, No. 83-7728, slip op. (2d Cir. Mar. 26, 1984) (available May 1, 1984, on LEXIS, Genfed library, Dist file), *aff'g*, 570 F. Supp. 908 (E.D.N.Y. 1983). *See infra* note 114.

114. Aetna Casualty & Sur. Co. v. Liebowitz, No. 81 Civ. 2616 (E.D.N.Y. Dec. 8, 1981). Although a preliminary injunction was granted under RICO in *Aetna Casualty & Sur. Co.*, an unreported decision, the issue whether RICO grants private parties injunctive relief was not contested and therefore was not discussed. After the case was settled, the court, however, defended its grant of injunctive relief under RICO, but in a decidedly halfhearted manner when the plaintiff sought attorney's fees under § 1964(c). Aetna Casualty & Sur. Co. v. Liebowitz, 570 F. Supp. 908 (E.D.N.Y. 1983), *aff'd*, No. 83–7728, slip op. (2d Cir. Mar. 26, 1984) (available May 1, 1984, on LEXIS, Genfed library, Dist file). In that case, the court denied the plaintiff's request for attorney's fees, because such awards are only available to the "prevailing party," and injunctive relief does not operate as a determination on the merits. *Id.* at 912–13. In reaching that decision, however, the court acknowledged that it had granted an injunction under RICO. The court noted that § 1964(a) gives the judiciary the power to issue "appropriate orders," that "[n]othing in the statute indicates that a preliminary injunction would not be an 'appropriate order' within the meaning of § 1964(a)," and that Congress's failure to pass an earlier version of RICO that included a provision for private equitable relief "was by no means a clear indication that Congress intended to deprive the district court of its traditional equity jurisdiction to grant preliminary injunctive relief to a plaintiff who could show irreparable injury resulting from a defendant's alleged violation of § 1962." *Id.* at 910. The court thus concluded that "whether a preliminary injunction is available to a private party under § 1964 appears at least to be an open question," *id.* at 911, a rather meek and qualified statement in light of the fact that the court had already granted precisely the equitable relief that it now could justify as no clearer than "an open question."

The Court of Appeals for the Second Circuit affirmed the district court's opinion on the question of attorney's fees but seemed to suggest that the district court's earlier grant of the injunction was proper. *See* Aetna Casualty & Sur. Co. v. Liebowitz, No. 83-7728, slip op. (2d Cir. Mar. 26, 1984) (available May 1, 1984, on LEXIS, Genfed library, Dist file) (framing the issue as "whether a plaintiff who obtains a preliminary injunction in a civil action under [RICO] . . . , and then settles the case, is entitled to an attorney's fee award").

granting equitable remedies to private RICO plaintiffs.[115] The third court to address the issue interpreted the legislative history similarly and refused to grant a permanent injunction, expressly stating, however, that its ruling did "not reach the issue whether preliminary injunctive relief would be available to a private RICO plaintiff in extraordinary circumstances.... "[116] Even though these last two courts' exegesis of the legislative records is instructive, it is not as conclusive as they believed. The legislative history on the question is no less ambiguous than the statute.[117] In sum, the propriety of granting private equitable relief under RICO has not been satisfactorily resolved and is the most significant question facing targets instituting takeover litigation under RICO.

IV. THE UNTESTED RAIDER RICO SUIT

To be sure, David Marantette and Carl Icahn did not relish being called "racketeers." They did not realize, however, that they too could have hurled their own RICO thunderbolts. For just as ingenious counsel for target management have parsed the RICO statute to suit their clients' purposes, counsel for prospective raiders should be able to do the same. Would not a complaint that adequately alleged that target management was conducting the affairs of the target through a pattern of securities, mail, or wire fraud give the raider a sufficient claim under RICO Section 1962(c)? And when the pattern of alleged predicate offenses relates to the target's attempt to thwart the takeover, should not the raider be able to plead injury by reason of the violation of Section 1962(c), thereby invoking RICO's civil remedies?

Consider the litigation in *Bayly* and *Marshall Field*. The *Bayly* court, in

---

115. Kaushal v. State Bank of India, 556 F. Supp. 576, 584 (N.D. Ill. 1983). Actually, the court said that "*[at] most* the statute is arguably ambiguous." *Id.* (emphasis added).

As an interesting aside, the authors are only too painfully aware that law review articles will never reach the best sellers' list. It is gratifying to note, however, that law review articles are not entirely ignored. In its discussion of private equitable relief under RICO, the *Kaushal* court deplored the lack of quality of law review articles on the subject. *See id.* at 481 n.16 (declaring that it is "distressing... that the academic community, blessed with more time for reflection and extended treatment than the judiciary, had not served us well."). One hopes that Judge Shadur, the author of the *Kaushal* opinion, will provide a more favorable review of this commentary if the occasion arises.

116. DeMent v. Abbott Capital Corp., 589 F. Supp. 1378, 1383 No. 3 (N.D. Ill. 1984).

117. *See* Tyson & August, *The Williams Act after RICO: Has the Balance Tipped in Favor of Incumbent Management?* 35 Hastings L. J. 53, at 81–82 n.143 (providing an in-depth discussion of the legislative history on this issue).

addressing allegations in a counterclaim filed by Marantette, held that Bayly and its directors had violated Section 13(e) and Rule 13e-4 of the Exchange Act by engaging in a series of transactions, the purpose of which was to make an issuer tender offer, without filing a statement (Schedule 13E-4) with the SEC.[118] These allegations could have supported a RICO claim.[119] The transactions involved a contract to sell Bayly securities, so an allegation of the predicate act of "fraud in the sale of securities" could have been made, and if a contract to sell is not a "sale" for purposes of the RICO statute, allegations of the predicate acts of mail and wire fraud should have been able to remedy the infirmity. And in either case, allegations of a "pattern" of offenses and scienter should have presented no difficulty.

In *Marshall Field*, the target's defensive tactic was not an issuer tender offer, but certain lock-up arrangements with a white knight that had already launched a tender offer to gain control of the target. The first of these arrangements was a stock purchase agreement committing Marshall Field to sell treasury stock to the white knight, and the second was an agreement by which Marshall Field conferred a right of first refusal on the white knight for the purchase of Marshall Field's most valuable properties. Icahn alleged, in that case, that these lock-up arrangements constituted manipulative practices in connection with a tender offer in violation of Section 14(e) of the Exchange Act.[120] To the extent that allegations could have been made that these lock-ups contained elements of fraud or deception, they would also

---

118. Bayly Corp. v. Marantette, [1982–1983 Transfer Binder] Fed. Sec. L. Rep. (CCH) ¶ 98,834, at 94,293 (D.D.C. Oct. 19, 1982).

119. *See In re* Action Indus. Tender Offer, 572 F. Supp. 846 (E.D. Va. 1983), in which shareholders who sold their stock in response to an alleged fraudulent issuer tender offer sued under RICO utilizing violations of § 13(e) as predicate offenses.

120. Marshall Field & Co. v. Icahn, 537 F. Supp. 413, 420–21 (S.D.N.Y. 1982). The facts in the *Marshall Field* case expose one troubling problem regarding the proper construction of RICO's provisions, a problem that is seemingly endemic to § 1962(c): can a corporation simultaneously be both the named defendant in a RICO suit and the "enterprise" whose affairs are conducted through a pattern of racketeering activity? Placed in the context of a raider RICO suit, can a raider sue, under § 1962(c), *both* the target corporation and its individual managers who are conducting its affairs unlawfully, or is the raider limited to suing only the individual managers? This question is of more than academic importance to a raider considering such a suit, because the possibility of a full recovery is enhanced if the corporation (a deep-pocket adversary) can be joined as a defendant. The balance of judicial analysis on this point seems to suggest that if a corporation "is the enterprise, it cannot also be the RICO defendant." Rae v. Union Bank, 725 F.2d 478, 481 (9th Cir. 1984). *See also* United States v. Computer Sciences Corp., 689 F.2d 1181, 1190 (4th Cir. 1982), *cert. denied*, 103 S. Ct. 729 (1983) (same); *In re* Action Indus. Tender Offer, 572 F. Supp. 846, 849 (E.D. Va. 1983) (same).

have supported fraud claims under RICO. The first lock-up would seem to have provided adequate basis for a claim of a pattern of mail and wire fraud or RICO securities fraud (assuming once again that the stock purchase agreement constituted a RICO "sale"); the second lock-up would seem to have sustained a claim of a pattern of mail and wire fraud (but not RICO securities fraud, because no securities were involved).[121]

The raider RICO suits that could have derived from the *Bayly* and *Marshall Field* litigations by no means exhaust the plausible RICO claims that could be alleged by a raider in takeover litigation. A careful scrutiny of a target's activities to forestall the success of the takeover attempt may reveal other types of conduct that can sustain a claim under RICO.[122] Oddly, however, no reported decision reflects the use of RICO by a raider.

V. CONCLUSION

As we have indicated, some district courts, expressing alarm at the proliferation of RICO suits in contexts seemingly far removed from that originally contemplated by Congress, have devised ways to avoid applying RICO's

---

121. In *Marshall Field*, the court refused to grant a temporary restraining order for the alleged violations of § 14(e) holding that Icahn had not shown irreparable harm, likelihood of success on the merits, or a balance of hardships. A RICO suit for damages, based on the alleged violations of § 14(e), however, may have been able to survive a motion to dismiss. The viability of such a RICO suit would necessarily hinge, as the text suggests, on a court's finding that the lock-ups in question constituted not only a violation of § 14(e) but also RICO fraud. In Mobil Corp. v. Marathon Oil Co., 669 F.2d 366 (6th Cir. 1981), the court applied a broad definition of § 14(e) "manipulation" in holding that certain lock-up arrangements used by a target company to thwart a tender offer constituted a violation of § 14(e). The lock-ups in *Mobil* (which gave a white knight an option to purchase treasury stock and the most coveted asset of the target) were admittedly more egregious than those involved in *Marshall Field* (which did not involve options but a firm agreement and a right of first refusal). Assuming that a court found the lock-ups in *Marshall Field* to be manipulative acts in violation of § 14(e), a court would then have to be persuaded that such manipulative acts constituted fraud within the meaning of RICO. Since the lock-ups in *Mobil* and *Marshall Field* may not have involved fraud or deception as a matter of law, a court may find that this type of violation of § 14(e) is not RICO fraud. In this regard, see Data Probe Acquisition Corp. v. Datatab, Inc., 722 F.2d 1 (2d Cir. 1983), which held that a lock-up was not even a violation of § 14(e), because there was no misrepresentation—an essential element, in the court's view, of a § 14(e) cause of action. Thus, because the ability of a raider to employ a target's lock-up agreement with a white knight as a basis for a suit under § 14(e) is still not settled, the viability of an analogous RICO suit is *a fortiori* an open question.

122. *See* Tyson & August, *supra* note 117, at 108–09.

broad civil remedies when the statute produces a result not to their liking.[123] But as we have also pointed out, the courts of appeals have generally rejected these attempts, recognizing both that the RICO statute expressly grants victims a new remedy and that the legislative history evinces a Congressional intent to extend RICO's reach to garden-variety commercial crime committed by white-collar businesspersons.[124] In our view, these latter decisions reflect the proper function of the judiciary in the interpretation and application of the RICO statute. In general, attempts to restrict RICO's scope constitute an inappropriate and unworkable usurpation of legislative power by the judiciary; problems with the scope of RICO should be solved by Congress rather than by the courts.[125]

Even if the judiciary follows that recommendation and refuses to impose restrictions on RICO's application, some observers may still not believe that RICO can have a potentially enormous and destructive impact on corporate takeover battles. It is our position that such a view is ill-founded, because it overlooks several important considerations that emanate from our previous discussion of the five decisions in which RICO was used, none of which imposed restrictions that directly affected the viability of the RICO claim.[126]

In both *Spencer* and *Hanna*, it should be recalled, the court granted the target's motion for a preliminary injunction to redress alleged violations of the Exchange Act. In *Spencer*, the court allowed the tender offer to proceed but required corrective disclosures. In *Hanna*, the court preliminarily enjoined the tender offer, but because the offeror was granted an expedited appeal, the preliminary injunction (which usually amounts to a final and conclusive determination of the litigation)[127] did not spell the certain doom

---

123. *See supra* notes 70, 83, 88, and 90 and accompanying text.

124. *See supra* notes 69, 84, and 91 and accompanying text.

125. There is, however, one situation in which it would be appropriate for the courts to intervene and restrict the scope of RICO. *See* Tyson & August, *supra* note 117, at 107–14 (arguing that a well-established doctrine of statutory construction should permit a court to preclude the use of violations of the Williams Act (Exchange Act §§ 13(d), 13(e), 14(d), 14(e), and 14(f)) as RICO predicate offenses, because such RICO litigation causes a conflict in the goals of two federal statutes to surface).

126. It will be recalled that the infiltration requirement imposed by the *Spencer* court had no real effect on the viability of the RICO claim. *See* note 93 and accompanying text. Although the plaintiffs were unsuccessful in *Marshall Field, Bayly,* and *Dan River*, their failure seems traceable to the weakness of their cases rather than to any findings on RICO. *See supra* text accompanying notes 96–117.

127.

> Obviously (although, if it is obvious to the courts, they have not mentioned it), no offerer can afford to spend hundreds of thousands of dollars litigating for two or three years when he can't have the slightest idea whether he will

of the tender offer. Yet, at a time when the success of their tender offers was still possible, the offerors in both *Spencer* and *Hanna* nevertheless settled their cases and agreed to withdraw the offers. Although there are few certitudes, it would seem that the threat of a massive RICO damages award dangling over each of the litigations catalyzed the settlements.

First, the targets had established not just a *prima facie* RICO damages claim; by dint of the courts' rulings that the targets had a reasonable likelihood of substantiating at trial the Exchange Act securities fraud allegations—which were at the same time the alleged underlying predicate offenses for the RICO claims—the targets, in effect, had also established a likelihood of proving the RICO damages claims at trial. Second, in *Spencer*, the target had satisfied the court that the alleged RICO violation had caused it "legally compensable injury." The RICO claim for damages was thus far from spurious. Moreover, had it not been for RICO, no other legal rubric would have been available to the targets in either case on which they could have based their damages claim against the raiders. A damages claim for the alleged Section 13(d) violation in *Spencer* and *Hanna* would not have been cognizable since no court has implied a right of action for damages for a target under Section 13(d).[128] And in *Hanna*, a claim for damages for the alleged violations of Section 10(b) (and similarly Rule 10b-5) would have been barred, since only purchasers or sellers of securities may bring a suit for damages under Section 10(b)[129]—and the target was neither a purchaser nor a seller. Similarly, in light of recent Supreme Court cases signaling dissatisfaction with the implication of private rights of action, especially for damages, under the federal securities laws,[130] the target in *Hanna* would have almost definitely lacked standing to sue for damages for the alleged Section 14(e) violations.[131] The RICO damages suit was indeed a potent weapon for the targets.

---

still have any desire at the end of that time to continue with the offer under then prevailing market conditions.

R. Jennings & H. Marsh, Securities Regulation—Cases and Materials 672 (5th ed. 1982) (footnote omitted).

128. *See* W. Painter, The Federal Securities Code and Corporate Disclosure § 10.08(b), at 79–80 (Supp. 1982).

129. Blue Chip Stamps v. Manor Drug Stores, 421 U.S. 723 (1975).

130. *See, e.g.,* Transamerica Mortgage Advisors v. Lewis, 444 U.S. 11 (1979); Touche Ross & Co. v. Redington, 442 U.S. 560 (1979); Sante Fe v. Green, 430 U.S. 462 (1977); Piper v. Chris-Craft Indus., 430 U.S. 1 (1977); Ernst & Ernst v. Hochfelder, 425 U.S. 185 (1976). *See generally* Pitt & Ain, Dirks *Deals Blow to SEC Inside Trading Program*, Legal Times (Wash.), July 11, 1983, at 10, col. 1.

131. *See* Wellman v. Dickinson, 475 F. Supp. 783, 816 (S.D.N.Y. 1979), *aff'd,* 647 F.2d 163 (2d Cir. 1981), *cert. denied sub nom.* Dickinson v. SEC, 103 S. Ct. 1522 (1983).

A RICO damages claim can potentially assume even greater significance than it did in the *Spencer* and *Hanna* litigation. Although the targets were granted standing to seek injunctive relief for claims under the Exchange Act in these two cases, standing under Section 13(d) is not yet a settled question and thus cannot be counted upon in every court. Again in a desire to keep in step with the Supreme Court's recent reluctance to imply rights of action, a large number of courts have felt compelled to deny standing under Section 13(d) to even a target seeking only injunctive relief[132] even though *Hanna* held that a target's standing for injunctive relief under Section 14(e) was unquestioned and *Spencer* assumed standing for injunctive relief under both Sections 14(d) and 14(e) without discussion, the issue of the target's standing to seek an injunction under these two sections would not seem to be entirely settled. Furthermore, as Hanna acknowledged, some cases hold that a target does not have standing to maintain an action for an injunction under Section 10(b) (and Rule 10b-5) because of the purchaser-seller requirement.[133] There is likewise no certainty that a target will be able to obtain injunctive relief for violations of other provisions of either the Exchange Act or other statutes. Recall, for example, the target's unsuccessful attempts in *Hanna* to obtain an injunction under Exchange Act Section 9(a)(2), certain federal antitrust legislation, and the state takeover statute. In sum, if the judicial hostility toward injunctive remedies against raiders continues, a RICO suit for treble damages may turn out to be the target's sole litigation weapon, thus assuming overwhelming significance in takeover litigation.

We have neglected, of course, the possibility of the target suing for an injunction under the RICO statute itself. Although the availability of RICO's equitable remedies to a private party, as we have seen, is not clear, if a

---

132. *See, e.g.*, Equity Oil Co. v. Consolidated Oil & Gas [1983–1984 Transfer Binder] Fed. Sec. L. Rep. (CCH) ¶ 99,425 (D. Utah June 24, 1983); Liberty Nat'l Ins. Holding Co. v. Charter Co., [1982 Transfer Binder] Fed. Sec. L. Rep. (CCH) ¶ 98,797 (N.D. Ala. Aug. 13, 1982); First Ala. Bancshares, Inc. v. Lowder, [1981 Transfer Binder] Fed. Sec. L. Rep. (CCH) ¶ 98,015 (N.D. Ala. May 1, 1981); American Bakeries Co. v. Pro-Met Trading Co., [1981 Transfer Binder] Fed. Sec. L. Rep. (CCH) ¶ 97,925 (N.D. Ill. Mar. 27, 1981); Gateway Indus. v. Agency Rent-A-Car, Inc., 495 F. Supp. 92 (N.D. Ill., 1980); Sta-Rite Indus. v. Nortek, Inc., 494 F. Supp. 358 (E.D. Wis. 1980); Stromfield v. Great Atl. & Pac. Tea Co., 456 F. Supp. 1084 (S.D.N.Y. 1980); Luptok v. Central Cartage, [1981 Transfer Binder] Fed. Sec. L. Rep. (CCH) ¶ 98,034 (E.D. Mich. 1979). *But see* Indiana Nat'l Corp. v. Rich, 712 F.2d 1180 (7th Cir. 1983) (granting standing for injunctive relief under § 13(d)); Dan River, Inc. v. Unitex Ltd., 624 F.2d 1216 (4th Cir. 1980) (same), *cert. denied*, 449 U.S. 1101 (1981); Chromalloy Am. Corp. v. Sun Chem. Corp., 611 F.2d 240 (8th Cir. 1979) (same).

133. *Hanna II*, [1982–1983 Transfer Binder] Fed. Sec. L. Rep. (CCH) ¶ 98,878, at 94,592.

court interprets RICO's provisions liberally, the RICO statute may do double duty for the target, providing not only a damages remedy but an injunctive one as well. In such event, by filling two possible remedial voids—one at law and the other in equity—the primacy of RICO in takeover litigation becomes undisputed.

Comparing the two successful RICO cases (in which the targets sought damages) with the three unsuccessful RICO cases (in which the target moved for a preliminary injunction) may lead one to conclude, however, that although a target is able to state a RICO claim for damages that can survive a motion to dismiss, RICO may not prove as useful when the target seeks the coveted remedy of a preliminary injunction and accordingly is put to its proof to establish a likelihood of success on the merits. It cannot be gainsaid that in *Marshall Field, Bayly*, and *Dan River*, where standing to obtain injunctive relief under RICO was not even at issue, the RICO claim foundered because the targets could not offer sufficient proof of the underlying predicate offenses. But obviously, one should not extrapolate from the inability of these three targets to supply sufficient proof that every future target will be handicapped by a similar inability. Indeed, had the targets in *Spencer* and *Hanna* moved for a preliminary injunction to redress the RICO violation and had the courts in those cases found that injunctive relief was available to private parties, the injunctions would have issued. The targets had satisfied the courts' requirements—likelihood of success on the merits and irreparable harm—for the grant of a preliminary injunction for the Exchange Act claims. Since the Exchange Act claims were the underlying predicate offenses for the RICO suit and since there is no basis for establishing stricter requirements for the grant of a preliminary injunction under RICO,[134] the target, *a fortiori*, had satisfied the requirements for a preliminary injunction under RICO.

The potency and significance of civil RICO in corporate takeover litigation seems plain. Given the burgeoning judicial recognition of the impropriety of imposing restrictions on RICO's use, it requires no great leap of imagination to suppose that the availability of RICO's remedies in corporate warfare will result in some tender offers being withdrawn and may deter others from ever being made. There is no indication in the legislative history of RICO that Congress was aware that a statute admittedly designed primarily to combat organized crime could have such an unanticipated side

---

134. It is possible, however, that injunctions should be awarded more easily under RICO than in other situations. *See* Blakey, *The RICO Civil Fraud Action in Context: Reflections on* Bennett v. Berg, 58 Notre Dame L. Rev. 237, 338 n.217 (1982) (arguing that when a federal statute authorizes an injunction, neither inadequacy of the remedy at law nor irreparable injury need be shown, whether the government or a private party is seeking the injunction).

effect. Would Congress have countenanced such an effect had Congress been more prescient? On the one hand, Congress certainly would have approved of RICO's use in corporate takeover litigation insofar as the statute had the potential to halt organized crime's acquisition of corporate entities. On the other hand, Congress clearly would not have approved of RICO's use solely in discouraging takeovers. Indeed, two years before RICO was enacted, Congress, recognizing that corporate takeovers served important societal interests by providing a method for ousting uninventive and inefficient entrenched management, passed, and incorporated into the Exchange Act, the Williams Act (Sections 13(d), 13(e), 14(d), 14(e), and 14(f)), which had as one of its major objectives the preservation of the viability of corporate takeovers. The RICO Congress's creation of an expansive tool for combatting organized crime, without doubt, contrasts, and thus is in some tension, with Congress's earlier action in adopting the Williams Act.

RICO has been on the books for fourteen years. In that time, a great deal of evidence has developed on how civil RICO can be, and ordinarily is, utilized. It is time for Congress to evaluate that evidence and to assess RICO's costs and benefits in the corporate takeover arena. In this assessment, we trust that one compelling fact will be evident: organized crime rarely infiltrates businesses through mail, wire, and securities fraud. It is thus not surprising that, in the realm of takeover litigation, these RICO predicate offenses have been used in a purported attempt to ensnare white-collar crime rather than organized crime. As a result, in practice, civil RICO fraud suits have served solely as litigation weapons for corporations targeted for takeover and, as such, can only discourage legitimate and socially useful corporate acquisitions.

With these considerations in mind, we recommend that Congress act quickly to curtail these uses of RICO in takeover litigation. Specifically, we recommend that Congress amend RICO to preclude the utilization of the RICO predicate offenses of mail, wire, and securities fraud in litigation involving any corporate acquisition governed by the Williams Act.[135] Such an amendment would eliminate what could develop into an enormously potent tool to discourage takeover attempts but would not, at the same time, diminish RICO's effectiveness in its area of primary concern—organized crime. Although Congress may be commended for creating a statute with teeth, RICO will bite more evenly if one of those teeth is removed.

---

135. Sections 13(d), 13(e), and 14(d) of the Williams Act apply only to acquisitions of, or tender offers for, a class of equity security that is registered under Exchange Act § 12, 15 U.S.C. § 78*l* (1982). Section 14(e) of the Williams Act, in contrast, applies to *any* tender offer.

VII

PROPOSALS FOR TENDER OFFER REFORM

The subject of tender offer reform has lately received increased attention.[1] Although the present regulatory framework has its staunch defenders,[2] the advocates for some meaningful change are becoming more vocal and apparently more persuasive.[3] Even among those urging modification of the current regulatory process, there is sharp disagreement as to the proper nature and extent of any such changes. This point may be seen by the Report of Recommendations by the SEC's Advisory Committee on Tender Offers, where the Separate Statements submitted by respected members of the Committee contrasted sharply with those of the majority.[4]

This section contains two commentaries addressing the need for tender offer reform.[5] In the first article, A. A. Sommer, Esq., a former SEC Com-

---

1. This is evidenced by the scholarly literature on the subject (see the Bibliography contained herein), the SEC's Advisory Committee Report on Tender Offers, the SEC's tender offer reform legislative package transmitted to Congress (reported in 16 Sec. Reg. & L. Rep. (BNA) 793 (1984), and the several bills that have been recently introduced. *See, e.g.*, bills discussed in 16 Sec. Reg. & L. Rep. (BNA) 913-915, 1102-1103 (1984).

2. *See, e.g.*, Lipton, *Takeover Bids in the Target's Boardroom*, 35 Bus. Law. 101 (1979); Steinbrink, *Management's Responses to the Takeover Attempt*, 28 Case W. Res. L. Rev. 882 (1978).

3. *See* sources mentioned in note 1 *supra*.

4. *Compare* the views of Justice Arthur J. Goldberg, Messrs. Frank H. Easterbrook and Gregg A. Jarrell, and Jeffrey B. Bartell, Esq., with those of the majority and with the other Separate Statements. See also Part I herein on the SEC Advisory Committee Report.

5. Stanley Sporkin, Esq., also addresses tender offer reform in the "Panel Discussion" contained herein.

missioner, provides a critical assessment of tender offer regulation. Mr. Sommer begins by supplying a historical overview of federal and state regulation of hostile takeovers, including a review of the Williams Act and the states' responses to this acquisition technique. He then examines recent developments, including such issues as state reaction to the Supreme Court's decision in *MITE*,[6] the increased frequency of leveraged buy-outs, and the broad interpretation given by courts to the business judgment rule. The author thereafter addresses the pros and cons of tender offer regulation. In so doing, he discusses the diverse views of other experts in this area. In the last section, Mr. Sommer recommends that a thorough multidisciplined inquiry, initiated by the private sector, is long overdue to examine and reach a consensus on the hostile tender offer phenomenon.

In the second commentary, Professor Marc I. Steinberg presents a number of his thoughts on tender offer regulation. Observing that "tender offers are not a game in which corporate managements are entitled to play roulette with shareholder equity, employee security, and community welfare," he focuses on four broad themes: application of the business judgment rule to target companies' managements, application of existing federal law to target management, abuses that should be corrected through federal legislation, and a tentative proposal for vesting primary jurisdiction over pending tender offers in the Securities and Exchange Commission. Addressing each of these subjects, Professor Steinberg analyzes the relevant statutory and case law and proffers recommendations for reform.

---

6. 102 S. Ct. 2629 (1982). For further discussion on *MITE* and related developments, see Part II herein on the constitutional dimensions of state takeover statutes.

Hostile Tender Offers: Time for a Review of Fundamentals

A. A. SOMMER, JR.*

I. INTRODUCTION AND HISTORY

A series of events, both legal and economic, has clearly indicated the necessity for a thoroughgoing, fundamental analysis of the hostile takeover phenomenon in the United States and a basic review of the entire regulatory structure of this increasingly common troublesome occurrence.

Forcible takeovers are not a latter day phenomenon. While it is difficult to identify the precise origins of this method of accomplishing a transfer of control of corporate assets, probably for as long as there have been publicly held corporations there has existed the possibility that an unwanted suitor would offer shareholders a price for their shares that would result in large numbers of them responding by exchanging their shares for the consideration offered and thereby vesting control in the offeror.

It has only been in the last couple of decades that this method has become the predominant means of gaining corporate control in the face of management opposition.[1] Before then, the far more common technique for changing corporate control was the proxy contest, a form of struggle for control that has only lately come back into prominence, in large measure because the high cost of money has made a tender offer prohibitively ex-

---

* A. A. Sommer, Jr., is a partner of Morgan, Lewis & Bockius, Washington, D.C. He formerly was a commissioner of the United States Securities and Exchange Commission.

1. See Appleton, *The Proposed Requirements*, 32 Bus. Law. 1381, 1381 (1977); Note, *Corporate Directors Liability for Resisting a Tender Offer: Proposed Substantive and Procedural Modifications of Existing State Fiduciary Standards*, 32 Vand. L. Rev. 575, 575 (1979).

pensive.[2] Before 1968, the regulation of tender offers largely depended upon the willingness of courts to extend the application of traditional doctrines and remedies to this mode of activity totally uncontemplated when the laws sought to be applied were written.[3]

The Securities and Exchange Commission and private litigants tried to persuade courts to apply the general antifraud provisions of Rule 10b-5 to tender offers with somewhat mixed results.[4] Among the anomalous consequences of this was the refusal of most courts to permit suit by a target company under the rule on the grounds that it was neither a buyer nor seller of securities and, hence, had no standing to complain of alleged misconduct on the part of the offeror.[5]

State securities administrators similarly tried to stretch existing laws to regulate the conduct of tender offers directed to shareholders in their states.[6] This often involved some imaginative distortions of the purposes and words of their blue sky statutes. In many instances the interest of the states went beyond protection of security holders; they were often more concerned with avoiding the loss of jobs and tax revenues if plants were moved and other disruptions that would result from the control of locally owned and managed industries passing to entrepreneurs who had no stake in, or emotional ties to, the potentially affected communities.[7]

---

2. Einhorn, *The Growing Importance of Proxy Contests: Is There a Renewed Interest in That Strategy?* Proxy Litigation and Contests Handbook 3-5 (New York Law Journal Press, 1981).

3. *See* Sowards and Mofsky, *Corporate Take-Over Bids: Gap in Federal Securities Regulation*, 41 St. John's L. Rev. 499, 504-06 (1967). Prior to 1968, the New York Stock Exchange had adopted rules that companies with securities listed there were required to follow in making tender offers.

4. *Id.; see* Comment, *The Regulation of Corporate Tender Offers under Federal Securities Law: A New Challenge for Rule 10b–5*, 33 U. Chi. L. Rev. 359 (1966); 2 Bromberg and Lowenfels, *Securities Fraud and Commodities Fraud*, Secs. 6.3 (700)-(900) and (1022) and cases cited therein (1983); Allied Artists Pictures Corp. v. D. Kaltman & Co., Inc., [1966-67 Transfer Binder] Fed. Sec. L. Rep. (CCH) ¶ 91,998 (S.D.N.Y. 1967); The Greater Iowa Corp. v. McLendon, 378 F.2d 783 (8th Cir. 1967); Pacific Ins. Co. v. Blot, 267 F. Supp. 956 (S.D.N.Y. 1967).

5. Sommer, *Tender Offers*, Sec. Reg. Guide (P-H) §§ 1101, 1104 (1971).

6. *See* Order of the Ohio Division of Securities, May 15, 1967, in Matter of Glidden Corp. (tender offer to Ohio residents must be made through dealers licensed in Ohio).

7. Pitt, *Hostile Tender Offers Now Omnipresent Fact of Life*, Legal Times (Wash.), July 19, 1982, at 16; Aranow, Einhorn and Berlstein, Developments in Tender Offers for Corporate Control vi (1977); Nathan and Moloney, *State Tender Offer Statutes: An Analysis of the Practical and Policy Considerations*, 23 N.Y.L. Sch. L. Rev. 647, 680 (1978).

In 1968, Congress adopted the Williams Act,[8] its first explicit attempt to regulate this increasingly prevalent mode of acquiring control of a corporation with significant amounts of stock in the hands of the public. The Williams Act, which was cast as an amendment to the Securities Exchange Act of 1934, relied, like most federal regulation of securities, principally upon disclosure and stated the minimal information offerors must disclose in connection both with their pre-offer accumulations of stock and their tender offers.[9] Among the information required was the intention of the offeror if it achieved control, the names and affiliations of those associated with the offeror in the offer, and the source of financing for the acquisition.[10]

The Williams Act did not stop with disclosure, however. It also prescribed substantive rules in several areas: the times when offerees could withdraw their shares once tendered,[11] rules governing the pro rata acceptance of shares tendered when the offer was for less than all shares,[12] and several other matters.[13] The avowed purpose of the Williams Act was to assure fairness among offerors, offerees, and target companies and to assure that investors were protected in making their judgment on how to respond to the tender offer.[14]

It was, of course, unrealistic to imagine that the delicate balance that Congress sought to achieve with the Williams Act would remain in perfect poise amid the raucous and heated encounters of targets and raiders in the courts and in other combat arenas. Federal and state securities laws do not define the entire universe of the law's concern with the conduct of parties in connection with tender offers. For one thing, while state corporation statutes typically do not deal expressly with tender offers, traditional concepts and rules, both statutory and judicial, have been applied by the courts to the conduct of parties to tender offers. For the most part, these concepts and rules have been applied to the conduct of targets. Foremost among these has been the business judgment rule, which has been repeatedly invoked to justify the actions of management and directors in resisting a hostile takeover.[15] The courts have been almost unfailingly generous

---

8. 15 U.S.C. §§ 78m(d)-(e), 78n(d)-(f) (1976). The Williams Act is the popular name of Pub. Law No. 90-439, 82 Stat. 454 (1968).

9. 15 U.S.C. §§ 78m(d), 78n(d) (1976).

10. 15 U.S.C. § 78m(d)(1).

11. 15 U.S.C. § 78n(d)(5) (1976).

12. 15 U.S.C. § 78n(d)(6) (1976).

13. See, e.g., 15 U.S.C. § 78n(d)7 (1976) providing that if a tender offeror increases the consideration offered to shareholders, the increased consideration must be paid to those who tendered prior to the announced increase.

14. S. Rep. No. 550, 90th Cong., 1st Sess. 3 (1967).

15. See Fleischer, *Business Judgment Rule Protects Takeover Targets*, Legal Times (Wash.), April 14, 1980, at 15.

in according to target officers and directors the protections of this rule.[16]

On the other hand, as the courts became steadily less inclined to intervene in these struggles through the use of injunctions and other relief,[17] clearly the offerors began to have an advantage. This judicial boost to offerors through inactivity reinforced the realities of the marketplace. Once an offer commenced, market forces quickly took over. Arbitrageurs bought heavily, often in the expectation that the initial offer might trigger another higher one or simply to profit from the lag in the market price of the target's shares catching up with the offering price, a lag sometimes resulting from legal or other uncertainties attending the offer.[18] Thus, not infrequently, the ultimate outcome of the contest was quickly resolved in fact, if not in public awareness, because the "arbs," who typically were concerned solely with short-term gains and had no enduring interest in the fate of the target, were so heavily committed and had the ability to deliver so much stock to a bidder that acquisition of the target by someone was virtually a foregone conclusion.[19]

The balance contemplated by Congress was further confounded by the states, which, confronted by what they perceived to be the danger of losing industry, employment, and tax revenues when a local business fell before the onslaught of a tender offer, entered the fray with aggressive legislation intended to provide a wall behind which their industries might be protected from unwanted attentions.[20] The first of this genre of legislation was Ohio's, which in large measure provided a pattern followed by many of the forty states that eventually adopted antitakeover legislation.[21] The Ohio statute, which was described by one commentator as "an interesting and useful experiment in state securities and corporation law legislation,"[22] provided for notification by a would-be offeror to the target company, a filing with the state securities authority of information concerning the proposed offer

---

16. *Id.*; 1 Fleischer, Tender Offers: Defenses, Responses, and Planning 177-184 and cases cited therein (2d ed. 1983).

17. *See, e.g.*, Rondeau v. Mosinee Paper Corp., 422 U.S. 49 (1975); Agency Rent-A-Car, Inc. v. Connolly, 686 F.2d 1029 (1st Cir. 1982).

18. *See* Aranow and Einhorn, *supra* n. 7, at 177-80 (1973); Henry, *Activities of Arbitrageurs in Tender Offers*, 119 U. Pa. L. Rev. 466 (1971).

19. *See* O'Boyle, *Changing Tactics in Tender Offers*, 25 Bus. Law. 863, 866 (1970).

20. Pitt, *supra* n. 7. At the peak, forty states had adopted legislation intended to impact in one degree or another tender offers made for the securities of companies having some nexus with the state. Some simply extended the disclosure requirements of the Williams Act, while others followed the pattern of the Ohio statute.

21. Ohio Rev. Code Ann. § 1707.041 (1978). The effective date of this statute was October 9, 1969.

22. Shipman, *Some Thoughts about the Role of State Takeover Legislation: The Ohio Takeover Act*, 21 Case W. Res. L. Rev. 722, 724 (1970).

and the offeror, and a public announcement of the terms of the offer, twenty days before commencement of the offer;[23] gave the state securities administrator power to compel a hearing on the adequacy of disclosure;[24] required fuller disclosure than was mandated under the Williams Act;[25] and posed the possibility of long delay before a takeover could be accomplished.[26] In addition, it placed a severe inhibition on an offer by anyone who had accumulated 5 percent or more of the target company's stock without having disclosed in advance its intention to acquire control.[27]

It was from the outset commonly believed that such statutes might well be unconstitutional[28] but that, until such time as they had been definitively determined to be such (and there were doubts that that time would ever come), they might well be the death knell of hostile tender offers because of the delays they would occasion. It was thought that such delays would jeopardize financing of an offer and eliminate the commonly believed to be all-important element of surprise.[29] The savants were half-right. Ultimately, thirteen years from the enactment of the Ohio statute, the Supreme Court did determine that the Illinois statute, which resembled most of those that had been enacted, was unconstitutional.[30]

However, during the meantime, the state statutes did not have the inhibiting effects it was thought they would. Financing did not dry up; targets, while advantaged to some extent (principally in being afforded more time to find a more compatible and perhaps more generous acquirer), nonetheless continued to topple; and offerors continued with relatively little hindrance their quest.

While through the 1970's there continued to be considerable attention paid to the tender offer phenomenon, it was accepted as an essential com-

---

23. Ohio Rev. Code Ann. § 1707.041(B)(1) (1978).

24. Ohio Rev. Code Ann. § 1707.041(B)(4) (1978).

25. *See* Shipman, *supra* n. 22, at 731-734.

26. Forty days could elapse from the time the Division of Securities ordered a hearing on the adequacy of the offerors' disclosure before one was held. An additional 20 days could go by after the hearing was concluded before an adjudication on the merits was mandated. Ohio Rev. Code Ann. § 1707.041(B)(4) (1978). *See also* Shipman, *supra* n. 22, at 735.

27. Ohio Rev. Code Ann. § 1707.041(B)(2) (1978).

28. Wilner & Landy, *The Tender Trap: State Takeover Statutes and Their Constitutionality*, 45 Fordham L. Rev. (1976); Note, *Commerce Clause Limitations upon State Regulation of Tender Offers*, 47 Calif. L. Rev. 1133 (1974); Note, *Securities Law and the Constitution: State Tender Offer Statutes Reconsidered*, 88 Yale L.J. 510 (1979).

29. Langevoort, *State Tender-Offer Legislation: Interests, Effects and Political Competency*, 62 Cornell L.Q. 213, 239 (1977); Vorys, *Ohio Tender Offers Bill*, 43 Ohio Bar 65, 73 (1970); Shipman, *supra* n.22, at 757-758.

30. Edgar v. MITE Corp., 457 U.S. 624 (1982).

ponent of a capitalistic economy, and, in general, while uncertainty continued to cloud the ultimate fate of state regulation, there was little serious
questioning of the basic premises upon which the federal regulatory scheme
was based.[31] The Commission did adopt some modifications of its rules,[32]
but, for the most part, these constituted little more than tinkering, reflecting
its experience in administering the Williams Act and its continuing search
for a careful balance of fairness between offerors and targets. In 1980, the
Commission, in response to the request of Congress, proposed statutory
amendments,[33] but even these did not question the fundamental premises
of the Williams Act.

II. RECENT DEVELOPMENTS

Recent events, both regulatory and economic, have combined to create
a situation in which fundamental questions about takeovers are being asked,
and it is imperative that they be answered.

In many quarters, not the least in Congress, disquiet has mounted as the
size of takeovers has steadily mounted, with the current "champion" the
takeover of Gulf Oil by Standard Oil of California for a total consideration
in excess of $13 billion.[34] Where once sheer size was thought to insulate
a company from possible attack, now few companies may feel comfortable
behind that assumption. Renewed cries are heard that the wave of takeovers
not only has an adverse effect on competition but that it creates other
economic dislocations as well.[35]

At a time when the high level of interest rates creates in the eyes of most
economists a danger to the resurgence of the economy, and when many
would-be homebuyers appear to be priced out of the market by such interest
rates, consumers and their representatives marvel at the ability of offerors
to assemble vast sums in the twinkling of an eye, not for the purpose of
expanding the economy or making it more productive but simply for the
purpose of rearranging the ownership of already existing industrial riches.[36]

---

31. One exception to this was the extremely perceptive article by Arthur L. Liman,
Has the Tender Movement Gone Too Far? 23 N.Y.L. Sch. L. Rev. 687 (1978).

32. Securities Exchange Act Release No. 16384 (Nov. 29, 1979), [1979-1980
Transfer Binder] Fed. Sec. L. Rep. (CCH) ¶ 82,373 (1979).

33. Memorandum of the Securities and Exchange Commission to the Senate Committee on Banking, Housing, and Urban Affairs proposing amendments to the Williams Act, Sec. Reg. & L. Rep. (BNA) No. 542 at 15 (Feb. 27, 1980).

34. Salmans, *Wall St. Changes and Oil Glut Hurt*, March 10, 1984 at 35.

35. *See* Buick, *The Hidden Trauma of Merger Mania*, Bus. Wk. (Dec. 16, 1982)
at 14.

36. Brobeck, The Impact of 1984 Mega-Mergers on Interest Rates (Submitted to
the Subcomm. on Telecommunications, Consumer Protection, and Finance of the
House Comm. on Energy and Commerce, May 2, 1984).

And there is concern that the ever-lurking danger of a takeover distracts management from longer-term considerations necessary to mobilize the economy for the fierce worldwide competitive struggle in which we are engaged, causing it instead to concentrate on a short-term performance record designed to raise stock prices to levels hoped to make the company a less-tempting target.[37]

The concern over the danger of a takeover has caused many managements to opt for the leveraged buy-out,[38] a new term for, and a refinement of, what was more popularly known in the mid-1970's as "going private." As then, these moves are often perceived by small shareholders as an unfair squeeze-out, which denies them the opportunity to share in the forthcoming prosperity of the enterprise, or more immediately, the premium associated with a tender offer.

And while unquestionably the public enjoys the drama of the battles of goliaths (else why the front-page coverage of the details of the struggles?), they are often scandalized at what they perceive as unbridled ruthlessness by captains of industry in pursuit of objectives that seem less related to shareholder or societal welfare than ego satisfaction or the preservation of valuable "perks." They see new high priests, possessed of seemingly exclusive access to the secrets of aggression and defense, getting multimillion-dollar fees (one investment banker received over $17 million for its work for Marathon Oil in beating off Mobil, and two firms shared $45 million for their work for Gulf Corp.[39] in connection with its struggle to escape the grasp of the less-conventional T. Boone Pickens in favor of the "old-school-tie" comfort of Socal's embrace). Again the public has been discomfited by the sight of wealthy and well-compensated executives awarding themselves handsome employment termination contracts—aptly, in many instances, called "golden parachutes" or "silver wheelchairs"—providing for benefits in the millions of dollars.[40] It is true that many of the dangers, real or imagined, perceived by the public are not unique to hostile takeovers, though the drama associated with them, as contrasted with negotiated acquisitions, has tended to identify the dangers with hostile activities. More-

---

37. Statement of Timothy Wirth, Chairman, Subcommittee on Telecommunications, Consumer Protection, and Finance, 4 (May 22, 1984).

38. In the typical leveraged buy-out, all of the assets or stock of the corporation are purchased for cash. The bulk of the financing is provided by institutional lenders, although a small amount of equity capital comes from operating management and an investor group. *See* Lederman, Morris & Weitman, *Leveraged Buy-outs—Overview and Structure*, Sixth Annual Securities Update—1984, 395 (1984).

39. Bleakly, *The Merger Makers' Spiraling Fees*, N.Y. Times, Sept. 30, 1984, § 3 at 1.

40. *See* Moore, *Golden Parachute Agreements Shelter Displaced Executives*, Legal Times, Oct. 25, 1982 at 1, col. 1; Morrison, *Those Executive Bailout Deals*, Fortune, Dec. 13, 1982 at 82.

over, it may well be that some of the concerns are unfounded, for example, many economists do not see an undesirable preemption of credit resources by massive acquisitions.[41] Notwithstanding, the concerns are realities, and they are the sort of realities to which Congress is wont to respond.

The stage has been further set for a searching reexamination of fundamentals by a number of legal developments. The Supreme Court in *Edgar v. MITE*[42] declared the Illinois antitakeover statute unconstitutional under the Commerce Clause of the Constitution. While theoretically the decision impacted only the Illinois statute, most of the existing state statutes were placed under a probably irremovable cloud, and a succession of district and circuit court cases has extended the Supreme Court's analysis to the statutes of other states.[43] This development was preceded by suggestions that perhaps, at least with respect to targets not having close shareholder identity with a state, there should be federal legislative preemption in the field of tender offers; such a provision was incorporated in the American Law Institute's Federal Securities Code with the support of the North American State Securities Administrators.[44]

While the Supreme Court's *MITE* decision undoubtedly disappointed the states which had adopted antitakeover measures, it has apparently not resolved the basic questions about the roles of the federal and state governments in regulating tender offers. Ohio was the first to seek to undo the effects of the *MITE* case. In a manner carefully crafted to avoid the infirmities identified by the Supreme Court, Ohio amended its General Corporation Law to provide that before anyone could acquire shares of a company incorporated in Ohio having 20 percent or more of the voting power, its proposal to do so would have to be submitted to a meeting of shareholders for approval, and, similarly, if a holder wished to "up" its holdings to a third or more, another vote would be required, as it would if someone wished to acquire a majority of the voting power.[45] By incorporating these provi-

---

41. Berry, *Big-Merger Borrowing Does Not Pull Capital from Productive Use*, Financier (April 1984) at 6; *Do Mega-Mergers Drive Up Interest Rates?* Bus. Wk. (April 16, 1984) at 14.

42. 457 U.S. 624 (1982).

43. Telverst v. Bradshaw, 697 F.2d 576 (4th Cir. 1983) (1980 Amendment to Virginia Takeover Bid Disclosure Act); Martin Marietta Corp. v. Bendix Corp., 690 F.2d 558 (6th Cir. 1982) (Michigan Takeover Offers Act); National City Lines, Inc. v. LLC Corp., 687 F.2d 1122 (8th Cir. 1982) (Missouri Takeover Bid Disclosure Act); Mesa Petroleum Co. v. Cities Service Co., 715 F.2d 1425 (10th Cir. 1983) (Oklahoma Takeover Bid Act); Bendix Corp. v. Martin Marietta Corp., 547 F. Supp. 522 (D. Md. 1982) (Maryland Corporate Takeover Law); Natomas Co. v. Bryan, 512 F. Supp. 191 (D. Nev. 1981) (Nevada Takeover Bid Disclosure Law).

44. 2 American Law Institute Federal Securities Code Annotated § 1904(c) at 962-3 and 967-9 (1978).

45. Ohio Rev. Code Ann. § 1701.831 (Page's Supp. 1983).

sions in its General Corporation Law, Ohio hoped to escape the knife of the Supreme Court on the basis of the traditional doctrine that the internal affairs of a corporation are governed by the laws of the state of incorporation.[46] Clearly, if an offeror were willing to pay a price sufficiently high to attract enough stock to fill its bid, then it could probably count on a sufficient vote to permit its offer to go forward. Hence, it may be said that the Ohio statute simply provides a procedural hurdle, not a complete bar or even high hurdle, to an offer that is sufficiently attractive. But clearly it does pose problems.

Maryland has followed with a statute, adopted in 1983, requiring an 80 percent vote for certain transactions with interested shareholders; essentially this is a codification of the familiar charter provision requiring a supermajority vote for certain transactions with interested shareholders.[47] Pennsylvania has adopted what may be the most stringent and inhibitive of any statute either of the earlier generation or this. This legislation embraces three provisions. The most notable one provides that, when anyone acquires more than 30 percent of the voting stock of a corporation incorporated in Pennsylvania and registered under the Securities Exchange Act of 1934, the other shareholders have the right to receive from the 30 percent plus shareholder (*not* from the corporation whose stock they own) the fair value of their shares, *including* any premium that would attach to control shares.[48] Obviously this provision introduces a significant element of uncertainty in the price an offeror might have to pay for the remainder of the stock over 30 percent. Moreover, it probably removes pressure on shareholders to respond to a tender offer, since they would probably be able to contend successfully that the tender offer price represented the fair value of their shares, including the control premium.

Whether the states succeed or not in their efforts to thwart the impact of *MITE*, the fundamental question still remains whether tender offers for companies which have no shareholder base in a state sufficient to justify state concern should be regulated solely by federal statute or by parallel efforts reflecting the respective interests of the federal and state governments. The SEC's Advisory Committee on Tender Offers recommended that state regulation of takeovers should be confined to "local" companies.[49]

Closely related to this problem is the involvement of state corporate law, both judicial and statutory, in tender offer contests, particularly the ree-

---

46. Restatement (Second) of Conflicts of Laws §§ 196-310 (1971).

47. Md. Corps. & Assn's Code Ann. § 3-602 (Cum. Supp. 1983).

48. Pennsylvania Business Corporation Law § 410. The Pennsylvania Act is discussed in detail in the commentaries contained in Part II *supra*.

49. SEC Advisory Committee on Tender Offers Report of Recommendations, Fed. Sec. L. Rep. (CCH) No. 1028 at 17-18, (extra ed., July 15, 1983) [hereinafter cited as Report of Recommendations].

mergent business judgment rule. While the business judgment rule has a long history and has been for decades a reliable guardian of directors against liability for their conduct, in the last decade it has been the subject of extensive litigation and renewed interpretation, basically in two contexts: (1) the termination of derivative actions[50] and (2) the efforts of directors of target companies: first, to erect shields against unwanted offers[51] and second, once an attack has been mounted, to ward it off.[52]

In this latter context the business judgment rule has indeed been a reliable protector of the directors of targets. Directors have been attacked, unsuccessfully, because they authorized the repurchase of shares at a premium from a menacing intruder;[53] the acquisition of companies where it appeared the purpose was to create an antitrust defense;[54] the initiation of litigation raising issues under the federal or state securities laws, the antitrust laws, and other relevant statutes;[55] the authorization of "golden parachute" contracts for executives;[56] sales of valuable assets ("crown jewels," in takeover parlance) to reduce the company's desirability as a target;[57] grants of sufficient options or sales of sufficient shares to permit a "white knight" to block effective control by an offeror;[58] the so-called Pac-Man defense, where the target makes a bid for the offeror;[59] the issuance of stock into friendly hands as consideration for an acquisition;[60] and creation of a stock option plan to dilute the interest of the offeror.[61] With very rare exceptions, the business judgment rule has impelled courts to dismiss charges against target management.[62]

---

50. *See* Dent, *The Power of Directors to Terminate Shareholder Litigation: The Death of the Derivative Suit?* 75 Nw. U.L. Rev. 96 (1980).

51. 1 Fleischer, *supra* n.16, at 177ff.

52. *Id.* at 178ff. and cases cited therein.

53. Cheff v. Mathes, 41 Del. Ch. 494, 199 A.2d 548 (Sup. Ct. 1964); Kos v. Carey, 39 Del. Ch. 47, 158 A.2d 136 (Ch. 1960); Kaplan v. Goldsamt, 380 A.2d 556 (Del. Ch. 1977).

54. Panter v. Marshall Field & Co., 646 F.2d 271 (7th Cir. 1981), *cert. denied*, 454 U.S. 1092 (1981).

55. *Id.*, 1 Fleischer, *supra* n.16, at 257-58.

56. R. Winter, M. Stumpf & G. Hawkins, Shark Repellants and Golden Parachutes: A Handbook for the Practitioner 433 (1983).

57. Whittaker v. Edgar, 535 F. Supp. 933 (N.D. Ill. 1982); GM Sub Corp. v. Leggett Group, Inc., No. 6155 (Del. Ch. 1980).

58. Buffalo Forge Co. v. Ogden Corp., 717 F.2d 757 (2d Cir. 1983).

59. Martin Marietta Corp. v. Bendix Corp., 549 F. Supp. 623 (D. Md. 1982).

60. *Chris-Craft II*, 480 F.2d 341 (2d Cir.), *cert. denied*, 414 U.S. 910 (1973).

61. McPhail v. L. S. Starrett Co., 257 F.2d 388 (1st Cir. 1958).

62. *See* Easterbrook and Fischel, *The Proper Role of a Target's Management in Responding to a Tender Offer*, 94 Harv. L. Rev. 1161, 1195 (1981).

The business judgment rule is a state judicial doctrine, not found explicitly in any state corporate law. The SEC's Advisory Committee on Tender Offers paid it strong lip service:

> Except to the extent necessary to eliminate abuses or interference with the intended functioning of federal takeover regulation, federal takeover regulation should not preempt or override state corporation law. Essentially the business judgment rule should continue to govern most such activity.[63]

> The Committee supports a system of state corporation laws and the business judgment rule. No reform should undermine that system. Broadly speaking, the Committee believes that the business judgment rule should be the principal governor of decisions made by corporate management including decisions that may alter the likelihood of a takeover.[64]

Having said that the Committee then ticked off a number of exceptions to its dedication to the business judgment rule: contracts with "change-of-control" compensation features once a tender offer has commenced should be prohibited,[65] certain repurchases of stock at a premium should be allowed only if approved by shareholders,[66] and certain matters should be period-ically submitted to shareholders for an "advisory vote"[67]—matters now committed to the judgment of directors operating under the protection of the business judgment rule.

To the extent it is ascertainable, it would appear that the underlying premise of the Advisory Committee was that tender offers by and large are good, that some interferences with them are sufficiently controlled by tra-ditional state law concepts, but that where the efficacy of those impediments seems too effective, then the federal government should make sure they are removed. The SEC has largely concurred in its Advisory Committee's judgments.

III. BASIC CONSIDERATIONS AND PROS AND CONS

There are few who have paid attention to the events of recent years who believe that the tender offer process as presently constituted and regulated is satisfactory. Their dissatisfactions extend from the details of the process

---

63. Report of Recommendations, *supra* note 49, at 18.
64. *Id*. at 34.
65. *Id*. at 39-40.
66. *Id*. at 46.
67. *Id*. at 37-41.

to the entire system as it now operates. Among the former are the bulk of the members of the Commission's Advisory Committee who apparently believe that with a few regulatory reforms accomplishable within the authority of the Commission, supplemented by some specific new federal legislative measures that would in some cases supersede conflicting state law, the present basic regulatory system would be adequate—adequate, to be sure, in smoothing the path for offerors.

There are critics at both ends of the spectrum. Some would have government, perhaps not all government but at least the federal government, lope to the sidelines and allow free market forces maximum latitude. This philosophy has been espoused by, among others, two members of the Advisory Committee, Professor Frank Easterbrook and Dr. Gregg Jarrell,[68] and a number of others, particularly scholars commonly identified with the so-called Chicago, or free market, school of economics.[69] Many of these would limit the capacity of directors to interfere with the prosecution of a tender offer on the grounds that the decision of the individual shareholder should be permitted to be made without hindrance, other than the intervention of government to prevent fraud or manipulation. The advocates of this position would take government off the playing field unless its intervention was necessary to prevent improper interference with the free choice of shareholders.

This position is not without appeal. One of the fundamental premises of our economy is embodied in this position, namely, the free alienability of property, uninhibited by government save for the most extreme cases. Among the prides of American securities markets have been their liquidity and the measures which have been taken to assure that—the specialist system on many exchanges, the concept of competitive marketmakers in the over-the-counter (OTC) market. One of the principal concerns of the SEC as markets have been increasingly institutionalized has been the preservation of this liquidity even when the market is confronted with large-block buy or sell orders.[70] As the need for this service has grown, members of the securities industry have responded and committed steadily larger amounts of capital to the process of facilitating the purchase and sale of blocks.

Of course, there is ample evidence in virtually every society, including

---

68. Report of Recommendations, *supra* note 49 (Separate Statement of F. Easterbrook and G. Jarrell), at 70.

69. Jarrell and Bradley, *The Economic Effects of Federal and State Regulation of Cash Tender Offers*, Journal of Law and Economics 371 (1980); Easterbrook and Fischel, *Auctions and Sunk Costs in Tender Offers*, 35 Stan. L. Rev. 1 (1982); Fischel, *Efficient Capital Market Theory, the Market for Corporate Control and the Regulation of the Cash Tender Offer*, 59 Tex. L. Rev. 1 (1978).

70. Institutional Investor Study Report of the Securities and Exchange Commission, H.R. Doc. No. 92-64, Part 4, 92d Cong., 1st Sess. 1956 (1971).

71. *See* Restatement (Second) of Property 2d §§ 3.1-3.4, 4.1-4.5 (1981).

our own, that in the interests of the larger society governments may cir-cumscribe the free alienability of property.[71] Shareholders may not be per-mitted to accept tender offers if the result would be a violation of the antitrust laws;[72] controlling persons may not sell their stock without com-plying with certain disclosure and filing requirements.[73]

The advocates of a largely hands-off attitude for directors see the tender offer situation simply as another instance in which market forces should be permitted to function without interference. The individual shareholder's decision to buy or sell in their eyes is a totally economic one dictated generally by his own economic interests, just as it is when he buys or sells on an exchange or in the OTC market or refrains from buying or selling.

The advocates of a hands-off posture, as a corollary of their position, say unequivocally that tender offers are almost invariably good, because they afford the shareholder a higher price than he would have been able to secure in the market immediately before the offer, and, as an additional fillip and justification, often the price of the offeror's shares move higher as an apparent consequence of the offer.[74]

This economic justification has been sharply disputed by Martin L. Lipton, a distinguished New York attorney, who, though he has on occasion rep-resented offerors, generally has been identified with defenses against tender offers. He has pointed out that surveys have shown that, in many instances, some time after a tender offer or the indication of a desire to make a tender offer (one of the outstanding examples of his thesis was the aborted offer by American Express for McGraw-Hill, Inc.) the price of the target's stock in the market exceeded the actual or indicated tender offer price and that the shareholders of the target were better off by not having had their shares purchased, even when dividends and the opportunity cost of what they would have received are taken into account.[75] Free market advocates, of course, would respond that even if the Lipton data are correct, whether to risk such a happy outcome of not tendering should be an owner's choice, not that of his employees who have been hired to run the business and not the portfolios of the shareholders.

However, there may be a profounder flaw in the position of the free market advocates. Their position is bottomed on the notion that the decision to buy or sell in a tender offer is essentially an individual one, no different from that of a shareholder buying or selling in the organized market. Is it?

---

72. Grumman Corp. v. LTV Corp., 665 F.2d 10, 16 (2d. Cir. 1981).

73. Frome and Rosenzweig, *Sales of Securities by Corporate Insiders—Impact of Rule 140 Series* 1 (1975).

74. Report of Recommendations, *supra* note 49, at 7 (Separate Statement of F. Easterbrook and G. Jarrell), at 109-113; 11 Journal of Financial Economics, Nos. 1-4 (April 1983).

75. Lipton, *Takeover Bids in the Target's Boardroom*, 35 Bus. Law. 101 (1979).

It is long-standing Anglo-American jurisprudence that corporations are juridically separate from their shareholders and that, as a consequence, the interests of the corporation as a juridical person are not identical with those of the body of shareholders as a whole, with those of the controlling shareholders, or with those of any other segment of the corporation. This is recognized in a number of ways, the most dramatic and obvious being seen in the principle of limited shareholder liability. Another is the present Code of Professional Responsibility, which says that an attorney representing a corporation represents the "entity" and not the directors, shareholders, or management.[76]

Moreover, long before tender offers made their appearance as a means of shifting control over corporate assets to new owners, state laws made provision for dispositions of corporate entities to others through two means: merger and the sale of all, or substantially all, of the corporation's assets. At one time such a transaction required unanimous consent of all shareholders.[77] This was obviously impracticable in the context of corporations with numerous shareholders, so corporation statutes typically provided that such transactions might be accomplished through the vote of the holders of a specified majority of shares outstanding.[78] But these statutes have typically required something more—namely, approval by the directors as a matter totally separate and apart from approval by the shareholders.[79]

The implications of this historic requirement are intriguing. The commonly accepted rule is that in making their determination on a proposed merger or disposition of substantially all assets (as is true in any of their actions) the directors are bound by a fiduciary duty to the shareholders and the corporation, while in exercising their franchise as shareholders, shareholders, other than one in control who might have fiduciary duties stemming from that status, could vote entirely in accordance with their self-interest without concern for the welfare of the other shareholders or the corporation.[80]

---

76. Model Code of Prof. Resp., EC 5-18 (1981).

77. Henn and Alexander, *Laws of Corporations*, § 340 at 951 (3d ed. 1983).

78. *Id.*, § 340 at 698.

79. *Id.*, § 341 at 700; 2 Model Business Corporation Act Annotated 354 (1971).

80. *Id.*, § 240 at 654-5. *See also* Tanzer v. International General Industries, Inc., 379 A.2d 1121 (Del. Sup. Ct. 1977); Ringling Bros.-Barnum & Bailey Combined Shows, Inc., et al. v. Ringling, 53 A.2d 441, 447 (Del. Sup. Ct. 1947). *See also* 5 W. Fletcher, Cyclopedia of the Law of Private Corporation § 2031 at 140 (Rev. Perm. Ed. 1976):

> At a stockholders' meeting, each stockholder represents himself and his own interests solely and in no sense acts as a trustee or representative of others, and his right to vote upon a measure coming before the meeting is not in any way affected by the fact that he has a personal interest therein different or

The clear implication is that the draftsmen of these statutes believed that the directors brought to the process something that the shareholders did not and that there were policy reasons for withholding from the shareholders *alone* the power to sell the corporation. And what was the ingredient the directors would bring? On this we can only speculate. Presumably it derived from the fiduciary duty that directors bear and their unique position as the custodians of the interests of all the shareholders and the corporation, hopefully uninfected with the sort of self-interest permissible to shareholders. Thus, it was apparently expected that in some cases the self-interest of shareholders might interfere with their own best interests and the good of the corporation considered as a separate entity. Obviously, shareholders sufficiently intent upon having their way might displace the recalcitrant directors at the next shareholder's meeting (with the advent of staggered boards this would take a bit more patience) and elect directors sympathetic to a proposed transaction, or they might call a special meeting in those jurisdictions where shareholders might do such and effect a change of directors then. But this would take time, during which the proposed transaction might disappear, and the new directors would still be under the same constraint of acting in accordance with their fiduciary duty rather than the self-interests of even holders of a majority of the stock.

In a tender offer, of course, there is no requirement for formal target director approval as a prerequisite to effective action in changing control of the corporation; the acceptance of the tender offer by holders of a majority, or even less, of the stock is enough to accomplish the shift of control. However, as is apparent from experience with tender offers, approval or disapproval of the directors of the target company is in many instances a significant factor in how, and how expeditiously, the transaction is accomplished, and upon their approval or disapproval the final outcome may depend. It is extremely rare for an acquisition proposal for merger or purchase of all of a corporation's assets approved by directors to be turned down by shareholders; if the directors disapprove, it never reaches the shareholders. On the other hand, directorial disapproval in and of itself, unaccompanied by overt opposition by the board, is rarely sufficient to kill a proposed tender offer unless the offeror for one reason or another— distaste for contests, philosophical aversion to unwanted acquisitions, pessimism about his ability to successfully withstand the onslaughts of the target's board if it decides to oppose, apprehension about the uncertainties deriving from charter or other antitakeover measures taken by the target— unilaterally decides to forego making the offer.

---

separate from that of the other stockholders or by the fact that he is related to interested persons. He may vote contrary to what other stockholders deem to be the best interest of the corporation, or even detrimental to it. This is equally true of a stockholder who is also a director voting as a stockholder.

But if the offeror does decide to proceed notwithstanding the opposition of the board, although that opposition would doom a merger or acquisition of assets proposal, the offeror may still carry the day. Once an offer starts, the effectiveness of director disapprobation derives not from any statutory power afforded the board but rather in large measure from the skill of the target's attorneys, investment bankers, publicists, and counter–tender offer solicitors in using the arsenal of multiple litigation, advertisements, countersolicitations and white knights. Thus, as matters are presently constituted in this country, the directors have a role in tender offers, but their effectiveness depends upon how well they and their janissaries fight clad in the near-impenetrable armor of the business judgment rule.

The responsibilities of directors are independent of the shareholders and any responsibilities they may have. For instance, no matter that the holders of a majority of the stock of a corporation may favor a sale of the corporation's assets to a would-be purchaser, the directors are bound to fulfill their responsibilities, and if they believe, for instance, that the would-be buyer would loot the corporation, they must oppose the sale even if the majority of the shareholders, knowing full well the proclivity of the buyer, favor the sale. Similarly, in all but a handful of jurisdictions, shareholders, regardless of number, may not ratify a fraud committed by an agent of the corporation.[81]

These precepts find another expression in the commonly held proposition that if the directors of a corporation believe that a proposed tender offer is contrary to the interests of the corporation or that the consummation of a transaction between the offeror and the target would be illegal, they have an obligation to oppose the offer.[82] If the conclusion is correct that the near-universal statutory requirement of directorial approval of mergers and sales of substantially all assets suggests that there are interests involved in such transactions that cannot be left to the self-interest of the shareholders alone and that there must be involvement of persons under the constraints of fiduciary duty, then should we not inquire whether perhaps the same considerations dictate that tender offers be subjected to some similar discipline? In other words, perhaps there are values and considerations involved in tender offers that require the intervention of a judgment untainted by the narrow economic interests of the shareholders.

Those who would shrink from prohibiting tender offers, or from severely inhibiting them, argue that unless such means for changing control were freely allowed, there would be an inadequate discipline upon management

---

81. *Id.*, § 194 at 515.

82. *See* Northwest Industries, Inc. v. B. F. Goodrich, 301 F. Supp. 706 (N.D. Ill. 1969); Heit v. Baird, 567 F.2d 1157 (1st Cir. 1977).

and inefficient stewards would be too secure in their positions.[83] The standard argument is that the only reason an offeror would offer more than the market price for the stock stems from a belief that the offeror can achieve, through synergism or better management, a more economic, efficient, and profitable use of the assets sought through the effort to acquire control. Judge, then Professor, Richard A. Posner, has summarized this position as follows:

> [T]he coalescence of ownership and control is not a necessary condition of efficient management. What is necessary . . . is that there be methods—the tender offer, the proxy fight, voluntary acquisition—by which investors (usually in this context, other large corporations) can obtain control of the board of directors and oust the present management. It is unimportant whether these mechanisms are employed often; indeed, the more effective a threat is as a deterrent, the less often it has to be carried out.[84]

Of course, these propositions are not without their adversaries. For one thing, many, perhaps most, of the recent tender offers have been directed against companies probably better managed than most or companies undergoing a desirable transition, for instance, Mead Corporation and McGraw Hill. As a matter of fact, many offerors are only interested in acquiring well-managed companies.[85] In a survey by Touche Ross & Company in 1981, 69 percent of a cross section of executives did not believe poor management made a company a likely takeover target.[86]

Moreover, there is no shortage of other disciplines for errant or inefficient managements. Increasingly, the independent directors of publicly held companies are quite willing to displace ineffective management;[87] the stock market quickly penalizes poor management, and the conduct, if not words, of large institutional investors makes itself felt in the inner circles;[88] lenders are sensitive to indications of poor management and are often uniquely effective in compelling changes. Thus, it is questionable whether in fact the

---

83. Easterbrook and Fischel, *supra* n.62, at 1169-1174.

84. Posner, Economic Analysis of Law 303-5 (3d ed. 1977).

85. Kissenger, *Against Forced Takeovers*, N.Y. Times, Jan. 22, 1978, § 4 at 9, col. 2.

86. The Effect of Mergers, Acquisitions, and Tender Offers on American Business, Touche Ross & Co. (1981).

87. *See Houston Natural Gas Chairman Quits; Transco Energy President Is Successor*, Wall St. J., June 7, 1984, at 2.

88. *See* Lorsch, *In Defense of the Corporate Defender*, N.Y. Times, May 20, 1984, at F3.

hovering threat of a tender offer adds significantly to the other forces that impose a discipline on the performance of management.

Finally, of course, there is always the proxy contest as an ultimate means of ousting management. Once the favored means of taking over control of a corporation, and then eclipsed by tender offers, proxy contests have reemerged as an effective tool for effecting changes of control. Though, like tender offers, they are carried out in a highly-charged and emotional atmosphere, with charges and counter-charges, still they focus principally upon the important issue: is the incumbent management competent, would the shareholders be better served with the proposed new management?

While there are many who would remove virtually all restraints on offerors, and many who would in one degree or another relax or tighten the restrictions on the conduct of offerors and targets, it is difficult to find anyone who seriously advocates the outright banning of hostile offers or the subjection of them to the same discipline as mergers, even though, according to a survey of a panel of business executives published in Dun's Business Month, chairmen and presidents of more than 200 major corporations by a margin of 7 to 1 appear to disapprove of them,[89] and even though a respectable argument can be made for the proposition that no acquisition should be permitted unless the traditional approvals—director as well as shareholder approval—have been secured. It does not appear that any serious academic study has espoused this position, and despite the misgivings of an apparently high proportion of executives, it is hard to find a pronouncement by any business, or other body, condemning hostile takeovers as such. The absence of proponents of this position is puzzling and necessarily gives rise to the question, why this void?

IV. A PROPOSAL

All this suggests that it would be a worthwhile endeavor to undertake an in-depth consideration of the proposition that a takeover bid for a company should not be allowed unless certain stringent conditions, such as director approval, are satisfied. Representative Peter Rodino recently, in an address to a National Association of Manufacturers group, suggested that consideration be given to requiring as a condition of a takeover that it be approved by a majority of the independent directors of the target.[90]

In recent years, there has been increasing emphasis upon independent directors and their importance in corporate America. Virtually all large, publicly held companies have substantial numbers of them, in many cases

---

89. Dun's Business Month, Nov. 1983, at 80.

90. Address of Hon. Peter J. Rodino, Jr., to the National Association of Manufacturers Issue Briefing Breakfast, March 3, 1984.

more than a majority; in some companies all save two or three are independent. Without any statutory change, in many respects the independent directors have been "institutionalized": more and more decisions of importance in corporations are being made by the independent directors acting as a body within the board to minimize charges of conflict of interest, and their unique role is being recognized by courts in several contexts, notably the dismissal of derivative suits. It may be that the time is indeed here for an explicit recognition of independent directors and a definition of their role in the tender offer context. Congressman Rodino suggested that any such legislative mandate be limited in duration to two years during which time the effectiveness of its operation could be observed and judgment reached whether indeed the directors did conduct themselves in a manner suggesting true independence. Such a testing would be prudent.

Putting aside for the moment, however, the merits of such a testing and considering only the proposal without that qualification, it is based on the assumption that "independent" directors (assuming a satisfactory definition of that term could be developed) would truly act independently. Experience in a number of takeovers suggests that that assumption may be subject to challenge. In many instances, it seems clear that only the most rigorous application of the business judgment rule has protected independent (as well as inside) directors from liability. This is perhaps best seen in the dissents in *Panter v. Marshall Field and Co.*[91] and *Johnson v. Trueblood*,[92] in both of which the dissenting judges made powerful arguments that suggest less than appropriate concern for the welfare of shareholders on the part of the boards (including independent directors) involved. Not surprisingly, independent directors usually become close allies of management, engaged as they are in a common endeavor and routinely associated with each other on a regular basis (this is, of course, not to deny that in numerous instances independent directors have often pursued highly independent courses, including terminating chief executive officers whose performance was not satisfactory), and often the judgments of management will heavily influence the course chosen by independent directors.

It may well be that for the Rodino proposal to be genuinely effective it would have to be combined with the proposal made by John Huber, Director of the SEC's Division of Corporation Finance, to put on directors a heavier burden of justifying their actions in a takeover contest, thereby denying them the awesome protections afforded by the business judgment rule.[93] It may be that the business judgment rule, necessary and appropriate as it is in most circumstances, is no longer an appropriate doctrine in the context

---

91. 646 F.2d 271, 299 (7th Cir. 1981), *cert. denied*, 454 U.S. 1092.

92. 629 F.2d 287, (3d Cir. 1980), *cert. denied*, 450 U.S. 999 (1981).

93. Remarks of John J. Huber to the American Bar Association Section of Corporation, Banking, and Business Law, April 7, 1984.

of contested takeover attempts. In some limited circumstances, courts have applied the so-called primary purpose test in assessing the propriety of directors' conduct. Under this doctrine, the court typically examines whether the primary purpose of the directors was properly a corporate one rather than one originating in personal or selfish considerations. The "primary purpose" test is encountered most commonly when there is a charge that the directors had a conflict of interest.

The allocation of the burden of proof when the primary purpose test is applied can have significant effect upon the outcome of the litigation. Not infrequently, the courts have placed the burden of proving the propriety of the action taken on the directors[94] and, in several cases, the courts have faulted the directors for their conduct notwithstanding assertions that the business judgment rule protected them against judicial interference.[95] It may be that the courts should invoke the primary purpose test more frequently than they have and place the burden of proving the propriety of the purpose on the directors. But, if the directors successfully sustain the burden, their opposition to a tender offer should be as conclusive as would their opposition to a merger or acquisition of assets proposal. On the other hand, if the directors fail to sustain their burden, then they should be precluded from taking action hostile to the accomplishment of the tender offer.

Regardless of the merits of the specific approaches suggested by Messrs. Rodino and Huber, it is clear that the time is indeed ripe—in fact, overripe—for a searching, deep, multidisciplined, free from cant and shibboleth, examination of the entire question of hostile takeovers. This inquiry should be isolated from the question of whether large takeovers, even when friendly, are good for society and the economy, and while, as a follow-up, specific measures to regulate hostile offers might be considered, the inquiry in its first stage should be concerned only with the most fundamental questions. Both the proposition that government should, to the maximum extent possible, let free market forces operate uninhibitedly in the takeover arena and the proposition that no takeover should be permitted unless approved by the target's directors (and the many positions in between) should be dispassionately examined and tested.

The study should avoid the myopic vision of many economists that define the value of tender offers solely in terms of the riches bestowed upon shareholders of the target company and instead examine a much broader range of values and interests: the impact of tender offers and the fear of them on managerial conduct in a world of steadily increasing international

---

94. 1 Fleischer, *supra* n. 16, at 195ff. and cases cited therein.

95. Telvest, Inc. v. Olson, No. 5789 (Del. Ch. 1979); Consolidated Investment Co., Ltd., v. Rugoff, [1978-1979 Transfer Binder] Fed. Sec. L. Rep. (CCH) ¶ 96,584 (S.D.N.Y. 1978).

competition, the extent of the resources (including managerial time and attention) absorbed by the many aspects of tender offers, and the extent to which the corporate governance processes and the capital structures of corporations are becoming distorted as corporations seek new and more effective means of thwarting takeover attempts.

The approach of the United Kingdom deserves careful study. Many of the abuses which have manifested themselves in this country have been avoided in England as a result of the creation of the Panel on Takeovers and Mergers.[96] This is a voluntary organization created by the principal financial powers in the United Kingdom for the purpose of regulating the conduct of the parties to a takeover. Through wise administration of the process, England has largely escaped the proliferation of the litigation that has customarily accompanied takeovers in this country, the efforts to manipulate time to advantage, and many of the other "violences" that are commonplace to the process here. Clearly the English model cannot, because of cultural, financial, and political differences, be transplanted intact to this country. However, there is much in their experience which, prudently adapted to our soil, might go far to civilize the process and make it what it essentially is—a business phenomenon—instead of a modern version of trial by combat.

Reconciling the interests of states and the federal government is a problem as old as our nation and is constantly in a state of adjusting to emerging needs in our society. Hence, it is too much to expect that a study, no matter how intense, will yield a single or enduring solution to this problem in the context of tender offers. However, any study of the problem in depth must pay heed to the needs and claims of the elements of our federal system. Our economy is a national economy; most tender offers for publicly held companies affect shareholders in many states and may impact the economies of many states.

It may be that the interests of shareholders and the nation necessitate some measure of federal supersession of traditional corporate law. If so, ideally the conclusion should be reached in the context of a study more basic and far reaching than the one done by the SEC's Committee in four months, and the extent of the supersession should not be determined on the basis of relatively unarticulated visceral responses to the varied means usable by management in thwarting or fighting off unwanted attentions.

This may be one of the areas in which the consequences of mergers in general must be carefully isolated from the problems unique to tender offers. The friendliest of acquisitions may wreak economic catastrophe on a city; hence it may well be that such phenomena should not be a part of the consideration of how, if at all, and by whom tender offers should be regulated.

---

96. *See* DeMott, *Current Issues in Tender Regulation: Lessons from the British*, 58 N.Y.U. L. Rev. 945 (1983) for a thorough discussion of the British model.

It is not only the question of the relationship of state and federal law that must be examined; state corporate law must also be subjected to critical scrutiny to determine whether traditional concepts, conceived and nurtured in a far different environment, should continue to be carried over into the takeover world. Particularly, of course, the role of the business judgment rule, and its adequacy, in the takeover context must be critically examined. Directors should be insulated properly against the horrendous damages that would accrue if their defensive maneuvers were found to be unlawful or contrary to the interests of shareholders, but the protection of them in that regard does not necessitate the conclusion that their actions cannot be faulted in the context of a determination of whether the particular conduct should be permitted. For example, the directors of Marshall Field might well have been prevented from undertaking various of the antitakeover measures they authorized without exposing them after the fact to a liability measured, perhaps, by the difference between the pre-offer price of the stock and the tender offer price, an appalling figure which if ever imposed as a liability on directors would chill the enthusiasm of any but the judgment-proof for serving on a board.

The sort of inquiry proposed will be a hard and demanding one. It will need the one ingredient denied to the Commission's Advisory Committee by Congress's impatience, time. It will require the talents of lawyers, including not just specialists in tender offers but experts on state law and other relevant disciplines within the law, investment bankers, and economists (and hopefully some who are able to determine the benefits and negative effects of tender offers with a measure having more dimensions than simply financial benefits to shareholders). Most of all, it will need the talents of people, whatever their particular discipline and background, who can "see things large" and who will be able to understand all the dimensions of the problem. The problems transcend simply providing a "level playing field" for the contest, protecting the interests of shareholders, protecting the mobility of capital; these are important, but none are all-important.

There are no panaceas. That there are none should not deter or delay the effort. The issues are too compelling and in many instances too central to our future as a nation. Who should initiate the effort? It is perhaps best if the initiative comes from the private sector. In this respect we can indeed borrow a leaf from the British book and have the initiative come from a powerful coalition including the exchanges and the National Association of Securities Dealers (NASD), the business community (the Business Roundtable, the Business Council, and the National Association of Manufacturers are likely candidates), the American Bar Association, the Federal Reserve Board, the political sector, both legislative and executive, both state and federal. While the multiplication of interests involved increases the difficulty of reaching a consensus, it is imperative that the effort have the benefits of many inputs and broad participation. And when should the effort commence? Tomorrow is not too soon.

Some Thoughts on Regulation of Tender Offers

MARC I. STEINBERG*

The proliferation of hostile bids for corporate control has resulted in the emergence of defensive and offensive maneuvers limited only by the ingenuity of counsel and investment bankers. The terms for some of these maneuvers, including "golden parachutes," "shark repellant" provisions, "lockups," "poison pills," "scorched-earth" tactics, "white knights," and the recently coined "Pac-Man" defense,[1] suggest that there is something fundamentally wrong with the process. In short, tender offers are not a game in

---

*Marc I. Steinberg is a professor at the University of Maryland School of Law. A.B., University of Michigan; J.D., University of California, Los Angeles; LL.M., Yale University. He is a member of the California and District of Columbia Bars.

Thanks are extended to Ralph C. Ferrara, Esq., Professor Oscar S. Gray, Ellen F. Kandell, Esq., Stanley Sporkin, Esq., and Professor Gordon G. Young for their helpful comments. The views expressed herein are those of the author.

1. Definitions of some of these maneuvers are provided in Appendix 3 to Justice Goldberg's Separate Statement for the SEC Advisory Committee Report on Tender Offers, U.S. SEC, Report of Recommendations 140-41 (1983):

Crown Jewel	The "crown jewel" is the most prized asset of a corporation, i.e. that which makes it an attractive takeover target. A defensive tactic against a hostile tender offer may be to sell this asset to another party, thereby removing the [key] asset that the unfriendly bidder was hoping to acquire and encouraging [it] to cease [its] offer without purchasing any shares of the subject company.
Golden Parachute	A generous severance package that protects certain key executives if control of [the subject] company changes.
Lock-Up	An arrangement, made in connection with the proposed acquisition of a publicly held business, that gives the proposed acquiror an advantage in acquiring the subject company over

which corporate managements are entitled to play roulette with shareholder equity, employee security, and community welfare. Unfortunately, managements on both sides of these so-called battles for corporate control more than occasionally neglect these important responsibilities. Target managements all too often have blindly fended off offers at substantial premiums while irretrievably wasting corporate assets and depriving shareholders of

	other potential acquirors. Lock-ups may take the form of: a) a stock purchase agreement for treasury or unissued shares, b) options to purchase treasury or unissued shares, c) an option to buy certain assets (See "Crown Jewel"), d) a merger agreement, e) agreements providing for liquidated damages for failure to consummate an acquisition, f) options and stock purchase agreements between the "white knight" and principal shareholders, and g) other similar provisions.
Pac-Man Defense	A tender offer by the subject company for the securities of the original bidder.
Scorched Earth Defense	Actions taken by the directors of the subject company to sell off the subject company's assets or failing this, to destroy the character of the company to circumvent the bidder's tender offer.
Two-tier Offer	A two step acquisition technique in which the first step (front end) is a cash tender offer and the second step (back end) is a merger in which remaining shareholders of the subject company typically receive securities of the bidder valued below the cash consideration offered in the first step tender offer. Despite the reduced consideration being offered in the merger, the merger is certain to be approved by the subject company's shareholders as the bidder, due to [its] acquisition of a controlling interest in the subject company through the tender offer, will vote in favor of the merger.
Poison Pill	A class of securities of the target company convertible upon consummation of any merger [or other enumerated] transaction into the common stock of the [target].
Greenmail	The purchase of a substantial block of the subject company's securities by an unfriendly suitor with the primary purpose of coercing the subject company into repurchasing the block at a premium over the amount paid by the suitor.
Shark Repellants	Amendments to a potential [target] company's certificate of incorporation or by-laws that have been devised to discourage unsolicited approaches from unwanted bidders.
White Knight	The party sought out by the subject company [in an attempt to fend off the unwanted bidder. Action taken by a white knight may include purchasing a large block of the target company's stock or making a competing tender offer].

an opportunity to tender their stock.[2] Some offeror managements also have delinquently utilized questionable practices to make tender offers amounting to several million dollars, sometimes after employees have made significant salary and benefit concessions.[3]

The recurrence of this kind of irresponsible behavior, and provocative comments made by others on particular abuses associated with hostile tender offers,[4] prompt me to offer a few of my own thoughts on the subject. These thoughts are loosely grouped under four headings: application of the business judgment rule to target companies' managements, application of existing federal law to target management, abuses that ought to be the

---

See also Goldberg, *Regulation of Hostile Tender Offers: A Dissenting View and Recommended Reforms*, 43 Md. L. Rev. 225 (1984). For discussion of various defensive maneuvers and their application, *see* M. Steinberg, Securities Regulation: Liabilities and Remedies § 11.08 (1984); Block & Miller, *The Responsibilities of Corporate Directors in Takeover Contests*, 11 Sec. Reg. L.J. 44, 52-66 (1983). *See also* Friedenberg, *Jaws III: The Impropriety of Shark-Repellent Amendments as a Takeover Defense*, 7 Del. J. Corp. L. 32 (1982); Gilson, *The Case against Shark Repellent Amendments: Structural Limitations on the Enabling Concept*, 34 Stan. L. Rev. 775 (1982); Riger, *On Golden Parachutes—Ripcords or Ripoffs? Some Comments on Special Termination Agreements*, 3 Pace L. Rev. 15 (1982).

2. *See, e.g.*, Panter v. Marshall Field & Co., 486 F. Supp. 1168 (N.D. Ill. 1980), *aff'd*, 646 F.2d 271 (7th Cir.), *cert. denied*, 454 U.S. 1092 (1981). There, prior to the time that Carter-Hawley's tender offer proposal for Marshall Field stock was made at $42.00 per share, Marshall Field stock was selling in the market at approximately $22.00 per share. Marshall Field's management successfully fended off the proposal by, *inter alia*, engaging in a number of dubious "defensive" acquisitions and filing an antitrust suit against Carter-Hawley. After Carter-Hawley withdrew the offer prior to it becoming effective, the price of Marshall Field stock declined to $19.76 per share. *See* R. Jennings & H. Marsh, Securities Regulation 676 (5th ed. 1982). The Seventh Circuit on appeal, over a vigorous dissent, affirmed the district court's grant of the defendant's motion for a directed verdict. Approximately one year later, Marshall Field was taken over in a friendly transaction by Batus, Inc., at a price of $30.00 per share. *See* Marshall Field & Company v. Icahn, 537 F. Supp. 413 (S.D.N.Y. 1982).

3. Prior to U.S. Steel's 1981 offer for Marathon Oil Co., for example, employees of the former company had agreed to significant concessions. United Steel Workers v. United Steel Corp., 492 F. Supp. 1, 8 (N.D. Ohio 1980). *See generally* Millspaugh, *Plant Closings and the Prospects for a Judicial Response*, 8 J. Corp. L. 483, 491-92 (1983). *Cf.* Hymowitz & O'Boyle, *Two Steel Mills Gird for Result of Merger Bid*, Wall St. J., Feb. 22, 1984, at 35, col. 3 (A worker at one of U.S. Steel's plants remarked that "[w]e gave [U.S. Steel] concessions and finally got back to work. I thought the bad times were finally over. But now with this [proposed] merger [between U.S. Steel and National Steel Corp.], I don't know if I have a job or not." *Id.*). The Wall Street Journal article also noted that some of U.S. Steel's employees are bitter about what they view as the company's inadequate investment in modernizing its plants.

4. *See* authorities cited *supra* note 1, *infra* notes 11, 14-15, 24, 31, 83.

subject of additional federal legislation, and a tentative proposal for vesting primary jurisdiction over pending tender offers in the Securities and Exchange Commission (SEC).[5]

I. APPLICATION OF THE BUSINESS JUDGMENT RULE TO TARGET MANAGEMENT

In general, the courts have not adequately redressed the misconduct of target managements in connection with hostile tender offers. Target managements have been protected by, *inter alia*, the mantle of the business judgment rule, under which corporate fiduciaries responsible for taking defensive actions have been shielded from liability for the ensuing consequences.[6] The courts have failed to recognize that, particularly when such actions deprive shareholders of the right to tender their stock, the basic premise underlying the business judgment rule is not valid in this context and application of the rule therefore is inappropriate.[7]

The business judgment rule provides that corporate officers and directors will be shielded from judicial inquiry into the propriety of their decisions and from liability for harm to the corporation resulting from their decisions, so long as (1) the decisions were within management's authority to make and (2) such corporate fiduciaries have "[a] informed [themselves] and made reasonable inquiry with respect to the business judgment[s]; [b] acted in good faith and without a disabling conflict of interest; and [c] had a rational basis for the business judgment[s]."[8] As the Supreme Court of Delaware

---

5. The purpose of this commentary is not to present a comprehensive analysis of the many issues raised by federal regulation of tender offers. The work is offered instead as a reflection upon selected problems associated with tender offers, with suggestions for remedial action. It is hoped that its contents will stimulate further discussion of the problems noted and that the ideas set forth will prove to be among the elements of an effective overall solution to inequities in the tender offer process.

6. *See, e.g.*, Panter v. Marshall Field & Co., 646 F.2d 271 (7th Cir.) (applying Delaware law), *cert. denied*, 454 U.S. 1092 (1981); Treadway Cos. v. Care Corp., 638 F.2d 357 (2d Cir. 1980) (applying New Jersey law); Crouse-Hinds Co. v. InterNorth, Inc., 634 F.2d 690 (2d Cir. 1980) (applying New York law); Berman v. Gerber Products Co., 454 F. Supp. 1310 (W.D. Mich. 1978) (applying Michigan law). *See generally* M. Steinberg, Corporate Internal Affairs: A Corporate and Securities Law Perspective 225-239 (1983).

7. With the benefit of the business judgment rule and restrictive federal court decisions construing the Williams Act, target managements usually are able to successfully fend off hostile bidders. *See* Austin, *Tender Offer Movement Off in 1982*, Nat'l. L.J., Jan. 16, 1984, at 15, col. 1, 36 ("In 1982, only 21.9 percent of the contested tender offers were completely successful. On the other hand, 53.1 percent of all the contested offers were completely unsuccessful.").

8. Principles of Corporate Governance and Structure: Restatement and Recommendations § 4.01(d) (Tent. Draft No. 1, 1982) [hereinafter cited as ALI Draft

recently pointed out,[9] the doctrine is an acknowledgment of the managerial prerogatives of corporate directors under state law. "It is a [rebuttable] presumption that in making a business decision the directors of a corporation acted on an informed basis, in good faith and in the honest belief that the action taken was in the best interests of the company."[10] That presumption is inappropriate however, with respect to decisions made by target managements that preclude shareholders from tendering their stock in response to a hostile tender offer.[11]

Because target management is likely to have a disabling conflict of interest,[12] the business judgment rule should not be applied to defensive actions undertaken by target companies in response to or in anticipation of tender offers, particularly where such actions materially impede or preclude shareholders from tendering their shares. Directors and officers of the target corporation know that they are likely to be replaced if an offer

---

Restatement]. For discussion of the ALI's draft formulation of the business judgment rule, see Steinberg, *The American Law Institute's Draft Restatement on Corporate Governance: The Business Judgment Rule, Related Principles, and Some General Observations*, 37 U. Miami L. Rev. 295 (1984). For other formulations of the business judgment rule, *see* Arsht, *The Business Judgment Rule Revisited*, 8 Hofstra L. Rev. 93, 111-12 (1979); Steinberg, *Application of the Business Judgment Rule and Related Judicial Principles: Reflections from a Corporate Accountability Perspective*, 56 Notre Dame Law. 903, 904-05 (1981).

9. Aronson v. Lewis, 473 A.2d 805, No. 203, 1983 (Del. Mar. 1, 1984), discussed in *Delaware Court Clarifies Demand Requirement for Derivative Suits*, 16 Sec. Reg. & L. Rep. (BNA) No. 10, at 480 (Mar. 9, 1984).

10. Aronson v. Lewis, 473 A.2d 805, No. 203, 1983, slip op. at 12. The Court also stated that "under the business judgment rule director liability is predicated upon concepts of gross negligence." *Id.* at 14. *See generally* Veasey & Manning, *Codified Standard—Safe Harbor or Uncharted Reef?* 35 Bus. Law. 919, 926-30 (1980) (discusses inconsistent indications in the cases as to whether the standard of care required of corporate directors under Delaware law is ordinary care or merely avoidance of gross negligence).

11. *E.g.*, M. Steinberg, *supra* note 6, at 237-39; Easterbrook & Fischel, *Takeover Bids, Defensive Tactics, and Shareholders' Welfare*, 36 Bus. Law. 1733, 1745-47 (1981). *See generally* Comment, *The Misapplication of the Business Judgment Rule in Contests for Corporate Control*, 76 Nw. U.L. Rev. 980 (1982). *Cf.* Lowenstein, *Pruning Deadwood in Hostile Takeovers: A Proposal for Legislation*, 83 Colum. L. Rev. 249, 313-14 (1983) (the courts' use of the business judgment rule in the context of hostile tender offers necessitates a legislative solution); Note, *Tender Offer Defensive Tactics and the Business Judgment Rule*, 58 N.Y.U. L. Rev. 621 (1983) (a less deferential version of the business judgment rule ought to be applied in the tender offer context).

12. Crane Co. v. Harsco Corp., 511 F. Supp. 294, 305 (D. Del. 1981). *But cf.* Northwest Indus. v. B. F. Goodrich Co., 301 F. Supp. 706, 712 (N.D. Ill. 1969) ("[W]henever a tender offer is extended and the management of the threatened company resists, the officers and directors may be accused of trying to preserve

succeeds. "Inside" directors[13] therefore have a personal financial interest in defeating tender offers, unless the impact of a successful offer upon them has been ameliorated by "golden parachutes"[14] or some other form of protection.[15] Even "inside" directors who have such protection and "outside" directors who may not be deemed financially interested nonetheless may be "interested" in maintaining their

> positions of power, prestige and prominence.... They are "interested" in defending against outside attack the management which they have, in fact, installed or maintained in power.... And they are "interested" in maintaining the public reputation of their own leadership and stewardship against the claims of "raiders" who say that they can do better.[16]

---

their jobs at the expense of the corporation.... Yet, management has the responsibility to oppose offers which, in its best judgment, are detrimental to the company or its stockholders.").

13. "Inside" directors include those who hold positions as officers of the corporation, or who are otherwise employed by the company, e.g., as in-house corporate counsel. "Inside" directors are also those directors who may be said to have a pecuniary interest in the corporation's affairs greater than that arising from ownership of a less-than-controlling block of the corporation's shares. See Cheff v. Mathes, 199 A.2d 548, 554-55 (Del. 1964). Burden of proof as to whether a stock repurchase was in the corporate interest was not as great for directors who were merely "substantial shareholders" as for those who were the chief executive officer and corporate counsel, since the former did not have "a personal pecuniary interest in the decisions made by the board of directors...." Id. at 554.

14. The use of "golden parachutes" has generated extensive criticism. These executive compensation agreements, which generally provide generous severance remuneration for key officers or directors upon a change in corporate control, have been attacked as constituting a waste of corporate assets, as unconscionable self-dealing and hence a breach of the duty of loyalty, and as an unwarranted antitakeover device. See, e.g., Goldberg, supra note 1, at 128; Riger, supra note 1, at 25-39. On the other hand, proponents assert that such compensation agreements may benefit shareholders by enabling the corporation to retain high-quality management and more securely aligning management's interests with those of the shareholders when a hostile bid is made. E.g., Advisory Comm. on Tender Offers, U.S. SEC, Report of Recommendations 39 (1983) [hereinafter cited as Advisory Committee Report]. Professors Easterbrook and Jarrell assert: "Perhaps such [golden parachute] guarantees are 'unseemly,' but they grease the skids of offers by decreasing the role managerial self-protection plays in defending." Id. at 103 (Separate Statement of Easterbrook & Jarrell). See generally Note, Golden Parachutes: Executive Employment Contracts, 40 Wash. & Lee L. Rev. 1117 (1983).

15. Some have taken the position that defeat by target management of a tender offer virtually is never in the best long-term interests of shareholders as a whole. See Easterbrook & Fischel, The Proper Role of a Target's Management in Responding to a Tender Offer, 94 Harv. L. Rev. 1161, 1174-75 (1981).

16. Panter v. Marshall Field & Co., 646 F.2d 271, 300-01 (7th Cir.) (Cudahy, J., concurring in part, dissenting in part), cert. denied, 454 U.S. 1092 (1981).

In addition, the element of structural bias is ever present.[17] Incumbent management's control of the proxy machinery and general informational processes,[18] combined with its control of the methods for selecting outside directors,[19] frequently result in undue directorial loyalty to management rather than the exercise of independent judgment.[20]

Target management therefore has an inherent conflict of interest when faced with a hostile tender offer.[21] Drawing on traditional common law

---

17. "Structural bias" may be defined as "inherent prejudice... resulting from the composition and character of the board of directors [and management]." Note, *The Business Judgment Rule in Derivative Suits against Directors*, 65 Cornell L. Rev. 600, 601 n.14 (1980) [hereinafter cited as Note, *Derivative Suits*]. For further discussion of the concept of structural bias, see *id*. at 619-26. *Cf*. Clark v. Lomas & Nettleton Financial Corp., 625 F.2d 49, 53-54 (5th Cir. 1980), *cert. denied*, 450 U.S. 1029 (1981) (recognizing the possibility of structural bias, the court held that, due to conflicts of interest, the board was incompetent to compromise the plaintiff shareholders' derivative claims); Miller v. Register and Tribune Syndicate, 336 N.W. 2d 709, 716-18 (Iowa 1983) (recognizing structural bias problem in refusing to dismiss derivative suit against corporate fiduciaries where members comprising the special litigation committee were appointed to the committee by defendant fiduciaries).

The inherent problem of structural bias is discussed at length in Note, *The Propriety of Judicial Deference to Corporate Boards of Directors*, 96 Harv. L. Rev. 1894 (1983) [hereinafter cited as Note, *Judicial Deference*]. Drawing upon studies of group dynamics, the author of the Note concluded: "Given cohesiveness and informational dependence in the boardroom, directors are likely to conform to the expectations both of management and of their fellow board members." *Id*. at 1901.

18. *See, e.g.*, Mace, *Directors: Myth and Reality—Ten Years Later*, 32 Rutgers L. Rev. 293, 297-303 (1979) ("C.E.O.'s continue to control board functions through the proxy process."); Note, *Judicial Deference, supra* note 17, at 1898 ("Confronted by difficult issues of business policy and largely dependent upon management for information about these issues, directors are likely to believe that management's views and judgments are worth adopting.") (footnote omitted).

19. *See* Comment, *supra* note 11, at 1002 n.106 (outside directors are selected by C.E.O.s partially on the basis of whether they can be expected "not to rock the boat"; the problems arising from management's control over directors may be mitigated, but not entirely eliminated, by utilizing nominating committees of disinterested directors to control the corporate proxy machinery).

20. *See* Note, *Derivative Suits, supra* note 17, at 619-22. *Cf*. Note, *Judicial Deference, supra* note 17, at 1896-1902 (discussing the pressures on directors to conform their judgments to those of management).

21. *See, e.g.*, Crane Co. v. Harsco Corp., 511 F. Supp. 294, 305 (D. Del. 1981) ("in the context of a tender offer, the directors have an inherent conflict of interest.") (citation omitted.)

The Supreme Court of Delaware has recognized that a similar conflict of interest may arise when, on the recommendation of a special litigation committee comprised of nondefendant directors, a corporation seeks dismissal of a shareholder derivative suit. In Zapata Corp. v. Maldonado, 430 A.2d 779 (Del. 1981), that court held that,

standards,[22] as well as the more recent "interested director" statutes,[23] it may be argued that the burden should be placed on target management to show both the substantive and procedural propriety of its conduct. Hence, to pass muster under state law, target management should be required to prove that its actions were taken for the corporation's best interest and were intrinsically fair to the corporation and other affected parties.[24]

---

in cases where demand on the board is excused, a two-step test should be applied in determining whether to grant the corporation's motion to dismiss: first, the court should inquire into the special litigation committee's independence and good faith and the bases supporting its conclusions, with the burden of proof on the corporation; second, providing that the first step is satisfied, the court should apply "its own independent business judgment" and "should, when appropriate, give special consideration to matters of law and public policy in addition to the corporation's best interests." *Id.* at 788-89. *See* Aronson v. Lewis, 473 A.2d 805, No. 203, 1983 slip op. at 16 (Del. Mar. 1, 1984) (the chancery court "must" apply both steps).

22. *See, e.g.,* Geddes v. Anaconda Copper Mining Co., 254 U.S. 590, 599 (1921); Pappas v. Moss, 393 F.2d 865, 867 (3d Cir. 1968); Petty v. Penntech Papers, Inc., 347 A.2d 140, 143 (Del. 1975); Guth v. Loft Inc., 5 A.2d 503, 510-12 (Del. 1939). As the Supreme Court of Delaware stated in *Guth*: "The occasions for the determination of honesty, good faith and loyal conduct are many and varied, and no hard and fast rule can be formulated. The standard of loyalty is measured by no fixed scale." *Id.* at 510.

23. *See, e.g.,* California Corps. Code § 310 (West 1977); Delaware Code Ann. tit. 8, § 144; Maryland Corps. & Ass'ns Code Ann. § 2-419 (1975 & Supp. 1983); Model Business Corp. Act § 41 (1982); N.Y. Bus. Corp. Law § 713 (McKinney 1963). For judicial decisions construing these interested director statutes, see Remillard Brick Co. v. Remillard-Dandini Co., 109 Cal. App. 2d 405, 241 P.2d 66, 74-76 (1952); Fliegler v. Lawrence, 361 A.2d 218, 221-22 (Del. 1976). *See generally* Bulbolia & Pinto, *Statutory Responses to Interested Directors' Transactions: A Watering Down of Fiduciary Standards?* 53 Notre Dame Law. 201 (1977).

24. *Cf.* Treadway Cos. v. Care Corp., 638 F.2d 357, 381-83 (2d Cir. 1980) (Under New Jersey law, the business judgment rule should be applied when the issuance and sale of shares to a white knight is challenged, but after the plaintiff has shown that a majority of the issuer's directors either expected that the transaction would serve to perpetuate their own control or approved the transaction under the domination or control of directors who had such a personal control interest, the burden of proof will shift to the directors who then must prove that the transaction was fair to the corporation. Plaintiff failed to meet the initial burden of proof, however, and so the burden did not shift.) Cheff v. Mathes, 199 A.2d 548, 554-55 (Del. 1964) (Directors who authorized an issuer's repurchase of shares from a dissident shareholder necessarily had a conflict of interest when a threat to the directors' control was involved, and the burden of proof was upon them to show that the purchase was in the corporation's interest. Defendants whose interests were not clearly pecuniary were not held to as high a standard of proof as those with "personal and pecuniary interest in the transaction," however. *Id.* at 555.)

If the approach recommended in the text is not adopted, at least courts should

One might note in this context that shareholders who are denied the opportunity to tender their shares at a substantial premium must find application of the business judgment rule to be egregiously unfair. Under Delaware law, for example, the presumption of good faith and care is rebuttable only by showing that management's sole or primary purpose for its conduct was to retain control.[25] Corporate fiduciaries who are given the benefit of the presumption almost always will be able to proffer a "legitimate" business purpose for their actions, including actions employed solely to perpetuate incumbent management's position.[26] This outcome is even more assured if management uses expert counsel and investment bankers to lay a foundation for and to structure its actions.[27]

Some may argue that the duties imposed upon corporate fiduciaries by state law counterbalance any potential conflict of interest on the part of target management and thus make application of the business judgment rule appropriate.[28] This response is deficient in at least two respects. First, if the principles of corporate governance, shareholder welfare, and market integrity are to have practical meaning in this context, management cannot be permitted to invoke a presumption of disinterested decision making in a situation in which its interests are so likely to conflict with those of the

---

inquire whether the decision to oppose the tender offer and to engage in defensive tactics was made primarily by disinterested directors or by those directors whose livelihoods and economic interests depended on the continued separate existence of the subject corporation. *See* Gelfond & Sebastian, *Reevaluating the Duties of Target Management in a Hostile Tender Offer*, 60 B.U.L. Rev. 403, 468-69 (1980); Williams, *Role of Directors in Takeover Offers*, 13 Rev. Sec. Reg. 963, 965 (1980). Such an approach generally is not advised, however, for the reasons given in notes 12-16 *supra* and accompanying text.

25. *See, e.g.*, Panter v. Marshall Field & Co., 646 F.2d 271, 293-95 (7th Cir. 1981) (plaintiff must show either bad faith or predominance of an improper control motive to prevent application of the business judgment rule on a motion for directed verdict under Delaware law); Johnson v. Trueblood, 629 F.2d 287, 292-93 (3d Cir. 1980) (also construing Delaware law).

26. The rule's underlying presumption is especially likely to be a cover for abuse if management's consideration of noninvestor interests is deemed to be within the presumption. *See infra* note 41.

27. Lowenstein, *supra* note 11, at 314; Steinberg, *supra* note 10, at 906-07. As discussed earlier, target management usually is successful in fending off hostile offers. See *supra* note 7.

28. Certain actions taken by corporate managers which have the effect of perpetuating their control may be held invalid under state law. *See, e.g.*, Lerman v. Diagnostic Data, Inc., 421 A.2d 906 (Del. Ch. 1980) (holding that a board of directors could not set the date of an annual stockholder meeting so as to leave insufficient time for submission of materials required of nominees under antitakeover amendments to the corporation's bylaws). *See generally* Gelfond & Sebastian, *supra* note 24, at 433-49.

shareholders.[29] Second, certain investment decisions are to be made by shareholders, without undue management intervention, absent good reason otherwise. Two common examples are a shareholder's decision to sell shares in the open market[30] and the decision to tender stock in response to a particular takeover bid.[31] Given the nature of the shareholder's traditional interest in disposing of his stock ownership, fiduciary duties do not entitle management to preempt such decisions absent foreseeable harm caused by the purchaser.[32] As one court has pointed out:

> What is sometimes lost sight of in these tender offer controversies is that the shareholders, not the directors, have the right of franchise with respect to the shares owned by them.... The Directors are free to continue by proper legal means to express to the shareholders their objection and hostility to the [subject] proposal, but they are not free to deny them their right to pass upon this offer or any other offer for the purchase of their shares.[33]

Notwithstanding target management's inherent conflict of interest when faced with a hostile tender offer,[34] there may be circumstances in which incumbent management, in accord with its obligations to shareholders, employees, and affected communities,[35] ought to be entitled to take certain

---

29. See supra notes 7-21 and accompanying text.

30. See Lowenstein, supra note 11, at 266 ("In a routine market transaction, there is no room for management to inject its views as to the price at which shares should trade and there is no 'corporate interest,' it is said, that would justify the target company management's using the corporate treasury to influence the transaction.").

31. See generally id. at 266-67; Cohn, Tender Offers and the Sale of Control: An Analogue to Determine the Validity of Target Management Defensive Measures, 66 Iowa L. Rev. 475, 509-24 (1981).

32. There are some exceptions. If a controlling shareholder sells out without making a reasonable investigation of its purchaser, for example, it may be held liable for damages incurred by the corporation and minority shareholders due to the purchaser's looting of the corporation. E.g.. DeBaun v. First Western Bank & Trust Co., 46 Cal. App. 686, 696-98, 120 Cal. Rptr. 354, 359-61 (1975); Gerdes v. Reynolds, 28 N.Y.S. 2d 622, 650-51 (Sup. Ct. N.Y. Co. 1941).

33. Conoco, Inc. v. Seagram Co., Ltd., 517 F. Supp. 1299, 1303 (S.D.N.Y. 1981) (dictum). See also infra notes 54, 55 and accompanying text.

34. See supra notes 12-16 and accompanying text.

35. See Herald Co. v. Seawell, 472 F.2d 1081, 1094-95 (10th Cir. 1972) (applying Colorado law in a shareholder derivative suit, the court stated that management of a corporation engaged principally in the publication of a large metropolitan newspaper had duties to the stockholders, the employees, and the public); Pa. Stat. Ann. tit. 15 § 408 (Purdon, 1967), as amended by Act No. 1983-92, 1983 Pa. Legis. Serv. 773, 774 (Purdon) (corporate fiduciaries "may, in considering the best interests of

defensive actions to fend off detrimental takeover bids. State law provisions may be needed, moreover, to ensure that the risk of incurring potentially astronomical monetary liability will not lead target managements to avoid taking defensive actions even when they are appropriate. Two proposals are offered here: First, if otherwise appropriate, the business judgment rule may be applied in its entirety to actions that do not materially impede or preclude shareholders from tendering their stock. Hence, management may enjoy the benefit of the rule's presumption when it recommends that the hostile offer be rejected,[36] raises its dividend rate,[37] induces a white knight to enter the fray,[38] or takes other actions which do not interfere with the shareholders' freedom to accept any tender offer of their choice.[39] Second, if defensive maneuvers do materially impede or preclude shareholders from tendering their shares to a particular bidder,[40] management should be required to prove that its actions were fair to the corporation and its shareholders, subject to two provisos: management may take noninvestor interests into account,[41] and a ceiling may be placed on the amount of damages

---

the corporation, consider the effects of any action upon employees, suppliers and customers of the corporation, communities in which offices or other establishments of the corporation are located and all other pertinent factors."); *See infra* notes 41, 82-85, and accompanying text.

36. *Cf.* Humana, Inc. v. American Medicorp, Inc., [1977-1978 Transfer Binder] Fed. Sec. L. Rep. (CCH) ¶ 96,286 (S.D.N.Y. Jan. 5, 1978) (applying a fairly lenient standard in determining whether the target's press releases were false or misleading).

37. *Id.*

38. A "white knight" generally is a "friendly" party which comes to the aid of incumbent target management in its efforts to fend off a hostile takeover bid by, for example, purchasing a large block of the target's authorized but unissued stock or making a competing tender offer at a higher price.

39. See M. Steinberg, *supra* note 6, at 225-28.

40. For examples of defensive maneuvers that materially impeded or precluded tender by shareholders to a particular bidder and were held to give rise to liability, see Mobil Corp. v. Marathon Oil Co., 669 F.2d 366, 374-76 (6th Cir. 1981) (options to sell substantial block of the company's stock and its "crown jewel"); Applied Digital Data Sys. v. Milgo Elec. Corp., 425 F. Supp. 1145, 1157-61 (S.D.N.Y. 1977) (issuance of substantial block of shares to a friendly third party); Royal Indus. v. Monogram Indus., [1976-77 Transfer Binder] Fed. Sec. L. Rep. (CCH) ¶ 95,863 (C.D. Cal. Nov. 29, 1976) (acquisition of another enterprise to interpose antitrust obstacles to a tender offer). *But see* Panter v. Marshall Field & Co., 646 F.2d 271, 297 (7th Cir. 1981) (acquisition of another enterprise in the context of a tender offer held to be protected by the business judgment rule); Whittaker Corp. v. Edgar, 535 F. Supp. 933 (N.D. Ill. 1982) (sale of an asset resulting in making target company less attractive to bidder held to be protected by the business judgment rule).

41. *See generally* Pa. Stat. Ann. tit. 15 § 408 (Purdon, 1967) *as amended by*, Act No. 1983-92, 1983 Pa. Legis. Serv. 773, 774 (Purdon); O'Boyle & Carey, *Gulf's Departing Pittsburgh Would Deal a Harsh Blow to City's Economy and Pride*, Wall

recoverable from corporate fiduciaries.[42] To protect adequately the competing interests at stake, the ceiling on damages should be high enough to deter corporate malfeasance but not so exorbitant as to dissuade courts from imposing liability.[43]

St. J., Mar. 9, 1984, at 33, col. 4 ("Standard Oil Co. of California's $13.3 billion bid to acquire the oil giant has brought shudders to Pittsburgh charities, university presidents, tax officials, ministers and everyone else who benefits from Gulf's financial and civic might." *Id.*). It is important that the burden of justification be placed on corporate fiduciaries when they take noninvestor interests into account. Otherwise, the presumption of the business judgment rule would be further extended, making it a nearly insurmountable barrier for any aggrieved party. Application of the business judgment rule in this context thus would represent an overly solicitous approach to target management. *See generally infra* notes 82-85 and accompanying text.

42. *Cf.* ALI Draft Restatement, *supra* note 8, at § 7.06(d)(e) (establishing a ceiling on damages in duty of care cases in the absence of culpability surpassing that of negligence).

43. *See infra* notes 99-104 and accompanying text. *Cf.* ALI Draft Restatement, *supra* note 8, at § 7.06(e), which sets forth the following monetary limits for the maximum recovery available in duty of care cases where the defendant's culpability is no greater than negligence:

> (i) in the case of a director who, at the time of the events giving rise to the action, was not otherwise an employee or officer of the corporation in whose name the action is brought, or of any corporation possessing control over, controlled by, or under common control with, such corporation, the ceiling shall not exceed (A) $200,000, nor fall below (B) $50,000; and

> (ii) in the case of any other defendant whose liability is based upon a duty owed to the corporation as an employee or as a corporate fiduciary, the range shall not exceed (A) the higher of (1) $200,000 or (2) twice such defendant's gross compensation from the corporation for the most recently ended calendar year, nor fall below (B) such defendant's gross compensation from the corporation for the same year; provided, however, that the court may utilize a different recent year if it finds that such compensation was artificially understated for the most recently ended year.

(citation omitted).

The question arises what standard should apply and what relief should be available when incumbent management, with disinterested shareholder approval, induces the corporation to adopt antitakeover (or shark repellant) provisions prior to the presence of a hostile bid. It may be argued that disinterested shareholder approval accompanied by full disclosure should insulate the provisions from successful challenge. *Cf.* Rivoli Theatre Co. v. Allison, 396 Pa. 277, 152 A.2d 449, 451 (Pa. 1959) (conversation with a single stockholder fell short of the full and frank disclosure to all stockholders necessary for ratification of contracts); State *ex rel.* Hayes Oyster Co. v. Keypoint Oyster Co., 64 Wash. 2d 375, 385, 391 P.2d 979, 986 (1964). Within the framework set forth in this article, however, the business judgment rule should

It should be evident that by taking the position that the business judgment rule should not be applied to certain defensive actions by target management, I am by no means urging the rule's abrogation. The business judgment rule serves important policy considerations when it is applied in appropriate settings,[44] and its continued use in those settings is desirable if this country's economy is to function efficiently. In the context of "show-stop" maneuvers in tender offers,[45] however, the rule serves as a sword to pierce legitimate shareholder interests rather than as a justifiable shield for management's conduct and, thus, should not be applied.[46]

---

apply only as to those shark repellant provisions which do not materially impede or preclude hostile bidders from coming forward with a viable offer. *See generally* Alcott v. Hyman, 208 A.2d 501, 506-07 (Del. 1965). To the extent such provisions materially impede or preclude the making of hostile offers, courts should scrutinize their terms to determine whether they are fair to shareholders. "Preclusive" shark repellant provisions may be analogized to certain self-dealing transactions that, by their very nature, involve constructive fraud, waste of corporate assets, or palpable overreaching. In such cases, shareholder approval does not inhibit the courts from evaluating the intrinsic fairness of the transaction. *See generally* Schreiber v. Bryan, 396 A. 2d 512, 518 (Del. Ch. 1978) (only unanimous stockholder ratification is sufficient to justify a waste or gift of corporate assets); Pappas v. Moss, 393 F.2d 865, 868 (3d Cir. 1968) (under New Jersey law, there can be no effective ratification where a majority of shares is held by those "interested" in the transaction). Providing that no monetary losses have been incurred (which normally would be the case when suit is brought challenging the validity of antitakeover provisions prior to the emergence of a hostile bidder), judicial relief normally should be limited to the invalidation of the subject provisions and the issuance of an injunction against enforcement of those and similar provisions which might otherwise be adopted in the future.

44. At least three policy considerations support appropriate application of the business judgment rule:

> First, if management were liable for mere good faith errors in judgment, few capable individuals would be willing to incur the financial and emotional risks of serving in such roles. Second, courts are generally ill equipped to evaluate business judgments. Finally, management has the expertise to discharge the responsibility of making such determinations.

M. Steinberg, *supra* note 6, at 236, *citing* Abramowitz v. Posner, 672 F.2d 1025, 1032 (2d Cir. 1982), Auerbach v. Bennett, 47 N.Y.2d 619, 629, 393 N.E.2d 994, 1000, 419 N.Y.S.2d 920, 926-27 (1979), and *Corporate Director's Handbook*, 33 Bus. Law. 1591, 1603-04, 1615 (1978).

45. A "show-stop" maneuver is any action taken by target management, such as the sale of the company's crown jewel, which has the effect of materially impeding or precluding shareholders from tendering their stock to the "hostile" bidder.

46. *See* Steinberg, *supra* note 8 at 904-07, 915.

II. APPLICATION OF FEDERAL LAW TO TARGET
MANAGEMENT

Under the Williams Act[47] and SEC regulations implementing the Act,[48] both offeror and target managements must disclose certain information relevant to a subject tender offer.[49] An offeror must disclose, *inter alia*, certain prior transactions between the offeror and the target, the source of funds to be used in the acquisition, and, if material, the applicability of antitrust laws and pending legal proceedings related to the tender offer.[50] The target company must disclose, *inter alia*, any material contract, agreement, or "understanding" between the target company, its officers or directors, and the bidder company, its officers or directors.[51] The target company also must state whether it is advising its shareholders to accept or to reject the offer, whether it is remaining neutral with respect to the offer, or whether it is unable to take a position regarding the offer. Whatever the recommendation advanced, the target corporation must disclose the reasons for its position.[52]

The disclosure provisions of the Williams Act were intended by Congress to ensure that shareholders, after hearing from both the offeror and target corporations with neither side having an unfair advantage over the other, would have sufficient information to make informed decisions in determining whether to tender their shares.[53] As former SEC Chairman Cohen testified, the Act's purpose was "to provide the investor, the person who is required to make a decision, an opportunity to examine and to assess the

---

47. The Williams Act was enacted in 1968 as an amendment to the Securities Exchange Act of 1934. Pub. L. No. 90-439, 82 Stat. 454 (codified as amended at 15 U.S.C. §§ 781(i), 78m(d), (e), 78n(d)-(f) (1982)).

48. *See, e.g.*, 17 C.F.R. § 240.14d-1 to .14d-101, 240.14e-1 to .14e-2 (1983).

49. 15 U.S.C. § 78n(d)(1), (4)(1982); 17 C.F.R. §§ 240.14d-3, .14d-6, .14d-9, .14d-100, .14d-101, .14e-2 (1983).

50. 17 C.F.R. § 240.14d-3(a)(1)(1983); SEC Sched. 14D-1, Items 3, 4, 10(c), 10(e) (codified at 17 C.F.R. § 240.14d-100 (1983)).

51. 17 C.F.R. §§ 240.14d-9(a)(1), (c) (1983); SEC Sched. 14D-9, Item 3(b) (codified at 17 C.F.R. § 240.14d-101 (1983)).

52. 17 C.F.R. §§ 240.14d-9(a)(1), (c), (d)(1)(i), .14e-2(a) (1983); SEC Sched. 14D-9, Item 4 (codified at 17 C.F.R. § 240.14d-101 (1983)).

53. *See* House Comm. on Interstate and Foreign Commerce, Disclosure of Corporate Equity Ownership, H.R. Rep. No. 1711, 90th Cong., 2d Sess. 4, *reprinted in* 1968 U.S. Code Cong. & Ad. News 2811, 2813; Senate Comm. on Banking and Currency, Full Disclosure of Corporate Equity Ownership and in Corporate Takeover Bids, S. Rep. No. 550, 90th Cong., 1st Sess. 3 (1967) [herinafter cited as Corporate Takeover Bids]. *See also* Edgar v. MITE Corp., 457 U.S. 642 (1982) (Illinois Business Takeover Act held unconstitutional under the commerce clause), in which Justice White stated:

relevant facts and to reach a decision without being pressured and without being subject to unwarranted techniques which are designed to prevent that from happening."[54] As noted elsewhere, "[d]isclosure, no matter how extensive, matters little if the target's management can employ defensive tactics that deprive or otherwise materially impede the investor's freedom of choice."[55] It follows logically that target management properly should be permitted to take defensive actions under the Williams Act that do not preclude or materially impede shareholders from tendering their stock so long as there is full disclosure.[56] On the other hand, maneuvers by target management that deny shareholders an opportunity to tender their shares should be held to violate the Williams Act, absent evidence that the offeror would inflict some clearly foreseeable harm upon the target corporation.[57]

The Williams Act may be applied in either of two ways to ensure that target shareholders normally have an opportunity to accept or reject a tender offer. First, conduct by management that deprives shareholders of

---

We...agree with the Court of Appeals that [in passing the Williams Act] Congress sought to protect the investor not only by furnishing him with the necessary information but also by withholding from management or the bidder any undue advantage that could frustrate the exercise of an informed choice.

...Looking at [the history of the Act] as a whole, it appears to us, as it did to the Court of Appeals, that Congress intended to strike a balance between the investor, management, and the takover bidder. The bidder was to furnish the investor and the target company with adequate information but there was no "intent[ion] to do...more than give incumbent management an opportunity to express and explain its position." Once that opportunity was extended, Congress anticipated that the investor, if he so chose, and the takeover bidder should be free to move forward within the time frame provided by Congress.

Id. at 634 (citations omitted) (quoting Rondeau v. Mosinee Paper Corp., 422 U.S. 49, 58 (1975)).

54. Corporate Takeover Bids, *supra* note 53, at 15 (statement of Manuel F. Cohen, Chairman, SEC). For additional legislative history supporting this view, see the sources gathered in Lynch & Steinberg, *The Legitimacy of Defensive Tactics in Tender Offers*, 64 Cornell L. Rev. 901, 911-12 (1979).

55. Lynch & Steinberg, *supra* note 54, at 911.

56. *Id.* at 927.

57. *Cf.* Mobil Corp. v. Marathon Oil Co., 669 F.2d 366, 376-77 (6th Cir. 1981) (grant of lock-up options to a white knight held to be manipulative acts within § 14(e) of the Williams Act); Joseph E. Seagram & Sons, Inc. v. Abrams, 510 F. Supp. 860 (S.D.N.Y. 1981) (temporary restraining order granted to prevent possibly improper manipulation under § 14(e) in the form of selling off target's assets or destroying its corporate charter to defend against a hostile offer). *But see* cases cited *infra* note 65.

an opportunity to tender may be held to constitute "constructive fraud" within the meaning of Section 14(e) of the Williams Act.[58] Although the Supreme Court held in *Santa Fe Industries, Inc. v. Green*[59] that "mere" breaches of fiduciary duty not amounting to "manipulation" or "deception" do not violate Section 10(b) of the Exchange Act and Rule 10b-5 promulgated thereunder,[60] Section 14(e) ought to be interpreted differently. Unlike Section 10(b), Section 14(e) by its terms prohibits "fraudulent" acts or practices.[61] This difference in statutory language and the legislative history of Section 14(e)[62] support giving it a broader reach than Section 10(b).[63] Second, defensive tactics, the practical effect of which is to prevent share-

---

58. 15 U.S.C. § 78n(e) (1982). *See* Loewenstein, *Private Litigation under Section 14(e) of the Williams Act* in Part VI of this volume; Steinberg, *Fiduciary Duties and Disclosure Obligations in Proxy and Tender Contests for Corporate Control*, 30 Emory L.J. 169, 226 (1981). *Cf.* SEC v. Capital Gains Research Bureau, Inc., 375 U.S. 180, 185 (1963) ("scalping" by registered investment advisor held to constitute a "fraud" upon clients within the Investment Advisors Act).

59. 430 U.S. 462 (1977).

60. *Id.* at 471-74. Section 10(b) is codified at 15 U.S.C. § 78j (1982) and provides in part that it is unlawful "[t]o use or employ, in connection with the purchase or sale of any security . . . any manipulative or deceptive device or contrivance. . . . " The statute, to a significant degree, has been interpreted and enforced by the SEC under 17 C.F.R. § 240.10b-5 (1983), known as Rule 10b-5. For discussion of *Santa Fe* and its ramifications, see Ferrara & Steinberg, *A Reappraisal of* Santa Fe: *Rule 10b-5 and the New Federalism*, 129 U. Pa. L. Rev. 263 (1980).

61. 15 U.S.C. § 78n(e) (1982) (making it unlawful for any person, *inter alia*, "to engage in any fraudulent, deceptive, or manipulative acts or practices" in connection with a tender offer). Although Rule 10b-5 does include fraudulent conduct within its prohibition, the Supreme Court held in Ernst & Ernst v. Hochfelder, 425 U.S. 185, 212-14 (1976), that the scope of the rule is subject to the reach of the statute upon which it is based, namely, Section 10(b).

62. See *supra* notes 53-57 and accompanying text.

63. *See* Loewenstein, *supra* note 58:

> In light of the meticulous attention the [Supreme] Court has paid to statutory language in its recent securities law decisions, one can easily imagine the Court saying that if Congress wanted Section 14(e) to be construed identically to Section 10(b), it could have easily done so by utilizing identical language. Failing to do this, and having purposefully used the ambiguous term 'fraudulent,' Congress 'intended' the courts to give broader meaning to Section 14(e) than to Section 10(b).

(footnotes omitted). Although Professor Loewenstein ultimately rejects the above argument, because "it presumes too much regarding Congressional intent," he concludes that, based on legislative intent, Section 14(e) has a broader reach than Section 10(b).

holders from tendering in response to a bid, may be viewed as "manipulative" under Section 14(e). Under this rationale, target management may be found to have engaged in "manipulative" practices proscribed by Section 14(e) when it undertakes maneuvers that artificially impede the operation of a fair market for the corporation's stock, such as granting options on valuable corporate assets to friendly third parties.[64] Unfortunately, a number of courts have declined to adopt either of the above rationales.[65] Congress therefore should consider enacting additional legislation to make more explicit the protective policies of the Williams Act.

Even absent Congressional action, the Act's legislative history suggests that the SEC could exercise its broad rulemaking power under Section 14(e) to the same effect. Section 14(e) grants the SEC authority to promulgate rules and regulations which are "reasonably designed to prevent such acts and practices as are fraudulent, deceptive, or manipulative."[66] Although the Commission has used this authority to promulgate a number of rules,[67] it

---

64. *See* Mobil Corp. v. Marathon Oil Co., 669 F.2d 366 (6th Cir. 1981); Jordan v. Global Natural Resources, [1982-1983 Transfer Binder] Fed. Sec. L. Rep. (CCH) ¶ 99,179 (S.D. Ohio Apr. 19, 1983); Hanna Mining Co. v. Norcen Energy Resources Ltd., 574 F. Supp. 1172 (N.D. Ohio 1982); Joseph E. Seagram & Sons, Inc. v. Abrams, 510 F. Supp. 860 (S.D.N.Y. 1981); Nelson, Mobile Corp. v. Marathon Oil Co.: *The Decision and Its Implications for Future Tender Offers*, 7 Corp. L. Rev. 233 (1984); Weiss, *Defensive Responses to Tender Offers and the Williams Act's Prohibition against Manipulation*, 35 Vand. L. Rev. 1087 (1982); Note, *Target Defensive Tactics as Manipulative under Section 14(e)*, 84 Colum. L. Rev. 228 (1984). *See also* Prentice, *Target Board Abuse of Defensive Tactics: Can Federal Law be Mobilized to Overcome the Business Judgment Rule?* 8 J. Corp. L. 337 (1983); Silberberg & Pollack, *Are the Courts Expanding the Meaning of "Manipulation" under the Federal Securities Laws?* 11 Sec. Reg. L.J. 265 (1983); Note, *Lock-up Options: Toward a State Law Standard*, 96 Harv. L. Rev. 1068, 1069-72 (1983).

65. *See, e.g.*, Schreiber v. Burlington Northern, Inc., [1984 Transfer Binder] Fed. Sec. L. Rep. (CCH) ¶ 91,407 (3d Cir.) *cert. granted*, 105 S. Ct. 81 (1984); Data Probe Acquisition Corp. v. Datatab, Inc., 722 F.2d 1, 4-5 (2d Cir. 1983), *cert. denied*, 104 S. Ct. 1326 (1984); Buffalo Forge Co. v. Ogden Corp., 717 F.2d 757, 760 (2d Cir.), *cert. denied*, 104 S. Ct. 550 (1983); Panter v. Marshall Field & Co., 646 F.2d 271, 283-87 (7th Cir.), *cert. denied*, 454 U.S. 1092 (1981); Martin Marietta Corp. v. Bendix Corp., 549 F. Supp. 623, 628-30 (D. Md. 1982); Berman v. Gerber Products Co., 454 F. Supp. 1310, 1317-18 (W.D. Mich. 1978); Marshall Field & Co. v. Icahn, 537 F. Supp. 413 (S.D.N.Y. 1982); Altman v. Knight, 431 F. Supp. 309, 314 (S.D.N.Y. 1977).

66. 15 U.S.C. § 78n(e) (1982).

67. *See, e.g.*, 17 C.F.R. §§ 240.14e-1 to .14e-3 (1983). For discussion of these rules, *see* M. Steinberg, *supra* note 1, at §§ 3.06, 11.07; Bloomenthal, *The New Tender Offer Regimen, State Regulation, and Preemption*, 30 Emory L.J. 35, 35-57 (1981).

thus far has declined to address the serious "fraudulent, deceptive, [and] manipulative" misconduct that prevails in the tender offer context.[68]

On the other hand, recent SEC actions may indicate that the Commission is becoming more cognizant of its responsibility to mandate more meaningful disclosure of potentially abusive target managerial practices. For example, Commission rules now require that the terms of "golden parachute" agreements be disclosed.[69] In a recent enforcement action, the SEC also emphasized the need for management to disclose the material effects of antitakeover proposals.[70] These actions are laudable, but much information within the possession of target management and important to shareholders

---

68. *But see* SEC v. Carter Hawley Hale Stores, Inc., 16 Sec. Reg. & L. Rep. (BNA) 749 (1984) (SEC effort to have target's defensive stock repurchases defined as a "tender offer"). Indeed, the Commission recently asserted that the business judgment rule should not be the principal governor of decisions made by target management in the midst of a tender offer. *See SEC Faults Advisory Panel's Reliance on Business Judgment Rule in Takeovers*, 16 Sec. Reg. & L. Rep. (BNA) No. 11, at 495-96 (Mar. 16, 1984).

69. *See* SEC Exchange Act Release No. 20220 (Sept. 23, 1983), Amendment to Item of Regulation S-K, Item 402, 48 Fed. Reg. 44,467 (1983) (to be codified at 17 C.F.R. § 229.402) (requiring disclosure in Item 402(e) of any remuneration plan exceeding $60,000 for any corporate fiduciary included in the "cash compensation table," where such plan becomes effective on the resignation, retirement, or other termination of employment of such person, a change in control of the company, or a change in such person's responsibilities subsequent to a change in control).

70. *See* SEC v. Dorchester, [1983-1984 Transfer Binder] Fed. Sec. L. Rep. (CCH) ¶ 99,613 (D.D.C. Jan. 9, 1984). *Accord*, SEC Securities Act Release No. 6504 (Jan. 13, 1984), 3 Fed. Sec. L. Rep. (CCH) ¶ 23,120B. There, the Commission stated:

> The Commission again wishes to emphasize the need for adequate and accurate disclosure with respect to anti-takeover and other defensive measures ("anti-takeover measures"). Such measures are designed to deter contests for control or unfriendly takeovers, by making the subject company unattractive as a potential target and by making it more difficult to change a majority of the board of directors or to remove management. The anti-takeover measures also may help management to insulate a proposed corporate transaction, such as a merger or acquisition, from unwanted competition.

> Companies must disclose all the material effects of anti-takeover measures, including their impact on any proposed corporate transaction, whether hostile or friendly. It is also important that management's interest in the corporate transaction (including the existence of any actual or potential conflicts of interests) and the ultimate effect of the anti-takeover measures on shareholders be disclosed. Absent such disclosure, shareholders will be unable to make informed voting decisions on the matters being proposed. It is especially important, when management is considering or pursuing a leveraged buy-out with its attendant serious conflicts of interest, that full and fair disclosure of the impact of the anti-takeover measures on the proposed transaction be made.

remains undisclosed.[71] Hopefully, the SEC will continue to exercise its rule-making and adjudicatory authority under the Act to fill the disclosure gap.[72]

Another potential problem associated with the use of defensive maneuvers by subject corporation management is the ready access to the courts that is granted to management on both sides of a takeover struggle. Despite the Supreme Court's holding in *Piper v. Chris-Craft Industries*[73] that a defeated tender offeror does not have standing under Section 14(e) to bring an action for damages,[74] a majority of lower federal courts have permitted actions for injunctive relief under Sections 13(d)[75] and 14(e).[76] This approach, on the

---

71. For example, specific SEC rules and regulations should require disclosure of the underlying purposes and ultimate effects of defensive maneuvers taken both prior to and during a takeover bid, the existence of any managerial policy designed to maintain the corporation as an independent entity, and the costs of conducting and defending takeover bids, including attorney and investment banker fees.

72. Certain SEC rules and regulations require that "purpose" be disclosed. *See, e.g.*, Schedule 13D, 17 C.F.R. § 240.13d-101c, Item 4 (1983); 17 C.F.R. § 240.13e-1(a)(2)(1983); Schedule 13E-3, 17 C.F.R. § 240.13e-100H, Item 7(a)(1983). As to disclosing the "effect" of the transaction, see SEC Exchange Act Release No. 15230 (Oct. 13, 1978)[1978 Transfer Binder] Fed. Sec. L. Rep. (CCH) ¶ 81,748. For further discussion, see M. Steinberg, *supra* note 1, at § 1.04.

73. 430 U.S. 1 (1977).

74. *Id.* at 24-42.

75. Courts have permitted actions brought by target managements for injunctive relief under Section 13(d). *See, e.g.*, Indiana National Corp. v. Rich, 712 F.2d 1180 (7th Cir. 1983); Treadway Cos. v. Care Corp., 638 F.2d 357, 380 (2d Cir. 1980); Dan River, Inc. v. Unitex, Ltd., 624 F.2d 1216, 1222-24 (4th Cir. 1980), *cert. denied*, 449 U.S. 1101 (1981); Chromalloy Am. Corp. v. Sun Chem. Corp., 611 F.2d 240, 246 (8th Cir. 1979). *But see* Schnell v. Schnall, [1981 Transfer Binder] Fed. Sec. L. Rep. (CCH) ¶ 97,927 (S.D.N.Y. Mar. 30, 1981). *See generally* Note, *An Implied Right of Action for Issuers under Section 13(d) of the Securities Exchange Act of 1934*, 61 B.U.L. Rev. 933 (1981) [hereinafter cited as Note, *An Implied Right of Action*]; Note, *Private Litigation under the Williams Act: Standing to Sue, Elements of a Claim and Remedies*, 7 J. Corp. L. 545, 559-61 (1982); [hereinafter cited as Note, *Private Litigation*]; Note, *Implied Private Rights of Action for Equitable Relief under Section 13(d) of the Williams Act*, 1981 Utah L. Rev. 869 [hereinafter cited as Note, *Implied Private Rights of Action*]; Note, *Section 13(d) of the '34 Act: The Inference of a Private Cause of Action for a Stock Issuer*, 38 Wash. & Lee L. Rev. 971 (1981).

Generally, Section 13(d)(1) of the Exchange Act and Rule 13d-1 promulgated thereunder require any person or group of persons who acquire beneficial ownership of more than 5% of a class of equity securities registered under Section 12 of the Act to disclose, within 10 days, specific information by filing a Schedule 13D with the SEC and by sending copies to the issuer and to each exchange on which the security is traded. For further discussion of Section 13(d), see M. Steinberg, *supra* note 1, at § 9.03[5].

76. Courts have permitted both target and offeror managements to bring actions

whole, seems correct. The target corporation often may be the only party with the readily available resources and motivation necessary to maintain a successful injunctive action against a bidder who would harm the company and its shareholders.[77] Granting standing to an issuer therefore may be a practical approach to protecting the integrity of the marketplace and the interests of shareholders.[78]

It should not be presumed, however, that noble motives always lie behind subject companies' suits for injunctive relief. Target managements may seek access to the courts not to vindicate shareholder interests but rather to seek delay, thereby gathering the time needed to develop successful strategies for defending and perpetuating their control.[79] Indiscriminately granting standing to such parties to bring actions for injunctive relief may be

---

for injunctive relief under Section 14(e). *See, e.g.*, Mobil Corp. v. Marathon Oil Co., 669 F.2d 366, 376 (6th Cir. 1981); Weeks Dredging & Contracting, Inc. v. American Dredging Co., 451 F. Supp. 468, 475-76, 486 (E.D. Pa. 1978); Humana, Inc. v. American Medicorp, Inc., 445 F. Supp. 613, 614-16 (S.D.N.Y. 1977). *See generally* Comment, *Preliminary Injunctive Relief and Tender Offers: An Analysis under the Williams Act*, 49 Geo. Wash. L. Rev. 563 (1981).

77. The SEC is a proper party to seek injunctive relief for disclosure violations under Sections 13(d) and 14(e). Given the Commission's heavy workload and its manpower shortages, however, the SEC often lacks the resources to act on a timely basis. *See* J. I. Case Co. v. Borak, 377 U.S. 426, 432-33 (1964). It may well be necessary to grant standing to competing bidders seeking injunctive relief, particularly if target management is aligned with the friendly offeror. In such a situation, a competing offeror may well be the only available party willing to bring a suit for injunctive relief which will ultimately benefit the target corporation and its shareholders. See Mobil Corp. v. Marathon Oil Co., 669 F.2d 366, 371 (6th Cir. 1981). *See also* Lowenstein, *supra* note 11, at 301; the Business Roundtable, *The Role and Composition of the Board of Directors of the Large Publicly Owned Corporation*, 33 Bus. Law. 2083, 2099-2101 (1978).

78. *See, e.g.*, Mobil Corp. v. Marathon Oil Co., 669 F.2d 366, 371 (6th Cir. 1981); Treadway Cos. v. Care Corp., 638 F.2d 357, 380 (2d Cir. 1980); Dan River, Inc. v. Unitex, Ltd., 624 F.2d 1216, 1225 (4th Cir. 1980), *cert. denied*, 449 U.S. 1101 (1981); Chromalloy Am. Corp. v. Sun Chem. Corp., 611 F.2d 240, 248 (8th Cir. 1979); Weeks Dredging & Contracting, Inc. v. American Dredging Co., 451 F. Supp. 468, 476 (E.D. Pa. 1978); Humana, Inc. v. American Medicorp, Inc., 445 F. Supp. 613, 616 (S.D.N.Y. 1977). *See also* Note, *An Implied Right of Action*, *supra* note 75, at 963-64; Comment, *supra* note 76, at 576-77; Note, *Private Litigation*, *supra* note 75, at 561; Note, *Implied Private Rights of Action*, *supra* note 75, at 881.

79. *Cf.* Easterbrook & Fischel, *Antitrust Suits by Targets of Tender Offers*, 80 Mich. L. Rev. 1155 (1982). "When managers face the sort of conflict that every tender offer presents, a conflict between investors' interests and managers' continued employment, it is altogether too easy for managers to find—to their delight—that some ethical principle enables them to take the high road of defending against the acquisition." *Id.* at 1176.

detrimental, rather than helpful, to the shareholders who are the primary beneficiaries of the Williams Act. Courts therefore should grant standing only after independently determining that the party seeking to invoke injunctive relief is acting for the target corporation's and shareholders' benefit.[80]

As set forth above, the primary beneficiaries of the Williams Act are the target corporation's shareholders who are entitled to make informed investment decisions without being unduly hampered by techniques and maneuvers employed by the offeror(s)' and subject corporation's managements. There ought, however, to be a narrow, implicit exception to such an interpretation of the Williams Act. That exception would permit target management to take appropriate action to defeat a hostile offer if it could demonstrate affirmatively that the offeror represented a clear threat to the corporation's business, including the equity interests of its shareholders. Although not apparently permitted under the Act,[81] Congress should also allow target management to consider noninvestor concerns that merit protection, such as the job security of the corporation's employees and the viability of the communities in which it primarily operates.[82] Because the individual shareholder is concerned principally with his own investment, management may be deemed the most appropriate decision maker to assess these larger societal concerns.[83]

---

80. *Cf.* Zapata Corp. v. Maldonado, 430 A.2d 779 (Del. 1981), discussed, *supra* note 21.

81. The Williams Act has been interpreted as intended solely for the benefit of investor shareholders. *See, e.g.*, Piper v. Chris-Craft Indus., 430 U.S. 1, 26-35 (1977) ("[T]he sole purpose of the Williams Act was the protection of investors who are confronted with a tender offer." *Id.* at 35); Rondeau v. Mosinee Paper Corp., 422 U.S. 49, 58 (1975) ("The purpose of the Williams Act is to insure that public shareholders who are confronted by a cash tender offer for their stock will not be required to respond without adequate information regarding the qualifications and intentions of the offering party."). Given this judicial interpretation of the Act, allowing target management to take action based upon nonshareholder interests could well be viewed as antithetical to the Act's purpose and thus not permitted.

82. These interests may include the stake of loyal employees in continued employment, the corporation's responsibility to the environment, and the community's reliance on the corporation as a local employer. *See, e.g.*, Herald Co. v. Seawell, 472 F.2d 1081, 1094-96 (10th Cir. 1972) (applying Colorado law); *supra* notes 35, 41 and accompanying text.

83. *See, e.g.*, Lipton, *Takeover Bids in the Target's Boardroom*, 35 Bus. Law. 101, 130 (1979); Williams, *supra* note 24, at 963; *supra* notes 77-80 and accompanying text. Lipton goes so far as to argue that, regarding management's response to a hostile tender offer, "[n]ational policy is a proper consideration." Lipton, *supra*, at 130. Directly opposed to the views of Lipton are those of Professors Easterbrook and Fischel who contend that, because cash tender offers are beneficial and lead to more efficient management, any attempt by the subject corporation's management

If enacted, such an exception must be carefully limited. If the statutory language of an exception based on noninvestor interests were unduly broad, target management, in practically all instances, could argue plausibly that a takeover bid would harm employees, customers, suppliers, and the community. Legislative or judicial acceptance of the asserted protection of such noninvestor interests, without careful scrutiny, would provide a smoke screen masking target management's actual motives. To reconcile the competing considerations, the framework proposed permits the subject corporation's management to undertake defensive maneuvers based on noninvestor interests but only if such maneuvers are warranted. That is, management must prove that the tender offeror presents a clear threat to deserving societal interests.[84]

III. ADDITIONAL LEGISLATIVE PROPOSALS

In addition to the foregoing suggestions, it would be appropriate for Congress to act to remedy other deficiencies in the tender offer process. Two-tier offers, for example, have not been viewed as "fraudulent" or "manipulative" by the few courts to have considered the issue.[85] Such offers nevertheless constitute a coercive tactical ploy that enables an offeror to acquire control through a partial tender offer at one price and then to squeeze out minority shareholders at a substantially lower price.[86] Partial

---

to impede such an offer should be proscribed. Easterbrook & Fischel, *supra* note 15, at 1164. *See* Gilson, *A Structured Approach to Corporations: The Case against Defensive Tactics in Tender Offers*, 33 Stan. L. Rev. 819, 862-65 (1981).

84. A lesser standard would only increase the opportunities for corporate malfeasance, thereby conflicting with the rationale underlying the Williams Act as well as with management's fiduciary duties under state law. *See* Lynch & Steinberg, *supra* note 54, at 913 n.55.

85. *See, e.g.*, Martin Marietta Corp. v. Bendix Corp., 549 F. Supp. 623, 630-31 (D. Md. 1982); Radol v. Thomas, 534 F. Supp. 1302, 1314 (S.D. Ohio 1982).

86. One justification sometimes given for the higher front-end tender offer price is that the differential between the first and second tiers represents a premium paid for control. *See generally* Easterbrook & Fischel, *Corporate Control Transactions*, 91 Yale L.J. 698 (1982); Toms, *Compensating Shareholders Frozen Out in Two-Step Mergers*, 78 Colum. L. Rev. 548 (1978). The payment and receipt of premiums for control have received judicial approbation in nontender contexts. *See, e.g.*, Zetlin v. Hanson Holdings, 48 N.Y.2d 684, 397 N.E.2d 387 (1979) (controlling interest may be purchased and sold at a premium over market price). Front-end—loaded offers nonetheless provide potential for abusive tactics and practices, since shareholders recognize that they must either tender or be relegated to a substantially lower second-step, squeeze-out merger price if the takeover bid is successful. *See* Advisory Committee Report, *supra* note 14, at 24-26; Brudney & Chirelstein, *Fair Shares in Corporate Mergers and Takeovers*, 88 Harv. L. Rev. 297 (1974); Finkelstein,

tender offers may have become too firmly established to be eliminated, even if their elimination were desirable,[87] but basic principles of fair dealing should be applied to the takeover process. Fairness requires that an offeror who obtains control pursuant to a partial tender offer normally be permitted to acquire no additional equity securities of the subject corporation unless (1) the offeror proves that changed economic cirucmstances justify the lower price or (2) the offeror pays the same or higher price for the shares in the second step as it paid for the shares tendered.[88]

Antitakeover Protection against Two-Tier and Partial Tender Offers: The Validity of Fair Price, Mandatory Bid, and Flip-Over Provisions under Delaware Law, 11 Sec. Reg. L.J. 291, 293 (1984). At least five states, Maryland, Michigan Ohio, Pennsylvania, and Wisconsin, have enacted statutes that address the potential abuses associated with second-step, squeeze-out mergers. *See* Md. Bus. & Assoc. Code §§ 3-202, 3-601-03; 8-301(12)-(14); Mich. S. Bill No. 541 (1984); Ohio Rev. Code §§ 1701.01, 1701.831; Pa. Stat. Ann. §§ 408, 409.1, 910; Wisc. Stats. §§ 180.69, 180.725. In connection with the constitutional concerns raised by these statutes, see Edgar v. MITE Corp., 457 U.S. 624 (1982) (Illinois Business Takeover Act declared unconstitutional on interstate commerce grounds; Chief Justice Burger and Justices White and Blackmun also would have held the state act unconstitutional under the Supremacy Clause). *See generally* Sargent, *On the Validity of State Takeover Regulation: State Responses to* MITE *and* Kidwell, 42 Ohio St. L.J. 689 (1981); Scriggins & Clarke, *Takeovers and the 1983 Maryland Fair Price Legislation*, 43 Md. L. Rev. 266 (1984); Steinberg, *The Pennsylvania Anti-Takeover Legislation*, 12 Sec. Reg. L.J. 184 (1984).

87. Justice Goldberg, pointing to the English regulatory framework, recommends that the two-tier offer be prohibited, unless there are exceptional circumstances present. Goldberg, *supra* note 1, at 130-131. Although there is merit to this suggestion, such an approach would preclude an offeror from making a tender offer for an inefficiently managed target corporation if the offeror lacked the funds necessary to acquire the entire company. I believe that society, on the whole, benefits from permitting the acquisition of controlling interests in these and related circumstances. *See* Advisory Committee Report, *supra* note 14, at 24-25. Moreover, shareholders wishing to tender in a partial offer normally can be adequately protected by (1) having their shares accepted on a pro rata basis throughout the duration of the offer and (2) requiring that any second-step, squeeze-out transaction be at the same price. *See* SEC Rule 14d-8, 17 C.F.R. § 240.14d-8 (1985).

88. Maryland recently passed legislation designed to protect nontendering minority shareholders from being unfairly squeezed out in second-tier transactions. Act of June 2, 1983, Ch. 1, Sp. Sess. (codified at Md. Corps. & Ass'ns Code Ann. §§ 3-202, 3-601 to 3-603, 8-301 (12)-(14) (1975 & Supp. 1983)). Under the new legislation, most second-tier transactions must be approved by a supermajority vote ($^4/_5$ of all votes entitled to be cast *and* $^2/_3$ of votes entitled to be cast by shareholders who are neither "interested" nor "affiliated" with interested shareholders). *Id.* § 3-602. The supermajority vote requirement does not apply, however, if nontendering minority shareholders receive at least as much for their shares as tendering shareholders received for theirs, and if certain additional conditions are met, or if the

Another inequity under current law is that a beneficial owner of more than 5 percent of a subject security need not disclose such ownership until ten days after attaining that status.[89] Persons are free to seek additional acquisitions through privately negotiated transactions and open market purchases during that ten-day period as long as the acquisitions do not constitute a "tender offer."[90] This makes possible the rapid accumulation of securities, representing a potential shift in corporate control without notification and disclosure of pertinent information to the marketplace, and is inconsistent with the purpose of Section 13(d).[91] Congress should close this loophole by either (1) prohibiting additional accumulations above the

---

corporation otherwise qualifies for an exemption. *Id.* § 3-603(b)-(e). *See generally* Scriggins & Clarke, *supra* note 86.

89. 15 U.S.C. § 78m(d)(1) (1982); 17 C.F.R. § 240.13d-101 (1985). *See* M. Steinberg, *supra* note 1, at § 9.03[5]. The information required by Schedule 13D includes

> the identity of the issuer and the security, the identity, background and citizenship of the reporting persons, the source and amount of funds used to acquire the securities, the purpose of the transaction, the reporting person's interest in the securities including trading history for the last 60 days and any contracts, arrangements, understandings or relationships with respect to the securities to which the reporting person or group is a party.

Bialkin, Attura & D'Alimonte, *Why, When and How to Conduct a Proxy Fight for Corporate Control*, in Proxy Contests and Battles for Corporate Control 117 (Practising Law Institute 1981).

90. A number of courts have addressed the question of what constitutes a tender offer. *See, e.g.*, Wellman v. Dickinson, 475 F. Supp. 783, 818-24 (S.D.N.Y. 1979), *aff'd on other grounds*, 682 F.2d 355 (2d Cir. 1982), *cert. denied*, 103 S. Ct. 1522 (1983); Kennecott Copper Corp. v. Curtiss-Wright Corp., 584 F.2d 1195, 1206-07 (2d Cir. 1978); Brascan Ltd. v. Edper Equities Ltd., 477 F. Supp. 773, 789-92 (S.D.N.Y. 1979); Financial Gen. Bankshares, Inc. v. Lance, [1978 Transfer Binder] Fed. Sec. L. Rep. (CCH) ¶ 96,403 (D.D.C. Apr. 27, 1978); S-G Securities, Inc. v. Fuqua Inv. Co., 466 F. Supp. 1114, 1126-27 (D. Mass. 1978).

In determining whether a tender offer was made, the general criteria utilized by the courts include: "(1) whether the transactions place pressure on the solicited shareholders to sell without deliberation; (2) the sophistication of the selling shareholders; (3) the opportunity for negotiation; and (4) access of the solicitees to the kind of information generally available in connection with a tender offer." Bloomenthal, *supra* note 67, at 42. The SEC proposed for comment but took no further action on rules which sought to define the term "tender offer." *See* SEC Exchange Act Release No. 16385, Proposed Amendments to Tender Offer Rules, 44 Fed. Reg. 70, 349 (1979). *See also* H.R. 5693, introduced in May 1984 by Congressman Wirth at the request of the Commission, which represents the latest SEC effort to define this term in the context of golden parachute arrangements. *See* 16 Sec. Reg. & L. Rep. (BNA) No. 21, at 914 (May 25, 1984).

91. *See, e.g.*, Treadway Cos. v. Care Corp., 638 F.2d 357, 380 (2d Cir. 1980).

5 percent level unless there has been prior disclosure of the requisite information[92] or (2) deeming acquisition of more than 10 percent, or some other appropriate level, of beneficial ownership of a security, with certain exceptions, to constitute a tender offer, thereby triggering the disclosure and dissemination requirements of the Williams Act.[93]

"Greenmail" is another practice which merits Congressional attention.[94]

---

92. *See* Senate Comm. on Banking, Housing, and Urban Affairs, 96th Cong., 2d Sess., Securities and Exchange Commission Report on Tender Offer Laws, 55, 56 (Comm. Print 1980) [hereinafter cited as Tender Offer Laws]. *Cf.* Advisory Committee Report, *supra* note 14, at 21-22. The Advisory Committee would prohibit additional purchases above the 5% level unless the requisite information has been on file with the SEC for at least a forty-eight-hour period. This position is unwise. Preacquisition delay of that sort would provide target management with substantial time to implement defensive maneuvers, thereby undermining the neutrality, as between offeror and target, that Congress built into the Williams Act. *See* Edgar v. MITE Corp., 457 U.S. 624, 633-39 (1982). *See also* Piper v. Chris-Craft Indus., 430 U.S. 1, 29-31 (1977); Rondeau v. Mosinee Paper Corp., 422 U.S. 49, 58-59 (1975).

93. Although the 10% level of benefical ownership proposed in the text is arbitrarily set, a shareholder with that percentage of voting shares may exercise what amounts to a controlling or a substantial influence in some publicly held corporations. This is especially true when stock ownership is combined with the persuasive authority of, e.g., a position as a corporate officer. *See generally* L. Loss, Fundamentals of Securities Regulation 445-56 (1983). Of course, certain transactions, such as purely privately negotiated purchases, should be permitted without requiring the prospective acquirer to make a tender offer. In 1980, the SEC proposed legislation to require that acquisition of more than 10% of a subject corporation's shares generally be made only by means of a tender offer. *See* Tender Offer Laws, *supra* note 92, at 62 ("The Commission proposes to amend Section 14(d) by defining the term 'statutory offer' to mean all offers to acquire the beneficial ownership of equity securities of a public issuer by a person who is or could thereby become the beneficial owner of more than 10 percent of the class. Exceptions to the definition are made for: (1) offers pursuant to a statutory merger or acquisition, (2) the solicitation of voting proxies, (3) acquisitions of 2 percent per year, (4) acquisitions from the issuer, (5) acquisitions from no more than 10 persons in any 12 months pursuant to privately negotiated transactions."). *Cf.* Advisory Committee Report, *supra* note 14, at 22-23 (acquisitions which would give the acquirer more than 20% of the voting power in a corporation should be permitted only if obtained from the offeror or by means of a tender offer); SEC Tender Offer Bill, H.R. 5693 (introduced by Congressman Wirth in May 1984 at the request of the Commission), *discussed in*, 16 Sec. Reg. & L. Rep. (BNA) No. 21, at 914 (May 25, 1984) (defining the term tender offer in the context of golden parachute arrangements as an unconditional offer to purchase at least 10% of the target's stock for a 25 or greater percent premium).

94. "Greenmail" has been defined as "[t]he practice of buying a portion of a company's stock and threatening the company with a hostile takeover fight unless management agrees to buy back [the] shares at a premium." *SEC Faults Advisory*

When a subject corporation's incumbent management causes the corporation to repurchase, at a substantial premium, the stock acquired by a
potential bidder, management should be deemed to have a conflict of interest that precludes application of the business judgment rule. Unfortunately, present law is not clear on this point.[95] Congress therefore should
consider adopting legislation which requires incumbent management to
prove affirmatively that such a stock repurchase was in the corporation's
best interests and at a fair price.[96] Shareholders should be provided a cause
of action similar to that available under Section 36(b) of the Investment
Advisors Act to enable them to challenge these repurchases.[97]

As a policy matter, Congress also should establish a ceiling on monetary
damages assessed against corporate fiduciaries under the Williams Act, except where there has been egregious misconduct. In all practicality, courts
have declined to construe the Williams Act and state fiduciary law restrictively wherever a finding of liability would result in astronomical monetary
damages.[98] The Seventh Circuit's unduly narrow interpretation of federal

---

Panels' Reliance on Business Judgment Rule in Takeovers, 16 Sec. Reg. & L. Rep.
(BNA) No. 11, at 496 (Mar. 16, 1984).

95. *Compare* Panter v. Marshall Field & Co., 646 F.2d 271, 293-94 (7th Cir.),
cert. denied, 454 U.S. 1092 (1981) (broad application of the business judgment rule
in the context of a tender offer), *and* Johnson v. Trueblood, 629 F.2d 287, 292-93
(3d Cir. 1980) (same), *with* Crane Co. v. Harsco Corp., 511 F. Supp. 294 (D. Del.
1981) (the burden is on directors to justify the issuer's repurchase of shares in a
hostile tender offer situation).

96. Alternatively, Congress should adopt the Advisory Committee's recommendation that "[r]epurchase of a company's shares at a premium to market from a
particular holder or group that has held such shares for less than two years should
require shareholder approval." Advisory Committee Report, *supra* note 14, at 46.
Although this alternative is an improvement over the application of the business
judgment rule, particularly if the shareholder vote is required to be disinterested
and informed, a court's careful scrutiny of the fairness of the transaction arguably
will better protect the integrity of the takeover process and shareholder protection.
See generally supra notes 22, 23 and accompanying text.

97. *See* 15 U.S.C. § 80a-35(b) (1982). Section 36(b) generally permits an action
to be brought by the SEC, or by a security holder of a registered investment company
on behalf of such company, to recover from the investment advisor, any person
affiliated with such investment advisor, and certain other persons any compensation
or payments, "for breach of fiduciary duty in respect of such compensation or
payments paid by such registered investment company or by the security holders
thereof to such investment adviser or person." *See also* Daily Income Fund, Inc. v.
Fox, 104 S. Ct. 831, 842 (1984) (demand on board of directors of registered investment company not required in suit brought by shareholders pursuant to Section
36(b)).

98. *See, e.g.*, Panter v. Marshall Field & Co., 646 F.2d 271, 286 (7th Cir.), *cert.
denied*, 454 U.S. 1092 (1981); Lewis v. McGraw, 619 F.2d 192 (2d Cir. 1980);

and state law in *Panter v. Marshall Field & Co.*,[99] for example, might best be viewed in light of the fact that plaintiffs sought damages exceeding $200 million.[100] A finding of liability in such an amount could not only bankrupt the subject company and its management[101] but also wreak havoc upon our system of corporate governance. Few corporate directors would be willing to mount even minimal opposition to detrimental takeover bids; indeed, outside directors could be expected to resign their positions rather than risk financial catastrophe.

Congress should recognize the importance of the policy considerations involved in this unique context by enacting an appropriate ceiling on damages. Such a ceiling must be high enough to deter target management from viewing violation of the law as a mere business expense. To further inhibit management from pursuing its own survival at all costs,[102] the limit on damages should not be applicable in cases of egregious misconduct.[103]

Other commentators, including Justice Goldberg, have suggested more fundamental changes that Congress might make in the tender offer regu-

---

Berman v. Gerber Products Co., 454 F. Supp. 1310 (W.D. Mich. 1978). *See also* Mobil Corp. v. Marathon Oil Co., 669 F.2d 366, 374-75 (6th Cir. 1981) (court's construction of "manipulation" was formulated where no monetary liability recovered).

99. 646 F.2d 271 (7th Cir.), *cert. denied*, 454 U.S. 1092 (1981).

100. 646 F.2d at 283. Plaintiffs in *Marshall Field* apparently were seeking the benefit of their bargain. For recent application of the benefit-of-the-bargain measure of damages in securities litigation, *see* Hackbart v. Holmes, 675 F.2d 1114, 1121-22 (10th Cir. 1982); Osofsky v. Zipf, 645 F.2d 107, 111-15 (2d Cir. 1981). For further discussion on *Marshall Field, see supra* note 2; M. Steinberg, *supra* note 6, at 212-16.

101. The extent of adverse consequences for the subject parties would depend on whether the defendant corporate fiduciaries were entitled to be indemnified by the corporation and whether insurance were available to cover the damages assessed. *See* Model Business Corp. Act § 5 (1982); Del. Code Ann. tit. 8, § 145, (1983); Bishop, *Sitting Ducks and Decoy Ducks: New Trends in the Indemnification of Corporate Directors and Officers,* 77 Yale L.J. 1078 (1968); Johnson, *Corporate Indemnification and Liability Insurance for Directors and Officers*, 33 Bus. Law. 1993 (1978); Hill, *Lloyd's Offers U.S. Concerns Insurance for Costs of Fighting Hostile Takeovers*, Wall St. J., May 12, 1980, at 14 ("A policy will pay 80% of most costs associated with fending off an unwanted takeover up to $1 million. One big catch: A company must win to collect on the insurance." *Id.*)

102. *See* Nagelvoort, *Kudos for Management, Not Darts*, N.Y. Times, April 1, 1984, at F.3 (referring to criticism leveled against Gulf's failure to use all defensive options in its arsenal to ward off offerors, including Standard Oil Co. of California, as "distorted because it focuses on 'survival at all costs' rather than on the proper responsibilities of managers in public corporations." *Id.*).

103. It is beyond the scope of this article to propose an appropriate ceiling. Note, however, the ceiling built into the ALI Draft Restatement, set forth in note 43 *supra*.

latory framework.[104] Imposition of substantially longer time periods for offers to remain open, appointment of an independent reviewer to evaluate the fairness of tender offers, and provision of a "freeze" period sufficient to enable shareholders to make informed decisions all are meritorious concepts which deserve Congressional attention.[105] Justice Goldberg also astutely perceives that for too long the interests of the offeror's shareholders have been overlooked.

Tender offers frequently resemble mergers in their practical effect, yet the rights of the offeror's shareholders vary greatly depending upon which form a transaction takes.[106] Shareholders normally have the right to approve mergers,[107] and federal legislation assures that the proxy disclosure process will provide them with sufficient information to do so knowledgeably.[108]

---

104. *See, e.g.*, Goldberg, *supra* note 1, at 127-32.

105. *Id.* at 127-30. Some of these concepts are not as novel as they may appear. For example, the Advisory Committee itself recommended that the bid time periods be lengthened but not to the extent suggested by Justice Goldberg. Advisory Committee Report, *supra* note 14, at 27-28 (recommending a minimum offering period of 30 days for an initial bid, 20 days for a subsequent one). Under current SEC rules, tender offers must be held open for at least twenty business days. 17 C.F.R. § 240.14e-1(a)(1983). The concept of a "freeze" period also has been advanced by Lowenstein, *supra* note 11, at 317-18. The concept of a special review person has received approbation from both the Supreme Court of Delaware and the SEC in the going-private context. *See* Weinberger v. UOP, Inc., 457 A.2d 701, 709 n.7 (Del. 1983); *In re* Spartek, Inc., SEC Exchange Act Release No. 15,567 (Feb. 14, 1979).

106. Somewhat analogously and apparently without good reason, there are significantly more regulatory impediments to undertaking an exchange offer (in lieu of a cash tender offer) than to making a cash tender offer. *See* Advisory Committee Report, *supra* note 14, at 16. Because of this inequality of regulation, there are far more cash tender offers than exchange offers. *See* Austin, *supra* note 7, at 15, 36. The SEC Advisory Committee concluded that the more extensive regulation of exchange offers is unnecessary for shareholder protection and recommended that "[c]ash and securities tender offers should be placed on an equal regulatory footing so that bidders, the market and shareholders, and not regulation, decide between the two." Advisory Committee Report, *supra*, at 16.

107. *See, e.g.*, Del. Code Ann. tit. 8 §§ 251-(c),(f), 252(c),(e) (1983); Md. Corps. & Ass'ns Code Ann. § 3-105(d) (1975 & Supp. 1983); Model Business Corp. Act § 73 (1982).

108. 15 U.S.C. § 78n(a) (1982); 17 C.F.R. §§ 240.14a-1 to .14a-102 (1985). *See* Mills v. Electric Auto-Lite Co., 396 U.S. 375, 381 (1970)(noting that the underlying purpose of Section 14(a) of the Exchange Act is to promote " 'the free exercise of the voting rights of stockholders' by ensuring that proxies [are] solicited with 'explanation to the stockholder of the real nature of the questions for which authority to cast his vote is sought.' ") (quoting H.R. Rep. No. 1383, 73d Cong., 2d Sess. 14 (1934), and S. Rep. No. 792, 73d Cong., 2d Sess. 12 (1934)). *See also* TSC Indus. v. Northway, Inc., 426 U.S. 438, 444 (1976); J. I. Case Co. v. Borak, 377 U.S. 426, 431 (1964).

In contrast, the offeror's shareholders usually have neither voting nor disclosure rights in connection with tender offers. One might argue that this is a matter of internal corporate governance that should be left to state regulation,[109] but in the analogous proxy setting Congress has recognized that the disclosure and dissemination of adequate information to shareholders is a proper subject of federal regulation.[110] Hence, Congress should consider requiring offerors to disclose to their shareholders, at the time that a tender offer is publicly announced, information sufficient to allow them to determine whether the takeover bid is in the corporation's best interests from both a short- and long-term perspective.[111]

IV. SOME FINAL THOUGHTS

The analysis and proposals set forth in this commentary are a response to current judicial and SEC thinking on tender offers, which frequently presumes that subject corporations' managements are acting in their shareholders' best interests. Unfortunately, the converse is all too often true. Management, when anticipating, or in the midst of, a tender offer, sometimes acts in its own interests, neglecting the valid interests of shareholders, employees, and affected communities. Judicial and SEC deference to managerial processes and decision making therefore is unwarranted. If the courts and the SEC choose not to face this stark reality, then Congress should act to reaffirm that the primary beneficiaries of the Williams Act, the subject corporation's shareholders, normally are entitled to make their investment decisions without being preempted by defensive maneuvers.

---

109. *See generally* Ferrara, Starr & Steinberg, *Disclosure of Information Bearing on Management Integrity and Competency*, 76 Nw. U.L. Rev. 555, 563 (1981).

110. *See* M. Steinberg, *supra* note 6, at 77, 83, 103; Ferrara, Starr & Steinberg, *supra* note 109, at 559; authorities cited *supra* note 108.

111. Failure to make truthful and accurate disclosure of information would be actionable in suits for injunctive relief and actions for damages pursuant to Section 14(e). Moreover, if shareholders receive adequate information, they could seek an injunction against the tender offer in state court based on management's alleged breach of fiduciary duty or take other appropriate measures to protect themselves from financial injury. Federal courts have found nondisclosures to be material where adequate disclosure would have enabled shareholders to obtain state court relief or take other protective measures. *See, e.g.*, United States v. Margala, 662 F.2d 622, 625-27 (9th Cir. 1981); Healey v. Catalyst Recovery of Pa., Inc., 616 F.2d 641, 647-48 (3d Cir. 1980); Goldberg v. Meridor, 567 F.2d 209, 219-20 (2d Cir. 1977), *cert. denied*, 434 U.S. 1069 (1978). As an alternative measure, albeit frequently a futile one, aggrieved shareholders may bring an action against management for waste or seek to vote the "rascals" out in the next election. For a restrictive view, see Gaines v. Haughton, 645 F.2d 761, 776-79 (9th Cir. 1981), *cert. denied*, 102 S. Ct. 1006 (1982).

The expansive construction given by many courts to the business judgment rule,[112] in conjunction with state antitakeover statutes which protect
incumbent management,[113] strongly suggests that any meaningful shareholder protection and reforms in the tender offer area must come from
existing federal law and implementation of further Congressional and SEC
action. In view of this situation, the unduly narrow interpretation given by
a number of federal courts to the Williams Act[114] is unfortunate. By constituting Section 14(e) as solely a disclosure statute, these courts are ig-
noring the Act's legislative history, which indicates that its provisions are
to have a broader reach.[115] As important, by relegating aggrieved shareholders to state court processes where it is unnecessary to do so, such
federal courts in all practicality are ensuring that shareholders with meritorious claims are left without a viable remedy.

Consideration also ought to be given to whether the entire administrative
and judicial framework for the resolution of tender offer disputes needs
restructuring. It may be argued that federal district courts, on the whole,
understandably have little expertise in dealing with the complicated issues
surrounding tender offers. In any given tender offer situation, furthermore,
suits may well be brought in a number of district courts situated throughout
the country.[116] The net result is potentially inefficient, time-consuming,
costly, and non-uniform litigation. In light of these problems, Congress
should consider vesting with the SEC exclusive original jurisdiction to bring
administrative enforcement actions[117] and to resolve disputes arising between private parties in the tender offer setting, except where a damages
remedy or injunctive relief is sought after a takeover bid has been consummated or defeated.[118] As with administrative matters under present law,

---

112. *See* authorities cited *supra* notes 6-12.

113. *See supra* note 86 for discussion of these state statutes.

114. *See* cases cited *supra* note 65.

115. *See supra* text and accompanying notes 53-72.

116. During the Bendix–Martin Marietta struggle, for instance, actions were brought
in two federal courts in New York, the federal court in Maryland, a federal and a
state court in Michigan, and two state courts in Delaware. Martin Marietta Corp. v.
Bendix Corp., 549 F. Supp. 623, 626 (D. Md. 1982).

117. Congress recently enacted legislation, the Insider Trading Sanctions Act,
which, *inter alia*, provides the Commission with authority to bring administrative
proceedings against subject persons who file misleading statements with the SEC in
connection with proxy and tender offer contests.

118. Unless Congress legislates to preempt state regulation of takeovers, as the
SEC Advisory Committee recommended (Advisory Committee Report, *supra* note
14, at 17), suits could be brought in the state courts even if the SEC obtains exclusive
original jurisdiction in the federal regulatory setting. *See supra* note 112. The propriety of preempting state tender offer regulation by means of federal legislation is

legislation could provide for appeal of the Commission's decisions to the United States Courts of Appeals.[119] The suggested approach, if successful, would provide the SEC with a meaningful enforcement mechanism to protect the investing public and the integrity of the securities markets in this fast-moving context. It also would provide corporations and their shareholders with expeditious and uniform decisions by an expert body and the right to federal appellate court review. In theory, implementation of the proposal would result in a significant improvement over our present system.

In order for this proposal to be successfully implemented, the SEC would have to be provided with sufficient resources to enable the agency to adjudicate these matters on an expedited basis. Such a framework is based on a number of underlying assumptions which, although not tested empirically, appear plausible. These assumptions include that the SEC's expanded oversight and adjudicatory authority in the tender offer area would not be unduly expensive; would result in more expeditious, uniform, and sound interpretations; and would be administratively feasible. Admittedly, all of these propositions are subject to challenge. The proposal is offered nonetheless as an arguably attractive alternative to the present system and as a useful vehicle for considering how the present tender offer regulatory system can be improved.

---

beyond the scope of this commentary. Nonetheless, while such state regulation continues in effect, the proposal advanced herein still offers a more attractive approach than the present federal regulatory framework.

119. *See, e.g.*, Securities Act of 1933, § 9, 15 U.S.C. § 77i(a) (1982); Securities Exchange Act of 1934, § 25, 15 U.S.C. § 78y(a) (1982).

VIII

REGULATION OF TENDER OFFERS: A PANEL DISCUSSION

On September 22, 1983, the University of Maryland School of Law and the Section of Corporations, Banking, and Business of the Maryland State Bar Association cosponsored a program on tender offer regulation. Participants were Professor Marc I. Steinberg,[1] who served as the moderator and presented an overview of tender offer developments; Ms. Paula Chester,[2] who addressed the impact of tender offers on small issuers as well as the definition of the term "tender offer"; Mr. Ralph C. Ferrara,[3] who discussed "manipulation" under the Williams Act; Professor Ted J. Fiflis,[4] who presented an analysis of the SEC Advisory Committee Report on Tender Offers; Mr. L. P. Scriggins,[5] who addressed the recent Maryland legislation; and Mr. Stanley Sporkin,[6] who presented a proposal for tender offer reform. Only the individual presentations are contained herein.

PROFESSOR STEINBERG:

Welcome and I thank you for coming. We have a distinguished panel here and hopefully will have an interesting program. Basically, each of us will

---

1. Professor, School for Law, University of Maryland.
2. Partner, Baskin and Steingut, P.C., New York City.
3. Partner, Debevoise & Plimpton, Washington, D.C. Formerly, General Counsel, Securities and Exchange Commission.
4. Professor, School of Law, University of Colorado.
5. Partner, Piper & Marbury, Baltimore, Maryland.
6. General Counsel, Central Intelligence Agency. Formerly, Director of Enforcement, Securities and Exchange Commission.

give a short presentation of 20 minutes, followed by a discussion panel among us. I am going to begin with an overview of tender offer developments.

First, turning to state regulation, one of the key issues in the tender offer setting is the applicability of the business judgment rule. The question is whether target management has a disabling conflict of interest that precludes application of the rule. Most of the recent decisions have involved federal courts construing the applicable state law. These decisions basically have applied the business judgment rule to target management's conduct. These decisions include, for example, the *Marshall Field* decision in the Seventh Circuit,[7] the *Gerber Products* decision in the Western District of Michigan,[8] and the *Treadway*[9] and *Crouse-Hinds* decisions in the Second Circuit.[10] The types of actions that have been given protection under the rule include the target corporation engaging in defensive acquisitions, the filing of antitrust suits against the bidder, and the sale of a large block of stock to a friendly third party.

One question that arises is what does the plaintiff have to show to overcome the presumption of the business judgment rule. Both the Third Circuit in *Johnson v. Trueblood*[11] and the Seventh Circuit in the *Marshall Field* case held that the presumption of the business judgment rule is rebutted only when the plaintiff shows that a director's sole or primary purpose for undertaking the action is to retain control. This standard no doubt imposes a heavy burden upon the complainant. There were, however, dissents in these decisions, the strongest of which was by Judge Cudahy in *Marshall Field*, where he was very critical of the broad application of the business judgment rule rendered by the majority.

The Delaware Supreme Court has not rendered a recent decision on this issue in the tender offer area. I think it significant, though, that in *Zapata Corporation v. Flynn*,[12] which involved special litigation committees, the Delaware Supreme Court refused to apply the business judgment rule to the committee's recommendation to terminate a shareholder's derivative suit against fellow directors where demand on the board of directors was excused. Although this is different from a tender offer situation, nevertheless it indicates that the Delaware courts, in appropriate circumstances, will not apply the business judgment rule.

---

7. 646 F.2d 271 (7th Cir.), *cert. denied*, 454 U.S. 1092 (1981).
8. 454 F. Supp. 1310 (W.D. Mich. 1978).
9. 638 F.2d 357 (2d Cir. 1980).
10. 634 F.2d 690 (2d Cir. 1980).
11. 629 F.2d 287 (3d Cir. 1980).
12. 430 A.2d 779 (Del. 1981).

The next key issue is the propriety of state tender offer legislation. Larry Scriggins is going to speak about the Maryland legislation. In *Edgar v. MITE Corp.*,[13] the U.S. Supreme Court declared the Illinois Business Takeover Act unconstitutional under the Commerce Clause, because the Act imposed burdens on interstate commerce that were excessive in light of the local interests the Act purported to further. However, the Illinois legislation was quite broad. First, the Act applied to target corporations which had relatively minimal contacts with Illinois. For example, the Act applied if Illinois shareholders owned 10 percent of the class of securities that were subject to the offer. Second, the Illinois legislation imposed a substantial, namely a twenty-day, precommencement notification requirement on the offeror. And third, the Act entitled the Illinois secretary of state to hold a fairness hearing and to prevent the offer from going forward if he found that the tender offer was inequitable.

The plurality opinion in *MITE* also found the Illinois Act unconstitutional on preemption grounds. However, a majority of the Court did not join this aspect of the holding. Therefore, the issue apparently remains open whether other types of state takeover legislation that may be distinguished from the Illinois statute are valid. While a number of state statutes have been struck down, some may be upheld.[14] On a different front, the SEC Advisory Committee Report, on which Ted Fiflis will speak, recommended that state regulation of takeovers should be confined solely to local companies. Jeffrey Bartell, a member of the Committee and a former Wisconsin state securities commissioner, sharply disagreed with the Committee's recommendation.

Turning to federal regulation, a key issue is the effect of *Sante Fe Industries*,[15] a 1977 Supreme Court decision, in the tender offer context. There, the Supreme Court held that breaches of fiduciary duty that do not amount to manipulation or deception do not violate Section 10(b) of the Securities Exchange Act and Rule 10b-5 promulgated thereunder. A number of courts have extended the principles of *Sante Fe* to Section 14(e) of the Exchange Act,[16] which is the basic antifraud provision regulating tender offers. These decisions generally stand for the proposition that in order to state a Section 14(e) claim there must be a material misrepresentation or nondisclosure. In other words, these courts construe Section 14(e) as solely a disclosure provision. Other types of misconduct must be redressed, according to these

---

13. 102 S. Ct. 2629 (1982).

14. *See, e.g.*, Cardiff Acquisitions, Inc. & Hatch, 16 Sec. Reg. & L. Rep. (BNA) 1892 (8th Cir. 1984); Agency Rent-A-Car v. Connolly, 686 F.2d 1029 (1st Cir. 1982). For further discussion on this issue, see the commentaries herein addressing state legislation.

15. 430 U.S. 462 (1977).

16. *See e.g.*, Altman v. Knight, 431 F. Supp. 309, 314 (S.D.N.Y. 1977).

courts, under state law. One case that has so held is *Martin Marietta v. Bendix*,[17] which was decided here in Maryland.

Some courts, however, have construed Section 14(e) more flexibly, relying particularly on the term "manipulative." The key decision, which Ralph Ferrara will discuss in greater depth, is the *Mobil Corporation* case decided by the Sixth Circuit in 1981.[18] That decision involved two options that Marathon had granted to U.S. Steel, one of which was an option to purchase Marathon's crown jewel, a 48 percent interest in Marathon's major oil field. This option could only be exercised if a party, other than U.S. Steel, obtained control. If either Marathon remained independent or if U.S. Steel gained control of Marathon, then U.S. Steel would not exercise the option. A second option was for U.S. Steel to purchase approximately 17 percent of Marathon's authorized but unissued shares. The Sixth Circuit held both these options to be manipulative under Section 14(e), because they created an artificial ceiling in the tender offer market for Marathon's shares and served as an artificial and significant deterrent to competitive bidding for a controlling interest in Marathon. As Ralph will point out, this decision has been heavily criticized.[19] However, one recent case, *Data Probe Acquisition Corp.*,[20] basically followed *Marathon* but limited its scope. There, in construing Section 14(e), the court said that the legality of the defensive tactic should be judged on whether the tactic materially impeded or precluded the shareholder from tendering his shares. In other words, defensive tactics that precluded shareholders from tendering their stock would be manipulative under the Williams Act. Other tactics that did not have this effect would be valid so long as there was full disclosure.

Another key issue in federal tender offer regulation concerns proof of reliance in private litigation brought for alleged violations of Section 14(e). Generally, courts have held that under Section 14(e), in order for a plaintiff to recover for damages, the element of reliance must be met. A number of

---

17. 549 F. Supp. 623 (D. Md. 1982).

18. 669 F.2d 366 (6th Cir. 1981).

19. Indeed, shortly after this panel discussion was held, the Second Circuit criticized *Marathon*. *See* Buffalo Forge v. Ogden, 717 F.2d 757 (2d Cir. 1983), *cert. denied*, 104 S. Ct. 550 (1984). *Accord*, Data Probe Acquisition Corp. v. Datatab, Inc., 722 F.2d 1 (2d Cir. 1983), *cert. denied*, 104 S. Ct. 1326 (1984) (rejecting *Marathon*).

20. [1983-1984 Transfer Binder] Fed. Sec. L. Rep. (CCH) ¶ 99,451 (S.D.N.Y.). Subsequent to the panel discussion, this decision was reversed by the Second Circuit. *See* 722 F.2d 1 (2d Cir. 1983), *cert. denied*, 104 S. Ct. 1326 (1984). *Accord*, Schreiber v. Burlington Northern, Inc., [1984 Transfer Binder] Fed. Sec. L. Rep. (CCH) ¶ 91,407 (3d Cir.), *cert. granted*, 105 S. Ct. (1984).

these decisions, including the *Marshall Field* decision in the Seventh Circuit and the *McGraw-Hill* decision in the Second Circuit,[21] stated that no reliance can be shown when the tender offer is withdrawn before the plaintiffs have an opportunity to tender their stock. Arguably, these decisions signify that, if target management engages in defensive tactics that induce the potential offeror to withdraw the offer prior to it becoming effective, then target management will be insulated from private liability insofar as Section 14(e) violations are concerned. A policy rationale underlying this approach undoubtedly is that astronomical damages would otherwise be available. For example, in the *Marshall Field* case, the plaintiffs sued for $200 million in damages, not exactly a small sum!

There are a number of other controversial issues that I wish to point out at this time, hopefully to be dealt with at greater length during the course of the panel. These issues basically concern the proper role of federal and state legislation. The first such issue deals with the two-tier offer. Basically, the two-tier offer involves a tender offer for 51 percent of a target's stock with a subsequent forced merger at a substantially lower price. The recent Maryland legislation, as Larry Scriggins will discuss, addresses two-tier offers. Also, the argument has been made that these offers are manipulative under Section 14(e). Thus far, this claim has been rejected.[22]

A second issue is the sale of crown jewels. Should the business judgment rule be the only source of regulation in regard to such transactions? That is basically what the SEC Advisory Committee recommended. On the other hand, the Sixth Circuit's decision in *Marathon* suggests that the federal securities laws, namely Section 14(e), may be invoked. Arguably, the policy underlying this approach is that federal regulation is appropriate where the lax application of the business judgment rule practically assures that the defensive tactics of corporate managers will be uniformly insulated from successful challenge.

The third issue is the practice of greenmail. Greenmail occurs when the target corporation's incumbent management causes the corporation to repurchase at a substantial premium stock acquired by a potential bidder. One question concerns whether such repurchases should be approved by the shareholders before they are consummated. Other questions involve management's potential conflicts of interest in this situation and whether management should be required to show that the transaction is fair and reasonable to the corporation.

---

21. 646 F.2d 271 (7th Cir. 1981); 619 F.2d 192 (2d Cir. 1980). For a further analysis of these issues, *see* M. Steinberg, Corporate Internal Affairs: A Corporate and Securities Law Perspective (1983).

22. *See, e.g.*, Radol v. Thomas, 534 F. Supp. 1302 (S.D. Ohio 1982).

A fourth subject is that of golden parachute agreements, which basically provide substantial compensation packages for corporate executives to take effect only upon a change in corporate control. In this context, there arise such issues as the need to disclose the terms of such agreements,[23] possible state law liability premised on breach of fiduciary duty, and the much broader corporate accountability concerns.

The fifth issue is the role of the SEC in this process. Although the SEC has promulgated a number of tender offer rules, it generally has declined to address the serious fraudulent, deceptive, and manipulative practices in this area. Although the Commission is unlikely to act in the present era of deregulation, nevertheless, the issue should be raised whether the SEC should regulate more substantively in the tender offer area.

Now we will turn to Paula Chester's presentation on the impact of tender offers on small issuers. To tell you a little bit about Paula, most important, she is a graduate of this law school. She is currently with Baskin and Steingut in New York City. Previously, Paula was at the Securities and Exchange Commission for four years, during two of which she was special counsel to the Office of Small Business Policy and helped draft Section 4(6) of the Securities Act and Regulation D. She has also spoken on a number of ABA and FBA panels. She is going to discuss *Wellman v. Dickinson*,[24] dealing with the definition of tender offer, and the application of Regulation D in this context. Also, Paula will address the difference in regulation insofar as the small corporation is concerned between exchange offers on one hand and cash tender offers on the other.

MS. CHESTER:

Thanks, Marc. Someone asked me, as a matter of fact Professor Gibson who is an old friend of mine, why I was asked to speak here. I told him that "my practice generally relates to small companies," and he said, "Does your practice involve tender offers?" I indicated to him that it didn't, and he said, "What are you doing here?" I said, "Well, I'm going to discuss how to structure a transaction to avoid the tender offer rules to begin with." As you heard from Marc's discussion, the panoply of different arrangements that are possible (including crown jewels, golden parachutes, and various lock-up arrangements), can present quite a problem for the small company.

---

23. Shortly after the panel discussion was held, the SEC issued a release which, *inter alia*, promulgated disclosure requirements in regard to such golden parachute agreements. *See* Securities Exchange Act Release No. 20220, [1983-1984 Transfer Binder] Fed. Sec. L. Rep. (CCH) ¶ 83,425 (S.E.C. 1983).

24. 475 F. Supp. 783 (S.D.N.Y. 1979), *aff'd on other grounds*, 682 F.2d 355 (2d Cir. 1982).

The strategy involved in these arrangements is in addition to the full, extensive regulation under the federal securities laws.

Consider your client's proposed transaction. Probably a lot of you who are in practice here in Baltimore have a similar type of practice to ours: small business, venture capital–type clients. I've noticed somehow that small entrepreneurs are big dreamers; they are the most optimistic people in the hardest of times. They come to your office and say, "You know I'd like to gain control of this company." You ask them what company they would like to take over, and they tell you "IBM." The regulations governing tender offers can present a problem for the small issuer. As counsel to the small company, we have to say, "Let's lower your goals a little bit and let's see what we can do to help."

If your client wants to grow through the acquisition process rather than the capital formation process, it may want to take over a small company by the means of purchasing the controlling shares. Suppose your client wants to purchase the shares of a small company for cash. If the target company is a Section 12(b) or 12(g) company, then the full deck of disclosure requirements contained in Regulation 14D will come into play. However, suppose you were to go for a nonreporting company or even a Section 15(d) company. I think the Chicago Cubs are a prime example. In this case, you would not come under Regulation 14D. Of course, however, you would be subject to Section 14(e) of the 1934 Act which is principally an antifraud provision. Note, however, that although it is principally an antifraud provision, Regulation 14E contains some important time periods to which the bidder must adhere. For example, there are minimum periods that the tender offer must be held open, including certain minimum periods after an increase in the consideration. Moreover, Regulation 14E requires a statement of the target company's position with respect to the offer.

Suppose your client is really small or has limited financial resources. It is trying to acquire controlling interest in another company but has no cash. For example, suppose your client wants to acquire controlling interest in a nonpublic company and the acquisition is valued at approximately $6 million. To effect this offer, your client intends to exchange its securities for the securities of the target company. The only way that can be done is to register those shares under the 1933 Act, unless there is an available exemption. Because your client has limited cash resources and must exchange securities, it is subject to the registration requirememts of Section 5 and the liability provisions of Section 11 of the 1933 Act. This is extremely onerous for a small company. Greater attention needs to be paid to this discriminating effect. Clearly, as of now, regulation is in favor of the cash-heavy acquirer.

Turning to a related subject, in such a counseling role, the attorney must determine whether the client is in fact engaging in a tender offer. For example, counsel must determine whether a proposed purchase of controlling shares would necessarily be deemed a tender offer, thus triggering the applicability of Regulation 14E, or would be viewed as a privately negotiated transaction.

There is no clearly established definition of a tender offer. The Williams Act gives no guidance. Even though the Commission has set forth a number of factors to be considered in deciding whether the subject transaction constitutes a tender offer, the term remains elusive. In many situations, such as the *Marshall Field* and *Mobil* cases, there is no question; those transactions are clearly tender offers. It's sort of like pornography—you know it when you see it. If it's in the Wall Street Journal, it's a tender offer. But what about the small transaction? When is your client engaging in a tender offer? If the target company is a small company with a small float, with perhaps 50 or 60 percent of the shares held by insiders, the purchase of those shares may be a privately negotiated transaction or may, in fact, be a tender offer.

With this in mind, I'm going to explore the *Wellman v. Dickinson*[25] case to see whether or not the transaction can be structured to avoid the applicability of the tender offer rules. The Commission has set forth seven elements, which were adopted in *Wellman*, of a tender offer. These are: Is there a general solicitation of the shareholders? Is the solicitation for a substantial percentage of the issuer's stock? Is there a premium paid for the stock over the prevailing market price? Are there firm terms that are being offered, or is there an opportunity to negotiate those terms? Is your client's offer contingent on receipt of a fixed number of shares, or will the client take as many as it can get? Is there a limited period of time for the offer? In other words, is the client saying to those shareholders, "let me know in two days or the deal's gone." And, finally, is the offeree subjected to pressure to sell the stock, either to take the deal or not, or is there room for negotiation?

The Commission has also stated that there is an eighth characteristic: Do public announcements precede or accompany rapid accumulations of large numbers of shares? However, courts have obviously not applied this eighth characteristic when the issue is whether the subject transaction is privately negotiated or a tender offer.

If you look at those characteristics of a tender offer that I just mentioned, you will note striking similarities with the negotiated transaction for control of a small company. Your client is not likely to try to purchase the shares unless it is going to get control—that's the whole point of the deal.

Suppose your client intends to pay a premium for that stock. With control comes a price! Obviously, in a privately negotiated transaction it is not unusual to have a premium paid for the shares. Moreover, it is not unusual

---

25. 475 F. Supp. 783 (S.D.N.Y. 1979), *aff'd on other grounds*, 682 F.2d 355 (2d Cir. 1982).

to make a purchase contingent on obtaining control. There is no point in commencing any kind of offer if you're only going to end up with 2 percent of the stock. Clearly, the contingency nature of procuring control is something that is normally involved in a privately negotiated transaction. Thus, your proposed transaction has already taken on two of the stated attributes of a tender offer.

The courts, however, have indicated that there are other factors that must be addressed separately to determine whether or not a tender offer has been made. In *Wellman v. Dickinson*, the court reviewed the same factors that I have discussed but emphasized the extent to which the offerees had time to consider the transaction and negotiate the terms of the sale. In that particular transaction, the attorney's had devised two scripts, one for the institutional investors and one for the individual investors. The solicitors used the actual scripts, and there was no deviation from them. Clearly, those solicitors who made the phone calls or other contacts were not in a position to negotiate. They had no authority.

In addition, the district court in *Wellman* reasoned that negotiating the transaction would have bogged down the deal. Clearly, it was the Sun Oil Company's intention to get this deal done in ten days. Hence, negotiation would clearly have defeated the whole transaction. The court also looked at the fact that the price was so good that there really was no room to negotiate. I don't feel very comfortable with that as a determining factor in considering whether or not there was the ability to negotiate. If you've got a company with no earnings and no dividends and it hasn't done anything for twenty years, anything may look good. The fact that someone is willing to pay a good price for shares in a company with no earnings should not, in my view, be a determining factor in assessing whether there is negotiation. Nevertheless, the *Wellman* court reasoned that the pressure to sell, evidenced by a good price requiring a hurried response, defeated the ability to negotiate the transaction.

In addition, the court used another standard which I find fairly interesting—namely, whether or not there was a public solicitation. In making this determination, the court turned to those factors under Section 4(2) of the 1933 Act which have been used in deciding whether there has been a private offering of securities. The court observed that the Supreme Court's seminal decision in *Ralston Purina*[26] distinguished a public from a private offering by determining whether the class of persons affected needed protection under the Act; in other words, can they fend for themselves? Although the qualification of the offerees is an issue in determining whether or not such class of persons need the protection of the 1933 Act, the *Wellman* court reasoned that sophistication standing alone is of no import

---

26. 346 U.S. 119 (1953).

if those sophisticated offerees are not given access to the information that they need to make an informed investment decision. Sophistication, therefore, is not a substitute for access to information. (There have been 1933 Act cases that have had similar holdings: one example is the *Hill York* case.[27]) Therefore, the court in the *Wellman* case said that the furnishing of material information, or at least access to such information, is essential in determining whether there is a public solicitation–tender offer or whether there is a privately negotiated transaction.

The *Wellman* case was decided in 1979. The question that I'm going to pose is would the case be any different in view of the adoption by the Securities and Exchange Commission of Regulation D?

For those who may not know, Regulation D was adopted pursuant to Sections 3(b) and 4(2) of the Securities Act. In short, it changes the status of private offerings. Basically, it permits persons who are deemed to be accredited investors to participate in a private transaction. In such a transaction, there can be an unlimited number of accredited investors. In addition, there are no specific informational requirements, because such persons are presumed to be able to ask for and receive the information they need to make an informed investment decision, to fend for themselves. Who are the individuals that are accredited investors? In addition to certain institutional–type investors, such as banks, insurance companies, investment companies, certain venture capital companies, tax-exempt organizations, and directors and executive officers, they include any natural person with a net worth of $1 million, persons with individual gross incomes of $200,000 per year, and persons who purchase at least $150,000 of the securities being offered (provided the total purchase price does not exceed 20 percent of the purchaser's net worth).

What does the accredited investor status do to the *Wellman* reasoning of access to information? Would you as counsel advise your corporate client that it could offer to exchange cash for securities of persons who may be deemed to be accredited? It's never been addressed. Presumably, however, since sophistication alone dosen't suffice under the *Wellman* case, the lack of sufficient information or access to such information remains key. Even though accredited investors may be presumed to be able to ask for and receive such information as they may deem material to their investment decision, the pressure to sell coupled with other factors evidencing an inability to negotiate terms may defeat the presumption of access to material information. Therefore, the deregulatory mode that the Commission has been taking lately to reduce impediments facing small business would seem to have little effect in the tender offer context. While sophistication of offerees, standing alone, has been considered a factor in determining whether there has been a privately negotiated transaction as opposed to a tender offer, these cases have involved principally institutional investors. For ex-

---

27. 448 F.2d 680 (5th Cir. 1971).

ample, in the *Kennecott*[28] case there were only a handful of institutions involved in the transaction. Thus, it would appear that the individual accredited investor definition of Regulation D would have little application to the tender offer context.

As a practitioner, therefore, I'm going to try to suggest some things that you should be doing to make sure your client's proposed acquisition is not a tender offer. Make sure that your client's offer is not firm and leaves room for negotiation. Perhaps you can make sure that there are meetings with the shareholders that have large blocks of shares. There, an opportunity can be given to ask questions and make a counteroffer. Further, make sure that the shareholders know who the acquirer is. A number of the cases have said that there is a need for an investor to know who the acquirer is and what its financial resources are. If you're providing that information to begin with, there's less need for a court to find that there is a tender offer. Make sure also that your solicitors are not using scripts and that there's adequate time for the shareholder to decide whether to participate in the transaction. Possibly one of the key elements is whether there is enough time to make an informed investment judgment. You have to give those shareholders time—eliminate the pressure. By following these suggestions, although certainly not sureproof, your client appears to have entered a privately negotiated transaction, rather than a tender offer. That way, you don't have to worry about crown jewels, lock-up arrangements, or other such demons. You can just go and take control of IBM.

PROFESSOR STEINBERG:

Thank you, Paula.

I had the pleasure of serving as Ralph Ferrara's special counsel for two and a half years at the SEC. Ralph is currently a member of the New York law firm of Debevoise and Plimpton and is a resident partner in the firm's D.C. office. Prior to joining Debevoise, Ralph was general counsel at the SEC. He has spoken numerous times at professional conferences and has authored a number of law review articles in prominent journals including the Northwestern and Pennsylvania Law Reviews. Speaking from personal experience, Ralph Ferrara was a very highly regarded general counsel. Ralph is going to address manipulation under the Williams Act.

MR. FERRARA:

Thank you, Marc. My assigned topic is to discuss manipulative tactics used in tender offers and to assess how the federal, and indeed the state, courts are dealing with that subject. Essentially, my job is to review the body count that has resulted from the offensive and defensive tactics used

---

28. 584 F.2d 1195 (2d Cir. 1978).

in the tender offer context between the *Mobil-Marathon* and the *Martin Marietta* cases.

In doing this, I will touch on several of the buzz words that are unique to this area of our practice. Today, for example, we speak of lock-ups, defensive options, bait and switch, poison pills, standstills, sales of assets, two-tier pricings, Pac-Man maneuvers, shark repellants, and ransoms.

In 1981, the Sixth Circuit created quite a stir with the *Mobil-Marathon* decision.[29] This case held that certain lock-up devices, even though fully disclosed, could violate Section 14(e) of the Williams Act. Section 14(e) is the in-house antifraud provision of the SEC's tender offer rules and regulations. It says, essentially, "Thou shalt not commit fraud of any variety in the context of a tender offer." In the immediate aftermath of *Mobil-Marathon*, it seemed that virtually any device that target management used in fending off an unwanted bid would result in a charge of manipulation. In the two years since the *Mobil-Marathon* decision, however, virtually every court that has considered the issue has read the term "manipulative acts and practices" (as it appears in Section 14(e)) somewhat more narrowly, and in many cases very much more narrowly, than the *Mobil-Marathon* case did. Nonetheless, courts today are as much at sea as to what manipulation is in the context of a tender offer as they were at the time of the *Mobil-Marathon* decision. It may be that Section 14(e) requires not only disclosure but sets some standard of normative conduct for the parties to the tender offer. It is unclear, though, how high those normative standards actually are. The factual situation in *Mobil-Marathon* when juxtaposed with that of *Martin Marietta* will illustrate this point.

In the *Mobil* case, Marathon, seeking to defend a hostile takeover bid from Mobil, induced U.S. Steel to make an offer for 51 percent of Marathon's stock at $125.00 per share. Marathon did this by dangling two big carrots in front of U.S. Steel. First, Marathon gave U.S. Steel an option to purchase 10 million authorized but previously unissued Marathon shares, representing about 17 percent of the company, for $90 per share. U.S. Steel knew its bid of $125 per share for 51 percent of Marathon was being competed against by third parties but, because of this option, could grab 17 percent of the stock at a bargain basement price of $90 per share without competition. The second carrot that was dangled in front of U.S. Steel to induce it to come into the deal was an option on Marathon's "crown jewel," namely a 48 percent interest in the Yates gas field in Texas, at a price of $2.8 billion. I'm not an oil and gas lawyer, but I understand that the Yates field is one of the biggest booms that has ever hit the oil and gas business.

The Sixth Circuit held that Mobil had shown a likelihood of success in proving that the 17 percent lock-up and the crown jewel option were "manipulative" in the sense that Section 14(e) of the Williams Act uses the

---

29. 669 F.2d 366 (6th Cir. 1981).

term. This was because the options gave U.S. Steel a huge advantage in the takeover contest. U.S. Steel obtained 17 percent of Marathon at a bargain basement price, and there was at least some evidence in the record that the Yates oil field was worth a great deal more than the $2.8 billion that U.S. Steel would have to pay for it. Regrettably, though, the court's legal analysis wasn't very astute. The court looked at the term "manipulative conduct" as it is used in the federal securities statutes generally, it talked about the classic forms of securities manipulation (such as washed sales and matched orders), and then just reached the conclusion that the two options granted to U.S. Steel were manipulative in the same sense. The *Mobil* court did not discuss the legislative history of the Williams Act to justify its result, nor did it look (nor could it have looked) to any other cases to support its theories.

It is granted that the two options had the effect of discouraging other companies from competing with U.S. Steel for Marathon. The court, however, never raised some terribly important questions. First, did the options serve a critical function by bringing U.S. Steel into the deal? If so, why should they be considered artificial? Second, if U.S. Steel had advised Marathon that it would not make the $125 per share bid for 51 percent of the stock had it not received the options, where would Marathon shareholders have been? From this perspective, wasn't the lock-up option given by Marathon to U.S. Steel really something that benefited everybody in the transaction with the possible exception of Mobil, its hostile bidder? Third, what would have happened if the options hadn't been given; would U.S. Steel have gone away and not entered the fray? Interestingly enough, when the Sixth Circuit struck down the options, U.S. Steel didn't go away. I suppose a cynic would say, however, that the granting of the options already had their effect. By the time the Sixth Circuit struck the options down, U.S. Steel was so far ahead of the game, it could afford to go forward without the options.

Perhaps the most celebrated decision since the *Mobil-Marathon* case is *Martin Marietta v. Bendix*,[30] decided in the Federal District Court of Maryland. This bloody battle involved an offer by Bendix for Martin Marietta and, as a defensive maneuver, an offer by Martin Marietta for Bendix. Bendix charged that Marietta's counter offer was a scorched-earth defensive tactic and constituted manipulative conduct under Section 14(e). The Maryland court rejected the argument, holding in effect that Section 14(e) permits a target to use every last farthing in its defense if it deems it appropriate. The court read relevant Supreme Court cases as saying that Section 14(e) was meant to benefit target shareholders and provided no help to a hostile bidder. The court said that it wouldn't have made any difference at all if the Martin Marietta offer had not succeeded, because Section 14(e) is solely a disclosure statute. So long as you tell all, there can be no "manipulation."

---

30. 549 F. Supp. 623 (D. Md. 1982).

This holding specifically rejects *Mobil-Marathon*. The Sixth Circuit and the Maryland District Court are thus on opposite sides of the fence. The *Mobil-Marathon* court held that the lock-up options in that case were manipulative irrespective of the disclosures involved. The *Martin Marietta* court, in a hurried but well-reasoned opinion, held that Section 14(e) is solely a disclosure provision. So long as the lock-ups or other defensive manipulative tactics are disclosed, they can't be manipulative in the Section 14(e) sense.

No reported decision since *Martin Marietta* (with the possible exception of the *Data Probe* case[31]) has held that a fully disclosed tender offer tactic could be violative of Section 14(e). Most courts, however, do not go as far as the Maryland court did. A good example is the *Dan River v. Icahn* case.[32] In that case, the Fourth Circuit held a "bait and switch" tactic to be not manipulative and not violative of Section 14(e). Carl Icahn, the so-called 21st century corporate raider, had made an offer for Dan River for $18 per share, but stated that if management did not capitulate to the offer, he was going to lower his offer to $15 per share. This put the Dan River directors in the position of having to choose between fighting Icahn in court or defending a shareholder suit for allegedly raising a frivolous defense. The Dan River directors chose to sue Icahn on the grounds that this bait and switch tactic was manipulative under Section 14(e). The district court judge agreed, but the Fourth Circuit lifted the injunction granted by the district court on the grounds that Dan River didn't have much of a chance of prevailing on the merits of the litigation. The court examined the recent cases (*Martin Marietta* in particular) and held that Section 14(e) could not be used to challenge the "substantive goodness" of a tender offer tactic. The court essentially ruled that Section 14(e) was a disclosure provision but did not go quite as far as the Maryland court did. The *Dan River* court distinguished the "manipulation" in *Mobil* from that of Icahn, reasoning that the two options Marathon gave to U.S. Steel were negotiated face-to-face outside of the marketplace. Since Icahn's so-called manipulation was in the marketplace and did not artificially affect anything, the Fourth Circuit Court felt that it did not have to go as far as the *Mobil-Marathon* court.

Judge Pierre Lavalle of the Southern District of New York has also disagreed with the Sixth Circuit's *Mobil-Marathon* decision, calling it questionable legal theory.[33] Judge Lavalle declined an invitation to apply the *Mobil-Marathon* rationale to the lock-ups granted in the Batus acquisition

---

31. [1983-1984 Transfer Binder] Fed. Sec. L. Rep. (CCH) ¶ 99,451 (S.D.N.Y.), *rev'd*, 722 F.2d 1 (2d Cir. 1983), *cert. denied*, 104 S. Ct. 1326 (1984).

32. 701 F.2d 278 (4th Cir. 1983).

33. Marshall Field & Co. v. Icahn, [1982 Transfer Binder] Fed. Sec. L. Rep. (CCH) ¶ 98,616 (S.D.N.Y.). The Second Circuit subsequently has rejected *Marathon*. *See* cases note 19 *supra*.

of Marshall Field. In that case, Carl Icahn was on the offensive, charging that the actions of Batus and Marshall Field were manipulative in the sense of Section 14(e). The *Batus* case is a good example of an attempt by attorneys to apply the *Mobil-Marathon* holding to a slightly different situation. In this case, Marshall Field agreed to sell two million authorized but unissued treasury shares to Batus, its white knight. Note that this was not an option to purchase but an absolute sale to Batus. Of course, Batus had some outs, one being that if it didn't takeover the company, it didn't have to go through with the sale. Marshall Field also went on to give Batus a right of first refusal on the Marshall Field crown jewels, its downtown Chicago properties. This was not a crown jewel option in the Yates oil field sense; rather, it was a right of first refusal. It provided that if anybody (such as Carl Icahn) acquired Marshall Field and wanted to dispose of its properties, there was to be a right of first refusal given to Batus. Both of these features were put in to inhibit the Icahn bid and to ingratiate shareholders to the Batus bid for Marshall Field. Judge Lavalle made an effort to distinguish the *Mobil-Marathon* case saying that there are options in one case and an actual sale of assets and a right of first refusal in the other. Upon close inspection, however, Judge Lavalle's decision stems more from his belief that the tender offer laws do not bar management from taking offensive or defensive actions in the course of a takeover.

In *Whittaker v. Brunswick*,[34] the federal district court for the Western District of Illinois distinguished the *Mobil-Marathon* case in a different way. This case arose when Whittaker Corporation commenced a hostile tender offer for Brunswick. Brunswick looked for a white knight, but it was only partially successful. Brunswick found that American Home Products (AHP) wasn't interested in Brunswick as a whole but was interested in its major asset, the Sherwood Medical Products subsidiary. Brunswick then signed an agreement with its white knight calling for American Home to commence a tender offer in competition with the outstanding hostile bid for 51 percent of the target's stock. Brunswick also agreed that if American Home Products received the 51 percent, then AHP would purchase (by trading its 51 percent of the stock with Brunswick) the Sherwood Medical Products subsidiary. After examining this transaction, the court found that it was not manipulative, because it was an actual sale and not an option in the Yates field sense. The court also stated, a proposition that is debatable, that this agreement did not inhibit or artificially restrict any tender offer activity.

There are other cases that are fascinating in this area. The bottom line is that, with minor exceptions, most of these offensive and defensive strategies are passing muster. So long as corporate management and their counsel are

---

34. 535 F. Supp. 933 (N.D. Ill. 1982).

careful in the way they construct their offensive and defensive strategies, they're likely to have an advantage when they come before a federal court.

PROFESSOR STEINBERG:

Thank you, Ralph. The next speaker is Ted Fiflis who is a professor of Law at the University of Colorado Law School. This year Ted is visiting at American University and is also teaching at the University of Pennsylvania Law School. He is the chairman of the National Institute of Securities Regulation and is also the editor in chief of the Corporation Law Review. He has visited at a number of other law schools in addition to those that I mentioned, including New York University, University of California at Davis, University of Chicago, University of Virginia, and Duke University. Ted has also coauthored with Professor Homer Kripke the well-known casebook on accounting for lawyers and has published extensively in the field.

PROFESSOR FIFLIS:

Thank you, Marc. My task is to describe the Tender Offer Report of the task force that was appointed last February by the SEC to consider whether fundamental change is required in the tender offer area. I want to begin by reminding us all of a little bit of the political history of tender offers. Before 1968, there was no tender offer regulation at the state level or at the federal level. In fact, in the two or three years prior to 1968, there had been several bills submitted in Congress, all of which were defeated in committee. What finally brought about federal and state tender offer legislation in 1968?

In the late 1960's, the shortage of companies that were willing to be taken over became acute. As a result, many companies became potential involuntary victims of takeovers. Those companies and their counsel lobbied in Congress for tender offer legislation which would inhibit tender offers by protecting target company incumbent managements. Those efforts were beaten back in 1966 and 1967. In 1968, however, it became apparent that, rather than a need primarily to protect the target or the bidder corporations, there was a need to protect the people that had invested in such target companies. The federal tender offer legislation known as the Williams Act was thus adopted. It has basically two aspects.

First, the Act requires full disclosure, where appropriate, by both the bidder and target of information deemed material to the target company's shareholders. Second, the Act creates substantive protections, adopted in order to inhibit or avoid perceived abuses in the tender offer process. For example, investors who tender their shares to the bidder may withdraw those shares for a specified period which commences at the beginning of the tender offer. The Williams Act also contains a proration provision which comes into effect when the bid is for less than 100 percent of the target company's stock. For instance, assume that the tender offer is for 60 percent of the stock, but there is an oversubscription so that 80 percent of the shares are tendered. Before the Williams Act, the bidder could select which shareholders it would honor with payment. The Williams Act prohibits this; there must now be proration of all of the shares tendered. In the example, each shareholder will thus have three-fourths of his tendered shares accepted by the bidder. Finally, the Williams Act contains an equal price provision which prohibits an abuse that had previously occurred. Under the Act, once a tender offer is made at a certain price, if that price is later increased, then all persons who submit their shares in that offer must receive the highest ultimate price actually paid.

The Williams Act was said to favor neither the targets nor the bidders. The pressure for nonneutral legislation, however, continued. The target companies (who had lost in Congress with the Williams Act) succeeded in getting legislation adopted by a majority of the states which would have substantially inhibited tender offers if the legislation were valid. These laws provided all sorts of stumbling blocks to the bidder company. The U.S. Supreme Court, however, in *Edgar v. MITE*[35] struck down the Illinois legislation under the Commerce Clause. Language in that opinion suggested that other state tender offer legislation is also preempted by the federal legislation. So far, though, the Supreme Court has not ruled on this issue.

In this regard, the present SEC rules, among other things, require tender offers to commence within five days after public announcement, probably having the effect of preempting many state statutes which require delays of more than five days. To the extent that state statutes prohibit tender offers from going forward after the five-day period, they are clearly inconsistent with federal law. In view of *Edgar v. MITE*, however, a number of states have sought to engineer their legislation so as to give target companies some way of fending off hostile bidders. It remains to be seen whether these most recently enacted statutes will be held constitutional.

In addition to target company incumbent managements and the bidders, there are probably two other constituencies that are now being served. Because of the debate that has been going on for the past fifteen years, a public interest element has emerged. There are academics, government regulators, and others who purport to act on behalf of the investor in proposing tender offer rules, regulations, and principles. In addition, there is a fourth group that has grown up. These are the tender offer "professionals," the law firms and investment banking firms (and government regulators for that matter) who have attractive jobs because there is substantial regulation in the tender offer area. These professionals have come to have an important interest in the regulation of tender offers and have a substantial voice in the creation of legislation.

---

35. 102 S. Ct. 2629 (1982).

The tender offer situation with these constituencies seemed to come to a head last year during Bendix's attempted takeover of Martin Marietta. The public finally began to see that there may be something wrong with allowing these four interest groups to tell us what the law ought to be. Substantial pressure developed for another look at the fundamental problem of what, if any, regulation should apply to tender offers. The SEC perceived this substantial public interest but appointed the Advisory Committee task force consisting mainly of those same tender offer professionals. The group was appointed to study the tender offer problem from a fresh vantage point and to consider questions ranging from whether tender offer regulation should be eliminated to whether regulation should be increased in favor of targets, bidders, or investors. The result of the task force effort is the Report of Recommendations consisting of 50 specific suggestions for change. It has been said that these suggestions are largely of cosmetic effect and that they are not of great consequence. Though this appears at first glance to be the case, upon a closer look, the changes may have farreaching effect.

The fifty different proposals can be categorized into three parts. First, there are proposals that inhibit target companies and what they can do to defend against tender offers. Second, several proposals regulate bidders and inhibit them in their activities. Third, a single proposal is aimed at the market professionals.

The task force recommended that the business judgment rule should continue to regulate what a board of directors can do to defend against a takeover. For example, suppose that a target's board of directors decides, after a tender offer is made, to acquire a company, which is a substantial competitor of the bidder, with the objective of providing an antitrust stumbling block to the takeover. The task force suggests that the key question should then be whether the board of directors of the target has exercised its good faith business judgment. On this point, the task force is merely adopting the current law.[36]

In three specific areas, however, the task force suggests what may be substantial changes. The first deals with the adoption of "golden parachutes" by the target companies. Under a "golden parachute," the executives of the target company are awarded contracts by the company which provide that, upon a change in corporate control, very substantial payments would be made to the departing executives. The task force suggests that golden parachutes be totally prohibited once a tender offer has commenced. In other words, if no golden parachute contract is in effect and a tender offer is then made, the task force suggests that such golden parachutes should be prohibited by law. Second, although the task force would continue to regulate most lock-up arrangements by the business judgment rule, it would treat

---

36. *E.g.*, Panter v. Marshall Field & Co., 646 F.2d 271 (7th Cir.) (applying Delaware law), *cert. denied*, 454 U.S. 1092 (1981).

one type of lock-up differently. The task force suggested that lock-up arrangements that include the issuance of stock should be subject to shareholder vote if the shares issued would amount to 20 percent or more of the voting power of the target company. Third, the task force proposed that if a target company seeks to repurchase some of its own shares in competition with the bidder, the repurchase should be subject to approval by a vote of target company shareholders.

The task force Report further recommended that state statutory change-of-control provisions, such as state antitakeover legislation, should be prohibited. The task force would also prohibit certain charter and bylaw provisions that are popularly called "shark repellants." One example of a shark repellant would be a bylaw providing that once a person or group acquires more than a certain percentage of the shares of a corporation, instead of having a per share voting right, its voting right would be limited to a certain maximum. This is a very common shark repellant. Another device which the Report would eliminate through federal law is high quorum and vote requirements, the so-called supermajority shark repellants. These require, for example, that before a merger following a tender offer can be consummated, 90 percent of the shares must vote for the merger. The task force would require moreover that, until supermajority voting is eliminated, any supermajority provision in the bylaws must itself be passed by an equivalent supermajority of the shareholders.

The Report contains other proposals concerning the defenses that target companies may establish to avoid takeovers. The Report suggested that a "non–per share" voting provision (as discussed above) be submitted to an advisory vote of the shareholders every year. This would be a nonbinding advisory vote, one that simply gives a straw poll verdict to the board of directors as to whether the existing shareholders think that it is appropriate to inhibit a takeover with such a provision. The task force also recommended that long-term standstill agreements be submitted to an annual advisory vote by the shareholders. Finally, the task force recommended that golden parachute arrangements that were established before a takeover should also be submitted to an advisory shareholder vote.

The task force made a specific recommendation on one other kind of target company tactic, the "Pac-Man" defense. When a Pac-Man defense is used, tender offers are made not only by the bidder for target stock but also by the target for the bidder's stock. The task force recommended that this tactic should continue to be subject to the business judgment rule, unless the first bidder has made a 100 percent cash tender offer for the target. In that case, the Report would not permit a Pac-Man defense to be mounted by the target company's management.

Several recommendations of the task force have to do with the bidder company. Perhaps for the advantage of potential bidders, the task force suggested that "paper" tender offers (offers of stock or debentures or other paper of the bidder for the target company's shares) should be put on an equal basis with cash tender offers. At the present time, when there is an offering of paper, it is likely to be subject to the registration requirements of the 1933 Act. There is thus a period of delay and expense, and the bidder consequently loses the advantage normally associated with cash tender offers. The task force suggested that the law should be changed so that there is not this kind of delay for paper offers. The Report, therefore, recommended that a paper offer should be permitted to go forward from the time of the filing of the registration statement rather than, as today, from the time of the effective date of the registration statement.

Another proposal of the task force would regulate the bidder but would do so to its disadvantage. All "13(d)" acquisitions (non–tender offers that are acquisitions of 5 percent or more of the equity securities of the target) today require that, within ten days after the acquisition of the 5 percent, the acquirer must file a report with the SEC. The consequence is that during the interim ten-day period, the bidder may go ahead and continue to acquire shares and could conceivably acquire 100 percent before the ten day period expires. The task force would prevent that situation from occurring. The Report suggested that once 5 percent of the stock has been acquired, all further acquisitions would be stopped for at least forty-eight hours. This forty-eight-hour period would begin after a notice has been filed with the SEC of the acquisition of the 5 percent. Thus, no longer would bidders be able to acquire much more than 5 percent before there is any public notice of the transaction.

With respect to partial tender offers where less than 100 percent of the shares of a target are sought by the bidder, the task force recommended that some small disadvantage be imposed upon bidders. The rationale for this penalty is the substantial criticism currently existing on partial bids. It also has been argued unsuccessfully that these transactions are manipulative.[37] The task force recommended in such a situation that two weeks' extra time be given for all purposes to the target company's shareholders. Thus the minimum period that the offer is to be open must be extended two weeks longer than the minimum period for a 100 percent tender offer. The task force would similarly extend the periods for proration and withdrawal of shares for partial tender offers.

The task force made two final recommendations with respect to bidders. The first is a recommendation that any acquisition of more than 20 percent of a target must be made by means of a tender offer. The sole exception to this proposal is that, if the shares are purchased from the target company itself, then, of course, no tender offer would be required. The task force also felt that the public investor and target companies do not have enough time to consider offers, especially under the complex arrangements that

---

37. *E.g.*, Radol v. Thomas, 534 F. Supp. 1302 (S.D. Ohio 1982).

are being set forth today. The task force thus recommended increases in the minimum offer and withdrawal periods from their current time periods.

The third category of the task force's recommendations addressed the perceived abuses of certain market professionals. One such abuse is the short tendering of shares, prohibited under SEC Rule 10b-4.[38] For example, if a stockholder owns 100 shares of stock and a partial tender offer is made for only a certain amount of the shares of the target, providing that the offer is oversubscribed, that stockholder will find that he is left holding some shares because of the proration requirement.[39] To avoid this, many professionals decided a few years ago to tender more shares than they actually had so that their shares would be prorated down to somewhere around the amount actually owned. The difference could be covered by buying options. Although the SEC prohibited this practice, this did not prevent a process called "hedged" tendering. Hedged tendering occurs when the market professional, concerned that its shares will be prorated, tenders all shares owned, followed by the sale of a portion of those shares in the market. Because the task force viewed both short and hedged tendering as giving an unfair advantage to market professionals, it recommended that the SEC prohibit both of these practices.

On the whole, the task force Report seems acceptable—but only acceptable. However, in a Separate Statement, Professors Easterbrook and Jarrell assert that the Advisory Committee failed to grapple with the fundamental issues. Basically, Easterbrook and Jarrell contend that tender offers are a good thing, since everybody benefits by them. They claim that the financial economists have established that per share prices of targets are enhanced, roughly 30 percent on the average, when a tender offer occurs. They also argue that not only are target shares enhanced 30 percent but the bidders' shares are also enhanced, 4 percent on average. Therefore, they say, everybody wins when tender offers are made, and tender offers should be encouraged to the maximum extent possible. Anything that discourages tender offers should thus be eliminated. The Williams Act as it presently exists, however, inhibits tender offers. Furthermore, the task force's suggestions really amount to nothing more than increased regulation; they would inhibit tender offers to an even greater extent. This is why Easterbrook and Jarrell feel that the Report is destructive of positive values and should not be followed.

On this, I believe, despite Easterbrook and Jarrell, the tender offer task force's Report is adequate—not great, not terrible, but adequate. This is the situation only because the economists haven't done enough of their homework yet.

---

38. The SEC subsequently prohibited "hedged" tendering pursuant to Rule 10b-4. *See* Securities Exchange Act Release No. 20799 (March 29, 1984).

39. *See* SEC Rule 14d-8. For further discussion, *see* the commentary herein addressing the SEC proration rule.

All of the economists' work to date has been based only on price analysis. As a consequence, all the economists can say right now is that the target company's price is enhanced on the average 30 percent by tender offers and that the bidder's price is enhanced on the average by 4 percent. They can't yet say anything about the long-term effect on the prices of the bidder, the target, or the combined companies after a successful tender offer. Nor can they say anything yet about the fairness of the division of that enhancement in "value," namely, the distribution of that enhanced value among present and former shareholders and other various participants in the takeover process. Once more evidence is collected as to the economic effects, it should dictate our policies with respect to tender offers. Easterbrook and Jarrell are probably going to end up being correct in their belief that the Williams Act was a drastic mistake and that we ought to eliminate all regulation of tender offers and go back to 1967. Right now no one can say that that will be the correct result.

PROFESSOR STEINBERG:

Thank you, Ted. Our next speaker is Larry Scriggins. After graduating from the University of Chicago Law School, Larry clerked for the Honorable Frederick W. Brune, Chief Judge of the Court of Appeals of Maryland. Thereafter, he joined the firm of Piper & Marbury, where he has been a partner for a number of years. He has been very active in bar activities and has published a number of articles in the Business Lawyer, which, of course, is the professional journal of the ABA Section of Corporation, Banking, and Business Law. Larry will speak on the recently adopted Maryland legislation.

MR. SCRIGGINS:

Thank you, Marc. Let me begin with a few thoughts to partially set the stage. First of all, the notion that the Williams Act created a level playing field is nonsense. Second, the Advisory Committee Report is inadequate. Many people have thought for a long time that tender offer regulation has imposed a tremendous time pressure advantage to a bidder without a sufficient setting for target management to respond properly. There is a recent proposal by Professor Lowenstein in a Columbia Law Review article[40] in which he concludes that tender offers ought to be open for six months and that targets ought to be restrained from some of the more drastic tactics during that period in order to create a substantial period of time for evaluation and for a true auction process to come forward. This is a very interesting proposal.

---

40. Lowenstein, *Pruning Deadwood in Hostile Takeovers: A Proposal for Legislation*, 83 Colum. L. Rev. 249 (1983).

Turning to the subject matter of my talk, the new Maryland legislation is not really tender offer legislation.[41] Further, the terms front-end–loaded tender and two-tiered pricing of tenders do not really refer to pricing of tender offers. What they do refer to is a tender offer like the Bendix tender offer. In such a situation, the bidder buys 51 percent of the stock for say $80 per share, obtaining a bare majority. The acquiring company then takes advantage of the particular state statute to vote its shares, thereby effecting a forced merger for stock, debentures, or cash. The price paid per share in such a forced merger is usually far less than the tender offer price. This second step isn't a tender offer at all; it is the use of the evolution of state law to allow the controlling owner to fix the price and force out the others in the second step at a lower price through its voting power. The Maryland statute as amended simply says that, if a company wants to do something like that, the second-step, forced transaction has to be at the same price as the first-step tender offer. Otherwise, the law makes the bidder surmount a tremendous supermajority vote provision. There are, though, certain exceptions. One of the important exceptions is that any transaction which is recommended by the board of directors prior to the time 10 percent or more of the stock is acquired is exempt from the equal price provision. The transaction is covered by the normal state law process for the voting of fundamental corporate changes.

The statute contains a whole series of complex transitional rule, exemption, and election provisions which were designed to respond in part to criticisms that crept up at the last minute. Although I will not address these complex provisions, I do want to emphasize the important point that this statute is valid. It is a proper exercise of the legislative power of the state and is not aimed at tender offers per se.

It is important to go back here and take a historical view of corporation law. At one time, any fundamental change in a corporation, such as a merger or consolidation, required the approval of all shareholders. Even after the vested rights theory eroded, the usual sequence was for companies to come together, the successor's stock to be distributed, and, usually, both sides of the transaction to have appraisal rights. In the last thirty or forty years, however, those statutes have been amended to create the capacity to do reverse and forward triangular mergers; to do swap transactions for stock, debentures, or cash; to allow 90 percent or some similar percentage ownership by a parent of a subsidiary company to merge out the small minority at the will of the parent, without bothering with a stockholder vote; and to eliminate appraisal rights if the company is listed on a national securities exchange, sometimes even if it is only traded over the counter.

---

41. H.B. 1, 1983 Special Session, §§ 3-202, 3-601-03, 8-301(12)-(14) of the Md. Corps. & Ass's. Code (1983).

All of these changes in the law were designed to facilitate more imaginative business combinations during the 1960's. They created a whole panoply of modern devices and methodologies to do acquisitions in new and novel ways with combined forms of consideration. They also allowed a majority, usually a simple majority, to impose a voted will in order to get rid of the minority. In this case, the small investor's stock is taken away from him by the vote of the controlling shareholder, frequently without appraisal rights and without permitting him a free choice on whether he will or will not sell. By contrast, a pure tender offer is a classic transaction in which the bidder offers to buy the stock and the investor can say yes or no.

The Maryland statute does not regulate the pure form of tender offer. It is an attempt by the legislature to change the evolution of state law away from making it easier for the acquiring company to outvote the minority shareholders and take their stock without a consensual decision. The statute specifically attempts to redress the balance of voting power in front-loaded or two-tier tender offer situations where there can be an immense amount of coercion. Because of the short periods of time involved (which have now been lengthened only slightly), under the tender offer rules, the bidders, arbitrageurs, and other market professionals gain an overwhelming advantage over the small stockholder who receives complex information ten days later in the mail. Even if the small shareholder happens to figure the situation out, he has to go down to the bank, retrieve the stock from the safe deposit box, have his signature guaranteed and send everything to some New York bank. In the meantime, the professionals have all gotten into the proration pool, and they alone benefit.

There is no question that this Maryland legislation will be a deterrent to partial tenders. Presumably it will be a large deterrent to the so-called two-tier–type transaction, since it inhibits the bidder from using many of the mechanics of state law to outvote minority shareholders who are reluctant to tender. One further point that should be kept in mind is that the Maryland statute, like those in several other states, contains the so-called stock exchange exemption to appraisal rights.[42] This provision was inserted with the mistaken idea that the open market is always a true measure of value. The recent Maryland legislation wisely takes away that exemption in this kind of transaction.

PROFESSOR STEINBERG:

Thank you, Larry. We are delighted to have Stanley Sporkin with us tonight. Prior to becoming the general counsel of the Central Intelligence Agency in 1981, Stan was director of the Division of Enforcement at the

---

42. § 3.202(c) of the Md. Corps. & Ass's. Code (1983).

SEC from 1974 to 1981. During that time, as you well know, the SEC's voluntary disclosure program relating to questionable foreign payments took place. Stan seems to have been the recipient of practically every award possible for one to receive if one is a federal employee. For example, he's the recipient of the President's award for distinguished federal civilian service, the highest honor that can be granted to a member of the federal career service. He also received the Rockefeller award for public service in 1978. In addition, he received from the SEC the distinguished service award and the supervisory excellence award. In 1979, he was awarded the Alumnus of the Year award by his alma mater, the Pennsylvania State University.

MR. SPORKIN:

Thank you, Marc. I'd like to spend a few minutes to present a few thoughts. Prior to 1968, when the first Williams Act was passed, there was no real regulation of tender offers. The only thing we had was Rule 10b-5. Things were so bad then that we at the SEC, as well as the investing public, could not even learn the identity of the person making the takeover, because it was not deemed to be material under the rule. On that point, I would have to disagree with Ted. I believe that the Williams Act was and is very important legislation, even though the original Act was a very weak one with a few disclosure provisions. Even with subsequent amendments to the Act, acquiring companies are still being very predatory in their acquisitive activities.

I was recently at a conference at Harvard sponsored by the Kennedy School and the New York Stock Exchange. Attending were a number of corporate presidents as well as investment bankers and lawyers who specialize in the takeover area. One of the views expressed at that meeting was that the current takeover climate created a mistaken perception of reality. I dispute that view. The problem is a real one and is largely one of an abuse of process. There should be another round of legislation or SEC-imposed reforms.

I would like to give you my ideas of what I believe is required. First, I am not prepared to suggest any radical surgery or structural reforms. I think that the measured evolutionary approach that has been in effect since the first Williams Act is the right track to take. Let us try to define where the problems exist and then try to devise an appropriate solution to those problems. One of the major problems I see is the tremendous creative ability of the specialists that perform in this field. They always seem to come up with a new offensive tactic or new defensive response. How else does one explain the acquiring methodology used in the *Dickinson* case[43] and

---

43. 475 F. Supp. 783 (S.D.N.Y. 1979), *aff'd on other grounds*, 682 F.2d 355 (2d Cir. 1982).

the very creative Pac-Man defense utilized in the recent *Bendix* case?[44] What is the solution to this problem? While I agree that we should normally be in favor of creativity, not so in this field. The rules need to be firm and the SEC needs to exercise its rulemaking power to assure that corrective measures are adopted on a real time basis. As soon as the SEC sees that one of the so-called takeover sharpshooters has reinvented the wheel, the SEC should act swiftly to readjust the rules. As an adjunct to promptly bringing about the necessary rule adjustments, the SEC must also assume a greater role in monitoring and policing tender offers. The hands-off policy it has taken in recent years, while understandable at times, should be altered. The corporation finance and enforcement divisions should keep tighter reins over the process in individual cases. This point is proven by the discussion here today. Other than mentioning the Advisory Committee, the SEC has not been mentioned as a tender offer "player" by any of the panelists.

It seems to me that the acquiring company, as Larry mentioned so effectively, has a tremendous edge in a hostile takeover, because it has the time advantage in which to shape its first strike. It sits back there; it lines up its money and the people that it's going to take with it. This is a tremendous advantage over the target company which doesn't know what is coming. Adjustments need to be made with respect to getting an earlier public notice of the takeover. One method would be to immediately require notificiation after 5 percent of the stock has been acquired and then to stop any purchases over 5 percent during a cooling-off period. This period needs to be more than 48 hours so that people can think and digest what has happened. Also, the various state statutes that had a notification period might work on the federal level. It is argued that tender offers of necessity require quick action. There were, however, a number of state statutes with 20- or 30-day notification periods which did not seem to cause too much of a problem.

Furthermore, there is too ready access to our courts in tender battles. It is a misapplication of judicial resources for a corporation to be able to rearrange court dockets and delay cases that have been scheduled for years simply because it's involved in a tender offer. The SEC should be designated as the initial or principal forum in effect to act as referee as to whether there has been an abuse of the regulations.

The problem of greenmail must also be corrected. In this scenario the so-called acquirer comes in and takes a percentage of a company with the sole motive of forcing the board to buy back the stock of the company at a premium over what it paid. To correct this abuse, I think that a company should be precluded from buying back its stock unless an offer is made to all the shareholders and they are given the same opportunity. The credit area is another major problem. I disagree with the Advisory Committee's

---

44. *See* 549 F. Supp. 623 (D. Md. 1982).

position that there is no credit problem. While I am not an economist, I am quite concerned that a company about to take over another can go into a bank and get all the money it requires at a time when there is a tremendous rationing of credit with respect to the general public. The golden parachute problem, of course, makes no sense. If a corporation is going to give all of these benefits, then they ought to be given during a time when there's no tender offer on the horizon. Much has been said about the Pac-Man defense. This should not be done away with, because it can be used in situations like the very gallant, courageous, and successful fight raised by Martin Marietta.

Finally, the foreign takeover problem is particularly significant. It is a very dangerous situation when there is the possibility of a foreign takeover of a defense company. There has not been much said on this, but the area should be examined. There is almost no limitation on a foreign company that wants to takeover any corporation in this country. There might be something in the Federal Communications Commission (FCC) area, but there is little in the defense contracting area. To lessen this danger, the President should be given the right to deny the acquisition by a foreign organization or entity, either directly or indirectly, where such an organization seeks to obtain over 5 percent of a defense-contracting organization or any other organization that is important to the national defense of this nation.

PROFESSOR STEINBERG:

Thank you, Stan. Before we conclude, I'd like to thank certain individuals, in addition to our excellent panelists, for making this program possible. In particular, I extend my appreciation to Dean Michael Kelly of the Maryland Law School for his strong support and encouragement and to Ms. Mary Jo Rodney and Ms. Doreen Sekulow for their invaluable assistance in planning the program. Also, I extend my thanks to Mr. Kenneth Lundeen, Chairman of the Maryland State Bar Section of Corporations, Banking, and Business, for his very helpful cooperation and advice.

Conclusion

Perhaps no area in corporate/securities law has evoked such controversy as the subject of tender offers. As we have seen, the issues raised in this context have been vigorously debated. They include, for example, the procedural and mechanical aspects of the tender offer process, the legitimacy of defensive tactics as well as maneuvers employed by the offeror, the propriety and extent of state and federal regulation, and proposals for modification of the regulatory framework. Due to the diversity of viewpoints held and the continuing search for the ultimate resolution of these issues, the commentaries herein are, of course, not the "final word" on the subject. Rather the objectives of this project are to provide a greater understanding of the issues involved in the tender offer setting and to add meaningfully to the dialogue now taking place. It is hoped that, in seeking to meet these objectives, the book will serve as a useful source for the ongoing tender offer debate.

Bibliography

ACQUISITIONS

Books

Business Acquisitions: Planning and Practice (J. Herz & C. Baller eds., 1981).

Fox, Byron E. & Fox, Eleanor M. Corporate Acquisitions and Mergers (1968).

Freund, James C. Anatomy of a Merger: Strategies and Techniques for Negotiating Corporate Acquisitions (1980).

Articles

Bialkin, Kenneth J. & Kramer, M. J. *Lock-Ups, Proxy Contests, Counter-Tender Offers and Other Acquisition Techniques.* 14 Institute on Securities Regulation 189 (1983).

Chazen, Leonard. *Fairness from a Financial Point of View in Acquisitions of Public Companies: Is "Third Party Sale Value" the Appropriate Standard?* 36 Business Lawyer 1439 (1981).

Fleischer, Arthur, Jr., & Sternberg, Daniel. *Corporate Acquisitions.* 12 Review of Securities Regulation 937 (1979).

Freund, James C. & Easton, Richard I. *The Three Piece Suitor: An Alternative Approach to Negotiated Corporate Acquisitions.* 34 Business Lawyer 1679 (1979).

Freund, James C. & Greene, Edward F. *Substance over Form S-14: A Proposal to Reform SEC Regulation of Negotiated Acquisitions.* 36 Business Lawyer 1483 (1981).

Herzel, Leo, Sherck, Timothy C. & Colling, Dale E. *Sales and Acquisitions of Divisions.* 5 Corporation Law Review 3 (1982).

Note, *The Conflict between Managers and Shareholders in Diversifying Acquisitions: A Portfolio Theory Approach.* 88 Yale Law Journal 1238 (1979).

Note, *Partial and Selective Reacquisitions of Corporate Securities.* 15 California Western Law Review 264 (1979).

Schipper, Karen & Thompson, Rex. *Do Shareholders Benefit from Acquisition Programs?* 18 Mergers and Acquisitions 65 (1983).

Schulman, Stephen H. & Schenk, Alan. *Shareholders' Voting and Appraisal Rights in Corporate Acquisitions,* 38 Business Lawyer 1529 (1983).

Tobin, James M. & Maiwurm, James J. *Beachhead Acquisitions: Creating Waves in the Marketplace and Uncertainty in the Regulatory Framework.* 38 Business Lawyer 419 (1983).

BUSINESS JUDGMENT RULE

Articles

Arsht, S. Samuel. *The Business Judgment Rule Revisited.* 8 Hofstra Law Review 93 (1980).

Block, Dennis & Barton, Nancy. *The Business Judgment Rule as Applied to Stockholder Proxy Derivative Suits under the Securities Exchange Act.* 8 Securities Regulation Law Journal 99 (1980).

――――. *The Business Roundtable, the Role and Composition of the Board of Directors of the Large Publicly Owned Corporation.* 33 Business Law 2083 (1978).

Carney, William J. *Fundamental Corporate Changes, Minority Shareholders, and Business Purposes.* American Bar Foundation Research Journal 69 (1980).

Comment, *Director Liability under the Business Judgment Rule: Fact or Fiction?* 35 Southwestern Law Journal 775 (1981).

Comment, *The Misapplication of the Business Judgment Rule in Contests for Corporate Control.* 76 Northwestern University Law Review 980 (1982).

Fleischer, Arthur, Jr. *Business Judgment Rule Protects Takeover Targets.* Legal Times (Washington), April 14, 1980, at 15.

Gruenbaum, Samuel H. *Defensive Tactics and the Business Judgment Rule.* 4 Corporation Law Review 263 (1981).

Lynch, John J. *The Business Judgment Rule Reconsidered.* 17 Forum 452 (1981).

Note, *The Business Judgment Rule in Derivative Suits against Directors.* 65 Cornell Law Review 600 (1980).

Pitt, Harvey L. & Israel, Carol Herndon. *Recent Cases Chart Use of Business Judgment Rule.* Legal Times (Washington), Jan. 2, 1981, at 33.

Steinberg, Marc I. *The American Law Institute's Draft Restatement on Corporate Governance: The Business Judgment Rule, Related Principles, and Some General Observations.* 37 University of Miami Law Review 295 (1983).

――――. *Application of the Business Judgment Rule and Related Judicial Principles: Reflections from a Corporate Accountability Perspective.* 56 Notre Dame Lawyer 903 (1981).

Enforcement

Articles

Comment, *Equitable Remedies in SEC Enforcement Actions.* 123 University of Pennsylvania Law Review 1188 (1975).

Comment, *Scope of Review or Standards of Proof—Judicial Control of SEC Sanctions & Steadman v. SEC.* 93 Harvard Law Review 1845 (1980).

Eisenberg, Jonathan. *SEC Injunctive Actions.* 14 Review of Securities Regulation 901 (1981).

Farrand, James R. *Ancillary Remedies in SEC Civil Enforcement Suits.* 89 Harvard Law Review 1779 (1976).

Hazen, Thomas L. *Administrative Enforcement: An Evaluation of the Securities and Exchange Commission's Use of Injunctions and Other Enforcement Methods.* 31 Hastings Law Journal 427 (1979).

Long, Joseph C. *A Guide to the Investigative and Enforcement Provisions of the Uniform Securities Act.* 37 Washington and Lee Law Review 739 (1980).

Mathews, Arthur F. *Effective Defense of SEC Investigations: Laying the Foundation for Successful Disposition of Civil Administrative and Civil Proceedings.* 24 Emory Law Journal 567 (1975).

———. *Litigation and Settlement of SEC Adminstrative Proceedings.* 29 Catholic University Law Review 215 (1980).

Pitt, Harvey L. & Markham, Jerry W. *SEC Injunctive Actions.* 6 Review of Securities Regulation 955 (1973).

Steinberg, Marc I. *SEC and Other Permanent Injunctions—Standards for Their Imposition, Modification, and Dissolution.* 66 Cornell Law Review 27 (1980).

———. *Steadman v. SEC: Its Implications and Significance.* 6 Delaware Journal of Corporate Law 1 (1981).

Treadway, William E. *SEC Enforcement Techniques: Expanding and Exotic Forms of Ancillary Relief.* 32 Washington and Lee Law Review 637 (1975).

INSIDER TRADING

Articles

Allen, Samuel N. *The Scope of the Disclosure Duty under SEC Rule 14e-3.* 38 Washington and Lee Law Review 1058 (1981).

Anderson, Allison. *Fraud, Fiduciaries, and Insider Trading.* 10 Hofstra Law Review 341 (1982).

Barry, John F., III. *The Economics of Outside Information and Rule 10b-5.* 129 University of Pennsylvania Law Review 1307 (1981).

Branson, Douglas M. *Discourse on the Supreme Court Approach to SEC Rule 10b-5 and Insider Trading.* 30 Emory Law Journal 263 (1981).

Brom, Thomas. *Bad Tip? Sue Your Broker!* 4 California Lawyer 17 (1984).

Brudney, Victor. *Insiders, Outsiders, and Informational Advantages under the Federal Securities Laws.* 93 Harvard Law Review 322 (1979).

Brunelle, George. *Disgorgement of Insider Trading Profits in SEC Injunctive Proceedings.* 11 Securities Regulation Law Journal 371 (1984).

Carlton, Dennis W. & Fischel, Daniel R. *The Regulation of Insider Trading.* 35 Stanford Law Review 857 (1983).

Dooley, Michael P. *Enforcement of Insider Trading Restrictions.* 66 Virginia Law Review 1 (1980).

Easterbrook, Frank H. *Insider Trading, Secret Agents, Evidentiary Privileges, and the Production of Information.* Supreme Court Review 309 (1981).

Ferber, David. *Short-Swing Transactions under the Securities Exchange Act.* 16 Review of Securities Regulation 801 (1983).

Freeman, Milton V. *The Insider Trading Sanctions Bill: A Neglected Opportunity.* 4 Pace Law Review 221 (1984).

Gruenbaum, Samuel H. *Disclosure of Inside Information in Tender Offers.* 5 Corporation Law Review 357 (1982).

————. *The New Disclose or Abstain from Trading Rule: Has the SEC Gone Too Far?* 4 Corporation Law Review 350 (1981).

Haft, Robert J. *The Effect of Insider Trading Rules on the Internal Efficiency of the Large Corporation.* 80 Michigan Law Review 1051 (1982).

Heller, Harry. Chiarella, *SEC Rule 14e-3 and* Dirks: *Fairness versus Economic Theory.* 37 Business Lawyer 517 (1982).

Hiler, Bruce. Dirks v. SEC: *A Study in Cause and Effect.* 43 Maryland Law Review 292 (1984).

Karjala, Dennis S. *Statutory Regulation of Insider Trading in Impersonal Markets.* 1982 Duke Law Journal 627 (1982).

Koprucki, Jane Huffman. *Market Insiders' Duty under Section 10(b), Rule 10b-5 and Rule 14e-3 to Disclose Material Nonpublic Market Informtion.* 50 University of Cincinnati Law Review 558 (1981).

Langevoort, Donald C. *Insider Trading and the Fiduciary Principle: A Post-* Chiarella *Restatement.* 70 California Law Review 1 (1982).

Levmore, Saul. *Securities and Secrets: Insider Trading and the Law of Contracts.* 68 Virginia Law Review 117 (1982).

Morgan, Richard J. *The Insider Trading Rules after* Chiarella: *Are They Consistent with Statutory Policy?* 33 Hastings Law Journal 1407 (1982).

Morrison, Peter H. *Silence is Golden: Trading on Nonpublic Market Information.* 8 Securities Regulation Law Journal 21 (1980).

Note, *Damages for Insider Trading Violations in an Impersonal Market Context.* 7 Journal of Corporation Law 97 (1981).

Note, *Trading on Material, Nonpublic Information under Rule 14e-3.* 49 George Washington Law Review 539 (1981).

Rosenbaum, E., Simmonds, R. L., Simpson, J. H., & Vaidila, D. P. *Corporate and Investment Attitudes towards Insider Trading in Canada.* 8 Canada Business Law Journal 485 (1984).

Roth, Paul N. & Watterson, Paul N. *Section 16(b) Business Combination Transactions.* 16 Review of Securities Regulation 822 (1983).

Wang, William K. S. *Post-* Chiarella *Developments in Rule 10b-5.* 15 Review of Securities Regulation 956 (1982).

————. *Trading on Material Nonpublic Information on Impersonal Stock Markets: Who is Harmed and Who Can Sue Whom under SEC Rule 10b-5?* 54 Southern California Law Review 1217 (1981).

MERGERS

Books

Borden, Arthur M. Going Private (1981).

Freund, James C. Anatomy of a Merger: Strategies and Techniques for Negotiating Corporate Acquisitions (1980).

Kinter, Earl W. Primer on the Law of Mergers (1973).
Lipton, Martin & Steinberger, Erica H. Takeovers and Freezeouts (1984).

Articles

Ashman, Allan. *Delaware Stiffens Rules on Parent-Subsidiary Business Mergers.* 69 American Bar Association Journal 966 (1983).

Atkins, Peter A. *Defense against Creeping Acquisitions.* 13 Institute on Securities Regulation 57 (1982).

Austin, Douglas V. & Boucher, James R. *Tender Offer Update: 1982.* 17 Mergers & Acquisitions 48 (1982).

Berger, Carolyn & Allingham, Thomas J., II. *A New Light on Cash Out Mergers: Weinberger Eclipses Singer.* 39 Business Lawyer 1 (1983).

Bialkin, Kenneth J. & Kramer, M. J. *Lock-Ups, Proxy Contests, Counter-Tender Offers and Other Acquisition Techniques*, 14 Institute on Securities Regulation 189 (1983).

Brudney, Victor. *Equal Treatment in Corporate Distributions and Reorganizations.* 71 California Law Review 1072 (1983).

Brudney, Victor & Chirelstein, Marvin A. *Fair Shares in Corporate Mergers and Takeovers.* 88 Harvard Law Review 297 (1974).

———. *A Restatement of Corporate Freezeouts.* 87 Yale Law Journal 1354 (1978).

Cann, Jr., Wesley A. *The New Merger Guidelines: Is the Department of Justice Enforcing the Law?* 21 American Business Law Journal 1 (1983).

Carney, William. *Shareholder Coordination Costs, Shark Repellants and Takeover Mergers: The Case against Fiduciary Duties.* 1983 American Bar Foundation Research Journal 341 (1983).

Comment, *Rule 13e-3 and the Going-Private Dilemma: The SEC's Quest for a Substantive Fairness Doctrine.* 58 Washington University Law Quarterly 883 (1980).

Comment, *The Standard of Care Required of an Investment Banker to Minority Shareholders in a Cash-Out Merger.* 8 Delaware Journal of Corporate Law 98 (1983).

Connolly, Leonard L. *New Going-Private Rule.* 13 Review of Securities Regulation 975 (1980).

Elfin, Rodman M. *Changing Standards and the Future Course of Freezeout Mergers.* 5 Journal of Corporation Law 261 (1980).

Finkelstein, Jesse A. *Antitakeover Protection against Two-Tier and Partial Tender Offers: The Validity of Fair Price, Mandatory Bid and Flipover Provisions under Delaware Law.* 11 Securities Regulation Law Journal 291 (1984).

Fisher, Alan A., Lande, Robert H., & Vandale, Walter. *Afterward: Could a Merger Lead to Both a Monopoly and a Lower Price?* 71 California Law Review 1697 (1983)

Gannon, Christopher R. *An Evaluation of the SEC's New Going Private Rule.* 7 Journal of Corporation Law 55 (1981).

Greene, Edward F. *Corporate Freeze-Out Mergers: A Proposed Analysis.* 28 Stanford Law Review 487 (1976).

Grisham, Lynn A. & Rake, Doug. *Future Executive Bailouts: Will Golden Parachutes Fill the American Business Skies?* 14 Texas Tech Law Review 615 (1983).

Hammermesh, Lawrence A. *Going Private Merger after UOP.* 16 Review of Securities Regulation 943 (1983).

Harrison, Gilbert. *Retail Mergers*. 17 Mergers and Acquisitions 40 (1983).

Herzel, Leo & Colling, Dale. *Squeeze-Out Mergers in Delaware: The Delaware Supreme Court Decision in* Weinberger v. UOP, Inc. 7 Corporation Law Review 195 (1984).

Lipton, Lytle Susan. *High Technology Acquisitions*. 17 Mergers and Acquisitions 30 (1982).

Lorne, Simon M. *A Reappraisal of Fair Shares in Controlled Mergers*. 126 University of Pennsylvania Law Review 955 (1978).

Manning, Bayless. *The Shareholder's Appraisal Remedy: An Essay for Frank Coker*. 72 Yale Law Journal 223 (1962).

Meister, Kurt J. *Time for a Change in Anti-Trust Laws Affecting Mergers*. 3 Harvard Journal of Law and Public Policy 225 (1980).

Mirvis, Theodore N. *Two-Tier Pricing: Some Appraisal and Entire Fairness Evaluation Issues*. 35 Business Lawyer 485 (1983).

Moore, Charles L. *Corporate Freezeouts—1980*. 13 Review of Securities Regulation 939 (1980).

Nathan, Charles M. *Lock-ups and Leg-ups: The Search for Security in the Acquisitions Marketplace*. 13 Institute on Securities Regulation 1 (1982).

Note, *Corporations-Mergers-Delaware Redefines "Entire Fairness" Test for Cash-Out Mergers and Suggests More Liberal Appraisal Remedy*. 28 Villanova Law Review 1049 (1983).

Note, *Lock-up Options: Toward a State Law Standard*. 96 Harvard Law Review 1068 (1983).

Note, *Regulating Going Private Transactions: SEC Rule 13e-3*. 80 Columbia Law Review 782 (1980).

Payson, R. K. & Inskip, G. A. Weinberger v. UOP, Inc.: *Its Practical Significance in the Planning and Defense of Cash-out Mergers*. 8 Delaware Journal of Corporate Law 83 (1983).

Power, Daniel Joseph. *Acquisition Decision Making*. 18 Mergers and Acquisitions 63 (1983).

Prickett W. and Hanrahan, M. Weinberger v. UOP: *Delaware's Effort to Preserve a Level Playing Field for Cash-Out Mergers*. 8 Delaware Journal of Corporate Law 59 (1983).

Rothschild, Steven J. *Going Private*, Singer, *and Rule 13e-3: What Are the Standards for Fiduciaries?* 7 Securities Regulation Law Journal 195 (1979).

Sardell, William. *Cash-out Mergers*. 7 Corporation Law Review 72 (1984).

Schipper, Karen, & Thompson, Rex. *Do Shareholders Benefit from Acquisition Programs?* 18 Mergers and Acquisitions 65 (1983).

Schulman, Stephen H. & Schank, Alan. *Shareholder's Voting and Appraisal Rights in Corporate Acquisitions*. 38 Business Lawyer 1529 (1983).

Sparks, A. Gilchrist, III. *State Law Developments Concerning Defensive Techniques*. 14 Institute on Securities Regulation 229 (1983).

Steinberg, Marc I. *State Court Decisions after* Santa Fe. 8 Securities Regulation Law Journal 79 (1981).

Steinberg, Marc I. & Lindahl, Evalyn. *The New Law of Squeeze-Out Mergers*. 62 Washington University Law Quarterly 351 (1984).

Watson, Fred J. & Chung Kwang S. *Do Mergers Make Money? A Research Summary*. 18 Mergers and Acquisitions 40 (1983).

Weiss, Elliott J. *Balancing Interests in Cash-Out Mergers: The Promise of* Weinberger v. UOP, Inc. 8 Delaware Journal of Corporate Law 1 (1983).
————. *The Law of Take-out Mergers:* Weinberger v. UOP, Inc. *Ushers in Phase Six.* 4 Cardozo Law Review 245 (1983).
Werden, Gregory J. *Market Delineation and the Justice Department's Merger Guidelines.* 1983 Duke Law Journal 419 (1983).

PROXY CONTESTS

Books

Aranow, Edward Ross, & Einhorn, Herbert A. Proxy Contests for Corporate Control (1968).
Proxy Contests and Battles for Corporate Control (PLI, 1981).
Proxy Litigation and Contests (Law Journal Seminars Press, 1981).

Articles

Eisenberg, Jonathan. *Current Application of the Shareholder Proposal Rule.* 15 Review of Securities Regulation 903 (1982).
Elliot, Robert M. *The Remarriage of Corporate Ownership and Management Accountability: Rebuilding the Foundations of Corporate Government.* 3 University of Bridgeport Law Review 49 (1981).
Hazen, Thomas L. *Corporate Management and the Federal Securities Act's Antifraud Provisions: A Familiar Path with Some New Detours.* 20 Boston College Law Review 819 (1979).
Note, *Negligence or Scienter? The Appropriate Standard of Liability for Outside Accountants for Misleading Proxy Statements under Section 14(a) of the Securities Exchange Act of 1934.* 7 University of Dayton Law Review 437 (1982).
Note, *Proxy Regulations Ensuring Accurate Disclosure through Negligence Standard.* 50 Fordham Law Review 1423 (1982).
Schwartz, Michael W. & Tillman, Sharon L. *Proxy Contest Developments: Bust-up Proposals Designed to Force Corporate Sale or Liquidation Have Generated Some Novel Tactics. The Outcome is Determined by Litigation.* 16 Review of Securities Regulation 789 (1983).
Steinberg, Marc I. *Fiduciary Duties and Disclosure Obligations in Proxy and Tender Contests for Corporate Control.* 30 Emory Law Journal 169 (1981).

RICO

Articles

Blakey, Robert. *The RICO Civil Fraud Action in Context: Reflections on* Bennett v. Berg. 58 Notre Dame Law Review 237 (1982).
Blakey, Robert & Gettings, Brian. *Racketeer Influenced and Corrupt Organizations Act (RICO): Basic Concepts—Criminal and Civil Remedies.* 53 Temple Law Quarterly 1009 (1980).

Bradley, Craig M. *Racketeers, Congress, and the Courts: Analysis of RICO.* 65 Iowa Law Review 837 (1980).

Comment, *Civil RICO Actions in Commercial Litigation: Racketeer or Business-man?* 36 Southwestern Law Journal 425 (1982).

Glanz, Michael N. *RICO and Securities Fraud: A Workable Limitation.* 83 Columbia Law Review 1513 (1983).

Long, Louis C. *Treble Damages for Violations of Securities Laws: A Suggested Analysis and Application of the RICO Civil Cause of Action.* 85 Dickinson Law Review 201 (1981).

MacIntosh, Jeffrey. *Racketeer Influenced and Corrupt Organizations Act: Powerful New Tool of the Defrauded Securities Plaintiff.* 31 Kansas Law Review 7 (1982).

Morrison, Peter H. *Old Bottle—Not So New Wine: Treble Damages in Actions under the Federal Securities Laws.* 10 Securities Regulation Law Journal 67 (1982).

Note, *Application of the Racketeer Influenced and Corrupt Organizations Act (RICO) to Securities Violations.* 8 Journal of Corporation Law 411 (1983).

Note, *Civil RICO: The Temptation and Impropriety of Judicial Restrictions.* 85 Harvard Law Review 1101 (1982).

Note, *RICO and the Liberal Construction Clause.* 66 Cornell Law Review 144 (1980).

Pickholz, Marvin & Friedman, Paul. *Civil RICO Actions.* 14 Review of Securities Regulation 965 (1981).

Strafer, Richard G., Massumi, Ronald R. & Skolnick, Holly R. *Civil RICO in the Public Interest: "Everybody's Darling."* 19 American Criminal Law Review 655 (1982).

Tarlow, Barry. *RICO: The New Darling of the Prosecutor's Nursery.* 49 Fordham Law Review 165 (1980).

SANTA FE AND ITS PROGENY

Articles

Block, Dennis J. & Schwarzfeld, Neal. *Corporate Mismanagement and Breach of Fiduciary Duty after* Santa Fe v. Green. 2 Corporation Law Review 91 (1979).

Campbell, Rutherford B., Jr. Santa Fe Industries, Inc. v. Green: *An Analysis Two Years Later.* 30 Maine Law Review 187 (1979).

Comment, Santa Fe Industries v. Green *Revisited: A Critique of Circuit Court Application of Rule 10b-5 to Breaches of Fiduciary Duty to Minority Shareholders.* 28 UCLA Law Review 564 (1981).

Ferrara, Ralph C., & Steinberg, Marc I. *The Interplay between State Corporation and Federal Securities Law:* Santa Fe, Singer, Burks, Maldonado, *Their Progeny, and Beyond.* 7 Delaware Journal of Corporate Law 1 (1982).

———. *A Reappraisal of* Santa Fe: *Rule 10b-5 and the New Federalism.* 129 University of Pennsylvania Law Review 263 (1980).

Gorman, Thomas O. *At the Intersection of Supreme Avenue and Circuit Street. The Focus of Section 10(b) and* Santa Fe's *Footnote Fourteen.* 7 Journal of Corporation Law 199 (1981).

Hazen, Thomas L. *Corporate Mismanagement and the Federal Securities Act's Anti-Fraud Provisions: A Familiar Path with Some New Detours.* 20 Boston College Law Review 819 (1979).

Jacobs, William R. *Rule 10b-5 and Self Dealing by Corporate Fiduciaries: An Analysis.* 48 University of Cincinnati Law Review 643 (1979).

Krendl, Cathy S. *Progeny of* Santa Fe v. Green: *An Analysis of the Elements of a Fiduciary Duty Claim under Rule 10b-5 and a Case for a Federal Corporation Law.* 59 North Carolina Law Review 231 (1981).

Note, Goldberg v. Meridor: *The Second Circuit's Resurrection of Rule 10b-5 Liability for Breaches of Corporate Fiduciary Duties to Minority Shareholders.* 64 Virginia Law Review 765 (1978).

Note, *Liability for Corporate Mismanagement under Rule 10b-5 after* Santa Fe v. Green. 27 Wayne Law Review 269 (1978).

Note, *Suits for Breach of Fiduciary Duty under Rule 10b-5 after* Santa Fe Industries, Inc. v. Green. 91 Harvard Law Review 1874 (1978).

Roberts, William M. *The Status of Minority Shareholders' Remedies for Oppression after* Santa Fe *and* Singer *and the Question of "Reasonable Investment Expectation" Valuation.* 6 Delaware Journal of Corporate Law 16 (1981).

Sherrard, Thomas J. *Federal Judicial and Regulatory Responses to* Santa Fe Industries, Inc. v. Green. 35 Washington and Lee Law Review 695 (1978).

Steinberg, Marc I. *State Court Decisions after* Santa Fe. 8 Securities Regulation Law Journal 79 (1981).

SECURITIES AND EXCHANGE COMMISSION

Books

Karmel, Roberta S. Regulation by Prosecution: The Securities and Exchange Commission versus Corporate America (1982).

Kripke, Homer. The SEC and Corporate Disclosure: Regulation in Search of a Purpose (1979).

Phillips, Susan M. & Zecher, J. Richard. The SEC and the Public Interest (1981).

Seligman, Joel. The Transformation of Wall Street: A History of the Securities and Exchange Commission and Modern Corporate Finance (1982).

Articles

Steinberg, Marc I. *The Securities and Exchange Commission's Administrative, Enforcement, and Legislative Programs and Policies—Their Influence on Corporate Internal Affairs.* 58 Notre Dame Law Review 173 (1982).

Wolfson, Nicholas. *A Critique of the Securities and Exchange Commission.* 39 Emory Law Journal 119 (1981).

TENDER OFFERS

Books

Aranow, Edward Ross, Einhorn, Herbert A. & Berlstein, George. Developments in Tender Offers for Corporate Control (1977).

Axinn, Stephen M., Fogg, Blaine W. & Stoll, Neal R. Acquisitions under the Hart-Scott-Rodino Antitrust Improvements Act (1979).

Bloomenthal, Harold S. Securities and Federal Corporate Law (1980).

Bromberg, Alan & Lowenfels, Louis. Securities Fraud and Commodities Fraud (1983).
Fleischer, Arthur. Tender Offers: Defense, Responses and Planning (1983).
Lipton, Martin L. & Steinberger, Erica H. Takeovers and Freezeouts (1984).
Steinberg, Marc I. Corporate Internal Affairs: A Corporate and Securities Law Perspective (1983).
————. Securities Regulation: Liabilities and Remedies (1984).

Articles

Generally

Arsht, S. Samuel. *The Delaware Takeover Statute: Special Problems for Directors*. 32 Business Lawyer 1461 (1977).

Austin, Douglas V. *Tender Offer Movement Off in 1982*. National Law Journal, Jan. 16, 1984, at 15.

Bebchuck, Lucian A. *The Case for Facilitating Competing Tender Offers*. 95 Harvard Law Review 1028 (1982).

Block, Dennis J. & Miller, Yvette. *The Responsibilities and Obligations of Corporate Directors in Takeover Contests*. 11 Securities Regulation Law Journal 44 (1983).

Bloomenthal, Harold S. *The New Tender Offer Regimen, State Regulation, and Preemption*. 30 Emory Law Journal 35 (1981).

Brudney, Victor. *A Note on Chilling Tender Solicitations*. 21 Rutgers Law Review 609 (1967).

Brudney, Victor & Chirelstein, Marvin A. *A Restatement of Corporate Freezeouts*. 87 Yale Law Journal 1354 (1978).

Brunelle, George. *The Lost Tender Offer Opportunity and Section 14(e)*. 9 Securities Regulation Law Journal 285 (1981).

Cohn, Stuart R. *Tender Offers and the Sale of Control: An Analogue to Determine the Validity of Target Management Defensive Measures*. 66 Iowa Law Review 475 (1981).

Comment, *Buying Out Insurgent Shareholders with Corporate Funds*. 70 Yale Law Journal 308 (1960).

Comment, *Preliminary Injunctive Relief and Tender Offers: An Analysis under the Williams Act*. 49 George Washington Law Review 563 (1981).

Comment, *Senate Bill 510 and the Cash Tender Offer*. 14 Wayne Law Review 568 (1968).

DeMott, Deborah A. *Current Issues in Tender Offer Regulation: Lessons from the British*. 58 New York University Law Review 945 (1983).

Easterbrook, Frank H. & Fischel, Daniel R. *Antitrust Suits by Targets of Tender Offers*. 80 Michigan Law Review 1155 (1982).

————. *Auctions and Sunk Costs in Tender Offers*. 35 Stanford Law Review 1 (1982).

————. *The Proper Role of a Target's Management in Responding to a Tender Offer*. 94 Harvard Law Review 1161 (1981).

————. *Takeover Bids, Defensive Tactics and Shareholder's Welfare*. 36 Business Lawyer 1733 (1981).

Easton, Richard L. & Freund, James C. *The Three-Piece Suitor: An Alternative Approach to Negotiated Corporate Acquisitions*. 34 Business Lawyer 1679 (1979).

Fallon, W. Gerard. *Hostile Tender Offers and Injunctive Relief for 14(e) Manipulation Claims: Developments After* Mobil Corp. v. Marathon Oil Co. 40 Washington and Lee Law Review 1175 (1983).

Fenno, Nathan R. *Tender Offer Decisions: Effect of the Business Judgment Rule.* 45 Albany Law Review 1122 (1981).

Flom, Joseph H. *Forcing a Friendly Offer.* 32 Business Lawyer 1319 (1977).

Friedenberg, Ellen. *Jaws III: The Impropriety of Shark-Repellant Amendments as a Takeover Defense.* 7 Delaware Journal of Corporate Law 32 (1982).

Gilson, Ronald J. *The Case against Shark Repellant Amendments: Structural Limitations on the Enabling Concept.* 34 Stanford Law Review 775 (1982).

———. *A Structural Approach to Corporations: The Case against Defensive Tactics in Tender Offers.* 33 Stanford Law Review 819 (1981).

Glenn, D. Roger. *Rethinking the Regulation of Open Market and Privately Negotiated Stock Transactions under the Securities Exchange Act of 1934.* 8 Journal of Corporation Law 41 (1982).

Goldberg, Arthur J. *Regulation of Hostile Tender Offers: A Dissenting View and Recommended Reforms.* 43 Maryland Law Review 225 (1984).

Gruenbaum, Samuel H. *Defensive Tactics and the Business Judgment Rule.* 4 Corporation Law Review 263 (1981).

Gutman, Karoly Sziklas. *Tender Offer Defensive Tactics and the Business Judgment Rule.* 58 New York University Law Review 621 (1983).

Herzel, Leo & Schmidt, John R. *Is There Anything Wrong with Hostile Tender Offers?* 6 Corporation Law Review 329 (1983).

Hochman, Stephen A. & Folger, Oscar D. *Deflecting Takeovers: Charter and By-Law Techniques.* 34 Business Lawyer 537 (1979).

Jarrell, Gregg A. & Bradley, Michael. *The Economic Effects of Federal and State Regulations of Cash Tender Offers.* 23 Journal of Law and Economics 371 (1980).

Johnson, Henry F. *Disclosure in Tender Offer Transactions: The Dice Are Still Loaded.* 42 University of Pittsburgh Law Review 1 (1980).

Jupiter, Jay A. *An Analysis of Effects to Avoid Williams Act Requirements.* 9 Securities Regulation Law Journal 259 (1981).

Kelly, Thomas M., Maciejezyk, John M. & Wolfe, Sherrie. *Lock-up Options Employed by Target Corporations as a Defensive Technique to Unwanted Takeovers.* 58 Notre Dame Law Review 926 (1983).

Kreider, Gary. *Fortress without Foundation? Ohio Takeover Act II.* 52 University of Cincinnati Law Review 108 (1983).

Leiser, Harvey. *The SEC: A Black Knight for Target Management. An Analysis of Some Recent SEC Rules and Proposed Rules.* 7 Journal of Corporation Law 21 (1981).

Lipton, Martin. *Takeover Bids in the Target's Boardroom.* 35 Business Lawyer 101 (1979).

Loewenstein, Mark J. *Section 14(e) of the Williams Act and the Rule 10b-5 Comparisons.* 71 Georgetown Law Journal 1311 (1983).

Lowenstein, Louis. *Pruning Deadwood in Hostile Takeovers: A Proposal for Legislation.* 83 Columbia Law Review 249 (1983).

———. *Regulation of Tender Offers: A Critical Comment.* 16 Review of Securities Regulation 831 (1983).

Lynch, Gary G. & Steinberg, Marc I. *The Legitimacy of Defensive Tactics in Tender Offers*. 64 Cornell Law Review 901 (1979).

McIntyre, Julie C. *Shareholder's Recourse under Federal Securities Law against Management for Opposing Advantageous Tender Offers*. 34 Business Lawyer 1283 (1979).

McLaughlin, David J. *The Myth of the Golden Parachute*. 17 Mergers and Acquisitions 47 (1982).

Manges, Gary. *SEC Regulation of Issuer and Third Party Tender Offers*. 8 Securities Regulation Law Journal 275 (1981).

Manne, Henry G. *Cash Tender Offers for Shares: A Reply to Chairman Cohen*. 1967 Duke Law Journal 237 (1967).

Mencher, Eric M. *Section 14(e) of the Williams Act: Can There Be Manipulation with Full Disclosure or Was the* Mobil Court Running on Empty? 12 Hofstra Law Review 159 (1983).

Nathan, Charles M. & Ziegler, Richard F. *Issuer Stock Repurchases*. 14 Review of Securities Regulation 9 (1981).

Note, *Bank Fiduciary Duty and Takeovers*: Washington Steel Corp. v. TW Corp. 34 Southwestern Law Journal 739 (1980).

Note, *Bank Financing of Hostile Takeovers of Borrowers:* Washington Steel Corp. v. TW Corp. 43 Harvard Law Review 440 (1979).

Note, *Bank Financing of Involuntary Takeovers of Corporate Customers: A Breach of Fiduciary Duty?* 53 Notre Dame Lawyer 827 (1978).

Note, *The Business Judgment Rule in Derivative Suits against Directors*. 65 Cornell Law Review 600 (1980).

Note, *Lock-up Options: Toward a State Law Standard*. 96 Harvard Law Review 1068 (1983).

Note, *The Propriety of Judicial Deference to Corporate Boards of Directors*. 96 Harvard Law Review 1894 (1983).

Note, *Securities Law: Implied Causes of Action under Section 14(e) of the Williams Act*. 66 Minnesota Law Review 865 (1982).

Note, *Target Defensive Tactics as Manipulative under Section 14(e)*. 84 Columbia Law Review 228 (1984).

Phalon, Richard. *Tipping the Takeover Balance of Power*. 16 Mergers and Acquisitions 52 (1982).

Pitt, Harvey L. & Israel, Carol H. *Recent Cases Chart Use of Business Judgment Rule*. Legal Times (Washington), Jan. 29, 1981, at 33.

Pozen, Robert C. *Takeover Can Pose Tough Conflict for Officer-Trustee*. Legal Times (Washington), Jan. 11, 1982, at 18.

Prentice, Robert A. *Target Board Abuse of Defensive Tactics: Can Federal Law Be Mobilized to Overcome the Business Judgment Rule?* 8 Journal of Corporation Law 337 (1983).

Riger, Martin. *On Golden Parachutes: Ripcords or Ripoffs? Some Comments on Special Termination Agreements*. 3 Pace Law Review 15 (1982).

Roche, John J., Berkery, Rosemary T. & Hinman, William H. *Hostile Takeovers of Banks*. National Law Journal, Aug. 9, 1982, at 17.

Rosenzweig, Victor M. *The Legality of "Lock-Ups" and Other Responses of Directors to Hostile Takeover Bids or Stock Aggregations*. 10 Securities Regulation Law Journal 291 (1983).

Rowe, Richard H. *Tender Offer Regulations: Changing the Game Rules*. Legal Times (Washington), Dec. 31, 1979, at 9.

Scriggins, L. P. & Clarke, David. *Takeovers and the 1983 Maryland Fair Price Legislation*. 43 Maryland Law Review 266 (1984).

Silberberg, Henry J. & Pollock, David C. *Are the Courts Expanding the Meaning of "Manipulation" under the Federal Securities Laws?* 11 Securities Regulation Law Journal 265 (1983).

————. *"Manipulation": Should It Be Interpreted to Have a Different Meaning in Tender Offer than in 10b-5 Cases?* 12 Securities Regulation Law Journal 69 (1984).

Soderquist, Larry D. *Reconciling Shareholders' Rights and Corporate Responsibility: Close and Small Public Corporations*. 33 Vanderbilt Law Review 1387 (1980).

Sommer, A. A., Jr. *The SEC Advisory Committee on Tender Offers: Whatever Happened to State Law?* 16 Review of Securities Regulation 833 (1983).

Sommer, A. A., Jr., & Feller, Lloyd. *Takeover Rules: A Cohesive Comprehensive Code*. Legal Times (Washington) Dec. 17, 1979, at 18.

Sowards, Hugh L. & Mofsky, James S. *Corporate Take-Over Bids: Gap in Federal Securities Regulation*. 41 St. John's Law Review 499 (1967).

Stanford, Peter A. *The Future of Lock-ups after* Mobil v. Marathon Oil. 27 St. Louis University Law Journal 261 (1983).

Steinberg, Marc I. *Fiduciary Duties and Disclosure Obligations in Proxy and Tender Contests for Corporate Control*. 30 Emory Law Journal 169 (1981).

————. *The Pennsylvania Anti-Takeover Legislation*. 12 Securities Regulation Law Journal 184 (1984).

Steinbrink, William H. *Management's Response to the Takeover Attempt*. 28 Case Western Reserve Law Review 882 (1978).

Tobin, James M. & Maiwurm, James J. *Beachhead Acquisitions: Creating Waves in the Marketplace and Uncertainty in the Regulatory Framework*. 38 Business Lawyer 419 (1983).

Turner, Jeffrey Stephen. *Should Tender Offer Arbitrage Be Regulated?* 1978 Duke Law Journal 1000 (1978).

Tyson, William C. & August, Andrew A. *The Williams Act after RICO: Has the Balance Tipped in Favor of Incumbent Management?* 35 Hastings Law Journal 53 (1983).

Walsh, Patrick D. *Defensive Tactics and the Fiduciary Obligations of the Target Board of Directors*. 7 Journal of Corporation Law 579 (1982).

Weiss, Elliot J. *Defensive Responses to Tender Offers and the Williams Act's Prohibition against Manipulation*. 35 Vanderbilt Law Review 1087 (1982).

Williams, Harold M. *Role of Directors in Takeover Offers*. 13 Review of Securities Regulation 963 (1980).

Antitakeover Measures

Finkelstein, Jesse A. *Antitakeover Protection against Two-Tier and Partial Tender Offers: The Validity of Fair Price, Mandatory Bid and Flip Over Provisions under Delaware Law*. 11 Securities Regulation Law Journal 291 (1984).

Friedenberg, Ellen S. *Jaws III: The Impropriety of Shark-Repellant Amendments as a Takeover Defense*. 7 Delaware Journal of Corporate Law 32 (1982).

Gilson, Ronald J. *The Case against Shark Repellant Amendments: Structural Limitations on the Enabling Concept.* 34 Stanford Law Review 775 (1982).

Johnson, Henry F. *Anti-Takeover Actions and Defenses: Business Judgment or Breach of Duty?* 28 Villanova Law Review 51 (1982).

Moran, Marjery R. *Anti-Takeover Charter Changes Upheld by Courts.* Legal Times (Washington), March 24, 1980, at 22.

Rose, Ira B. & Collins, Richard S. *Porcupine Proposals.* 12 Review of Securities Regulation 477 (1979).

Sargent, Patrick C. *Anti-Takeover Maneuvers: Developments in Defense Tactics and Target Actions for Injunctive Relief.* 35 Southwestern Law Journal 617 (1981).

Antitrust Considerations

Axinn, Stephen M., Fogg, Blain V. & Stoll, Neal R. *Contests for Corporate Control under the New Law of Preacquisition Notification.* 21 Corporate Practice Commentator 547 (1980).

Easterbrook, Frank H. & Fischel, Daniel R. *Antitrust Suits by Targets of Tender Offers.* 80 Michigan Law Review 1155 (1982).

Fleischer, Arthur. *Buy or Be Bought: The Antitrust Defense.* 18 Mergers and Acquisitions 50 (1983).

Fraidin, Stephen & Franco, Joseph. *Lock-up Arrangements.* 14 Review of Securities Regulation 821 (1981).

Handler, Milton. *Antitrust: Myth and Reality in an Inflationary Era.* 50 New York University Law Review 211 (1975).

Kintner, Earl W., Griffin, Joseph P., & Goldston, David B. *The Hart-Scott-Rodino Antitrust Improvements Act of 1976: An Analysis.* 46 George Washington Law Review 1 (1977).

Lesser, Henry & McDonald, David G. *Premerger Notification: An Update.* 15 Review of Securities Regulation 967 (1982).

Millstein, Ira M. *Antitrust Aspects of Takeovers and Mergers: The Hart-Scott-Rodino Antitrust Improvements Act of 1976: A Panel.* 32 Business Lawyer 1517 (1977).

Sidak, Joseph Gregory. *Antitrust Preliminary Injunctions in Hostile Tender Offers.* 30 University of Kansas Law Review 491 (1982).

Titus, John Warren. *Stop, Look and Listen: Premerger Notification under the Hart-Scott-Rodino Antitrust Improvements Act.* 1979 Duke Law Journal 355 (1979).

Tomlinson, Timothy. *Premerger Notification under Hart-Scott-Rodino: Valuation of Assets and Voting Securities.* 26 UCLA Law Review 1321 (1979).

Banks and Financial Intermediaries

Comment, *Bank Financing of Hostile Takeovers of Borrowers*: Washington Steel Corp. v. TW Corp. 93 Harvard Law Review 153 (1980).

Comment, *Bank Use of Confidential Information to Evaluate Applications for Financing on Tender Offers*: Washington Steel Corp. v. TW Corp. 61 Boston University Law Review 245 (1981).

Cox, Charles & Linten, Albert. *Tender Offers*: Washington Steel Corp. v. TW Corp. 6 Journal of Corporation Law 225 (1980).

Greenberg, Stephen J., Mack, William C. & Scholte, Jeffrey L. *The Obligations of Banks in the Public Securities Markets.* 1980 Duke Law Journal 1063 (1980).

Hawke, Jr., John, Adler, Howard B. & Kaplan, Steven L. *Banks' Immunity to Hostile Takeovers Has Dissolved*. Legal Times (Washington), Aug. 10, 1981, at 45.

Herzel, Leo & Rosenberg, Richard M. *Loans to Finance Tender Offers: The Banks Legal Problems*. 96 Banking Law Journal 676 (1979).

Lowenfeld, Andreas F. *Bank Secrecy and Insider Trading: The* Banca della Svizzera Italian *Case*. 15 Review of Securities Regulation 942 (1982).

Mears, Rona R. *Bank Fiduciary Duty and Takeovers:* Washington Steel Corp. v. TW Corp. 34 Southwestern Law Journal 739 (1980).

Note, *The Responsibilities of Banks in Financing Tender Offer Takeovers of Customers*. 48 University of Chicago Law Review 439 (1981).

Constitutional Considerations

Kreider, Gary. *Fortress without Foundation? Ohio Takeover Act II*. 52 University of Cincinnati Law Review 108 (1983).

Langevoort, Donald. *State Tender Offer Legislation: Interests, Effects, and Political Competency*. 62 Cornell Law Review 213 (1977).

Sargent, Mark. *On the Validity of State Takeover Regulation: State Responses to* MITE *and* Kidwell. 42 Ohio State Law Journal 689 (1981).

Scriggins, L. P. & Clarke, David. *Takeovers and the 1983 Maryland Fair Price Legislation*. 43 Maryland Law Review 266 (1984).

Steinberg, Marc I. *The Pennsylvania Anti-Takeover Legislation*. 12 Securities Regulation Law Journal 184 (1984).

Wolff, Samuel. *The Unconstitutionality of the Arkansas Tender Offer Statute*. 36 Arkansas Law Review 233 (1983).

Definition Thereof

Glenn, D. Roger. *Rethinking the Regulation of Open Market and Privately Negotiated Stock Transactions under the Securities Exchange Act of 1934*. 8 Journal of Corporation Law 41 (1982).

Junewicz, James J. *SEC Blocked in Effort to Limit Takeover Defense Tactic*. Legal Times (Washington), May 14, 1984, at 31.

Korval, Neal I. *Defining Tender Offers: Resolving a Decade of Dilemma*. 54 St. John's Law Review 520 (1980).

Mather, Steve. *The Elusive Definition of a Tender Offer*. 7 Journal of Corporation Law 503 (1982).

Murphy, Lewis F. *Cash Tender Offers: A Proposed Definition*. 31 University of Florida Law Review 694 (1979).

Note, *The Developing Meaning of "Tender Offers" under the SEC Exchange Act of 1934*. 86 Harvard Law Review 1250 (1973).

Note, *What is a Tender Offer?* 37 Washington and Lee Law Review 908 (1980).

Sutherland, Colleen. *The Tender Offer Trap: A Transactional Proposal*. 45 Albany Law Review 464 (1981).

Wurzinger, Ida C. *Toward a Definition of Tender Offer*. 19 Harvard Journal on Legislation 191 (1982).

Golden Parachutes

Comment, *Golden Parachutes: A Perk That Boards Should Scrutinize Carefully*. 67 Marquette Law Review 293 (1984).

Herzel, Leo. *Golden Parachute Contracts: Analysis.* National Law Journal, Feb. 15, 1982, at 20.

Masters, Kim. *Execs' "Golden Parachutes" Await First Court Challenges.* Legal Times (Washington), Nov. 2, 1981, at 1.

Note, *Golden Parachutes: Executive Employment Contracts.* 40 Washington and Lee Law Review 1117 (1983).

Riger, Martin. *On Golden Parachutes: Ripcords or Ripoffs? Some Comments on Special Termination Agreements.* 3 Pace Law Review 15 (1982).

Lock-Ups

Bialkin, Kenneth J. *Court Casts Cloud over Option Tactic in Takeovers.* Legal Times (Washington), Jan. 11, 1982, at 19.

Bloomenthal, Harold S. *Lock-ups: Mobil Wins Battle; Loses War.* 4 Securities and Federal Corporation Law Report 97 (1982).

Brunelle, George. *Using the Lock-up to Defend against a Hostile Tender Offer: When Is It Manipulative?* 11 Securities Regulation Law Journal 76 (1983).

Fleischer, Arthur J. & Raymond, Elizabeth A. *Lockups Ease Acquisition, May Forestall Bidding War.* Legal Times (Washington), Oct. 24, 1983, at 13.

Fraidin, Stephen & Franco, Joseph. *Lock-Up Arrangements.* 14 Review of Securities Regulation 821 (1981).

Lewkow, Victor I. & Forrest, Neil P. *The Lock-Up under Exchange Act Section 14(e).* National Law Journal, March 26, 1984, at 15.

Nathan, Charles M. *Lock-Ups and Leg-Ups: The Search for Security in the Acquisition Market Place.* 13 Institute on Securities Regulation 1 (1982).

Note, *Lock-Up Options: Toward a State Law Standard.* 96 Harvard Law Review 1068 (1983).

Stanford, Peter A. *The Future of Lock-ups after* Mobil v. Marathon. 27 St. Louis University Law Journal 261 (1983).

Management's Conduct

Cohn, Stuart. *Tender Offers and the Sale of Control: An Analogue to Determine the Validity of Target Management Defensive Measures.* 66 Iowa Law Review 475 (1981).

Easterbrook, Frank H. & Fischel, Daniel R. *The Proper Role of a Target's Management in Responding to a Tender Offer.* 94 Harvard Law Review 1161 (1981).

————. *Takeover Bids, Defensive Tactics, and Shareholders' Welfare.* 36 Business Lawyer 1733 (1981).

Gelfond, Richard L. & Sebastian, Steven B. *Reevaluating the Duties of Target Management in a Hostile Tender Offer.* 60 Boston University Law Review 403 (1980).

Gilson, Ronald J. *Seeking Competitive Bids versus Pure Passivity in Tender Offer Defense.* 35 Stanford Law Review 51 (1982).

————. *A Structural Approach to Corporations: The Case against Defensive Tactics in Tender Offers.* 33 Stanford Law Review 819 (1981).

Hazen, Thomas. *Corporate Mismanagement and the Federal Securities Acts' Antifraud Provisions: A Familiar Path with Some New Detours.* 20 Boston College Law Review 819 (1979).

Herzel, Leo, Schmidt, John R. & Davis, Scott J. *Why Corporate Directors Have a Right to Resist Tender Offers.* 3 Corporation Law Review 107 (1980).

Lipton, Martin. *Takeover Bids in the Target's Boardroom.* 35 Business Lawyer 101 (1979).

————. *Takeover Bids in the Target's Boardroom: An Update after One Year.* 36 Business Lawyer 1017 (1981).

Lynch, Gary G. & Steinberg, Marc I. *The Legitimacy of Defensive Tactics in Tender Offers.* 64 Cornell Law Review 901 (1979).

Note, *Tender Offer Decisions: Effect of the Business Judgment Rule.* 45 Albany Law Review 1122 (1981).

Steinbrink, William H. *Management's Response to a Takeover Attempt.* 28 Case Western Reserve Law Review 882 (1978).

Williams, Harold M. *Role of Directors in Takeover Offers.* 13 Review of Securities Regulation 963 (1980).

Private Litigation

Aranow, Edward R., Einhorn, Herbert A. & Berlstein, George. *Standing to Sue to Challenge Violations of the Williams Act.* 32 Business Lawyer 1755 (1977).

Loewenstein, Mark J. *Section 14(e) of the Williams Act and the Rule 10b-5 Comparisons.* 71 Georgetown Law Journal 1311 (1983).

Note, *Implied Private Rights of Action for Equitable Relief under Section 13(d) of the Williams Act.* 1981 Utah Law Review 869 (1981).

Note, *An Implied Right of Action for Issuers under Section 13(d) of the Securities Exchange Act of 1934.* 61 Boston University Law Review 933 (1981).

Note, *Private Litigation under the Williams Act: Standing to Sue, Elements of a Claim and Remedies.* 7 Journal of Corporation Law 545 (1982).

Note, *Section 13(d) of the '34 Act: The Inference of a Private Cause of Action for a Stock Issuer.* 28 Washington and Lee Law Review 971 (1981).

Pitt, Harvey L. *Standing to Sue under the Williams Act after Chris Craft: A Leaky Ship on Troubled Waters.* 34 Business Lawyer 117 (1978).

Steinberg, Marc I. *Fiduciary Duties and Disclosure Obligations in Proxy and Tender Contests for Corporate Control.* 30 Emory Law Journal 169 (1981).

Proration

Greene, Edward F. & Nathan, Charles M. *The SEC's New Prorationing Rule Will Change "Partial" Tender Offers.* National Law Journal, Jan. 10, 1983, at 38.

Lederman, Lawrence & Vlahakis, Patricia. *Pricing and Proration in Tender Offers.* 14 Review of Securities Regulation 813 (1981).

Note, *Rulemaking under Section 14(e) of the Exchange Act: The SEC Exceeds Its Reach in Attempting to Pull the Plug on Multiple Proration Pools.* 36 Vanderbilt Law Review 1313 (1983).

Pozen, Robert C. *Extended Proration Time for Tender Offers Proposed.* Legal Times (Washington), July 12, 1982, at 15.

SEC Rules

Comment, *SEC Tender Offer Timing Rules: Upsetting a Congressionally Selected Balance.* 68 Cornell Law Review 914 (1983).

Decker, Grant R. *Kneeling to the SEC Rules: The Virginia Takeover Act and the SEC Tender Offer Rule 14d-2(b)*. 22 William and Mary Law Review 487 (1981).

Fleischer, Arthur. *SEC Rules Impose Obligations on Target Company's Managers*. Legal Times (Washington), April 27, 1981, at 25.

Friedman, Stephen. *Tender Offer Issues for 1982*. 14 Review of Securities Regulation 833 (1981).

Huffman, Diane. *States Charge SEC with Abuse of Power*. Legal Times (Washington), March 17, 1980, at 1.

Landau, W. Loeber. *New Tender Offer Rules Make Far Reaching Changes*. Legal Times (Washington), March 24, 1980, at 34.

Leiser, Harvey. *The SEC: A Black Knight for Target Management: An Analysis of Some Recent SEC Rules and Proposed Rules*. 7 Journal of Corporation Law 21 (1981).

Note, *The Effect of the New SEC Rules on the Constitutionality of State Takeover Statutes*. 8 Fordham Urban Law Journal 913 (1979-1980).

Rowe, Richard H. *SEC: New Legislation Instead of Tender Offer Rules?* Legal Times (Washington), April 7, 1980, at 15.

———. *Tender Offer Regs: Changing the Game Rules*. Legal Times (Washington), Dec. 31, 1979, at 9.

Sommer, A. A., Jr., & Feller, Lloyd H. *Takeover Rules: A Cohesive, Comprehensive Code*. Legal Times (Washington), Dec. 17, 1979, at 18.

Standstill Agreements

Bartlette, Joseph W. & Andrews, Christopher B. *The Standstill Agreement: Legal and Business Considerations Underlying a Corporate Peace Treaty*. 62 Boston University Law Review 143 (1982).

Bialkin, Kenneth J. *The Use of Standstill Agreements in Corporate Transactions*. 13 Institute on Securities Regulation 33 (1982).

State Regulation

Bloomenthal, Harold S. *The New Tender Offer Regimen, State Regulation and Preemption*. 30 Emory Law Journal 35 (1981).

Jarrell, Gregg H. & Bradley, Michael. *The Economic Effect of Federal and State Regulations of Cash Tender Offers*. 23 Journal of Law and Economics 371 (1980).

Kreider, Gary P. *Fortress without Foundation? Ohio Takeover Act II*. 52 Cincinnati Law Review 108 (1983).

Langevoort, Donald C. *State Tender Offer Legislation: Interests, Effects, and Political Competency*. 62 Cornell Law Review 213 (1977).

Malmgrem, Richard R. & Pelisek, Frank J. *Takeovers of Wisconsin Corporations: A New Era of Shareholder Protection*. Wisconsin Bar Bulletin, May 1984, at 26.

Note, *The Constitutionality of State Takeover Statutes: A Response to Great Western*. 53 New York University Law Review 872 (1978).

Note, *State Takeover Statutes: Edgar v. MITE Corp*. 96 Harvard Law Review 62 (1983).

Note, *State Takeover Statutes versus Congressional Intent: Preempting the Maze*. 5 Hofstra Law Review 857 (1977).

Note, *The Validity of State Tender Offer Statutes: SEC Rule 14d-2(b) and Post-Kidwell Federal Decisions*. 38 Washington and Lee Law Review 1022 (1981).

Profusek, Robert A. & Gompf, Henry. *State Takeover Legislation after* MITE: *Standing Pat, Blue Sky, or Corporation Law Concept?* 7 Corporation Law Review 3 (1984).

Rainey, Robin Antoinette. *State Regulation of Tender Offers Reexamined*. 19 Tulsa Law Journal 225 (1983).

Sargent, Mark A. *On the Validity of State Takeover Regulation: State Responses to* MITE *and* Kidwell. 42 Ohio State Law Journal 689 (1981).

Steinberg, Marc I. *The Pennsylvania Anti-Takeover Legislation*. 12 Securities Regulation Law Journal 184 (1984).

Webster, Susan. *State Regulation of Tender Offers for Insurance Companies after* Edgar v. MITE. 51 Fordham Law Review 943 (1983).

Two-Tier Offers

Finkelstein, Jesse A. *Antitakeover Protection against Two-Tier and Partial Tender Offers: The Validity of Fair Price, Mandatory Bid and Flip Over Provisions under Delaware Law*. 11 Securities Regulation Journal 291 (1984).

Mirvis, Theodore N. *Two Tier Pricing: Some Appraisal and Entire Fairness Valuation Issues*. 38 Business Lawyer 485 (1983).

Index

Contributors

ANTHONY AIN, a graduate of the University of Pennsylvania Law School, is associated with the firm of Fried, Frank, Harris, Shriver and Jacobson in Washington, D.C.

PETER BRENNAN is associated with the law firm of Mason, Griffin and Pierson in Princeton, New Jersey. He previously served as a Deputy Attorney General, White Collar Crime Section, of the New Jersey Attorney General's Office, as Legislative Counsel to the National Society of Public Accountants, and as Legislative Assistant to United States Senator William V. Roth.

MARC EDWARD CHAFETZ is an attorney at the Washington, D.C., Office of Ballard Spahr Andrews & Ingersoll.

PAULA A. CHESTER is a partner in the New York City law firm of Baskin and Steingut, P.C. She previously served as Special Counsel to the Office of Small Business Policy at the Securities and Exchange Commission.

ALAN B. COHEN is special counsel in the Office of the General Counsel of the Securities and Exchange Commission.

DEBORAH A. DeMOTT is Professor of Law at the Duke University School of Law. She has written extensively in the corporate and securities law area, including recent articles in the Duke and New York University Law Reviews, and she was the editor of *Corporations at the Crossroads: Governance and Reform* (1980).

RALPH C. FERRARA is a member of the New York City law firm of Debevoise and Plimpton and is a resident partner in the law firm's Washington, D.C., office. Mr. Ferrara previously served as the General Counsel of the Securities and Exchange Commission. He has authored several articles on the federal securities laws.

TED J. FIFLIS is Professor of Law at the University of Colorado School of Law. He also has taught at the law schools of Georgetown University, New York University, the University of California-Davis, Duke University, and the Universities of Chicago, Pennsylvania, and Virginia. Professor Fiflis has published extensively in the fields of real property law, corporations, securities regulation, and accounting. He is coauthor of *Accounting for Business Lawyers* (3d ed. 1984) and is the Editor-in-Chief of *The Corporation Law Review*.

DANIEL L. GOELZER is the General Counsel of the Securities and Exchange Commission. He has lectured and written extensively in the securities regulation area.

JAMES J. HARRISON, JR., is Vice-President, Secretary and General Counsel of McCormick and Company, Incorporated, and a member of its board of directors.

THEODORE A. LEVINE is a partner with Wilmer, Cutler and Pickering in Washington, D.C. He previously served as Associate Director in the Division of Enforcement at the Securities and Exchange Commission. Mr. Levine has authored several articles on the federal securities laws and is an Adjunct Professor at Antioch Law School and Howard University Law School.

MARK J. LOEWENSTEIN is Associate Professor of Law at the University of Colorado School of Law. He has written extensively in the securities regulation field, including recent articles published in the Duke and Georgetown Law Journals.

THOMAS J. LYKOS, JR., is Associate Minority Counsel to the United States House of Representatives Committee on Energy and Commerce. He formerly was an attorney in the Division of Enforcement at the Securities and Exchange Commission.

DAVID B. H. MARTIN, JR., is Counsel to Chairman John S. R. Shad of the Securities and Exchange Commission. Mr. Martin served as Secretary to the SEC Advisory Committee on Tender Offers.

LINDA C. QUINN is the Executive Assistant to Chairman John S. R. Shad of the Securities and Exchange Commission. She served as the Staff Director of the SEC Advisory Committee on Tender Offers. Ms. Quinn previously was the Associate Director of the SEC's Division of Corporation Finance responsible for the Office of Tender Offers.

MARK A. SARGENT is Associate Professor of Law at the University of Baltimore School of Law. Professor Sargent has published extensively in the corporate and securities law areas.

L. P. SCRIGGINS is a partner in the law firm of Piper and Marbury in Baltimore, Maryland. He has published a number of articles in the *Business Lawyer*, the professional journal of the American Bar Association's Section of Corporation, Banking and Business Law.

A. A. SOMMER, JR., is a partner in the law firm of Morgan, Lewis and Bockius in Washington, D.C. From 1973 to 1976, Mr. Sommer was a Commissioner of the Securities and Exchange Commission. He has written extensively and lectured frequently with respect to accounting, corporate, and securities law matters.

STANLEY SPORKIN is the General Counsel of the Central Intelligence Agency. He formerly was the Director of Enforcement of the Securities and Exchange Commission. Mr. Sporkin is the recipient of the President's award for distinguished federal civilian service, the highest award that can be granted to a member of the federal career service, and the Rockefeller award for public service. Mr. Sporkin also is an Adjunct Professor at Antioch Law School and Howard University Law School.

WILLIAM C. TYSON is an Assistant Professor at The Wharton School of the University of Pennsylvania. Professor Tyson has written extensively in the federal securities law area.

About the Editor

MARC I. STEINBERG is Professor of Law at the University of Maryland School of Law. He is an acknowledged expert in the securities field, having written numerous law review articles as well as two books, *Corporate Internal Affairs: A Corporate and Securities Law Perspective* (Greenwood Press, 1983) and *Securities Regulation: Liabilities and Remedies* (1984).